For Ursula

'... forsan et haec olim meminisse iuvabit.'

(*Aeneid*, I. 203)

SAM SOLECKI

The Last Canadian Poet: An Essay on Al Purdy

UNIVERSITY OF TORONTO PRESS
Toronto Buffalo London

© University of Toronto Press Incorporated 1999
Toronto Buffalo London

Printed in Canada

ISBN 0-8020-4715-7

Printed on acid-free paper

Canadian Cataloguing in Publication Data

Solecki, Sam, 1946–
   The last Canadian poet : an essay on Al Purdy

Includes bibliographical references and index.
ISBN 0-8020-4715-7

1. Purdy, Al, 1918–   – Criticism and interpretation.   I. Title.

PS8531.U8Z94 1999   C811'.54   C99-930994-3
PR9199.3.P8Z94 1999

10018 20 302

University of Toronto Press acknowledges the financial assistance to its
publishing program of the Canada Council for the Arts and the Ontario Arts
Council.

This book has been published with the help of a grant from the Humanities
and Social Sciences Federation of Canada, using funds provided by the Social
Sciences and Humanities Research Council of Canada.

University of Toronto Press acknowledges the financial support for its
publishing activities of the Government of Canada through the Book
Publishing Industry Development Program (BPIDP).

Canada

Contents

Preface

How many miles to Alexandria
from dusty Ameliasburg?

'I Think It Was Wednesday' (*CH*, 98)

A critical study of a major figure of a national literature doesn't need justification, but it may nevertheless be useful to explain some of the reasons why it was written. As will be obvious from the main part of the book, the primary reasons are my admiration for the poetry of Al Purdy and my general impression that despite his acknowledgment by creative writers – Margaret Atwood, Michael Ondaatje, George Bowering, Dennis Lee – and critics – Tom Marshall, George Woodcock – as probably the pre-eminent poet of our literature, he (like some other canonical poets) has been curiously ignored in recent years. With the exception of the special Purdy issue in *Essays on Canadian Writing* (Summer 1993), commissioned and assembled for the most part by Russell Brown and myself, there has not been a single article about Purdy – or Irving Layton, to broaden the sample – in *Canadian Literature, Canadian Poetry*, or *Essays on Canadian Writing* in this decade. Why canonization has been coextensive with neglect is clear, in part, from the titles and concerns of many of the essays in the journals: *in* are contemporary literature, feminism and feminist poetry, postmodernism, language poetry, colonial and postcolonial theory, and various so-called theoretical approaches; *out* are the poetry and fiction of the first generation of Canadian modernists, especially those whose work does not lend itself to these approaches. Put another way, the age of Layton and Purdy has given

way to that of Atwood and Ondaatje; Northrop Frye and George Woodcock have been succeeded by Robert Kroetsch, Frank Davey, and Linda
Hutcheon.

Frank Davey offers a succinct and accurate summary of the sea
change in poetry, though I disagree with his view that the poetry canon
has 'collapsed.' It still exists and most of the figures in it are self-evident,
but postmodern critics, caught in the epistemological contradictions of
their own relativism, are simply pretending that it isn't there. What *has*
collapsed is the importance or centrality of poetry.

... critical conceptions of twentieth-century Canadian poetry were dominated, at
least until the late 1970s, by two closely related ideologies. One was the aes-
thetic/humanist ideology that assumes that the writing of poetry reveals and
celebrates human creativity and the spiritual dimensions of a common humanity, and that the reading of it is morally beneficial through its enlarging of one's
understanding of humanity. This was the view of many of the initiators of the
institutionalized study of Canadian literature – Smith, Woodcock, and Frye in
particular. The second was a nationalist ideology in which it is not merely a
shared humanity that joins Canadian writers but a common humanity *as Canadians*. This Canadianness signified *difference*, a difference from other nationalities
... *homogeneity*, an identity with other Canadians, and *universality*, an impulse to
national identification that the Canadian also shares with other humans.[1]

One might question one or two of the details and emphases, but in general this is a fair comment on the major assumptions underlying Purdy's
poetics as well as the poetics of several of his contemporaries. Even if
they weren't nationalists in any obviously polemical or ideological
sense, they had a sense of the possibility of a national literature. The
questioning of humanism (including the humanist 'subject') and nationalism (by itself or as part of a postcolonial criticism) in the past three
decades by poststructuralist and postcolonial critics has, in a manner of
speaking, resulted in a critical amnesia about certain periods, writers,
and kinds of poetry. Graduate students and younger critics concerned
with Canadian literature, both here and in Europe, have tended to con-
centrate on writers, often minor or ephemeral, whose work is responsive to certain privileged subjects, critical theories, and discourses. Often
this has been coexistent with what Helen Vendler has described as 'a
jealous appropriation of literature into ... socially marked categories.'[2]
One of the ironic consequences of this development has been the recent
marginalization in criticism and in school curricula and courses of those

canonical writers whose work is less receptive or responsive to these trends. Courses in Canadian literature increasingly focus on contemporary writers more 'relevant' to and expressive of our new multicultural nation, with the predictable result that writers such as Dionne Brand or Rohinton Mistry are taught more often than E.J. Pratt or Hugh MacLennan, who are perceived as either irrelevant or having nothing but historical importance or both.

Layton, for instance, has been all but forgotten because of his belief in the humanist subject, in a hierarchy of values, and his politically incorrect attitude to women and feminism; Avison, a woman poet, has been ignored by feminists both because she's not interested in gender and because she's a Christian. (A more cynical observer might also be tempted to point out that young critics, trying to 'get published' as quickly as possible in today's Americanized academy, are more likely to work on a relatively accessible young writer with a handful of books than on a canonical one, such as Purdy or Layton, whose body of work numbers more than forty volumes, or Avison, who is notoriously difficult.) What's disturbing in this is not the fact that some writers are being dropped from the canon to be replaced by better writers. This, after all, has always happened: how many of Edward Dewart's selections are reprinted in today's anthologies? Does anyone remember John Pomfret, who has a not negligible page in Johnson's *Lives of the Poets*? They are being ignored or dropped either because their poetics are no longer fashionable (Kroetsch, a postmodern poet self-conscious about the subject and 'language,' is in; Layton, a belated Romantic, is out) or because they are ideologically suspect and do not write on the preferred topics (gender, homosexuality, language, postcolonialism, race, the native, etc.).

As I write this preface in December 1997, I still can't find major studies of Pratt, Smith, Avison, Layton, Page, and Purdy, all of whom are part of the national cultural memory and can now be read 'historically' because the phase of Canadian poetic modernism of which they were part ended in the late 1960s. Recent theses have tended to all but ignore them. As I suggest in my title and as I argue in the opening chapter, it is equally important to a reading of Purdy's work and its place in Canadian culture to recognize that a phase of Canadian culture and economic and political nationalism, in the broadest sense, has also come to a close at roughly the same time. At the very moment that Canadian cultural nationalism had, if not triumphed, then at least gained general acceptance – roughly the same historical moment in which Purdy articulated a national poetic – a crucial shift occurred in how we define the Canadian nation (and state) and how we view literature's relationship to it. As Robert Lecker suggests, 'most Canadian criticism written up to the 1980s ... refers us to the connection between writing, culture and nation,' and most of the criticism afterwards points us away from 'a national-referential aesthetic.'[3]

The three key terms in Lecker's statement – writing, culture, and nation – didn't disappear after 1980, they were simply redefined: writing became discourse, culture disappeared within cultural practices and cultural studies, and nation was filtered through postcolonial criticism and a soft version of multiculturalist politics that displaced Canadian nationalism with the various hyphenated nationalisms it had sheltered. The overall effect, as I have suggested, was to devalue the poetry, the criticism, and the ideology that took 'a national-referential aesthetic' seriously, the very 'aesthetic' that is central to Purdy's writing, though I don't want to be misunderstood as suggesting that his work is important for this reason alone. It is the overall argument of this book that Purdy is the Canadian poet with the strongest sense of a 'national patrimony,' in Whitman's words the one best 'fit to cope with our occasions,'[4] terms that will be less startling to Canadian readers and critics if they keep in mind not only Whitman and Purdy but also W.B. Yeats, Seamus Heaney, Czeslaw Milosz, and Derek Walcott.

Of Canadian poets who came to maturity in the 1940s and 1950s, Purdy seems to me to have as secure a critical reputation as any, a view that seems confirmed by his influence on younger poets such as Margaret Atwood, Michael Ondaatje, Bronwen Wallace, Tom Marshall, David McFadden and Tom Wayman, as well as by the critical responses of Woodcock, Atwood, Bowering, Marshall, and Lee. (The lack of an international reputation is, to be frank, troubling, but it is worth recalling that Williams was not published in England until after his death.) Still, with the exception of Bowering's monograph, published nearly thirty years ago, and Lee's seminal essay (an afterword to the 1986 *Collected Poems*), Purdy's major poems and his body of work have been for the most part neglected except for reviews and a handful of articles. If there is a debate about the poetry, it tends to surface over the extent to which Purdy's 'nationalist sentiments and subject-matter' are central to the poetic. For Lee, Purdy is a Canadian Whitman, who 'in his rootedness, his largeness, and his impulse to forge a native idiom for the imagination ... is one of a distinct breed: the heroic founders, who give their people a voice as they go about their own necessities.'[5] For Davey and, up to a point, for Bowering, 'this critical view works to transform Purdy's dynamic, random and questioning writings into a static caricature of some national Canadian archetype.'[6] It's not clear to me why poems with a national or nationalist theme or orientation cannot simultaneously be 'dynamic, random and questioning,' the defining terms of value in the Bowering-Davey poetics; the opposition strikes me as a factitious one, designed primarily to allow them to claim Purdy for their own view of a post-national North American poetic, deriving from Williams and Olson and grounded in *Tish*. Still, one is grateful for even a whiff of controversy around a body of poetry more often uncritically accepted than discussed.

One of the objectives of this book is to offer both an overview of Purdy's career and close readings of some of his major poems. Although I argue a case for Purdy's importance as a *Canadian* poet, the argument could not be ventured if I could not assert with some confidence and with the hope of general assent that, with or without the national adjective, he is a fine poet with an individual voice, vision, and what Vendler calls a 'compelling aesthetic signature.'[7] In other words, at the outset, the poems are important *not* because they are explicitly 'Canadian' or 'nationalist' or for any other thematic or ideological reason, but because they work as poems, and a book about Purdy *as a poet* is worth writing only if one thinks that he has produced a body of first-rate work that is important *as poetry* before it is important for any other reason. Otherwise, one might just as well write about Wilson MacDonald (a minor Vachel Lindsay) who also travelled across the country and wrote poems about the people and places he visited. This seems a difficult concept to communicate in an era in which poetry is often a function of identity politics or victim credentials, when more and more young poets treat their verse as a function of a place (a Manitoba poet), or way of life (an environmental poet), ideology (a feminist poet), or class (a working-class poet). Eliot's monition that 'a great poem survives its particular social purpose'[8] comes to mind too often when I read contemporary verse, though primarily as an adverse judgment on it. As should be obvious from my title, this doesn't mean, however, that I disagree with Lee over the centrality of Purdy's work for Canada and Canadian literature. On the contrary, as will be obvious throughout my reading, my debt to Lee is substantial, and there is a sense in which anyone writing on Purdy today is writing extended footnotes to his essay.

Among my 'footnotes' are the following:

1 I argue in part 1 that Purdy's poetry represents both the culmination
   and the close of the major phase of the Canadian literary tradition;
   hence the title, *The Last Canadian Poet*. The argument is coextensive
   with the suggestion that a phase of Canada's historical development –
   one that also entailed what could be called the founding vision of the
   nation – also ended in the 1970s. This section also describes a context
   for Purdy's career. Readers interested primarily or exclusively in the
   poetry may want to go directly to part 2.
2 Part 2 offers a detailed overview and reading of the poetry, including
   a description of the development of Purdy's Canadian 'poetics' (from
   Carman, Chesterton, and others through Thomas, Hopkins, and Eliot
   to Layton and Lawrence). Its seven chapters examine what seem to
   me the major issues and concerns raised by the work. It also argues
   the case for considering Purdy as a 'national poet.'
3 The annotated catalogue in the appendix demonstrates the extensive
   presence of the Canadian, American, and British poetic traditions in
   Purdy's work, and confirms my argument about the complexity of the
   poetic tradition in Purdy's poetry as well as in Canadian poetry as a
   whole.

Furthermore, the appendix, together with the drafts of poems quoted
in the text and notes, should help dispel the notion that Purdy is a
'natural,' or what Schiller would call a 'naive,' poet without craft or
craftsmanship. His poems may seem 'dynamic, random and questioning,' they may have several of the virtues of what Lawrence calls the
'poetry of the present' or what Bowering terms 'measure by tongue,' but
even the most cursory glance at the manuscripts in the archives will
reveal a poet who is a compulsive reviser.[9] Not coincidentally, among
his terms of highest praise in his reviews of the work of other poets is
'craftsman' ('Layton is a fine craftsman' [*SA*, 206]). The catalogue should
also put paid to the idea, if it still has any currency, that Purdy is no
more than an autochthonous poet, uneducated or under-educated and
self-created on railway boxcars during the late 1930s. What a close reading of the poetry reveals is a poet who may have dropped out of school
as a teenager but whose poems are informed by works from the entire
Western tradition, from *The Epic of Gilgamesh* and Homer to Milosz and
Márquez. One of the consequences of this is that while I shall be arguing
that Purdy is the most 'Canadian' of our poets, I shall often use non-
Canadian examples to illuminate his work.
  Though I refer to poems both published and unpublished, when quot-

ing I cite *The Collected Poems* whenever possible, simply because many of the earlier volumes are out of print and that is the edition most generally available. Finally, readers may wonder why some of the quotations tend to be quite long. There are two reasons: first, some of the poems are no longer in print and are probably known to few; and second, Purdy's poems, like those of Whitman, Jeffers, and Lawrence, tend to flow. Like Hopkins and Whitman he is a poet who works in the holophrase or rambling sentence because he often needs several lines to complete a sentence, finish a thought, or establish a cadence or rhythm. A note in his most recent collection confesses that 'longwindedness is a besetting fault' (*TPNA*, 129). Anyone who reads him out loud can feel this along the windpipe: his lines and sentences demand that the reader take a deep breath if a section of a poem is to be read as a unit. As a result he is not easy to excerpt. As Johnson said of a now forgotten poet, 'Particular lines are not to be regarded; the power is in the whole; and in the whole there is a magnificence of vast extent and endless diversity.'[10]

Though many people contributed in various ways to making this a stronger book than it otherwise would have been, my largest debt, both local and more general, is to W.J. Keith of the University of Toronto. He read and criticized the manuscript with a thoroughness and critical intelligence that I first experienced in his Victorian Poetry class at the University of Toronto thirty years ago. (It was also in his graduate class that I first read D.H. Lawrence.) Cynthia Messenger took time off from her comprehensive study of P.K. Page to cast a very critical eye on the entire manuscript, and especially on the appendix. Al and Eurithe Purdy answered various questions, and the poet remained patient through many letters and several interviews over the better part of a decade. My largest debts are to those who have written about Purdy during the past thirty years: Mike Doyle, Dennis Duffy, Margaret Atwood, Charles Taylor (*Radical Tories*), Dennis Lee, George Bowering, David McFadden, and the late George Woodcock. There is also a debt of a slightly different kind to F.W. Watt, whose 1968 undergraduate seminar on Canadian poetry included discussions of *Poems for All the Annettes* and introduced me to Canadian poetry. Russell Brown of the University of Toronto invited me to give a paper at the University of Toronto's 'Al Purdy Day,' and later involved me in a project we never completed (it became the *Essays on Canadian Writing* Al Purdy issue) but that nevertheless drew me further into the poetry. Also at the University of Toronto, Joaquin Kuhn and Father Owen Lee of St Michael's College helped locate allusions to Swinburne and to operas, respectively;

Heather Jackson helped with Coleridge; while David Shaw answered some questions about Browning.

Susan Addario, Margaret Calverley, Rosemary Sullivan, Karen Mulhallen, Linda Williams (my co-editor at McClelland and Stewart of *The Woman on the Shore*), Elias Polizoes, Anne Michaels, T.H. Adamowski (former Chair, Department of English, University of Toronto), Tamara Trojanowska (University of Toronto), Dr Gale Moore, David Little, Sandra Romeo, Mylissa Falkner, M.J. Morris, the late Hazel Belloni (University of Bordeaux), Nicoletta Scarpa (University of Udine), Maria-Jesus Llarena-Ascanio (University of La Laguna), and Andrea Werner-Thaler (University of Vienna) all contributed to a Purdy dialogue that has lasted since 1990. A particular note of thanks to Annick Hillger (University of Freiburg), who helped during the year of rewriting. A different kind of dialogue took place with André Solecki and Brendan Haley (both eighteen), whose interest in the poetry and prose leaves me optimistic about the future of Canadian literature. Audrey McDonagh (again), Freda Chayka, Susan Bartkiw, Ida Ferrinho, and Tina Colomvakos of the Office of the Dean (Arts and Science) helped with typing, faxes, and cheering in the background. As did my sister, Lydia Powers, who also keeps the candle burning during the dark times.

My copy editor, Darlene Money, made the text both more readable and presentable.

I am also grateful to the Department of English and the Social Sciences and Humanities Research Council for grants to travel to the Purdy papers at Queen's University and the University of Saskatchewan, and the McClelland and Stewart papers at McMaster University. My thanks to the staffs at these libraries for their patient help over several weeks; particular thanks to Glen Makahonuk at Saskatchewan and Carl Spadoni at McMaster.

At the University of Toronto, St Michael's College and University College provided a rewarding atmosphere for the research and writing. The latter also allowed me to try out some of the ideas in its weekly faculty seminars. My thanks for the invitation to Principal Lynd Forguson, Alan Bewell, and Glen Loney.

Parts of this book were tried out on students of two undergraduate and graduate seminars on Whitman, Lawrence, and Purdy (1994–5) at the University of Toronto. I wrote most of part 2 during an appointment as Visiting Professor at the University of Siena in 1992–3, where my hosts were Dr Sandro and Mrs Laura Forconi of the Centre for Canadian Studies. Sections of part 2 were given as lectures at the University of

Siena (1992–3, 1996), the University of Madrid (1994), the University of Venice (1996), the University of Trieste (1996), the University of La Laguna (1994, 1996), and the University of Vienna (1994, 1998). At Venice, where I taught a course in Canadian literature in the spring of 1996, I particularly want to thank Professor Rosella Mamoli Zorzi. At La Laguna (Canary Islands) I am grateful to Professor Bernd Dietz, the director of the Centre for Canadian Studies, for inviting me to be a Visiting Professor during the winter of 1996, and to Maria-Jesus Llarena-Ascanio, my unofficial host during my stay. At Vienna, my thanks to Professor Waldemar Zacharasiewicz, the director of the Canadian Studies Centre.

Part 1 was delivered as the first of a series of three lectures at the University of La Laguna in November 1996. Sections of part 2 have been published previously in the *Globe and Mail* (11 December 1983), *Essays on Canadian Writing*, number 49 (Summer 1993), and *La Rivista di Studi Canadesi* (Rome) (Winter 1997–8).

The main dedication records a different kind of debt, the kind that can never be paid.

SAM SOLECKI
UNIVERSITY COLLEGE
UNIVERSITY OF TORONTO

Abbreviations

THE LAST CANADIAN POET: AN ESSAY ON AL PURDY

PART I: POETRY, NATION, AND THE LAST CANADIAN POET

What, however, do we more definitely mean by New World literature?[1]

Walt Whitman

One can only reach out to the universe with a gloved hand – that glove is one's nation, the only thing one knows even a little of.[2]

W.B. Yeats

Though at first glance my title may seem polemical, indeed may seem to predict the end of Canadian poetry and, by extension, Canadian literature and perhaps Canada itself, it is not intended to sound quite that apocalyptic note. Its intended valence and resonance are more modest, though I'm assuming that by the end of the book many readers may be uneasy with some of the intimations and connotations surrounding both 'last' and 'Canada.' Perhaps a quick way of indicating where this argument is going would be to say that I see it as part of what some have called a post-national or postcolonial argument. In my reading, this assumes that a certain phase of Canadian history and the Canadian experience came to an end in the two decades between the 1967 centenary – called by Pierre Berton 'the last good year' – and the Canadian Multiculturalism Act in 1988 (Bill C-93), and that its passing was caused by forces both cultural and political, both national and international. Another way of putting this would be to suggest that on or about 8 October 1971, when Prime Minister Trudeau announced his government's support of multiculturalism, Canadian identity began to change. The Canadian state is still recognizably the same, but the nation – that often inchoate aggregate or complex of attitudes, values, and traditions – has significantly altered. I would suggest, in fact, that it has altered to the point that many of the constitutive assumptions and myths of our first century, as well as the questions we thought worth asking about identity, nation, and culture, no longer have the same frame of reference they once did. It's as if the key words – including nation and culture – have themselves shifted, and continue to shift, in meaning.

Take Canadian literature, for example. There is no doubt that over the past four decades it has achieved public and critical acceptance as well as institutionalization and canonization. It has done so, however, at precisely the time that both 'Canadian literature' and 'Canadian nation' have undergone radical redefinition, as have some of the assumptions about their relationship. Whether these are positive or questionable developments is of less moment than that they have happened. One of the consequences for literature is that we have diminished expectations of our poets, just as they have diminished expectations about their possible role in society. From the perspective of the 1990s it is obvious that the grand nationalist ambitions of Roberts, Pratt, and Purdy to write what can be called a national poetry belong to a particular historical phase. It was a phase in which writers and their audience gave credence to what could be called the master narrative of Canadian nationalism in literature, criticism, and politics. That narrative reached its peak of influence in the 1950s and 1960s, just before the end of its influence.

Today, I suspect that for most Canadian poets and readers outside Quebec the term 'national poet' would be puzzling, even if one pointed to Czeslaw Milosz, Aimé Césaire, Derek Walcott, and Seamus Heaney, all of whom would understand Milosz's comment 'What is poetry which does not save / Nations or people?'[3] Milosz would be the first to insist that not all poems, including some of his own, need to have this concern. Still, the couplet, from a poem written in 1945, calls for a certain kind of poetry complicit with the fate of nations, a complicity evident in Donald Davie's comments on the roles played by Heaney in Northern Ireland and R.S. Thomas in Wales.

Heaney has chosen to enter himself in a league that [Derek] Mahon ... has chosen not to compete in: that is to say, the competition as to what poet is the voice of his people. Heaney and Thomas have chosen to act out, in their lives as recorded in their writings, the role and the predicament imposed in our times on the Welshman in the one case, the Irishman in the other. This is presumptuous ... but in both cases the presumption is allowable, and indeed necessary, in the case of those who aspire to be *national* poets. The national poet holds up a glass in which his nation shall see itself as it is, not as it figures in the beguiling image available alike for internal and external consumption.[4]

With his characteristic good sense, Davie reminds us that not all poets share this aspiration and that those who do are presumptuous in both the positive and negative senses of the word. His description of their situation also reminds us of an obvious fact: the national poet is inseparable from an audience that thinks of itself as a nation brought to voice by his poetry and described in it 'as it is,' and, I would add, as it might be. In this sense, the poet's life, as it is figured in the poetry, is what Keats called 'a continual allegory' and stands in a metonymic relation with that of the nation.[5] The possibility of this sort of 'allegory' depends, however, on the conjunction of a particular kind of writer and a particular set of historical circumstances: an original poet with nationalist concerns and a nation at a critical moment in its formation.

The Canadian example is, of course, Purdy, described by Tom Marshall as our 'first truly native poet.'[6] Marshall's 'native' is synonymous with Canadian, indigenous, and national, and it encompasses both poetic vision and voice. In the remainder of this section, I want to explore some of the implications of these terms in our literature and history as a means of situating Purdy's poetry and gauging his achievement. This chapter as a whole is intended to establish several coextensive cultural, critical, and historical contexts for the reading of Purdy's poetry I offer in part 2. I have four interrelated concerns: 1. some of the significant constitutive characteristics of the Canadian experience and the Canadian literary tradition; 2. some of the characteristics, problems, and limitations of colonial and postcolonial literatures and of postcolonial criticism, in particular those prominent in effecting a change in how we view notions such as identity, canon, nation; 3. changing views of Canadian identity and the Canadian nation, and the introduction of multiculturalism; 4. the idea of the national poet and Al Purdy's central place in the Canadian literary tradition.

I should note at the outset that I use 'postcolonial' in the simple sense as defining a country that began as a colony and is now an independent state. 'Colony' and 'colonial' are slightly more ambiguous, but I try to restrict their frame of reference to two meanings: first, a state that is a political extension of an imperial power (that is, Canada East and Canada West before Confederation); (second, a state or nation that is politically independent but whose culture or economy or aspects of its politics are in some way dependent on or subservient to those of another influential and more powerful nation. In this second sense, Canadian fiction is colonial both before and after 1867, though, strictly speaking, the Dominion is an independent state after that date.

When Canada's centenary was celebrated in 1967, few anticipated, except perhaps for a handful of intellectuals, native leaders, and Quebec nationalists, that the country was about to enter an era of intense self-questioning and disunity, and that internal and external forces would lead to a gradual erosion of whatever national self-definition it possessed. The public mood was for the most part euphoric, and, if questioned, most Canadians would have predicted that in its second century the nation would build on the impressive achievements of the first. As I hope will become clear, I'm not beginning with an essentialist view of the nation or with the notion that prior to 1970 the country had a simple, homogeneous, and shared identity based on language, tradition, and history and accepted by all. I would assert, however, that for all its demographic and geographic diversity and despite the presence of French and aboriginal national minorities, the nation had what Ronald Dworkin calls 'a shared vocabulary of tradition and convention' and what Charles Taylor has termed common reference points of identity and 'a common purpose or project.'[7] I would even include in that 'shared vocabulary' the very questions about our differences, solitudes, and divisions that surfaced in 1885, 1917, and during the Second World War. These were primarily procedural and could be contained within an assumed vision of the nation. Since 1967, the new, important questions have become substantive, and have called into question the possibility of a shared national vision, the common national culture a nation needs 'if it is to be stable and command allegiance.'[8]

The following have been among the major agents of change.

1 The rise of the separatist movement in Quebec.
2 The Free Trade Agreement with the United States and Mexico, and the continuing and increasing domination by the United States of the Canadian economy and of Canadian mass culture.
3 The shift in immigration from Europeans to immigrants from the Caribbean, the Far East, Africa, and the Indian subcontinent.[9]
4 The development of the so-called global village unified by transnational electronic media such as the World Wide Web.[10]
5 The increasing official and intellectual acceptance of multiculturalism

and the multicultural model for the Canadian state, and the Canadian Multiculturalism Act's tacit indication that 'languages [and cultures] other than English and French' will have a real and symbolic status roughly equal to those of the two founding nations.

6 The rise in influence of deconstruction, postmodernism, and postcolonial theory in the humanities and social sciences, with their critique of the Western tradition in politics and culture, their radical redefinition of nation and nationalism, their valorization of difference and the margin over the centre, and their view of the equality of all value systems and identities.[11]

Whatever unity, 'identity,' and common project, however provisional or contingent, the country as a whole may have created in its first century have been massively challenged by these developments, which have created a 'legitimation crisis' in which Canadians almost continually question the beliefs and values essential to their existence as a nation. The referendums in Quebec, for instance, announce repeatedly the possibility of a fundamental change in the national situation, while challenging Canadians to reflect on or entertain the possibility that the country may be radically different in the future, both as nation and state.[12] Contributing to the confusion are several alternative views of the nation – usually grounded in postmodern, multicultural, or postcolonial assumptions about nationhood – not far different from and almost as unworkable as George Woodcock's earlier anarchist vision of a decentralized Canada. One doesn't have to be a committed conservative, humanist, or ego-psychologist to suspect that for a nation, postcolonial or not, to exist it needs a commitment to something more than a heterogeneous pluralism, a politics of difference, or a recognition of the equal value and validity of all of its cultures, languages, and traditions. One may believe in the value of difference and diversity, yet suspect that a community or nation cannot be founded on what Gad Horowitz has wittily termed a 'masochistic celebration of Canadian nothingness.'[13] Kieran Keohane's recent *Symptoms of Canada: An Essay on Canadian Identity* offers the curious argument that our openness to 'difference' is our constitutive and perhaps only characteristic. For Keohane, Canada is like Woody Allen's Zelig in that it has no native colouring, no distinctive characteristics, no personality until someone imposes them on the nation. The events and achievements of several centuries are simply ignored. Hugh Hood's comments on 'disunity' remind us what is wrong with this line of argument. 'For we must never forget that an imperilled unity is first of all a unity! That disunity cannot subsist in and of itself. The idea of the Canadian tradition lies exactly here. As soon as we created our unity, we began to put it in peril. Before the Canadian girl or boy is out of diapers, she or he starts to worry about our two founding cultures. When he or she has arrived at sixty, the Canadian understands that the debate is going to go on going on. The unity underpins the disunity, which has no other place to go.'[14] Recent uncritical advocates of decentralization, pluralism, multiculturalism, and even differentiated citizenship, who tend to approach the issue from a broadly cultural perspective, often pay little attention to the larger ideological and political implications of these. They also tend to be little concerned with the obvious discontinuity of these with the traditions and history that preceded them. That multiculturalism transplants forms of life generated by non-Canadian historical and cultural milieux to Canada seems to concern its proponents as little as the possibility, raised by Isaiah Berlin, that certain political and cultural goods, values, and goals may be not only incommensurable but even incompatible: freedom and equality, for instance, or a multicultural state and a strong nation.[15]

Hood's comment implicitly reminds us that even during its first century, Canada never lacked prophets to announce its end, from Goldwin Smith to Frank Underhill, both of whom anticipated a closer relationship, on whatever terms, with the United States as a positive development. A contrasting note can be heard in Harold Innis, Donald Creighton, Northrop Frye, George Grant, and Walter Gordon, all of whom 'lament,' however differently, the country's inevitable colonial status *vis-à-vis* the American empire and the end of its status as an independent state and nation. In their view Canada developed in its first century from colony to nation to colony. Even nationalists such as Mel Watkins, Abraham Rotstein, and Gordon suggested in the 1960s that Canada's status as nation and state would change, as the country entered a new phase, because of economic and technological changes. More surprisingly, Hugh MacLennan, whose nationalist credentials are impeccable, foresaw the possibility of a divided Canada with 'English-Canada' joining the United States. The following is from a 1965 letter to Jack McClelland.

Reasoning from the most hard-boiled point of view, though it negates the meaning of most of my life-work to say so, I think English-Canada might well be wise, right now, to tell Quebec that if she doesn't behave in a practical and adult fashion, it will be necessary to separate *from her*. If – but this is the big if – it were feasible for English-Canada to join the States.

Politically this is not feasible now because the States would not take us in.[16]

And, finally, an ending of sorts has also been announced during the past decade by Frank Davey, Philip Resnick, and Charles Taylor. Though his choice of novels could be questioned (where are Rudy Wiebe and Hugh Hood, for instance?) Davey suggests in *Post-National Arguments* that our recent novels announce 'the arrival of the post-national state – a state invisible to its own citizens, indistinguishable from its fellows, maintained by invisible political forces, and significant mainly through its position within the grid of world-class postcard cities.'[17] More sanguine, Resnick and Taylor recognize the challenges posed by, on the one hand, multiculturalism, and, on the other, the 'national' claims of Quebec and the aboriginal peoples, but they envision a possible transition to a future nation fully aware of and continuous with its complex historical heritage. Aware of the inevitability of a multicultural or poly-ethnic Canada, each emphasizes the importance of historical continuity and ideological unity for the idea of a national identity. Implicit in the work of both, as in Purdy's poetry, is the view that without these a nation is merely a state.

Taylor's richly suggestive essays of the past quarter century suggest, more optimistically, that the nation can survive, even prosper, if it is willing to find a unity 'based on a common purpose or project,' use the Charter of Rights as 'a common reference point of identity,' and adopt a pluralist model of the state that distinguishes between what he calls the 'deep diversity' of French Canadians and the First Nations and the 'first-level diversity' of other Canadians.[18] In Will Kymlicka's terms, French Canadians and the First Nations constitute national minorities, while other Canadians can be described as ethnic groups.[19] Taylor acknowledges that Quebecers and the aboriginal peoples have a prior membership in their own historical communities that predates their membership in Canada, and that that membership distinguishes them and gives them a status different from immigrant Canadians with other national origins.[20] He acknowledges the presence of a poly-ethnic Canada but resists the pressure – tacit or explicit in supporters of multiculturalism and postcolonial ideologies – to grant the same historical status to all groups of the Canadian mosaic. Looking at the situation from the perspective of English Canada, Resnick responds by insisting that 'English Canada is not some tabula rasa or blank sheet to be recast every time new cultural communities come along. These different communities must themselves make serious efforts to accommodate themselves to the ethos of the larger society.'[21] Like Taylor, Resnick rejects the radical pluralism implicit or explicit in some recent models of the state and nation, though, to be strictly accurate, Taylor, like Kymlicka, is sympathetic to the demands from nation groups for some sort of differentiated citizenship or group-differentiated rights. Still, while both Resnick and Taylor are relatively optimistic about the country's future, they acknowledge that in the next few years Canada will evolve politically and ideologically in new directions.

To cut to the chase, it is the argument of *The Last Canadian Poet* that Al Purdy is the major and perhaps last writer of the first phase – the major or constitutive phase – of the Canadian nation; to go further, that he is the major or central poet of our experience, the one who has given the strongest, most comprehensive, and most original voice to the country's cultural, historical, and political experiences and aspirations that have been at the heart of our various nationalist discourses since Confederation. If it makes sense to speak of 'the Canadian experience,' of our collective fabric, then he has been its most original and powerful poetic voice. Born in 1918, he belongs to the generation that, according to George Grant, took it for granted 'that they belonged to a nation. The character of the country was self-evident. To say it was British was not to deny it was North American. To be a Canadian was to be a unique species of North American. Such alternatives as F.H. Underhill's – "Stop being British if you want to be a nationalist" – seemed obviously ridiculous. We were grounded in the wisdom of Sir John A. Macdonald, who saw plainly more than a hundred years ago that the only threat to nationalism was from the South, not from across the sea. To be a Canadian was to build, along with the French, a more ordered and stable society than the liberal experiment in the United States.'[22]

Like other members of that generation – Donald Creighton, Robertson Davies, John Weinzweig, Pierre Trudeau, and Grant himself – Purdy found his voice during the period of the country's struggle for and evolution towards political and cultural nationhood and identity. What I want to suggest is that one of the ways of reading his body of work – the nearly fifty books he has published since 1944 – is as a vision of the nation, a poetic representation and record of one man's (Emerson's poet as 'representative man') encounter with his nation and the world. The words are a record of our sense of being in the world as Canadians, of being rooted in a particular landscape, way of life, and history. His writing is simultaneously an autobiography, an engagement with the national past, and a search for a personal and national voice – both a record and a vision.[23] To paraphrase Donald Davie, Purdy acts out in his life, as recorded in his writing, the role and the predicament imposed in our times on a Canadian.[24] It's a hallmark of the poetry's poise and authenticity that even as it articulates a comprehensive vision of nation – analogous to Whitman's or Milosz's – it simultaneously registers doubts and questions about nationhood as well as Purdy's awareness that the engagement with a national identity inevitably remains open-ended because of the predicaments of history. Read in chronological sequence, the poems reveal an individual discovering himself and his country, and in that act of discovery describing or 'mapping' it in its full complexity. Another, slightly more Wittgensteinian way of putting this, would be to say that in imagining a Canadian poetic Purdy simultaneously imagines a Canadian form of life.[25]

As Fernand Braudel points out in *The Identity of France*, 'any national identity necessarily implies a degree of national unity,' but at the same time its 'ambiguity is manifest: it stands for a string of questions – no sooner do you answer one than the next arises and so on *ad infinitum*.'[26] For Braudel, identity includes 'a string of questions,' an idea completely overlooked both by certain nationalists as well as supporters of multiculturalism who offer collective identities – African Canadians, European Canadians, French Canadians, etc. – that are radical simplifications of the complexities and contradictions of ethnic identity. Purdy's awareness of the open-ended nature of the discussion is evident in his poems' radical subjectivity, self-questioning, interest in other viewpoints, and resistance to closure. In the prose, one can see it in comments such as the following one to Milton Acorn (6 June 1973) about his vision of the nation: 'I write in my own way toward a society that will probably not come in my lifetime, perhaps never.'[27]

I use the phrase 'national identity' in this discussion aware of Purdy's impatient comment in the 1968 introduction to *The New Romans*:

there are few things I find more irritating about my own country than this so-called 'search for an identity,' an identity which I've never doubted having in the first place.

The environment, the land, the people, and the flux of history have made us what we are; these have existed since Canada's beginning, along with a capacity for slow evolvement into something else that goes on and on. And perhaps I would also include pride. Their total is all that any nation may possess. (iii)

I would suggest that Purdy could only make this assertion *after* a decade in which his poetry and prose had 'explored' and 'mapped' the country (a favourite image of his) and made it his own in words. In part 2, I try to substantiate my argument that Purdy's work is central to our national experience and to our sense of ourselves on the basis of some of the following terms: an idiom and voice whose rhythm, syntax, and texture sound Canadian and offer what Dennis Lee calls 'the local nature of cadence';[28] an attitude to the cultural tradition that mediates between, absorbs, and goes beyond both British and American influences; a sensitivity to what D.H. Lawrence calls 'the spirit of place' and a new-world desire to lift, in William Carlos Williams's words, 'an environment to expression'; a poetic stance grounded in Canadian geography, prehistory, and history; a poetic and a vision that take the local – 'starting from Ameliasburg' – or regional as the point of departure and as synecdoche for the national and universal; a desire to offer, in an era incapable of epic totality, a comprehensive vision of the nation – subjective, provisional, lyrical, fragmentary, syncretic, and open-ended; and influence within the tradition. Following Marshall and Lee, I also suggest that the sum of these qualities constitutes a Canadian poetic. I want to reiterate, however, that I assert the claim for Purdy's status not simply on the basis of content – if that were the criterion then one could replace Purdy with any number of poets or newspaper columnists – but on the basis of what used to be called 'achieved content' and what Helen Vendler calls a 'compelling aesthetic signature.'[29] Without the last a poet is not worth reading *as* poet.

Purdy came to prominence and wrote much of his strongest and most original work in the decade surrounding the centennial celebrations of Confederation. The optimism of the period, from John Diefenbaker's northern vision to Trudeaumania, as well as the nearly euphoric cultural nationalism are reflected in his poetic discovery of the country. Yet, as I mentioned earlier, the optimism of the period was counterpointed to significant voices uneasy about the country's postwar cultural and political status *vis-à-vis* the United States. It's worth recalling that Lee's seminal 'Cadence, Country, Silence: Writing in Colonial Space' (1974) is a testament to what he sees as the perhaps impossible struggle to write 'Canadian.' He emphasizes that that struggle takes place in a country that 'as a public space ... in the last 25 years ... has become an American colony.'[30] In other words, at the very moment when the nation had the best reasons since Confederation to celebrate itself and its culture – the artists and audience longed for by Dewart, MacMechan, Lampman, Brown, and others had finally appeared – it was entering a period when its idea of itself would be questioned, even undermined, and the major phase of its development was ending. The change in literary and cultural criticism is obvious if we recall the quotation from Frank Davey in the preface (x).

Part of the cultural optimism of the era was grounded in and was the culmination of nearly a century of cultural discourses and practices directed at creating a national culture that would, it was assumed, be the basis of a national identity. (Though some of the ground about to be covered is familiar to specialists in the field, it may be useful to take a few pages to sketch the evolution of a nationalist criticism and ideology since these form the matrix for my reading of Purdy's work.) As its earliest artists recognized, the young Dominion was a state in search of a national identity. Efforts to encourage and produce the latter can be seen in Canada First, the various anthologies of poetry like Dewart's *Selections from Canadian Poets* (1864), Carman's *Our Canadian Literature* (1922), and Smith's *Book of Canadian Poetry* (1943), as well as the various multi-volume series dealing with Canadian literature and history published earlier in this century. Furthermore, the CBC, the Governor General's Awards, the National Film Board, the Massey Commission Report, the Canada Council, McClelland and Stewart's New Canadian Library editions – all were part of a matrix of state and private apparatuses stimulating a new national self-awareness. In this context, Pratt's national epics of the 1940s and 1950s seem almost inevitable. The appearance in the 1950s and 1960s of writers as original as Irving Layton, Margaret Avison, Mavis Gallant, Mordecai Richler, Margaret Laurence, Margaret Atwood, Alice Munro, Michael Ondaatje, and Purdy seemed to herald the fulfilment of the hopes of the writers and editors of the previous century (Moodie, Dewart, Lighthall, MacMechan, Garvin, Sandwell, Deacon, and others) who, while lamenting the provincialism of Canadian culture, saw the work of their era as the seed-bed of what they hoped would become a distinct national literature. Lampman's ecstatic response to Roberts's *Orion and Other Poems* is too well known to need quotation, but a general comment on Canadian literature earlier in his 1891 lecture is worth recalling: 'A good deal is being said about Canadian literature, and most of it takes the form of question and answer as to whether a Canadian literature exists. Of course it does not. It will probably be a full generation or two before we can present a body of work of sufficient excellence as measured by the severest standards, and sufficiently marked with local colour, to enable us to call it a Canadian literature. It is only within the last quarter of a century that the United States have produced anything like a distinctive American literature.'[31] The realism and the optimism are echoed by Roberts nearly half a century later: 'When I was beginning to write, I was not aware of any such thing as Canadian literature ... but I did dream of *starting* a *Canadian* literature.'[32] Both Confederation poets simply make explicit the assumptions and hopes of many.

It is arguable that for a majority of writers – as different as Sangster, Roberts, Carman, Connor, Grove, MacDonald, Pratt, and F.R. Scott – Roberts's dream of a national literature was inseparable from the dream of a postcolonial nation. This is evident in the best work of minor and major writers (*Tecumseh, Brébeuf and His Brethren, Surfacing*) as well as in the mass of patriotic poetry written during the past century – from Sangster's poem on Sir Isaac Brock ('Oct. 12, 1859') to Roberts's 'Canada' and some of Purdy's weaker political poems – distinguished primarily by what Frye calls 'the gift of metrical gab.'[33] The dream of a national literature was inextricable from the dream of a nation. It was to be a literature that stood between British and American, and would articulate a national experience that, though rooted in the British tradition and unavoidably influenced by the American one, would be somehow different from both,[34] just as the citizens, though immigrants, would over the generations become 'Canadians.'[35] Lampman is again prescient and optimistic on the last point: 'Already there are many among us whose fathers and grandfathers have lived and died upon this soil, who are neither British, French nor German, but simply Canadians.'[36] Incidentally, he begins his lecture with a nod in the direction of those who are 'beginning to feel for Canada the enthusiasm of Fatherland,' an enthusiasm he hopes will be fostered by Canadian literature. To paraphrase Massimo d'Azeglio, he recognized that now that Canada had been created it was necessary to create (or invent) Canadians.[37]

In Eric Hobsbawm's sense of the terms, the artists I'm discussing were involved in creating and inventing the language and traditions that would put flesh on the skeletal state created by the British North America Act of 1867. Anticipating in 1966 Hobsbawm's notion of the invention of tradition, F.W. Watt described the situation as follows: 'To what extent have writers succeeded in inventing Canada and Canadians? If one thinks first of all of geography, the physical environment, the Canadian terrain, the answer is that Canada has been very successfully invented, but in a process as long and gradual as that by which this half-continent was explored, settled and mastered, both politically and by technology and communications.'[38] Watt emphasizes, in a nuanced discussion, that few writers have written with the explicit intention of 'inventing Canada' or from the standpoint of an explicit or self-conscious nationalist ideology, though from Mair, Sangster, and Roberts to Pratt, MacLennan, Purdy, Atwood, and Wayman there have been many who have seen themselves as cultural and political nationalists. And even those who did not were aware of the postcolonial dilemma of a 'Canadian' literature being written in the twin shadows of the British and American traditions. Watt, who is rightly uneasy with the idea of nationalism as a self-conscious motive for literary creativity, makes the important point, however, that 'nationalism may be influenced by writers who have no apparent interest in it and who would refuse to serve if invited.'[39] The poetry of P.K. Page, the David Milne of our poets, is a case in point. Written too often under the banner of aestheticism, it nevertheless contributed to the creation of a Canadian poetic tradition both by setting a high poetic standard and influencing poets in the next generation. Another example is Michael Ondaatje's *Coming through Slaughter* (1976); although dealing with a jazzman in New Orleans, it is as important to the 'tradition' as the more historical and political *In the Skin of a Lion*, which is set in 1920s Toronto and deals with the immigrants involved in the building of the city. To recall Lampman's lecture, Page and Ondaatje are important because their work shows 'sufficient excellence as measured by the severest standards,' though he might be uneasy about the lack of 'local [Canadian] colour' in Ondaatje's New Orleans novel. Watt's essay suggests that a national literary tradition is a relatively elastic concept that includes works that are intended to give voice to national issues as well as those whose primary concerns lie elsewhere.

It is worth recalling that most modern definitions of the nation are imprecise and inclusive except for essentialist ones that look back to the emphasis on *Volk* or race in Herder and Hegel. Most postcolonial nations, for instance, can't recognize themselves in Ernest Renan's comment that a 'nation is a soul, a spiritual principle' that is 'the culmination of a long past of endeavours, sacrifice, and devotion.'[40] Closer to the historical reality of a country like Canada are Eric Hobsbawm's suggestion that a nation 'is any sufficiently large body of people whose members regard themselves as members of a nation' and Rupert Emerson's view that a 'nation is a community of people who feel that they belong together in the double sense that they share deeply significant elements of a common heritage and that they have a common destiny for the future.' Even nations that claim a lengthy historical pedigree with origins shrouded in 'the mists of time,' perhaps especially such nations, are recent historical constructs that in their more myth-making moods have invented their own roots. Discussions of nation and nationalism need also to keep in mind Renan's warning that 'a nation's existence ... is a daily plebiscite' as well as Braudel's comment that a nation 'can have its *being* only at the price of being forever in search of itself ...'[41] I emphasize this point because I want to avoid leaving the impression that I am working with a fixed or simple idea of nation, nationalism, national literature, and national poet.

As one would expect in a country settled predominantly during its formative or constitutive years by European immigrants, Canadian assumptions about and definitions of a nation, nationalism, and a national culture have tended to reflect until recently European ones, especially those prevalent during the nineteenth century, the century of European nation making. In fact, I would even venture the guess that a concept of nation that doesn't reflect those assumptions to some extent will not be taken seriously by Canadians of European descent. Even while our more recent theorists debate the details of a new multicultural nationalism, it is probable that for most Canadians any argument over nation, nationalism, and identity will be conducted in the shadow of what Louis Dudek called 'the remnant of nineteenth century Romantic nationalism'[42] and Nathan Glazer the 'ghost nations' of Europeans in North America.[43]

Although our identity and the defining characteristics of the Canadian experience continue to be a subject of discussion, and the discussion itself often a topic of exasperation or ridicule, there is surprising agreement among our artists and intellectuals about them. For every writer like Joseph Levitt who does not 'believe there is such a thing as a Canadian national character,'[44] there are several who not only perceive one but also describe its genesis. W.L. Morton is even able to assert that 'there is no Canadian way of life' while nevertheless indicating the bases of a 'Canadian identity' in the well-known book with the same title.[45] We may lack what Robert Kroetsch calls a national 'meta-narrative or myth,' perhaps an impossibility for a modern nation neither tribal in origin nor founded by a revolution, but there is a certain coherence and congruence in the stories we tell about ourselves and a fundamental agreement about the constitutive historical, economic, and cultural events of our past.[46] Were this not so, I doubt that

Frye's 'Conclusion' would have the staying power that it does for our criticism.

For instance, the current generation of Canadians may know the land primarily as cottagers and tourists, but there is general agreement that, in Abraham Rotstein's words, the early relation to the land was the country's 'psychic crucible.'[47] Innis's and Creighton's geographical and economic determinism, Collins's 'savannahs,' Lower's northern vision and his version of Turner's frontier thesis, Diefenbaker's northern vision, Frye's 'garrison mentality' and the terror of the environment, Atwood's 'survival' and emphasis on space as a defining category, Pratt, Purdy, and the Group of Seven's attempts to evoke the cadences of the land – all these are part of the same ultimately convincing argument about one of the country's founding myths, French and English. Inseparable from this are the ideas and images of exile and immigration, French, British, European, and most recently Third World. There is also the heritage of what Charles Taylor calls 'Britishness' and Philip Resnick 'English Canada,' a language, set of attitudes, values, and cultural and political institutions that redefined the country after the Treaty of Paris of 1763, a heritage that today seems in particular danger of being neglected or even forgotten in the rush to redefine what aspects of history are relevant – or, more troublingly, irrelevant – for a multicultural or polyethnic Canada. And though I don't want to restrict Purdy's importance as a poet to this aspect of his work, its importance in his poetry should not be underestimated; if not quite the poet of Loyalism that Dennis Duffy and the other Charles Taylor suggest him to be, he is nevertheless a poet to whom that tradition has been of personal and creative importance, a constitutive aspect of an identity and a national vision that is interconnected with the prehistory of the land, the histories of Indians and Inuit (see 'Remains of an Indian Village,' 'Watching Trains,' and North of Summer), and, to a lesser extent, the French experience (see 'A Handful of Earth,' which is dedicated to René Lévesque).[48] Charles Taylor's comments on this tradition and its inescapable, though inevitably problematic presence today, are worth quoting at some length.

We have a commonly established self-image as being more rooted in the past than American civilization, with part of our society steeped in the British tradition (stemming from the Loyalists who refused the American revolution), and stemming from a French community cut off from the mother country before the revolution.[49]

We are all the Queen's subjects, but this seems to mean less to fewer people; and, more awkwardly, it still means quite a bit to some, yet nothing at all to others, and therefore cannot be the basis of unity. What binds Canada together outside Quebec is thus no longer a common provenance, and less and less is it a common history. But people find the bonding elements in political institutions and ways of being. This is not a total break from the old identity, because Britishness also defined itself largely in terms of political institutions: parliamentary government, a certain juridical tradition, and the like. The slide has been continuous and without a sharp break from the old to the new.[50]

While registering the pressures of the present situation, Taylor also reminds us of the unmistakable, living traces of once dominant traditions and hegemonies that constitute the historical matrix out of which the nation developed. These are not simply a nostalgic or archaic residue, but critical structural and, dare one say it, spiritual elements that provide something of 'the common provenance' or 'common history' no longer generally available or, at least, not in the once widely accepted social discourses and practices: political institutions, flags, religions, the names of villages and towns, royal visits, touring theatre companies, holidays, school texts, etc. If we want to understand who our Canadian ancestors thought they were, what kind of world they were living in, and what sort of nation and society they were creating – the future envisioned by our past – we need to understand this tradition. Simply to declare it irrelevant to the needs of the most recent immigrants and to replace it in school texts with more immediately 'relevant' material is to cut the nation's roots. More aware of political realities than most, Taylor emphasizes a view of national evolution 'without a sharp break from the old to the new.' His words could also be used to describe the sense of time and history in many of Purdy's poems, especially those in which the self, though located in the present, shifts easily back and forth between past, present, and future, exploring the unavoidable relations among them.

An analogous 'slide' occurs on the literary level. Whatever their differences of language, historical experience, or geography, colonial literatures of 'new' countries inevitably pass through similar overlapping stages of development, though they may do so within a time frame characterized by Frye as 'the foreshortening of history' and by Innis as 'cyclonics': the encounter with indigenes and the land; the dependence on a literature from 'home'; the puritanism of the colonial mentality; the struggle to create a national literature for the new nation; eventual international recognition. The political and cultural paradigm that most follow was established, though this is often forgotten, by the development of the United States and American literature. Emerson's 'The Poet' (1842–4) can be read as the manifesto of all postcolonial nations. It is worth quoting Emerson at some length because the tone and concerns of his essay will be echoed by countless writers, including Purdy, in most colonies of 'the white diaspora':[51]

I look in vain for the poet whom I describe. We do not, with sufficient plainness, or sufficient profoundness, address ourselves to life, nor dare we chaunt our own times and social circumstance. If we filled the day with bravery, we should not shrink from celebrating it ... We have yet had no genius in America, with tyrannous eye, which knew the value of our incomparable materials, and saw, in the barbarism and materialism of the times, another carnival of the same gods whose picture he so much admires in Homer; then in the middle age; then in Calvinism. Banks and tariffs, the newspaper and caucus, methodism and unitarianism, are flat and dull to dull people, but rest on the same foundations of wonder as the town of Troy, and the temple of Delphos, and are as swiftly passing away. Our logrolling, our stumps and their politics, our fisheries, our Negroes and Indians, our boasts, and our repudiations, the wrath of rogues, and the pusillanimity of honest men, the northern trade, the southern planting, the western clearing, Oregon, and Texas, are yet unsung. Yet America is a poem in our eyes; its ample geography dazzles the imagination, and it will not wait long for metres.[52]

Whitman's 'Democratic Vistas' (1867–8) will give Emerson's argument a more intensely democratic emphasis ('Literature, strictly considered, has never recognized the People'[53]) and a more religious orientation, but in essence it builds on three Emersonian points: America as a geographical place is different from Europe; the American social, political, and historical experience is unprecedented; and because America has yet to find its voice and its national poet, its literature remains inferior to Europe's. In other colonial literatures, the last concern will ironically become a lament that no local Whitman has yet appeared. In Canadian writing, for instance, E.K. Brown's well-known comment that 'Our Whitman is in the future'[54] was anticipated in 1928 by Leo Kennedy and has been echoed by critics for more than half a century, most notably in Dennis Lee's characterization of Purdy as our Whitman.

Though, with the possible exception of Frye's 'Conclusion' to *Literary History of Canada*, there is no text in Canadian literature with the symbolic and seminal importance of Emerson's and Whitman's essays, the colonial and postcolonial issues they engage are raised by almost all Canadian writers, from Frances Brooke and Julia Beckwith Hart (see the 'Preface' to *St Ursula's Convent* [1824], and 'Introduction' to *Tonnewonte* [1825]) to Roberts, Grove, MacLennan, Frye, Lee, and Atwood.[55] The discussion of these issues – and it continues in some form even today – has been constitutive of whatever it is that we mean when we refer to Canada, Canadian culture, and Canadian identity. The un-European nature of the land, for instance, was remarked on by explorers, evoked by Moodie's *Roughing It in the Bush* and Charles Mair's *Tecumseh*, and given memorable critical definition by Frye. T.E. Hulme's well-known comment that free verse was the appropriate metric for a description of the Canadian prairies recalls Emerson's and Whitman's assumption that America as a land requires a new kind of 'metre-making argument' and a new kind of poet. Poets as different as Mair, Pratt, Purdy, and Christopher Dewdney have assumed that a Canadian poetic would, in part, be based on some kind of expressive consonance with the land, similar perhaps to the relationship one senses between the texture of the paintings of the Group of Seven and the physiognomy of the landscapes they represent.[56] In one sense, this is part of a search for origins, the desire to articulate an aspect of the new land so primeval that it is untouched by the European historical and cultural experience.[57] It is a search for a style that will seem to be or will create the illusion that it is the voice of the spirit of place. Purdy sounds this note in 'A Handful of Earth' (1977), where he evokes 'our true language' as one that 'speaks from inside / the land itself' (*CP*, 245). Emphasis here, as throughout writing of this kind, is placed on the ontological priority of the landscape. In a sense, geography is a temporary substitute for what is sometimes perceived as an absent or inadequate history. It's a gambit that allows one to sidestep Henry James's well-known lament about the lack of 'society' in the New World and Frank Scott's acknowledgment that 'nothing great seemed to have been achieved in human terms' in the Canada of his youth.[58]

Though it may be unsettling to anyone asserting the uniqueness of the North American landscape and our relationship to it, there is a mystical quality in postcolonial discussions of the spirit of place analogous to the mystique of the soil one finds in the work of Johann Gottfried Herder and Romantic nationalists. Like the supposed remote ancestors of each of the European nations, the aboriginal peoples, though immigrants, are viewed as almost autochthonous and therefore coextensive with the land itself. The term 'First Nations' registers something of this. I linger over this point because the change in attitude towards the indigenous 'Other' during the past three decades is an important part of the ideological shift that brought what I have called the major phase of Canadian history to an end. How a literary critic views the prehistoric past often indicates his or her view of the canon, the nation, and national identity. Emerson's and Whitman's passing references to 'Indians' foreshadow contemporary movements in Canada, Australia, and New Zealand to integrate aboriginal writing into the still-forming national canons, and thus to find a ground for the latter in a non-European version of the *Volk*. The native inhabitants and their 'history' provide a human content to what is otherwise simply a natural landscape or geography. Similarly, so runs the argument, their myths and 'poems' provide an aboriginal poem of the land. Perhaps the most significant and also problematic recent development in Canadian literature has been the attempt not only to integrate native myths and songs into the anthologies and the canon but to use aboriginal materials in contemporary non-aboriginal writing in an attempt to form a continuity between immigrants who arrived at different times in history. Writing in 1960, James Reaney anticipated Frye and Bowering in insisting on the centrality of Indian art and myth to the Canadian experience.[59]

We have Indians: I've already glanced at their poetry, but the other things they've accomplished – the rituals, the sculpture, the design, just themselves – have always looked suggestive of development to me. The totem poles and the mounds seem so effortlessly to come out of the look of the country; but our culture, as yet, doesn't. When you compare Michelangelo's gigantic statues of Day and Night, Twilight and Dawn, when you compare them with the tense coloured oblongs by which in their ritual sand painting the Indians describe the same eternal truths, the difference between the genius of this continent and the genius of Europe becomes evident with a flash. And that difference contains the answer to the riddle of being an artist in this country.[60]

There's some idealization here, some reduction of different aboriginal cultures to a single model, and I'm uneasy with the suggestion that totem poles, mounds, and Michelangelo's statues 'describe the same eternal truths.' But Reaney's main point is clear: he wants to find a postcolonial equivalent to Indian art, a poetry with the same integral relationship to the land as the 'totem poles and mounds' that 'seem so effortlessly to come out of the look of the country.' Reaney, Frye, and Bowering are primarily interested in the uses to which non-indigenous artists and writers can put indigenous materials, including myths. Frye, for instance, suggests unconvincingly that Susan Musgrave 'shows throughout [her poems] strong imaginative links with a people she clearly thinks of as poetically her ancestors.'[61] A more radical version of this view carries the assumption that the North American landscape can only be adequately described by aboriginal peoples and their cultural artefacts. Only languages and modes of perception and being uncontaminated by the European cultural tradition, it is argued, can hope to express the spirit of place. A radically 'other' landscape can be adequately described only by a culture and a people who embody 'otherness' for the dominant culture and its discourses. In this instance, historical priority denotes ontological and epistemological authenticity and spiritual authority. At its most radical and its most questionable, as in the criticism of Robert Kroetsch, this attitude will lead to a dissatisfaction with European languages, a desire for a linguistic *tabula rasa* or ur-language directly expressive of 'American' being. (Whitman's preference for aboriginal names over European ones is part of the same impulse.) The result is a privileging of myth over mimesis and history, of metaphor over metonymy, a shift that then allows redefinitions of key terms such as literature, culture, canon, history, and truth. In this area one can understand why postcolonial and postmodern critics often share the same concerns and discourses.

They ignore, however, Hegel's warning in the *Aesthetics* that gods or myths that 'no longer have any *truth* for us' 'give us pleasure only for our imagination,' but we are unable 'to believe in them.'[62] George Grant may have had Hegel in mind in the following characteristically hard-headed comment:

The roots of some communities in eastern North America go back far in continuous love for their place, but none of us can be called autochthonous, because in all there is some consciousness of making the land our own ...

That conquering relation to place has left its mark within us. When we go into the Rockies we may have the sense that gods are there. But if so, they cannot manifest themselves to us as ours. They are the gods of another race, and we cannot know them because of what we are, and what we did. There can be nothing immemorial for us except the environment as object.[63]

For Grant, knowledge, expression, and continuity cannot be established on a substantive level between then and now, them and us, no matter how ecumenical our attitude, because of the radical difference between two peoples ('what we are') and because of the history of their relations ('what we did'). Though his concern is spiritual rather than more narrowly cultural, his comments point to differences in history and *mentalité* that prevent any simple continuity between the two traditions.

Whether aboriginal characters, events, and culture can be much more than an occasional subject-matter for non-aboriginal writers is a question as problematic as whether or not that body of myth and artefacts can be discussed in any meaningful way as part of a Canadian literary tradition. No one disputes that it constitutes an important and revealing response to the same environment later Canadian writers and artists describe, but if we think of a cultural tradition as involving not simply contiguity but continuity, transmission, and influence, then the aboriginal inheritance is more problematic than some postcolonial critics would have us believe. The materials in Musgrave's early Haida poems or Rudy Wiebe's *The Temptations of Big Bear* and *A Discovery of Strangers* are given at best a half-life in a borrowed language even if the poem or novel is an artistic success. A related problem is the fact that after four hundred years of a destructive, deracinating, and often murderous colonialism, the authenticity of some of the products of contemporary aboriginal culture is problematic. Is the majority of Inuit sculpture, for instance, truly indigenous? Or is it simply a response, initiated by James Houston in the late 1940s, to the economic needs of a people and the demands of an international art market? Authenticity is also an issue if we consider that most of us know the 'writings' of the First Nations in translation, and that most of the better-known writers – Thomas King, Tomson Highway, Daniel David Moses – write in English. What is the status of aboriginal writing as *aboriginal* writing if it is in English? To what extent is a writer still part of a literature or culture if he no longer writes in the language of that literature? Finally, if aboriginal writers consider themselves part of a North American, transnational, Amerindian tradition, are we justified in placing them in a Canadian or American or Mexican one?[64]

To repeat. If a national cultural tradition is something more than a simple, almost ethnographic collection of all the works of art produced by all individuals resident in one place over a period of time, if a tradition is to be a matter of influence, of the transmission of styles, values, a world-view, a body of art by several generations of people, then it isn't clear that aboriginal art – no matter of how high an artistic quality – and colonial and postcolonial art are part of the same tradition in any meaningful sense of the word. Our view of this issue has more than cultural implications or implications for the field we designate as Canadian literature. Inextricable from it is a view or definition of what we mean by the Canadian nation and Canadian identity. What I have been questioning above is what I call the soft or postmodern multicultural attitude. Its argument runs roughly as follows. Canada, despite the recent dominance of English and French languages and cultures, has always been a multicultural or polyethnic society. And if we agree that all value-judgments are relative, all cultures are therefore equally 'valid,' and all cultural artefacts are equally important or of equal value and relevance. No centre, no margin, no majority, no minority, everything and everyone of equal value and significance. This is a vision of the postcolonial culture and nation as an amorphous and ahistorical Whitmanian democracy. In culture, this reduces works of art to the status of paintings by kindergarten children – *all* efforts are put on display as of equal significance so that no group can feel excluded. Let me emphasize that what troubles me here is not the legitimate *political* desire to ensure that all groups have equal political or discursive representation or that certain historical wrongs are compensated but the attempt to politicize culture to make it do the work of identity politics and to make it part of a compensation package for historical wrongs or present anxieties.

This doesn't mean, of course, that postcolonial writers can't make effective use of indigenous materials, simply that they need to recognize the limits of what they can do with them. In fact, that recognition is often part of the theme of works by Wiebe, Purdy, and Kroetsch. More challenging and problematic is Kroetsch's well-known, though not closely examined, desire to 'un-name' the country in order to 'unhide the hidden' – that is, whatever was here prior to 1492. Because I discuss in the next chapter Purdy's concern with origins and with pre-linguistic modes of being and expression, I want to digress for a moment to look at ostensibly similar concerns in the criticism of Kroetsch and Lee. I write 'ostensibly' because Purdy's pragmatic attitude to language and the centrality of history to his vision divert him from their more radical and problematic acts of deconstruction. Kroetsch's neo-Heideggerian desire to unname, for instance, would at its most extreme disinherit us of Glenn Gould's versions of the *Goldberg Variations*, the music of John Weinzweig, colonial architecture and furniture, all painting before the Group of Seven, and all poetry prior to his own.

At one time I considered it to be the task of the Canadian writer to give names to his experience, to be the namer. I now suspect that, on the contrary, it is his task to un-name ...

The Canadian writer's predicament is that he works with a language within a literature, that appears to be authentically his own, and not a borrowing. But just as there was in the Latin word a concealed Greek experience, so there is in the Canadian word a concealed other experience, sometimes British, sometimes American.

In recent years, the tension between this appearance of being just like someone else and the demands of authenticity has become intolerable – both to individuals and to the society. In recent Canadian fiction the major writers resolve the paradox ... by the radical process of demythologizing the systems that threaten to define them. Or, more comprehensively, they uninvent the world.[65]

Kroetsch's linking of individuals and society alerts us to the political implications of his argument, though 'political' here – as in almost all poststructuralist writing – is far removed from any Canadian political reality. To be fair to Kroetsch it should be noted that several of his other essays and his poems stop short of what could be called the negative poetics of his most radical essay to offer a view of 'the Hidden' closer to what one finds in Purdy's more referentially oriented work.

While Philip Resnick doesn't refer to Kroetsch in *Thinking English Canada*, he nevertheless offers a strong possible response to the implications of unnaming, one that incidentally alerts us to the ahistorical dimension of Kroetsch's argument. Acknowledging the presence and pressure of multiculturalism and the historically unique status of the First Nations, Resnick nevertheless recognizes the limits of what is possible, and for him desirable, in the claims and assumptions of the postcolonial politics of pluralism. 'First, there can be no going back to the status quo ante, some earlier stage of civilization and social organization that existed before the Europeans arrived. Technology cannot be uninvented, English unlearned, Christianity extirpated, liberal democratic precepts cast aside, regardless of attempts to revive traditional notions of spirituality, to give a new lease on life to native languages, to allow aboriginals to touch base where possible with older tribal customs.'[66]

Resnick's immediate concern in this passage is with aboriginal rights, but the idea of 'going back to the status quo ante' makes his comments relevant to Kroetsch's desire for unnaming, authenticity, and some original language uninfected by English or American. Uneasy with the burden of inherited European myths, Kroetsch proposes another: the myth of the American Adam standing before all mythologies and all languages. If 'the demands of authenticity' have indeed become intolerable, then one wonders at what point Kroetsch's suggested 'demythologizing'

and un-naming can possibly stop. Do we change the names of all our cities or just those with names unacceptable to the new mythmakers? But,
then, why stop there? What are we to do with our inherited languages?
With our names? Surely names like Kroetsch, Woodcock, Ondaatje, or
Solecki are inauthentic according to these criteria that derive from what
could be called the demands of a North American poetics of presence
and authenticity? Taking his cue from Whitman, Lawrence, Williams,
and Olson, Kroetsch tries to imagine an 'authentic' language and nation
and finds himself in a theoretical cul-de-sac. If he is serious about
authenticity, he has only two realistic options if he keeps on writing in
English: either he wrestles with English in a manner foreshadowed by
Whitman and Twain and, in Australia, by Les Murray and the Jindy-
worobaks, or, despairing of ever being able to find a language adequate
to his experience and landscape, he lapses into silence. Anything else
represents compromise and a lapse into inauthenticity and bad faith.

Both alternatives are raised in Dennis Lee's more nuanced 'Cadence,
Country, Silence: Writing in Colonial Space.' Like Heidegger, whose
'dasein' becomes his 'cadence,' Lee is able to envision silence as a positive condition, either as an end in itself in which one confronts the
'cadence' or 'being' of self, earth, and 'here' or as a preparation for writing. Reading the essay, while keeping Lee's poems in mind, one senses
that it also explores what could be called his worst-case scenario for the
situation of the colonial and postcolonial writer, and it is as such that I
want to examine it. I want to emphasize that the passage I discuss below
represents a passing moment in Lee's criticism, which is qualified, for
the most part, in his essays and his poetry. But because it is representative of an attitude to the Canadian past common among contemporary
literary and cultural critics, I shall kidnap it for the sake of my argument. Like Kroetsch, though in a more historically inflected argument,
Lee senses that the stance or being-in-the-world as a writer that he
wants and the national language he envisions are simply not possible
for the postcolonial writer in an English-speaking society. He may
struggle with it and make of that struggle a subject for his writing, but
the linguistic matrix, no matter how reworked and violated by other
idiolects and local usage, will still carry for him the unavoidable burden
of colonialism, the British literary tradition and various other strong
echoes of empire. As Lee puts it in 'The Poetry of Al Purdy: An Afterword,' 'The very language of the metropolitan imagination has had to
be unlearned, even as it was being learned from' (CP, 390). An Espe-
ranto of colonial authenticity is not a possibility.

More troubling about both essays is the fact that, however seductive their rhetoric of neo-Adamic origins may be, neither can imagine the four-hundred-year tradition of colonial culture as anything but a burden or hindrance; in contrast to Purdy, each can offer only an either/or position. Kroetsch's desire to 'un-name' rejects everything – including language, history, and the conception of the self – inherited from the European tradition. It's tempting to see this as a chapter in the history of colonial anxiety of influence, similar to Herman Melville's insistence that Americans read Pop Emmons rather than Homer because Pop was home-grown, one of their own.[67] Melville jettisons the burden of the European past in order the clear a space for Pop Emmons and himself. Kroetsch's motives are probably as complex as Melville's: the insistence on an authentic American or Canadian literature is inextricable from the desire to escape from Homer and Shakespeare's shadow, and that includes escaping from a comparison that one loses even before it is made. It may be the mark of a strong writer like Purdy that, knowing the odds and the risks, he nevertheless invites the comparison.

Lee's description of his condition is more complex and slightly more responsive to the pressure of history, but no more than Kroetsch is he able to see that his past – no matter how colonial or populated by 'ancestors ... often mediocre or muddling'[68] – represents something of value, something that can be used in his writing not simply as part of a register of failure and oppression. Though he follows Grant and Purdy in acknowledging the importance of early Canadian history, Lee is so overwhelmed by Canada's postwar evolution into an American colony that he is unable to articulate the past except as a problem, even an impasse for the writer.

In fact, I conclude, the impasse of writing that is problematic to itself is transcended only when the impasse becomes its own subject, when writing accepts and enters and names its own condition as it is naming the world. Any other course ... leads to writing whose joints and musculature never work together, which remains constantly out of synch with itself. We have a lot of both in Canada.

Putting it differently: to be authentic, the voice of being alive here and now must include the inauthenticity of our lives here and now. We can expect no lightning or thunder to come down from heaven, to transform our past or our present. Part of the truth about us is that we have betrayed our own truths, by letting ourselves be robbed of them. To say that for real, the betrayal must be incorporated faithfully – in both sorrow and anger – in the saying.[69]

Two things trouble me here, even as I admire Lee's unsparing look at our past and find myself leaning towards most of his argument. The first has to do with the comment that 'we have betrayed our own truths.' On a more playful level one is tempted to ask, with Tonto, 'Who is this "we," Kemo Sabe?' In what sense, for instance, can the Group of Seven be accused of betraying 'our own truths'? Or Pratt? MacLennan? Purdy? More seriously, I wonder how 'truths' can be said to have been betrayed if one of the essay's assumptions is that they have yet to be dis-covered, articulated, and therefore brought to consciousness: can one betray something that doesn't yet exist in language and consciousness, that one doesn't yet know and that for historical reasons one and one's ancestors couldn't be expected to know? One of the reasons that we see what is missing or recognize the lacunae and failures Lee records is that, like Freud's flea, we stand on the shoulders of those ancestors who, in Purdy's words, 'Had their being once / and left a place to stand on' (ISOR, [90]). Furthermore, if the ancestors were 'mediocre or muddling' artists, surely it is too much to expect 'truths' of this kind from them? If Lee were to read the past in a slightly more dialectical manner, he would recognize that the ancestors' strengths and failings are coexten-sive and inseparable from their complex historical circumstances. The result would be a more sympathetic reading of the Canadian past of the kind that is pervasive in Purdy's work. As I suggested earlier, there's something curious in the postcolonial criticism of our earlier writers, almost all second-rate, for failing to do justice to the new continent in their work; the same objection can be applied to Lee. Though Lee strikes me as one of the more perceptive readers of our situation, his stance in the above passage, though not in his other work, isn't immune from the sort of criticism the historian J.G.A. Pocock directs at 'the lesser intellec-tuals of New Zealand, who are much like lesser intellectuals elsewhere, [and] seek to impose on themselves and others both the guilt of having been colonists and the victim status of having been colonised. They fas-ten on an overworked family of words, to bring the whole history of the country under the paradigms of "colonialism" and "decolonisation"; the latter in particular standing for an apparently nationalist rejection of a supposedly slavish subjection to British policy and culture.'[70] As I said, Lee, like the 'lesser intellectuals,' is unable to see the colonial past dialectically, to understand the inseparability of its positive and nega-tive aspects. When he refers to 'the words our absentee masters have given us' he makes, I would argue, too easy a judgment on the past. Our 'masters,' whether absentee or present, have passed on the culture – our enabling cultural and political discourses and institutions – that allows us to act, speak, and ask the difficult questions Lee is now posing. What's missing in 'Cadence, Country, Silence: Writing in Colonial Space' can be seen, I think, if we juxtapose Lee's comments to his own poems as well as to Pablo Neruda's reflections on the language he inherited from the Spanish who conquered South America.

What a great language I have inherited ... from the fierce conquistadores ... They strode over the giant cordilleras, over the rugged Americas, hunting for potatoes, sausages, beans, black tobacco, gold, corn, fried eggs, with a voracious appetite not found in the world since then ... They swallowed up everything, religions, pyramids, tribes, idolatries just like the ones they brought along in their huge sacks ... Wherever they went, they razed the land ... But words fell like pebbles out of the boots of the barbarians, out of their beards, their helmets, their horseshoes, luminous words that were left glittering here ... our language. We came up losers ... We came up winners ... They carried off the gold and left us the gold ... They carried everything off and left us everything ... They left us the words.[71]

This is impressive for a variety of reasons, not the least of which is its verbal and historical poise. Looking unflinchingly back at the past, Neruda understands – as too much postcolonial writing doesn't – that it is only possible to describe and judge today the razing of the land by the invading 'barbarians' because they also left the 'luminous words' (and I would add value systems) in which such an engagement can take place. Neruda sees his masters clearly, and his view of history is sufficiently ambivalent and complex to understand that no easy judgment of our past and our predecessors is possible. It is simply not possible to speak of 'them' and 'us,' since no clear line of demarcation exists between past and present. In Purdy's case, for instance, one of his 'masters,' after all, is Bliss Carman, in every sense a minor and derivative poet; yet he is as important as Lawrence or Yeats to the evolution of Purdy's poetry. In fact, it is arguable that, had Purdy not become 'enthralled with Bliss Carman's poetry' (*RBS*, 43) in high school, he would not have become a poet. As it is, Purdy's poetics would not be what they are without the influence of Carman and the tradition of conservative verse he represents. In other words, if the colonial 'masters' were provincial, limited, and/or repressive, they were also liberating, and the one quality cannot be conveniently separated from the other. Hegel, Nietzsche, or Freud would even insist that without the negative mastery, Lee's ability to articulate his and our situation would not have been possible. It is worth recalling that, in the end, Hegel's slave is more creative and vital than his master, but his eventual triumph is a function of his previous status as slave.[72]

Both Lee and Kroetsch seem to echo the American desire for a new beginning miraculously available on the other side of a colonial or post-colonial lustration or dispossession. Kroetsch's gesture is more purely 'American' and postcolonial: the inherited language, and the history and world-view embodied in it and inseparable from it are to be jettisoned like so much excess and irrelevant baggage in the search for 'the myth of the new world, the garden story. The dream of Eden.'[73] The images – warmed-up, belated Americana – place Kroetsch closer to the Americans in this discussion than to the Canadians, as does the Black Mountain poetic underlying his poems. Lee's version is more complex because of his insistence on the inevitability of a struggle with the heritage, though, to use Atwood's terms, one can't help wondering whether his writer is simply a victim (Hegel's slave) who has convinced himself that his enslavement is a temporary condition, a transition to masterhood. As I shall argue in the next section, Purdy escapes Kroetsch's and Lee's dilemma, and the former's ahistoric solution, in two ways. The first is his isolation during the 1940s and 1950s from the social and cultural movements that shaped Kroetsch's mind and the 'continentalism' or Americanization that were pervasive for Lee's generation. Secondly, Purdy has a more positive response to the Canadian past and makes use, however indirect and nuanced, of the tradition of poetry represented though not exhausted by Carman. His attachment to 'the old ones,' whether his grandfather, Ridley Neville Purdy, or Bliss Carman, roots him in Canadian history and prevents him from being tempted by what Jack Hodgins playfully calls the 'Eden swindle,' the new-world desire for a society and an art without antecedents. Purdy may be occasionally embarrassed by Carman's weaker poems, but he knows that he would not have become a poet without Carman's influence.

A good example of the North American longing for an art without precedents can be found in Mark Rothko's comment that contemporary American painters, the abstract expressionists, 'have wiped the slate clean. We start anew. A new land. We've got to forget what the Old Masters did.'[74] Missing in Rothko, however, is the writer's desire to represent the country, a desire evident in William Carlos Williams's seminal *In the American Grain*. 'Americans have never recognized themselves. How can they? It is impossible until someone invent the ORIGINAL terms. As long as we are content to be called by somebody else's

terms, we are incapable of being anything but our own dupes.'[75] 'ORIG-
INAL terms' could have been written by Kroetsch, while 'dupes' is from
the same nexus of feelings as Lee's 'betrayed.' As I suggested earlier, the
only original terms available belong to the native peoples, and English-
speaking poets can make use of them only within the matrix of a European language. If there is an origin it is available at a remove, just like
the works of the first peoples. To recast the situation in terms made
familiar by Schiller, the discussions of postcolonial writers like Williams
and Kroetsch are haunted by the desire for a 'naïve' national poet: themselves irrevocably 'sentimental' like Schiller himself – in the sense of
being belated, educated, and critical – they envision the 'naïve' poet as
one who can give the land and their experience an original and 'epic'
voice. One of the inescapable ironies of this is that, like Emerson's call
for an American poet, it reflects Romantic assumptions about a national
poet – Dante, Shakespeare, Goethe, Pushkin, Mickiewicz – able to imagine a national myth, a vision of a nation's experience and history.
Czeslaw Milosz's role in Polish poetry and Derek Walcott's in Caribbean literature are belated examples. Whitman, as suggested earlier and
as is obvious from Neruda's comments about him, is the model for postcolonial nations.

But the desire for a national Whitman also carries with it the expectation that he or she will relieve the colonial cultural inferiority and bring
to an end the postcolonial nation's version of the anxiety of influence or,
the same thing, an anxiety of tradition. That the culture of most colonies
is inferior in almost every sense is an inevitable fact of history, and it
cannot be altered by a critic's insistence on changing the viewpoint, dismissing all aesthetic value-judgment as the 'imperial' products of white
male Europeans, or insisting on an uncritical cultural relativism or pluralism (all hierarchies of value are ultimately either subjective or class-
specific and therefore ideological, that is, biased). The early colonial
writers are second-rate and provincial because they lack training and
talent and because they tend to reflect in their work the often belated
aesthetic assumptions of their society. In A.J.M. Smith's words, 'Colonialism is a spirit that gratefully accepts a place of subordination, that
looks elsewhere for its standards of excellence and is content to imitate
with a modest and timid conservatism the products of a parent tradition.'[76] Ironically, the postmodern and postcolonial refusal of critical
standards or insistence on the standards of identity politics, in which
some topics or ideologies are privileged over others, produces a critical
climate as 'provincial' as the one described by Smith and lamented by

some of our earliest critics. What needs to be added is the simple historical fact that the colonial artist by definition lacks the craftsmanship or talent – much less the 'genius' – to do anything but to be derivative or imitative. Confronted with the North American landscape, he or she can only fall back on a feeble imitation of the diction, styles, and genres of 'home.' Incidentally, it is worth reminding ourselves that almost all of these artists were minor, a point that raises some questions about the general claim that colonial or European artists were uniformly unable to depict North America. It might be more accurate to say that the new landscapes – whether North American, Australian, or African – proved intractable to minor talents rather than European artists in general. In *The Empire Writes Back*, for instance, the authors quote Joseph Howe's description of a moose ('the gay moose in jocund gambol springs, / Cropping the foliage Nature round him flings') to illustrate the point that the imperial poetic is incapable of offering an adequate account of the colonial landscape and experience. The fact that Howe is a *very* minor talent – a part-time and competent versifier rather than a poet – goes unmentioned. But if we keep in mind D.H. Lawrence's magnificent and widely praised evocations of the Australian landscape in *The Boy in the Bush* (1924) and *Kangaroo* (1925), we may be tempted to say that what Howe's poetry (or Moodie's or Mair's) really demonstrates are the limitations of a second- or third-rate writer. Do we have a study of the responses of major poets, novelists, travel writers, and painters (Delacroix, Flaubert, Gide) to foreign landscapes? Until we do, our discussions about the European colonial writers' response to the land may need to be more tentative and more nuanced than has been our custom.

If we turn from artists to readers or critics, from creation to reception, the colonial or postcolonial situation is equally complex. Some of the constitutive problems or questions posed by 'the founders' are still pertinent, though sometimes in a disguised or displaced form, to how we think of the canon and of the idea of a national writer and to how we situate and read individual authors. The crux of the matter for those concerned with nurturing a national literature, as Lampman implicitly recognized in the lecture quoted earlier, was how to maintain 'the severest standards' in a society whose finest artists were unable even to approach them.

Facing the same problem in 1855, Melville had resolved it nationalistically. 'Let America, then, prize and cherish her writers; yea, let her glorify them. They are not so many in number as to exhaust her goodwill.

And while she has good kith and kin of her own to take to her bosom, let her not lavish her embraces upon the household of an alien. For believe it or not, England, after all, is in many things an alien to us ... But even were there no strong literary individualities among us, as there are some dozens at least, nevertheless, let America first praise mediocrity even, in her children, before she praises (for everywhere, merit demands acknowledgment from everyone) the best excellence in the children of any other land. Let her own authors, I say, have the priority of appreciation.'[77] Melville's only criterion of value here is the 'Americanness' of the author and the work, and he is willing to praise even 'mediocrity' – Pop Emmons's *Fredoniad* – to encourage the development of a national literature. His dilemma of how to nurture a national literature, though not his uncritical solution, can be seen in Canadian readers as different as Moodie, Dewart, Lighthall, Roberts, and the neglected Archibald MacMechan, all of whom understood clearly that the writing produced in Canada in their time was provincial and colonial. Before I quote MacMechan's *Headwaters of Canadian Literature*, it's worth recalling that he taught one of the first courses in Canadian literature in the country – from 1923 on – and made one of the first attempts at describing a Canadian canon. He was also a noted medieval scholar and a very early champion of Melville's work, which he discovered in 1889! His nationalism is evident in the epigraph on his title page: *'ad maiorem patriae gloriam.'* I emphasize MacMechan's 'credentials' in part because there is a tendency today to condescend to earlier pre-theoretical critics in the tradition as if they were embarrassing, intellectually challenged, and ideologically blinkered aunts and uncles whose works need not be referred to. MacMechan was under no illusion about the quality of the work he was teaching, and his evaluation of the literature of the previous century – he writes in 1924 – is extreme but accurate: 'How much of the work produced in Canada during the last century is destined to live? How much will be read or remembered at the end of the twentieth century? The answer must be – very little. The bulk of it is ephemeral; it smells of mortality.'[78] (Samuel Johnson would have approved the visceral quality of the last clause.) His basic assumption – shared by Whitman and Milosz – was that 'literature is the voice of the people' because through it 'the life, the soul of a people may be known.' He also acknowledged the historical importance of what had been produced in Canada. But he insisted on criteria that reflected the word's etymology (*krites*), in part because he recognized the deleterious effect of a provincial criticism on the development of Canadian writing: 'Canadian authors are in the habit of looking across the border for appreciation. They value American approval because homegrown criticism is either cold, or so uniform and undiscriminating that it loses all savour.'[79] Though his point of departure was authors who had been born and/or educated in Canada and whose work had Canadian content, Mac-Mechan was as convinced as any evaluative critic, and contra-Melville, that only work that could stand comparison with the best poetry and fiction of other nations was of any ultimate importance. Everything else had at best a historical importance as a seed-bed for the first-rate work that he believed would eventually appear.

MacMechan's stance is worth recalling if for no other reason than that evaluative criticism has tended to be ignored among most of our critics (E.K. Brown, John Sutherland, George Woodcock, W.J. Keith, and John Metcalf are the obvious exceptions). There have been four reasons for this. First, as MacMechan recognized, colonial criticism tends to be 'undiscriminating' or, for understandable historical reasons, boosterish: it doesn't have the materials to which 'the severest standards' can be applied. Second, Canadian critics focused for the better part of this century on content and thematics in an understandable attempt to define what was distinctive in the literature and to argue that the literature articulated a national identity or character. Third, the influence of Northrop Frye's mythopoeic criticism nudged Canadian criticism in a neo-Aristotelian direction, insisting that if criticism was to be a 'science' it should avoid questions of value since these were subjective and belonged to the history of taste. And fourth, contemporary theories such as deconstruction, feminism, Marxism, new historicism, cultural studies, and postcolonialism tend to see evaluation as 1. irrelevant; 2. suspect because its criteria supposedly reflect and are embodied in the traditional western canon constituted by dead, middle- or upper-class, white European males; 3. aligned traditionally with the category of the aesthetic, which they treat as a mask for the political; 4. redefined in ideological terms so that the value of a text depends less on its craft or artistry than on its content, especially if that content reflects the experiences of oppressed or marginalized groups. In the fourth category, it is worth adding, literature tends to be appropriated into politically or socially marked categories and to be judged by the degree to which its content is expressive of their ideological assumptions. An extreme, though I would argue representative example of this, is Homi K. Bhabha's 'DissemiNation: Time, Narrative, and the Margins of the Modern Nation,' in which only one literary narrative – Salman Rushdie's *The*

Satanic Verses – is mentioned and then only to illustrate an abstract point.

Whatever the virtues of postcolonial theory, one of its obvious lacunae is a theory of literary or aesthetic value. If a text is an interplay of the aesthetic and the cognitive, postcolonial theory tends to privilege the latter over the former often to the point that the aesthetic disappears, absorbed within or redefined as the ideological-political. Its primary criterion for a work's relevance, importance or inclusion in the canon is explicitly ideological: the work reflects in some way – content, style, idiolect – the situation of someone who is a victim of or has been marginalized by European imperialism. Criteria pertaining to craft, aesthetic values, profundity, and comprehensiveness of vision are irrelevant or of secondary interest or to be dismissed as the irrelevant oppressive criteria of the empire. Consequently, it can only offer a description of a national culture that reflects an ethnographical monograph. In MacMechan's terms – 'uniform and undiscriminating' – postcolonial criticism is still a provincial criticism, though it now masks its anxiety of influence or tradition behind a morally valorized rhetoric of heterogeneous pluralism, 'otherness,' multiculturalism, and an ethnographic view of tradition based on temporal contiguity rather than value. Abandoned is the view of tradition, taken for granted by MacMechan and recently reiterated by Hood, as involving the preservation and transmission of something '*worthy* of preservation. Some sort of value, some human conviction about value is implied. When we go in search of a Canadian tradition, therefore, we are looking for valuable accomplishments or possessions ...'[80]

Value, hierarchy, and vision are precisely what the national poet establishes or brings; he is the strong poet who redefines the tradition, causing a shifting of chairs around the table of the nation's artists and establishing a poetic standard and a cadence against which all subsequent poetry in that national tradition will be heard and measured. The national poem is read as the founding vision of the nation, and it is not simply one among equals: though both were published in 1855, *Leaves of Grass* has literary, cultural, and national importance, *Hiawatha* is a historical curio, trotted out whenever critics want to demonstrate how dead white nineteenth-century males represented 'the indigene.' The great national work carries an aura important, as the Australian poet Alec Hope emphasizes, not only to readers but to other writers: 'There is something in a masterpiece – native, indigenous and speaking the same untranslatable language of a specific civilization – by which the writers of that country can measure themselves and feel the force of their talents in a way which they can rarely do with the masterpieces of other lands.'[81] Like the word 'genius,' 'masterpiece' is passing out of serious critical discourse and is found primarily on back-cover copy or in newspaper reviews, but it is worth recalling that both terms and their cognates are part of Schiller's conception of the 'naïve' poet, the orphic voice and founder of his community.

It is important to note, however, that where the major American writers emphasize the uniqueness of the American experience and of the new literature, Canadian writers, reflecting the Canadian historical experience and political situation, until very recently placed an almost equal emphasis on the continuity of Canadian literature with English. Similarly some of our historians – Creighton and Morton in particular – emphasized Britishness and the Commonwealth connection. Perhaps because of our historical belatedness, we have been less troubled by the idea of a 'sentimental' poetry than our neighbours. As well, in the distinction popularized by Edward Said, Americans have sought 'origins' while Canadians, more cautious and realistic, have made a series of 'beginnings' that incorporate the past. This is something recognized in Frye's more conservative – and Canadian – framing of the colonial situation in which continuity not rupture is emphasized. 'The Canadian poet cannot write in a distinctively Canadian language; he is compelled to take the language he was brought up to speak, whether French, English, or Icelandic, and attempt to adjust that language to an environment which is foreign to it, if not foreign to himself. Once he accepts a language, however, he joins the line of poets in the tradition of that language, at the point nearest to his immediate predecessors.'[82] For Frye, the tradition is inescapable, an idea whose extreme form can be seen in the criticism of Harold Bloom. Whatever violence the poet chooses to do to a language and to whatever degree he or she chooses to introduce 'original terms' and other idiolects into it, it will still carry the burden of its history, all the meanings, intimations, and suggestions acquired throughout its life. Not irrelevantly or coincidentally, the opposed attitudes to English mirror the very different ways in which each country gained independence from Britain. The lingering presence in the 1940s and 1950s of rhyme and metre among Purdy and other Canadian modernists and its easy coexistence with what Frye jokingly terms the American 'manly contempt of prosody' may be a sign both of colonial belatedness and of certain attitudes that on the level of the state manifested themselves as Confederation and the Britishness of our political heritage. Our culture on every level has tended to be inclusive and syncretic, and for our earlier critics and writers this meant anticipating a Canadian literature built on inevitable antecedents. One can see this quite clearly in Hugh MacLennan's prediction that Canadian literature would represent a third way between British and American within the tradition of literatures in English.[83] Similarly, the currently neglected John Sutherland suggested in 1947 that on the road to finding itself Canadian our poetry would pass through stages of influence, one British, one American.

As a sign of the times one would instance a contradiction in the nature of the English intellectual in Canada. His personality is not whole-heartedly English, but is divided between an English half and a half that is, or would like to be, American. His poetic self is English; his intellectual habits are borrowed from the mother country. But he is no longer quite satisfied with his poetic self, and is no longer certain that it represents him as he really is. There are ideas and attitudes, feelings and forms of expression, that sometimes cannot be conveyed by means of the polished and symmetrical vehicle of English poetry, but which attract him, because they seem more easygoing and natural – in short more American ...

... It is quite apparent that the American example will become more and more attractive to Canadian writers; that we are approaching a period when we will have 'schools' and 'movements' whose origin will be American. And perhaps it is safe to say that such a period is the inevitable half-way house from which Canadian poetry will pass towards an identity of its own.[84]

Arguing against A.J.M. Smith's seminal introduction to *The Book of Canadian Poetry* (1943), Sutherland insisted that 'there is no tradition of Canadian poetry,'[85] but presciently suggested that the beginnings of one could be perceived in the poetry of the 1940s. His historically accurate three-stage model of influence and genesis manages both a reconciliation of the 'Anglo' poetics of the *Preview* group and the 'proletarian' or North American poetics of the *First Statement* poets and a prediction whose final phase we are now experiencing, though in a form Sutherland could not have anticipated. Though in the years after his conversion to Catholicism and before his death in 1956 he argued that E.J. Pratt was the most important Canadian poet, there is little doubt that Pratt's work did not fulfil the criteria set out in the 'Introduction' to *Other Canadians*. Looking back from the vantage-point of half a century, I want to suggest that the body of work that best exemplifies Sutherland's predic-tion belongs to Purdy,[86] though it would be misleading to suggest that no other Canadian poets of his generation negotiated the passage sketched by Sutherland; Earle Birney, F.R. Scott, Ralph Gustafson, Mar-garet Avison, and Irving Layton are in this respect equally exemplary. All can be said to have responded to and assimilated the dual pressures of two powerful poetic traditions. Incidentally, I want to suggest that these constitutive pressures or influences began to decline during the very decade – the 1950s – that these poets reached their maturity. The deaths of Stevens (1955), Williams (1963), and Eliot (1965) and the decline in Auden's work marked the beginning of the end of a certain hegemony in Anglo-American poetry.

Though Les Murray locates the 'end' somewhat later than I do, his comments about the change in the situation of poetry in English make roughly the same point. 'While [Auden] was alive, English Literature could still be felt to have a centre, and all that High Table business of Fabers and Penguins and memories of the thirties and twenties still impinged upon our times. Now, since no living poet has the stature Auden enjoyed on both sides of the Atlantic, there is nothing to hold the illusion together any more, and what has long been true becomes plain as well. The power structure of literature is fragmented – not enough yet, but that's coming – and no one centre, geographical or intellectual, really rules the roost in English language poetry, though some pretend to.'[87] Though Murray doesn't discuss it, his poetry, like Purdy's, would probably have been a less rich and complex thing without the felt pres-sure of the tradition and poetics that Auden represented. For Purdy, at least, British poetry – Auden has been a life-long favourite – offered a countersong to the nearly overpowering siren call of the North Ameri-can style. He acknowledges as much in his reflections on his career in *Reaching for the Beaufort Sea*. 'I regard myself as an odd kind of main-stream poet, and much closer to the style of mainstream American writ-ers than British. And 'mainstream' may be regarded here, in my case, as eccentric-conventional ... Paradoxically, while I write more like Cana-dian and US poets in style and diction, I like the slightly older British poets much better than the American ones' (283).

As I shall discuss below, Purdy's involvement in American poetry is complicated by the fact that he comes to Whitman and Williams through D.H. Lawrence, whose poetics influenced a generation of American poets. Still, in various aspects of his poetry – subject-matter, idiom, voice, line, and verse paragraphs – he is close to the 'US poets.' On the other hand, the connection to Carman and 'the slightly older British poets' can be heard both in his occasional use of the iambic line (even in predominantly free-verse poems like 'Red Fox on Highway 500'), allusions to poets such as Noyes, Yeats, Housman, and Graves, and a nostalgia for rhyme and stanzas. Evident in Purdy is less an anxiety of influence or about one's postcolonial situation than a willingness to write with whatever materials come to hand – indigenous, Canadian, American, or European. An overview of his career suggests a poet who found his way to a Canadian stance, idiom, cadence, and style through his intense and often lonely engagement with the Canadian, the British, and the American traditions. There is more than a passing resemblance here to Murray: each has a sense of what could be called national proprietorship or national patrimony to be articulated by a national poetic, but each is willing to use whatever he needs of other literary traditions. Each realized that by itself the native tradition could not provide a nurturing and sustaining matrix for his work. And though Murray looks forward to a time when there will be no 'centre' for poetry, he is canny enough to realize that had such a centre not existed during his formative years, he would not have evolved into the original poet that he is. As I shall argue below, the same can be said of Purdy, an equally ambitious and original poet.

Since I want my reading of Purdy's poetry in the next section to make the case for my view of him as the poet of 'the Canadian experience' and his work as exemplifying a Canadian poetic, I end this section by looking briefly at a relatively unknown poem – 'On Canadian Identity' (1962) – in which we can hear anticipations of Purdy's mature poetic. It's not major Purdy, but one can hear clearly in it the decisive turn away from the derivative though important apprentice work of the previous decade, work in which the voice is that of a poetic ventriloquist – to paraphrase Eliot: 'He did the poems in different voices.' Prior to 1961–2, with a handful of exceptions, one has the impression of a poet uncertain not only about his voice, persona, and audience but even about his subject-matter. One also has the impression of a writer trying out styles and subjects and often not recognizing the lack of an organic connection between the two. Set against this body of work, 'On Canadian Identity' resonates on the ear like the work of another writer. Since it has never been republished after appearing in *Poems for All the Annettes* (1962), I quote it at some length.

On Canadian Identity:
(A Sentimental Monograph for the Daughters of the Empire)

Names if you like:
Illecillewaet and Medicine Hat,
Winnipeg's prairie sound –
the whoop and holler of Calgary,
Gun-a-noot's stammering outlawry,
the small wooded province Newfoundland – ...

History if you like:
Verendrye-Moses glimpsing something wonderful,
Mountains in the sky he thought were legendary;
Riel's pitiful, insular, Métis kingdom;
the socialist rebellion of '37;
Van Horne's railway hooting in the night
(laconic, mongoloid loneliness);
Macdonald too – Macdonald of course – ...

Legends? Oh, they're here alright,
ready to shine from the tv screen
for sweet profit's sake. Do you doubt it?

I'll tell you songs to sing and words to take to bed
that'll keep you warm as a wife with a sun-burned back –
Or – hell, I'll make these slovenly metrics sing
in a genuine American imitation of the real thing –
Bill Hickok, yet, Wyatt Earp maybe – ?
But all our heroes stayed dead god
rest their souls in the paradise
of the great north pole –

'The high school land' and 'A dull people' –
'A bridge between old land and new' –
But the critic judges by other achievements
than functional existence; seeks to label, define,
exhorts to be life-like – Ends puzzled.
For we have bounced no rockets off the moon,
swung west to loop the land with gold and steel,
or made a bloody pageant of our greatness,

or bought men's loyalty by giving or withholding –
we have not done any of these great things:
troubled, listening to other people's opinions,
becoming them, pinned to earth by them,
as if we were a focus and burning glass
for opinions, as if we were coming to birth somehow,
learning to love and to earn and to spend –
The worth of life being not necessarily noise
we kept unusual silence, and then cried out
one word which has never yet been said –   PAA, 47–8[88]

'On Canadian Identity' announces directly and unmistakably an original voice (at once cocky, self-questioning, and critical), a stance (rooted in a particular place), and a view of poetry as a public speech act by an anonymous first-person speaker concerned with our central issues. Later poems and essays will develop, more memorably, ideas latent in it. The idea that the poet names and maps the country ('lifting an environment to expression') will become almost a topos in Purdy's work, recurring several times in his 1993 autobiography, *Reaching for the Beaufort Sea* (160, 238, 249), in his review of *Literary History of Canada* (*SA*, 268), in his essay 'Disconnections' (*ECW*, 187), as well as in many poems of the past three decades. A recent and particularly memorable version of it occurs in 'Home Country,' the afterword to *To Paris Never Again* (1997), where Purdy remembers riding the freight trains across Canada in the 1930s: 'And the country itself began to take shape in my mind, even if I wasn't entirely aware of this ongoing process. Under those conditions it wasn't an abstraction either, not just names on a map but dirt under your fingernails. Places you've been and people you've known. Afterwards, of course, it's the mind and memory that create our known and loved places, that re-create what already is' (119). Here the 'names on a map' and the land itself – 'dirt under your fingernails' – are absorbed as a prelude to their recreation in poetry. Typically, in discussing the point in a letter to Dennis Lee (18 July 1972), Purdy both acknowledges having 'this sense of "opening up" the country, writing about places in a way that has not been done here before' and judges himself guilty of 'rank egotism' for making the assertion.[89] 'On Canadian Identity' also announces his intention of telling the narrative of a particular people, what Pound, borrowing from Kipling, called 'the tale of the tribe.' Describing in a letter to Earle Birney what he meant by 'a world poet,' Purdy insisted that to be one 'you hafta come from a country a place and a time, and be somewhat involved in those concerns' (11 June 1980).[90] Needless to say, the description also applies to a 'national poet.'

The title and the address to the reader in the first line – 'if you like' – announce this as a public poem. But it begins with a playful subtitle intended to deflect the criticism of those who might accuse the poet of being a simple nationalist or patriot like Roberts, perhaps – '(A Sentimental Monograph for the Daughters of the Empire).' If not quite an old-fashioned patriotic ode of the kind that Roberts wrote and that would have satisfied the much maligned Daughters of the Empire, 'On Canadian Identity' is nevertheless a poem whose syntax establishes an implicit dialogue with the reader and whose ending without closure invites the reader to look to the future and to speak the 'one word,' the name withheld throughout, the absent presence – Canada – that will include and sum up all the poem's names and events. Along the way the poem articulates, as well, the obstacles involved in speaking 'Canada' and 'in the Canadian grain': the need to overcome the temptation to 'sing / in a genuine American imitation of the real thing' as well as the inherent Canadian self-doubt about everything Canadian, whether historical or contemporary. The latter concern – one of our birthmarks, as it were – is subtly introduced in the two quotations in the fourth stanza's opening line: '"The high school land" and "A dull people."' The first is from Earle Birney's well-known 'Canada: A Case History: 1945,' while the second is from Irving Layton's 'From Colony to Nation.' The quotations perform a double function here: on the one hand, they allow Purdy to indicate the attitude *against* which his poem is written; on the other, they show a younger poet acknowledging his debts while establishing a space for himself within the tradition by questioning the wisdom of the tribal elders, each of whom was crucial to his poetic development during the previous decade.

Worth noting as well is the yoking of Verendrye and Moses with a hyphen; the pairing may be questionable but it anticipates later poems in which Canadian characters and events, private or historical, are often seen in contexts other than Canadian. Implicit here is a Canadian poetic that is open to other histories, poetries, and influences and that deals with a Canadian historical experience inseparable from the histories and prehistory that surround it. Also worth noting is the presence of French-Canadians and, in several of the names, of aboriginal peoples in the narrative. These are thematic hints that are developed in a handful of later poems about Quebec (especially 'Coffee with René Lévesque' [*SD*, 48] and 'A Handful of Earth' [CP, 245]) and more extensively in the 'aboriginal' poems in North of Summer (1967) and the unpublished translations of Haida myths. What the poem hints at on the level of content is the comprehensiveness, at least as far as Canada is concerned, of Purdy's vision. One of the more interesting developments in his work during the 1970s and early 1980s is the expansion of his concerns – the range of his stories and thematic interests – as he travels abroad. To stay with the Canadian poems for the sake of the present argument, I would also emphasize the extent to which they deal with almost every part of the Canadian experience: prehistory, aboriginal life, the pre-Confederation colonial past, the United Empire Loyalists, the First and Second World Wars, Quebec separatism, as well as various specific historical individuals ('Paul Kane,'[91] 'Who Killed D'Arcy McGee' [CP, 225], 'Stan Rogers' [NSM, 63]) and events ('The Battlefield at Batoche' [CP, 185]).

Though I wouldn't want to push this point, and there are better illustrative examples below, the poem carries traces of three poetic traditions: the quotations from Birney and Layton are Canadian; the vernacular diction, syntax ('Or – hell,') and strong, continuous enjambment show the direct or indirect influence of American free verse; while the iambic pentameter lines in the middle of the final stanza recall the English tradition ('For we have bounced no rockets off the moon' etc.). The extent of Purdy's relationship to these is discussed in the next section and is documented at length in the catalogue of allusions, quotations, and echoes in the appendix. The catalogue indicates clearly and, I think, decisively the extent to which Purdy is a 'literary' poet, one who, to use Schiller's terms, often appears 'naïve' but is 'sentimental.' In Smith's terms, he is simultaneously native (or national) and cosmopolitan (though in a slightly different sense than Smith's). More relevant to my argument, however, is the extent to which he has absorbed the two dominant traditions of poetry in English and used them to forge a Canadian poetic and a focus for the Canadian poetry canon. Since neither linguistics nor cultural theory provides the terms I need, I shall turn to Hegel's notion of aufheben or sublation, in which the third term in the dialectic simultaneously cancels out, supersedes, and preserves the two that preceded it. Here, I suggest, the English and American poetic traditions are sublated into a Canadian one that even as it still reveals their traces, nevertheless, constitutes something new. This reminds us, incidentally, that Purdy's anti-Americanism (see The New Romans [1968]) is predominantly political, not poetic: among his American influences are Robinson Jeffers (also important to Milosz), James Wright, and Charles

Bukowski. In his rejection of Charles Olson and the Black Mountain School – 'the overmen of Black Mountain'[92] – poetic concerns overlap with what could be called poetic-political ones. More on this below.

The poem's debt to the English and American poetic traditions also foreshadows Purdy's later discussion in prose and poetry of the tradition of poetry in English and his place in it. This is both a gesture acknowledging one's debt to significant predecessors – Wyatt to Layton – and an implicit indication of poetic values and critical standards. In these instances Purdy indicates the poets against whom he ultimately wants to be measured; these include Housman, Auden, Lawrence, and Yeats. Carman, Birney, and Layton were crucial early influences, but Purdy recognizes that they are not in the same class, and that in the final analysis neither is he. His view of the tradition has also influenced his version of the Canadian poetic canon when determined on the basis of 'the severest standards.' As the letter to Birney quoted earlier implies, he recognizes that he and his contemporaries are not in Yeats's class, but he nevertheless insists that a handful – Klein, Birney, Avison, and Layton – have written poems marked with an individual 'aesthetic signature' and a distinctive vision.

It is part of this book's argument that Purdy belongs in that list as the first among equals. In the next chapter I try to substantiate that claim, as well as the thesis that Purdy's is a poetry written 'in the Canadian grain,' by offering a close reading of his body of work.

PART II: THE POETRY OF AL PURDY

These are my history
the story of myself
for I am the land
and the land has become me.

'The Man without a Country' (*CP*, 314)

And every Space that a Man views around his dwelling-place,
Standing on his own roof, or in his garden on a mount
Of twenty-five cubits in height, such space is his universe;

William Blake, 'Milton,' plate 29, ll. 5–7

When Al Purdy began writing poems in the 1930s, the major active
Canadian poets were Sir Charles G.D. Roberts, Duncan Campbell Scott,
and E.J. Pratt. In retrospect, it's obvious that none of them could have
helped him, even if he had been ready, to develop into a modern poet.
On the other hand, both Roberts and Pratt had ambitions to write a
national or Canadian poetry and to be the national poet. Each might
have been sympathetic to the intention and the stance not only in 'On
Canadian Identity' but also in 'Canada,' one of Purdy's first publications
in his high school yearbook. Neither poem is vintage Purdy, but each
shows a poet trying, to paraphrase Whitman, 'to cope with our occasions' and concerns, to reflect, as Purdy did in various works throughout his career, on what it means to be a Canadian. And while none of the
above-named poets would play an important part in Purdy's development, his decision about how to respond to or how to use the tradition

of English poetry they represent played a crucial role in the evolution of his poetic. Tradition, both as something inherited and as something to be created, is a major issue throughout his career, and his complex and conservative response to it distinguishes him from most of his peers as well as most contemporary Canadian poets. In fact, the moment in which the postcolonial poet becomes conscious that the inherited poetic tradition may be an ambiguous heritage may be the moment that is constitutive for his development as a poet: will he become Poe or Whitman? Walcott or Brathwaite? Layton or Purdy? The temptation for the postcolonial poet – Whitman and Kroetsch – as for the revolutionary one – Mayakovsky – is to swerve away from the tradition, to pretend that one has forgotten or unlearned it on the road to a new poetry.

As I argued earlier, Purdy's response to the burden of tradition has been particularly complex, perhaps unavoidably so given the circumstances of Canadian history and his own conservative emphasis on continuity and the importance of the past. While emphasizing that 'Canadian' means something different from 'English' or 'American,' he nevertheless recognizes that in crucial ways it cannot be understood without taking them, especially the former, into account, because they left and continue to leave their traces on it. He makes the point in the polemical speech of a minor character in *A Splinter in the Heart*.

'This ain't England,' McPherson said with emphasis. 'And never think it is. It may have been England settled it; and the English sure did that along with Scotch, Irish, Dutch, German, and everyone else. Most of that in the last hundred years or so. And after they settled it, you know what happened?'

McPherson's glance impaled him on the thought, and he said again, 'You know what happened?'

Patrick shook his head, submissive, carried along by the urgency in the old man's eyes.

'What happened? They changed – the people who came here did. They weren't English, Irish, Dutch, or any other damn thing, not any more.' (151)

Purdy is enough of a realist to have McPherson add that some immigrants 'kept grumbling and grousing, how awful it was, how terrible it was, how it was like bein no place at all' (152). For those who 'changed,' 'Canadian' is what they changed into, even if the adjective resists easy definition. As I suggested earlier, one of the concerns of my reading of Purdy's poetry is to try to indicate what Purdy means by the adjective when it modifies substantives like tradition, literature, and nation.

Yet the very need to emphasize that '"This ain't England"' implicitly reveals an awareness of the unavoidable presence of England in Canada and of the need to come to terms with its manifold influence – everything from names and forms of public address to literature and the legal system. For a poet like Purdy, however, 'England' or the colonial past poses a double problem. On the one hand, as he searches for his voice and vision he needs to come to terms with English poetry without allowing himself to be restricted or overwhelmed by it; to do so would be to remain provincial or colonial. On the other, he is simultaneously confronted with the problem of how to respond creatively to and use the ambiguous colonial heritage left by 'ancestors ... often mediocre or muddling' (Dennis Lee's words). In both cases – they are essentially aspects of one complex situation – poetic concerns are inextricable from historical ones and the poetic imagination from its historical counterpart.

In the following pages I offer a critical overview of and commentary on Al Purdy's body of work within the contexts sketched both here and in the previous section. I have not tried to be exhaustive, and different readers will note different omissions. That there are several areas or concerns not dealt with is partly an indication of the limits of my approach and partly a testimony to Purdy's variety and his wide range of interests; to paraphrase Whitman, he is large and his poetry contains multitudes. He is also, it needs to be added at the outset, more uneven than any major Canadian poet except Layton: to be blunt, many poems simply do not merit serious critical engagement.

Though the section heads indicate my main concerns, it may be useful to provide a summary of this chapter's drift by saying that it begins with a discussion of Purdy's use of the English and American traditions in the evolution of his poetic; it then deals with some of the salient characteristics of the Purdy lyric and of Purdy's view of the poet and poetry; and it closes with three interrelated sections dealing with the poetry's engagement with the local, the national, and the universal or, in words drawn from the section titles, Ameliasburg, nation, and Being. The chapter, like the book, assumes that Purdy's body of work in poetry is as close to a national poem or classic as we have in verse. It also assumes, to quote Robert Lowell, that 'our classics ... must mean something, not by didactic pedagogy, propaganda, or edification – but by their action, a murky metaphysical historic significance. A sober intuition into the character of a nation – profundities imagined, as if in a dream, by authors who knew what they had written. Even to the Philistine *podesta*,

Dante was the soul of Italy.'[1] I have neither Lowell's confidence nor his authority, and am therefore reluctant to speak of the soul of Canada, but the idea of Purdy's work offering a 'sober intuition into the character of a nation' – both what it is and what it might be – seems to me just right. Ironically, this crucial body of work has appeared at a time when, in Randall Jarrell's words, 'the poet has a peculiar relation to [his] public. It is unaware of his existence';[2] when the idea of a national poetry is incomprehensible to most Canadians; and when, finally, the country itself seems on the verge of dissolution both ideologically and politically. It is no small measure of the poise and integrity of Purdy's vision that it includes an awareness of these. I would add to these dark possibilities the suggestion that he may be both the first and last of our poets.

1

Bliss Carman's Shadow

Either the passage of time or his characteristic reticence has prevented Purdy from dwelling on more than a handful of personal details about his youth. The most detailed and emotionally evocative accounts of what growing up in Wooler and Trenton, Ontario, was like – he was born on 30 December 1918 – are in the first two chapters of *Reaching for the Beaufort Sea* and in his novel *A Splinter in the Heart*. Both offer sketches of postwar small-town Ontario, a world not unlike the one described in greater detail in Robertson Davies's *Fifth Business*. Purdy's grandfather, as one would expect, is prominent, but his mother, who raised him alone, remains a surprisingly shadowy figure, as if even in old age the poet was unable to approach her too closely lest he bring into play guilt and other emotions dealt with only in a handful of poems. Since I'm primarily concerned with Purdy's development as a poet, what interests me in the memoir is the portrait of the poet as a young man – a fatherless, often spoiled, shy small-town Ontario boy becoming interested in books and writing in a town where 'there were no writers' (*RBS*, 38). The excitement that is palpable in Patrick Cameron's response to running in *A Splinter in the Heart* is similar to the young Purdy's response to poetry and reading. Even Patrick, who admits not liking school, is taken with Kipling, one of Purdy's lifelong enthusiasms. We know that at Dufferin Public School, Albert College, and Trenton Collegiate Institute, the lonely boy read whatever came his way, everything from the Edgar Rice Burroughs, Frank Merriwell, and pulp magazines to Bliss Carman. And at thirteen, for reasons the grown man still doesn't understand, he began to write. 'I was writing poems at that time, and getting them published in the school magazine, called the *Spotlight*. They were pretty bad poems, but I didn't know that, which was just as well. The magazine paid a dollar each for poems. Enthralled with Bliss Carman's stuff, I began to write at a furious rate, filling notebooks with them. Copying the poems on a neighbour's typewriter, I bound them into little leather-covered stapled books. These books contained some fairly long effusions, an epic on Robin Hood, another on the Norse myths, Thor, and Odin, etc.' (*RBS*, 43). The 'dollar each for poems' doesn't sound right – certainly not in the Depression – but other details, including a later comment that he wrote poems to impress the girls in the class, evoke a common enough situation. Similarly the enthusiastic response to Carman that Purdy describes is not unusual for a very young poet, as we can see if we juxtapose Purdy's various remarks on his early 'career' to Eliot's description of the very young poet's first encounters with poetry. 'At this period, the poem, or the poetry of a single poet, invades the youthful consciousness and assumes complete possession for a time. We do not really see it as something with an existence outside ourselves ... The frequent result is an outburst of scribbling which we may call imitation, so long as we are aware of the meaning of the word 'imitation' which we employ. It is not deliberate choice of a poet to mimic, but writing under a kind of daemonic possession by one poet.'[1]

Several of Purdy's longer early poems and collections, written under 'a kind of daemonic possession by one poet,' survive in seven small leather- or vinyl-bound manuscripts in the Purdy papers at the University of Saskatchewan, though they are all dated between 1939 and 1942. It's of some historical interest that as Purdy was writing and binding these booklets and dreaming of becoming a serious poet, Charles G.D. Roberts was receiving his first royalty cheque, for $26.20, for his *Selected Poems* (1936), and *New Provinces* was published stillborn from the press.[2] Had either Roberts or the *New Provinces* poets seen Purdy's titles they would probably have thought that they were dealing with a turn-of-the-century poet: 'The Road to Barbary,' 'The Dream That Comes No More,' 'Robin Hood,' and 'Songs of the Twilight Land' are as derivative and dismal as one would expect and as Purdy's own later account of them indicates. Like almost all of his poetry before 1960, they show little evidence on the level of diction or in their handling of metre, rhythm, imagery, and poetic thought that the writer is potentially even a competent versifier much less an important poet. In fact, the most remarkable thing about this early work is what *isn't* there: no awareness of modern poetry; no reference to his own life; a nearly complete blindness to the potential subject-matter in his own place; and none of the 'passionate pursuit of the Real' that Milosz defines as essential to poetry.[3]

Instead, the poems, and I include here his first publication, *The Enchanted Echo* (1944), reflect a belated late-Victorian and Edwardian poetic that still had a certain currency into the 1940s, as one can see from the Saturday Poetry Page of the *Vancouver Sun* and from the poetry selections of the *Vancouver Daily Province*. E. Agnes Norcross's 'England' (published on 14 October 1944) is worth quoting in part to indicate the tradition of popular taste within which Purdy's poems of the 1930s and 1940s were written and published, a tradition that he took seriously.

I would I were in England
  With its gracious countryside;
Yet I love our tow'ring mountains
  And mighty rivers' pride;
But the dear wild flowers of England,
  Meadows green and poppies gay,
Great tall foxgloves in the hedgerows
  Primrose, hawthorn, snow in May.

Purdy's 'The Poet's Rendezvous' appeared on the same page, and he was paid a dollar. A month later (25 November 1944) he published 'To Wendell Willkie,' an elegy for the 1940 Republican candidate for president. The second stanza is representative.

No sideline watcher when the pack goes by,
Or neutral in the stands.
A failure? No, his laurels rest with God,
And in no earthly hands.

It is necessary to read Purdy's early work by the side of poems by E. Agnes Norcross, Constance V. Cowell, and Hamish McTwigh in order to understand how far he had to come in order to make himself into a poet. Though the point about Purdy's unpromising beginning has been made by others, it is worth repeating, especially when almost none of his readers know either the poems of the late 1930s and early 1940s or the uncollected poems published in journals between the appearance of *The Enchanted Echo* (1944) and *Pressed on Sand* (1955). It should be noted that the poems published in the Vancouver newspapers are not listed in the ECW Annotated Bibliography even though it begins with 'Dramatis Personae,' a poem published in 1944. If we take into account the high-school poems, there is almost nothing of poetic value in the work of his first two decades. Louis MacKendrick's curious attempt to salvage something from the wreck strikes me as simply wrong: 'His first book, *The Enchanted Echo*, is not so completely dismissable in light of his later work, for among its conventionalities and regularities several poems hint of potential.'[4] If there's a single image or line that shows any poetic life, I haven't found it, and I doubt that, if challenged, MacKendrick could. As I argue below, the only thing that Purdy salvages from the wreck of his first volume is a lingering attachment to rhyme and the iambic line, both of which appear regularly in his work.

Williams and Stevens were equally forgettable poets at the same age, but they weren't writing in isolation. Williams knew that if he showed his first book to Pound – 'Ezra was silent, if indeed he ever saw the thing, which I hope he didn't'[5] – he would receive an educated and critical response. Purdy, the high-school dropout, had no one to fall back on but himself until he encountered Earle Birney and Curt Lang in Vancouver and then the Montreal poets – Layton, Dudek, Scott – in the mid-1950s. In his mid-twenties, Williams knew enough about poetry to be uneasy about his imitations of Keats; Purdy wouldn't know that he had been writing exercises in an outmoded poetic tradition until his own education in poetry reached Hopkins, Thomas, Pound, and Eliot in the early 1950s. This is one of the aspects of his career that brings him closer to Whitman than to any other poet; without formal education, each had to struggle to find his own way to a poetic. It would be difficult to overemphasize Purdy's isolation as a poet: he lived in a small town whose culture, such as it was, was colonial; he was a loner by temperament; he dropped out of high school; and he had no contact with writers and poetic movements or trends until the mid-1950s when he was already in his thirties. As with Whitman, however, the lack of contact with important contemporary poets gave him room to create at his own pace his own voice, poetic, and vision. Reading the poems of the 1940s and 1950s one can trace his self-education in poetry, especially the various false starts and dead ends evident in poems never reprinted. It's arguable, however, that he could find his voice only after trying and rejecting various styles, often learning something from them in the process. In other words, the isolation and the twenty years of failure are the precondition for Purdy's eventual success – the discovery of his own voice and the writing of the great poems of the 1960s.

In the face of Purdy's concern with everything represented by Ameliasburg, his national poems, and what could be called the sociability of his work, it may seem curious to emphasize his isolation and loneliness as somehow constitutive of the self and the poetry. But the suggestion will stand up to scrutiny if we simply recall how often the speaker in Purdy's poems emphasizes that he stands slightly apart, alone if not lonely, from what he is observing or remembering. Even granting that this is the basic stance of the lyric self in poets like Wordsworth, Whitman, and Hardy, it seems to me more than just part of the conventional baggage that lyric brings with it when we encounter it in Purdy. In the poetry and prose we find it in the scenes in which an individual lies in the grass looking up at the sky ('Group Photograph,' 'Ten Thousand Pianos' [SuD, 92, 96]), runs alone on country roads (the novel), stands at the door of a moving train ('Transient' [CP, 77]), drives a car down a country road to escape a bailiff, is lost in the woods ('Shall We Gather at the River' [SuD, 44]), or feels alone, even in company, simply because he knows that he doesn't belong. Even in the Ameliasburg poems written after the building of the cottage, the speaker regularly notes his ambiguous and marginal status in the region in which he was born, almost as if there is a liminal relationship between the A-frame and the human and non-human realms that surround it.

In retrospect, it is no exaggeration to call the achievement heroic, though during the lonely years of living in rental housing and in periods of mind- and body-numbing labour there must have been weeks and months of quiet desperation in the struggle to earn a living and to become a poet rather than a versifying dummy under the sway of a ventriloquist named Carman. Purdy deals with these years in the autobiography and in some poems ('Piling Blood' [CP, 287]), but his characteristic Upper Canadian reticence prevents him from discussing, and perhaps even probing certain events and emotions. As a result we know his later judgment on his first book, but we have no indications of what he thought of it or of poetry in general in the 1940s, since he didn't begin to write reviews until 1949 in Canadian Poetry Magazine. There must have been the normal excitement and pride that anyone feels on first publication, and some of that can be glimpsed in the fact that The Enchanted Echo was not only advertised on the Saturday Poetry Page of the Vancouver Sun but also offered as a prize for the best poem. Purdy's more serious thinking about poetry and poets is coextensive with the appearance of his breakthrough poems in the early 1960s. Not surprisingly, the archives contain no diaries, journals, or notebooks, just an occasional scribbled note on a scrap of paper abandoned between poetry work sheets. It's as if in that period he could only think about poetry in poetry but not in prose. Perhaps his earliest comment on poetry occurs in a 1947 letter to Earle Birney:

My idea of poetry is that it has no dateform [sic] or special identifying feature, it is a higher form of entertainment or enjoyment by the mind but nevertheless should be couched in the language of its own time. I believe anything that is stilted or grotesque in language is doomed to swift extinction UNLESS the message or beauty presented is so striking as to preclude this happening. Further I would say that anything stilted or grotesque militates against beauty. My whole contention is that poetry should use not every day but natural English. I have no doubt that you can marshal your words together and shake my arguments at their foundation because I have left many loopholes. Perhaps the reason is that I don't state my case in enough detail. I'm fully aware that because I don't like a thing does not signify that my opinion is universal. I believe that the only excuse for obscurity is if it adds something to the value of a poem which it may in the hands of the proper writer but obscurity coupled with the grotesque does not make a good combination.[6]

To Birney's credit, he encouraged the confused young poet to find his own way toward an adequate poetic, and their correspondence over the next decade is a record, in both prose and verse, of Purdy's development through what could be called several theories of poetry and his slow discovery of his own voice.

Purdy's first book, *The Enchanted Echo*, was more of an ending than a start. That he recognized it as such is indicated by the fact that he didn't publish – or try to publish – another volume until *Pressed on Sand* in 1955, and that no poems from it (and only one from its successor) were included in *The Collected Poems of Al Purdy* (1986). Today its value is primarily as an indication of the kind of poetry Purdy read and wrote at the Trenton Collegiate Institute and of the colonial or provincial poetic tradition that was representative of a branch of Canadian poetry until the 1940s and to which J.W. Garvin's *Canadian Poets* (1926) and Lorne Peirce and Carman's *The Book of Canadian Poetry* (1929) are monuments. Equally indicative of the nature of this tradition and of Carman's role in forming it is his choice of poets for *The Oxford Book of American Verse* of 1927. A glance at the table of contents shows the almost complete absence of the poets who would dominate American poetry through the century. Though *The Enchanted Echo* has echoes of Thomas Hardy ('Dramatis Personae' and 'Modern Parable'), Alfred Noyes, and A.E. Housman, and references to Sappho and Rudyard Kipling, its most obvious voice is Carman's, as Purdy has often acknowledged; in fact, the very title seems borrowed from the earlier poet. And if Purdy knew Sappho at this point in his career, it was probably in Carman's popular imitations of her lyrics in *Sappho: One Hundred Lyrics* (1904). It is noteworthy that Stevens also read the volume, though, as his letter to Elsie Moll reveals, by 1909 he was no longer uncritical of Carman. 'At the Library yesterday, I skipped through a half-dozen little volumes of poetry by Bliss Carman. I felt the need of poetry – of hearing again about April and frogs and marsh noises and the "honey-coloured moon" – of seeing "Oleanders / glimmer in the moonlight." You remember the fragments of Sappho. Carman has taken these fragments and imagined the whole of the poems of which each was a part. The result, in some instances, is immensely pleasant – although distinctly not Sapphic. Sappho's passion came from her heart. Carman's comes from a sense of warm beauty.' His poetic debt to Carman is evident in the following lines from his first 'Vagabondia' collection.

> These poets' Vagabondian airs,
> Recall how many of our own,
> That sang themselves, without a rhyme
> To stirrings of some secret chime.[7]

This could be a stanza from *The Enchanted Echo*. Many lines, images, and several of the titles in Purdy's first volume ('Summons to Vagabonds,' 'Votaries of April') are tropes for Carman's ghost, and the entire collection lacks, as do Carman's poems, what Ransom calls 'the rich contingent materiality of things.'[8] Sometimes, as in 'Erinna's Song,' an entire stanza seems to have been dictated from beyond the grave:

> In some dim age beside the sea
> She lived in Greek mythology;
> And no one knows from whence she came –
> Erinna of the lovely name.   *EE*, 14

You can almost see and hear the young poet counting off syllables and beats and checking off iambs. 'Votaries of April' begins as a pastiche of Housman – 'Oh, up my lads, 'tis April, and the boughs are all asway' – but ends echoing the less sombre Canadian poet:

> Oh, it's follow, follow, follow, the old allure returns,

A piper's song of other lands; the heart within me yearns;
And Arcady is nearly here, it's just beyond the ferns.   *EE*, 18

This, like much of the book, is pastoral, but completely different from that realistic or rural pastoral, rooted in Ameliasburg, that D.G. Jones sees as the focus of Purdy's later vision.[9]

One of the few moments the collection spends outside of 'Arcady' occurs in 'In Memoriam Engelbert Dolfuss [*sic*]' (the name of the Austrian Christian Socialist leader by itself wrenches Purdy's diction in a more modern direction) and in the nearly realistic two-stanza 'Self-Portrait' of the opening page, which seems written almost by another poet, perhaps the later Purdy:

Six foot three of indolence,
Two hundred pounds of weed:
My better judgment voted me
Least likely to succeed.

That is why I likely will,
If just to spite myself;
Contrary as a traffic light,
Inconstant as an elf.

The precision of detail in the height and weight, the mundane images 'of weed' and 'traffic light,' and the near colloquialism of 'Least likely to succeed' – based on a high-school yearbook cliché – all point in the direction of modern poetry before 'elf' pulls the book back to the turn of the century. There's not quite enough tension here to suggest self-contradiction or even a wrenching struggle to choose between two styles, but 'Self-Portrait' at least hints at the possibility of another kind of verse and voice, just as the realistic sketch of the moustached writer in uniform on the facing page seems out of place in a book titled *The Enchanted Echo*. (A point of interest: Whitman's portrait also appeared in the opening pages of the first edition of *Leaves of Grass*.)

It is conventional wisdom, encouraged by some of Purdy's own comments in his letters and essays (see 'Disconnections,' *Reaching for the Beaufort Sea*, and Dennis Lee's 'Afterword' to *The Collected Poems*), that Carman and the kind of poetry he represents were completely left behind when Purdy remade himself as a writer through the 1940s and 1950s. When Purdy writes about Carman in the 1980s and 1990s, he usually does so with a combination of admiration and embarrassment.[10] In *Reaching for the Beaufort Sea*, for instance, he lists Carman among the poets he loved and memorized in school:

So I memorized and memorized at school, much of it lost in the mind's over-flow. I immersed myself in Carman, Carman, Carman. And Byron:
  So we'll go no more a-roving
  So late into the night
  Though the heart be still as loving
  and the moon be still as bright.
And Browning, although I can't remember the last lines of 'Home Thoughts' any longer. And Tennyson:
  And I dipped into the future
  As far as the human eye could see
  Saw a vision of the world
  And all the wonder that would be.
(I am not, incidentally, consulting the book versions to ensure accuracy.) ... Remember, remember. And leave all the mistakes of quotation where they belong, uncorrected: and the lines glow like fireflies in your memory. (285–6)

He also quotes snatches of G.K. Chesterton, Hilaire Belloc, W.J. Turner, and Oliver St John Gogarty, none of whom is much read today except by specialists in the field, though Karl Shapiro refers to Turner in his *Essay on Rhyme*, while Chesterton's 'Lepanto' was a set text in Ontario high schools in the early 1960s. Letting himself go and not worrying about modernist critical orthodoxy, Purdy evokes in the above passage lovingly and sentimentally the lost world of the poetry on which he was nurtured and which, during a crucial decade in his development, he had to turn his back on in order to make himself a poet. *Reaching for the Beaufort Sea*, like the essays on Kipling and Carman (see *Starting from Ameliasburgh*), offers an unashamedly subjective rewriting of literary history, in which Carman, Chesterton, Belloc, Gogarty, and the completely forgotten Turner are as important as Byron, Browning, and Tennyson, and Chesterton's 'Lepanto' is as memorable as any poem in the century. Other than Auden, I can't think of another modern poet who writes as affectionately and strongly of poets normally, and justifiably, omitted from the canon and given at best cursory treatment in histories of modern poetry (David Perkins's is representative).

Writing more critically in 'Disconnections,' Purdy acknowledges the staying power in his memory of Carman's 'Low Tide on Grand Pré' but simultaneously places him tellingly as 'a less-intelligent Longfellow.' He also admits that 'scraps of several other Carman doggerels remain with me. One of them ... sententious and silly-reverberant ... I must again examine my own tastes every time I think of it' (*ECW*, 181–3). Carman is like a painting once popular, critically respectable (something by William Bouguereau or Puvis de Chavannes), and even loved, which one realizes has passed completely out of fashion. Purdy's ambivalent loyalty to him is that of a student who has surpassed his master and now clearly sees his limitations without, however, rejecting him for them. For Purdy, Carman is the predecessor who, in the end, represents a road he had to turn his back on, though it must be emphasized that doesn't mean that Carman, and the poetry he represents, will be completely absent from a body of work ostensibly radically different. Not the least of the ironies in Purdy's career is that he could not have found his eclectic mature poetic had he not made the mistake of following Carman for longer than he wants to remember. Echoes of Carman's line of English and early Canadian poetry function in the work of Purdy's maturity as reminders of one of the traditions that went into the making of his poetic, even if most of it was ultimately rejected. Perhaps a better way of putting this would be to emphasize not rejection but the act of using from one's past whatever comes in handy in the fashioning of one's own prosody and poetic. Even if there were no overt trace of this line in Purdy's later work, it could still be argued that the general influence is there in the simple fact that Purdy's poems are closer to *vers libéré* than to *vers libre*, since there is often a residue of traditional metre in them. That the 'residue' was often deliberate is clear from Purdy's 1967 comments, in a letter to Birney, about his revisions to a section of 'The North West Passage' slightly influenced by Coleridge's 'The Rime of the Ancient Mariner.'

In the above as a loose scheme, I was tryin two non-stress to a stress, but not rigidly, so it wouldn't be too apparent. The rhymes are off and may be a couple [of] syllables back or after the end, and not match the previous rhymes – ... It's there for the purpose of breaking up the rhythm of the main body of the poem, whether it succeeds in this. Also it's there a little for its own sake I suppose, and I do like it better than the Coleridge metre ... Besides it's damn easy to write metrical stuff, since I wrote Bliss Carman's poems for years that way. But it's not so easy when you start playin around with your metrics to make them do unforseen things. Eventually, like Camembert cheese is it? – you're liable to have no metrics at all and no poem and nothin but holes in yr cheese.[11]

Thus, however tempting it may be to place him among those poets who look back to Whitman as the key figure in the 'liberation' of poetry in English, an equally convincing case could be made that he also draws on the line that begins with Renaissance lyric, runs through Wordsworth and Hardy, and finds its twentieth-century voice in Auden and Larkin. The former group emphasizes individual talent, the latter tradition. Purdy characteristically uses both.

Finally, it may not be an exaggeration to say that his lingering nostalgia for the memorable and memorizable iambic, dactylic, and anapestic verses of his youth – their residue is often an undercurrent in his later poetry – prevented him from a wholehearted acceptance of the American free verse poetics of Whitman, Williams, and Olson; prevented him as well from becoming the poet of process and open form that both Davey and Bowering want him to be. I would even suggest that Purdy is one of the few contemporary poets writing predominantly in free verse who is nostalgic for the past, saddened by the fact that his poems – because of free verse – cannot be memorized and recited and therefore cannot be literally as memorable as the poems of his first model. I recall a dinner in Toronto in the early 1990s at which Josef Škvorecký and Purdy took turns reciting, in Czech and English respectively, long stretches of their favourite poems. First Jaroslav Seifert, then Bliss Carman; Jiří Orten followed by W.J. Turner; and so on. On the basis of that spontaneous public performance I have little doubt that Purdy would agree with Derek Walcott's comment that to quote from memory 'is the greatest tribute to poetry.'[12]

The poems Purdy recited were, as one would expect, from the line whose most characteristic representative for him is Carman. Again, I need to repeat that I'm thinking of Carman here as representing a body of traditional poetry – what in 1917 Eliot called 'Conservative Verse,'[13] – whether lyric or narrative, encompassing the work of poets as different as Carman, Kipling, Noyes, Housman, Chesterton, and, to compare small with great, Yeats. Other than belonging in Purdy's personal anthology of best-loved and memorized poems (the only anthology that ultimately counts for a poet), they have in common a commitment to a traditional poetic grounded in rhyme, stanzas, and the iambic line. And though one can't argue that they significantly influence Purdy's work after his first collection, they nevertheless continue to appear in some subtle form – a reference, an echo of an image, rhythm, or line – throughout his later work. An obvious imitation like 'Springtime' in *The Woman on the Shore* (1990), for example, is the product of a lifetime of reading Housman.

All the springs unite with this one
both the first one and the last
when the birds are winged flowers
and the flowers are singing birds

Every sunup's like a birthday
every sundown promised more
there are candles lit for noonday
and the darkness shines with stars

As for dying – when it's over
there'll be time to make a fuss
– but for now there's love and laughter
and the springtime is for us   83

Forty-five years after 'Votaries of April,' Housman reappears, without Carman, in a lyric written under his influence – Purdy's title carries the parenthesis '(After Housman)' – yet stepping slightly out of it in the refusal of the expected rhymes in the first two stanzas. It's almost as if Purdy denies us the anticipated rhymes to avoid either parody or pastiche. He only offers them, when it's obvious that the poem is his not Housman's, in the final stanza when, no longer expected as strongly, they both delight and surprise in capping the poem with a perfect rhyme between two words, one of which – 'fuss' – is never used by Housman.

Though Carman is mentioned together with Lampman in 'Bullfrogs' (*The Blur in Between: Poems 1960–61* [1962]), there is only one later poem on which his influence is decisive, though his ghost, and perhaps Whitman's, may linger in poems of 'vagabondia' like 'Transient' (*CP*, 77) and 'Riding West' (*WS*, 29). Otherwise, he seems left behind as completely as the diction, voice, form, and themes of Purdy's first book. Forty years later, however, Purdy calls back in *Piling Blood* (1984) not Carman's voice or manner but the example of a particular, and particularly untypical poem, 'The Green Book of the Bards,' in which Carman catalogues in rhyming quatrains the line of poets – from Moses to Whitman – in which he hopes to be included. It seems appropriate that in writing a *hommage* to the poets who have influenced him Purdy borrows the form and perhaps the topos from Carman (who may have borrowed it from William Dunbar), though he doesn't include his first master in the catalogue.[14] Carman's title is a metaphor for nature, which, according to

the poet, has been written about by all the great 'bards.' The poem ends
as follows:

> One page, entitled Grand Pré,
> Has the idyllic air
> That Bion might have envied:
> I set a foot-note there.

In Purdy's hands, 'The Green Book of the Bards' is combined with parts
of Auden's *New Year Letter* to become 'Bestiary [II].' Subtitled 'ABC of
P,' the poem is an alphabetically arranged catalogue of poets important
to Purdy, the tradition or canon that influenced his work and, equally
important, within which he implicitly hopes to be placed. One can
agree with Helen Vendler that 'writers and critics have historically
"excluded" from the canon those who publish feeble, conventional,
unmusical and unimaginative verse, no matter how intelligent or morally worthy or passionate its sentiments,'[15] and still recognize that each
writer acknowledges masters whose importance to him or her is all out
of proportion to their place in 'the canon.' Purdy's list begins with
'Whoever wrote "Tom O' Bedlam"' and ends with Yeats, with important stops at, among others, Auden, Housman, Jeffers (a particular
favourite), Lawrence, and Dylan Thomas. As the working papers in the
archives reveal, 'Bestiary [II]' is among Purdy's most heavily rewritten
poems. The stanza dealing with Jeffers, for example, exists in at least
twenty handwritten and typed versions, some on the backs of enve-
lopes.[16] 'Bestiary [II]' is a combination of poetic homage, breviary, and a
paying off of literary debts by a poet sufficiently established and confident of his own stature and authority to acknowledge them. It is also, as
a handwritten note in his papers indicates, an 'ABC of Poets I've Loved.'

Carman is mentioned neither in the poem nor in the nearly fifty pages
of manuscript in the files, though, as I have suggested, the original hint
for the poem comes from him as does its quatrain form (though unlike
Carman's, Purdy's stanzas are unrhymed). It's tempting to suggest,
however, on the basis of some comments in Purdy's letters to Mike
Doyle (4 September 1974) and George Johnston (10 August 1980) that
Carman and/or the kind of poetry Purdy associates with him are contained within the stanzas about the ballad poets, Housman, Kipling, and
in manuscript, Chesterton. In fact, it's arguable, as I mentioned earlier,
that the occasional presence of quatrains as well as lines with an iambic
base in Purdy's poetry – his commitment to open form and Laurentian

free verse is never complete – are a residual legacy of the poets he admired in his youth and who wrote much of his first book for him. In a sense, Purdy doesn't have to mention Carman in 'Bestiary [II]' because he has absorbed (and transformed) him and the tradition of poetry he represents into his own mature poetic. Carman's presence in Purdy is in the varied residue of 'the legacy of formal artifice'[17] that can be heard in a variety of ways throughout his work.

Purdy has acknowledged as much. Responding to Doyle's perceptive essay, 'Proteus at Roblin Lake,' Purdy concludes with the following remarks about *The Enchanted Echo* and rhyme and metre:

Anyway, it seems a good article to me – since I too find the contrast with that first book with the later ones a bit puzzling. I have specific reasons for the change – early models of form and rhyme seemed too simple and I grew dissatisfied with myself. I wasn't either lucky or unlucky enough to emerge fully formed from the mental egg, as some seem to do. And yet after whatever changes did occur, I found myself still in possession of some of the earlier traits and abilities, for instance the business of rhythms, iambic or otherwise, that may make a poem come off in three or four different rhythms. And I can't dismiss many earlier writers, Turner, Chesterton etc. as some do. I suppose I retain them forever. Whereas some young kids writing poems do not seem to read anything at all, except, say, Olson, Creeley and Pound and those allied to B.M.[18]

The style, form, and voice of *The Enchanted Echo* may have been left behind, but certain assumptions about rhythm, more specifically rhythms dependent on an iambic line, remained. I shall illustrate the point with some lines from poems of the 1970s and 1980s, but it is worthwhile to quote first Purdy's amplification of this idea six years after the letter to Doyle in an important letter to George Johnston. If not quite unique in the correspondence, it nevertheless shows him in the relatively rare mood of being willing to discuss more technical aspects of poetry. Mediating between Johnston's insistence on the importance of rhyme and Ezra Pound's rejection of it, Purdy offers a third way in which rhyme (and an iambic-based line) are used within free verse (neither quite *vers libre* nor *vers libéré*):

... I quite often use rhyme myself, and metre as well, trying to vary and conceal it within poems where it isn't expected and seems accidental if you do notice it. But I generally let a poem go where it seems to want to go, then touch it here and there deliberately, add metre say, or remove metre, add or remove a rhyme if too close to another rhyme. Perhaps it's not quite as artless as you seem to think? You say rhyme offers more variety, which to me is obviously absurd. How can a dozen poems all written in iambic offer variety? They go dah-dit, dah-dit in your head forever ...

But saying all that is not to say that rhyme is outdated as Pound did. But used wrongly it can sure be monotonous. It also removes all seeming spontaneity as well.[19]

If this isn't as unqualified an endorsement of rhyme and metre as would be offered by Philip Larkin or Richard Wilbur, it will nevertheless probably surprise most of Purdy's readers, both those who don't know of the existence of *The Enchanted Echo* – or, if they do, haven't read it – and those who tend to think of Purdy as almost exclusively a poet of *vers libre* and/or relatively open forms. The letter helps us understand why – with the exception of Robinson Jeffers and Lawrence, perhaps the single greatest influence on Purdy's poetic – the poets included in 'Bestiary [II]' belong, with two key exceptions, to the traditional line of English poetry. In Purdy's revisionist account of modernist poetry, W.B. Yeats, D.H. Lawrence, Robinson Jeffers, W.H. Auden, and Dylan Thomas are the key figures, though we shouldn't overlook his obvious affection for 'minor' poets and poems: 'Who could be contemptuous of Chesterton's "Lepanto" or Anon's "Tom O' Bedlam"? I still love some of those older poets, of whom Kipling is not the least' (*SA*, 314). The writers Purdy is ultimately interested in are those he can use or, as Harold Bloom puts it, those against whom he writes and hopes to supplant. Another way of putting this would be to say that this is also the tradition within which he wants to be read. Carman's 'The Green Book of the Bards' ends with the poet inscribing himself as the latest in the line of 'bards' stretching back to the beginnings of history.[20]

> And all these lovely spirits
> Who read in the great book,
> Then went away in silence
> With their illumined look,
>
> Left comment, as time furnished
> A margin for their skill, –
> Their guesses at the secret
> Whose gist eludes us still.
>
> And still in that green volume,
> With ardour and with youth

Undaunted, my companions
Are searching for the truth.

One page, entitled Grand Pré,
Has the idyllic air
That Bion might have envied:
I set a foot-note there.   *Pipes of Pan*, 8

Purdy, more reticent than his early mentor, leaves it to his readers to imagine a quatrain in 'Bestiary [II],' between the ones devoted to Pablo Neruda and Dylan Thomas, devoted to a Canadian poet whose name begins with 'P' (and it ain't Pickthall, Pratt or Page). 'Bestiary [II]' is an 'ABC of P[oetry],' an 'ABC of P[urdy],' and, up to a point, an answer to Pound's *ABC of Reading*.[21]

In this context, the use of an accentual-syllabic metre, stanzas, and rhyme – no matter how occasional – is, like reference, quotation, and allusion, an indication of allegiance, nostalgia, and a keeping faith with a particular poetic and cultural tradition. In one respect, the poem is an anticipatory elegy since the speaker includes himself in the line of already dead 'bards,' thus securing his place in the canon. The inevitable corollary is that he also imagines and places his poem among theirs by naming *them* and *theirs* in his. Unlike Purdy, Carman didn't realize that he didn't need to allude to his own work at the end of 'The Green Book of the Bards': the poem had already done this for him. That, in a manner of speaking, he was 'dead' as a poet when he wrote it is an unintended irony.

Like some of Purdy's other poems written for the most part in quatrains – 'My Cousin Don' (*CP*, 332); the first version of 'Across the Mary River' (*SB*, 64) – 'Bestiary [II]' denies at least one of the reader's immediate prosodic expectations by not being written in an iambic metre and not using rhyme. The poem is a good example of Purdy's eclectic and often surprising uses of the past. Here he needs a structuring principle that will both separate the poets and indicate their roughly equal status in his personal poetic pantheon: visually, as well as when read, each of the quatrains (Jeffers gets five lines) is also an epitaph. But he avoids the accentual-syllabic prosody we expect with it (with the exception of a handful of lines), probably because it would prevent him from speaking in his own 'natural' voice, the voice of the surrounding poems in *Piling Blood*. In a manner of speaking, he was confident enough in his early sixties to try to contain his canonical poets – a form of mastery – within the very voice that they helped create. The choppy syntax, incomplete sentences, and the occasionally slangy diction ('booze,' 'bloody hell') all produce a conversational tone far removed from Carman, an academic catalogue, a set of poetic portraits or formal elegies/epitaphs. The result is a stanza form pointing to one tradition in poetry, and a prosody indicating another. Mediating between the restrictiveness of the first and the freedom of the second is his reliance on what is for the most part an eight-syllable line with three stresses, though it can be as short as four syllables – 'Yeats for Maud Gonne' – and as long as sixteen – 'You have to remind yourself now and then this is literature.' Equally important is the mediation between British and American poets and traditions.

The poem's single finest stanza shows Purdy flirting with the restrictions of the stanza and the line, eliminating all connectives or transitional words, and producing a quatrain lapidary, terse, and nearly classical in its concision and borrowed energies.

> You, Gaius Valerius Catullus
> ' – here face down beneath the sun':
> an absent friend, lost in the centuries' dust
> next door, just stepped out for a minute –

Though I want to discuss this quatrain in some detail, it's worth pausing to look at some of its earlier versions to see the poet at work in his study. I'll quote them in what I take to be their order of composition, though I should point out that the manuscripts and typescripts are undated.

> 1.
> Catullus with several reservations
> but I've already forgotten nearly all of them
> He hated Caesar and all his life once
> was a lover of sparrows   (handwritten)

> 2.
> Catullus with several reservations;
> he was like a sour persimmon
> he hated Caesar, yet lived his life once
> loved a woman and envied power   (typescript)

> 3.
> [an absent friend, voice in the Roman dust]

voice in the Roman dust an absent friend,
in the next room, just stepped out a moment.   (handwritten)

4.
You, Gaius Valerius Catullus:
 – 'and here face down beneath the sun,' –
remember him in the new world and the old
[an absent friend, just stepped out]
just stepped out for a moment, returning soon
remember him like a friend   (handwritten)

5.
You, Gaius Valerius Catullus
'[and] here face down beneath the sun'
[remembered dust of our absent friend]
an absent friend, lost in the centuries' dust
next door, just stepped out for a minute –   (handwritten)

At every step – and I have noted only the major variants – revision has been pruning, refinement, and improvement. The early references to Caesar, based on Catullus XCIII,[22] are clearly a wrong scent as, less inevitably, is the interest in Lesbia in the second draft; she may have been eliminated because the succeeding stanza about Donne would focus on *his* love poems. The wistful 'voice in the Roman dust,' though a haunting image, is worth sacrificing for the quotation from Archibald MacLeish's 'You, Andrew Marvell.' The fourth version is interesting in showing Purdy tempted by and finally rejecting the possibility of a line of perfect iambic tetrameter – 'and here face down beneath the sun' – dropping the padding of the initial 'and' (it's in MacLeish's original) and thus increasing the deictic force of the first two lines each of which begins with a strong stress. I wonder, by the way, whether the stanza wouldn't have been stronger with a line from Catullus, perhaps from the intensely moving elegy for his brother. As fine as the line from MacLeish may be, its only connection with Catullus is the motif of death. Though there is a slight possibility that '"face down,"' 'absent friend,' and 'dust' may carry a vague memory for some readers of Catullus's elegy: 'Multas per gentes et multa per aequora vectus' (CI). Whatever the case, the stanza allows Purdy to pay tribute to three poets he admires: Catullus, MacLeish, and Marvell.

Mediating between the past and the present, like so many of Purdy's poems on various subjects, the stanza begins and ends by leaving the impression that the dead poet is still alive. The opening salutation evokes the Latin poet by way of one of Purdy's favourite modern poems as if he and the speaker exist in the same time, though the presence of Latin in his full Roman name simultaneously situates Catullus in his own era. And though his death is acknowledged in the immediately following quotation and in the third line's image of 'an absent friend, lost in the centuries' dust,' the quatrain ends with an open-ended line, the second part of which creates an impression of an interrupted present or timeless narrative soon to be resumed. Past and present, Catullus and Purdy, are linked by MacLeish and Marvell, and all four co-exist simultaneously within the poetic tradition Purdy is creating in the poem.

That Catullus is dead is, of course, never in question despite the efforts of the poem's grammar and imagery to make the reader momentarily suspend this knowledge; this, however, is deftly and sensuously counterbalanced by the music of the verse, which links with sibilants and plosive 't's' 'Gaius Valerius Catullus,' 'absent,' 'lost,' 'dust,' and 'stepped,' and establishes a firm connection between death and the poet with one of the poem's rare pararhymes, 'Catullus/dust.' (As if to confirm the association between poet/poetry and death, the last word then forms a perfect rhyme with the stressed 'Just' in the following quatrain:

> Donne, of course, Dean of St. Paul's
> Just the early stuff. That death portrait,
> sitting in his shroud, repels me:
> the godless lover is alive and warm.

With equal accuracy, the closing line of Donne's quatrain could be used to describe the Latin poet whose amatory career and love poems are already implicit in the hint of 'lust' in the near rhyme 'Catullus'/'dust.' It's not impossible that at least one other 'godless lover' is a ghost in the Catullus quatrain, the already mentioned Marvell: MacLeish's 'You, Andrew Marvell' may have brought Marvell's most famous poem, 'To His Coy Mistress,' further into Purdy's consciousness than it would have been had he opened the stanza in some other way. As a result, perhaps 'sun,' 'face down' (= Marvell's 'back'), and the rhyme 'lust'/'dust' are the residue of a half-conscious pressure of

> But at my back I always hear
> Time's winged chariot hurrying near:

And yonder all before us lie
Deserts of vast eternity.
Thy beauty shall no more be found;
Nor, in thy marble vault, shall sound
My echoing song: then worms shall try
Thy long-preserved virginity:
And your quaint honour turn to dust;
And into ashes all my lust.

Yet though we can not make our sun
Stand still, yet we will make him run.

Though 'Bestiary [II]' doesn't come off as a whole and contains some unusually flat lines – the last two in the Keats stanza, in particular – its importance lies in what it tells us about how Purdy reads the tradition and in its being representative of a large number of poems that show Purdy making unexpected use of the tradition he ostensibly abandoned in the eighteen years between *The Enchanted Echo* and *Poems for All the Annettes*, the period during which he educated himself in modern poetry and simultaneously remade himself as a poet. (I would add, however, that while Purdy may have found a voice and a stance in *Poems for All the Annettes*, the volume is primarily important as marking a point of departure for the more complex – in voice, theme, and structure – lyrics of the next three decades.) One way of charting Purdy's development as a poet from what Stevens would call an 'ephebe' to a master would be to look at the increasing skill and confidence with which he uses aspects of a more traditional prosody both in his more formal lyrics and, especially, in what are otherwise free-verse poems in which the reader doesn't expect them. This co-presence of what could be called the Carman and Lawrence strands in Purdy's poetic reminds us, poem by poem, of the two traditions he has brought together and reforged into his own voice. His development in traditional lyric can be gauged simply by juxtaposing 'Pause' from *The Blur in Between* (14) and 'Kerameikos Cemetery' from *Sundance at Dusk* (CP, 206).

Easily the leaves fall at this season
So numerous the eye arrests them
here – outside the past or present
they achieve a continual beginning.

What they have forgotten they have forgotten.
What they meant to do instead of fall
is not in earth or time recoverable –
the fossils of intention, the shapes of rot.

This is competent but undistinguished, and the first line of the second stanza is ponderous and rhythmically inert. By contrast, the placing of 'here' and 'rot' is dramatic and right, and 'the fossils of intention' wouldn't be out of place in one of the later poems about prehistory. The pararhymes of the second stanza show a sensitivity to nuance often missing from the earlier work ('forgotten'/'rot'; 'fall'/'recoverable'). But overall, the poem disappears a few minutes after being read, a judgment confirmed by Purdy's decision to rewrite the first stanza when it was included in *Poems for All the Annettes* (1968):

Uneasily the leaves fall at this season,
forgetting what to do or where to go;
the red amnesiacs of autumn
drifting through the graveyard forest.

This is stronger. 'Uneasily' introduces an intriguing though in the end unearned dramatic and affective quality, and the figure of the leaves as 'amnesiacs of autumn / drifting through the graveyard forest' is memorable though slightly forced, as is the anthropomorphism. One also doubts whether there is an organic connection between the form and content.

'Kerameikos Cemetery,' written roughly two decades later in the mid-seventies, is a stronger, more confident piece of work.

So old that only traces of death remain
for death is broken with the broken stones
as if convivial party-goers came
and talked so long to friends they stayed
to hear the night birds call their children home

All over Athens rooster voices wake
the past converses with itself and time
is like a plow that turns up yesterday
I move and all around – the marketplace
where something tugs my sleeve as I go by

By any standard, this is an accomplished piece of work, and Purdy could no more have written it in the 1940s and 1950s than Stevens could have written 'Modern Poetry' in the first decade of the century. This displays some of the qualities the New Criticism demanded of a lyric – objectivity, control, ambiguity – and yet is written in the strong rhythms of ordinary speech prevalent in Purdy's free-verse poems since the late 1950s. Both stanzas are closely organized and offer a loose counterpoint to each other: the first ends with 'the night birds,' the second opens with the raucous 'rooster voices,' which, picking up on the suggestion in the previous line of 'the night birds calling their children home' carries the trace of a suggestion of the rooster, as in *Hamlet*, warning the ghosts that dawn is about to break and that they should return to death's kingdom.

Closely organized though it is, the poem is nevertheless open at both ends: the first line is a grammatical fragment, while the last ends without punctuation and a declarative sentence made suggestive by the incremental effect of the preceding nine lines. The muted music of the near rhymes ('remain'/'came'; 'stones'/'home') is perfectly fitted to the setting and theme. The poem seems to take a risk with the repetition of two words – 'death' and 'broken' – in the first two lines, but the effect is not only a sentence that seems perfectly natural but a memorable and haunting line. Equally worth remarking is a trick of grammar and syntax common in the unpunctuated free-verse poems. I'm referring to the way in which key nouns in the second stanza simultaneously fulfil a double syntactic function: 'the past' is both object of the verb 'wake' and subject of the following clause 'the past converses with itself and time'; and 'time' then shifts or expands its syntactical function from object of the preposition 'with' to subject of the succeeding clause. Neither word is semantically ambiguous, and yet because of the two-way syntax a doubling of the stanza's denotative dimension occurs. The surprising and dramatic caesura in the ninth line disrupts the grammar dramatically and as a consequence allows a hint of mystery – 'something' from 'yesterday' – to enter the poem. What the poem says throughout is relatively clear even in its figurative lines, but what it means is suddenly made slightly mysterious as we cross the gap, marked by a dash, between 'around' and 'the marketplace,' a gap already present in the simile of the 'plow' cutting into the earth. A concrete and familiar situation is suddenly and surprisingly made strange by means of completely ordinary language, unforced figures of speech, and an unobtrusive music (see the linking of 'plow' and 'past'). To say that it is 'death' or a premonition of dying that 'tugs' his sleeve is probably accurate enough, though it also reminds us of one of the reasons why Cleanth Brooks was concerned with 'the heresy of paraphrase.'

Purdy's more traditional lyrics almost speak for themselves, and, to echo Donald Davie's comment on Hardy, one of their great virtues is that they usually give 'the exegete hardly anything to do'[23] beyond pointing out some aspects of their craftsmanship. Since my interest at this point is primarily in the persistence of a relatively conservative prosody in Purdy's mature work, I simply want to call attention to one more of the more traditional lyrics, 'Inside the Mill' (1976), in which Purdy's handling of stanzas and anapests seems particularly masterly, and in which, as in 'Kerameikos Cemetery,' the stanza form is essential to the theme.

> It's a building where men are still working
> thru sunlight and starlight and moonlight
> despite the black holes plunging down
> on their way to the roots of the earth
> no danger exists for them
> transparent as shadows they labour
> in their manufacture of light
>
> I've gone there lonely sometimes
> the way I felt as a boy
> and something lightened inside me
> – old hands sift the dust that was flour
> and the lumbering wagons returning
> afloat in their pillar of shadows
> as the great wheel turns the world
>
> When you cross the doorway you feel them
> when you cross the places they've been
> there's a flutter of time in your heartbeat
> of time going backward and forward
> if you feel it and perhaps you don't
> but it's voyaging backward and forward
> on a gate in the sea of your mind
>
> When the mill was torn down I went back there
> birds fumed into fire at the place
> a red sun beat hot in the stillness

they moved there transparent as morning
one illusion balanced another
as the dream holds the real in proportion
and the howl in our hearts to a sigh   *CP*, 208

As so often in Frost and occasionally in Les Murray, this could be called
a poem of rural ruins, the unexpected ruins of a young country.[24] In
Purdy's body of work it is almost a Canadian topos in which elegy is
simultaneously a record of loss and a resistance both to historical amnesia and the implicit devaluation of the historical past. Like many of these
poems, 'Inside the Mill' attempts to evoke an aspect of the not so distant
past, to use words to replace no longer existing people, objects, and
events. As I argue later, Purdy has no illusions about the limitations of
language and the imagination in such a project: when he describes 'the
flutter of time' in the reader's heartbeat when the past is encountered,
he's realistic enough to add almost immediately, 'if you feel it and perhaps you don't.' It's a signature gesture, often of doubt or ambivalence,
occurring in numerous poems, acknowledging the possibility of another
viewpoint, a response other than the one offered by the speaker. (Relevant here is Vendler's comment that 'what makes great poets "great" is
that they are always of two minds.'[25])

Each of the seven-line stanzas presents one facet of the poem's situation. The opening line's present tense creates the momentary illusion
that the 'men are still working,' an illusion to be gradually and reluc-
tantly undone by the rest of the poem and the narrator's finally explicit
admission that the mill no longer exists. And yet for three unpunctuated
stanzas the hypnotizing song-like lilt created by the rhythm and the
metre – a deft mix of iambs and anapests – keeps whole and real the first
stanza's dream image from the past. The reader's complicity in the
dream image is also secured in part by the deliberately ambiguous 'you'
running through the third stanza, which is simultaneously the speaker,
a synonym for 'one,' and, as so often in Purdy, an address to the reader.
The communion between past and present, the negation of transience in
the sense 'of time going backward and forward / ... / voyaging backward and forward / on a gate in the sea of your mind' is communicated
by the enjambment, the imagery, the lack of punctuation, and the con-
junctions building up to the three prepositional, anapestic phrases of the
stanza's final line.[26] The poem's last line repeats the syntax and the
rhythm – 'and the howl in our hearts to a sigh' – but the emotional quality is completely different, though, as we realize in retrospect, memory

or 'voyaging' in time – whether personal or historical – is rarely without emotional complications, and the 'howl' of the ending is as likely a result as any. From the poem's opening sibilant – 'It's' – to its final one in 'sigh,' from the anapest in the first line – 'It's a building' – to the one that closes the poem – 'to a sigh' – the lyric's tapestry is held together by a remarkably deft use of metre. (Purdy's comment to Birney on the metre is worth noting: 'I can adopt almost any rythm [sic] or conceitedly think I can – which made this poem seem a tour de force to me.'[27])

I don't want to leave the poem without remarking on the way the phrase 'pillar of shadows' colours the later clause 'birds fumed into fire,' implying the withheld ghost-image of a 'pillar of fire' shadowing the clause. 'Fumed,' incidentally, seems particularly daring and successful; it carries a slight suggestion of 'plumed' and leaves the impression of birds, resisting, 'angry,' being sucked into the smoke or fumes of the fire. The closing three lines – sudden, unexpected, and concentrated – belong with those endings in which Purdy avoids thematic closure with an enigmatic statement, image, or what David Shaw has called 'unconsummated symbolism.'[28] Returning to the demolished mill (or during its demolition), the narrator sees the ghosts of the workers once again and is left with the impression that they and he are equally illusory (and therefore, as in the rest of the poem, equally real) and equally necessary to each other. The syntax would seem to dictate that the last couplet be read something like this: 'as the dream holds the real in proportion / and [as the dream holds] the howl in our hearts to a sigh,' meaning, I think, that the dream (or the poem) contains the past and makes its loss somehow bearable. A childhood memory that began with a simple declarative sentence ends as an enigmatic meditation on our history and our mortality.

More unexpectedly, rhyme and iambic lines are also regularly present in the free-verse poems and are usually used to achieve a very specific set of effects. Because I look in some detail below at free-verse poems that make effective use of 'conservative verse' and the 'ghosts of metre,' I glance here at only one or two examples. In 'The Death Mask' (CP, 240), Purdy's poem about the so-called mask of Agamemnon, the several regular lines at the close lend the poem the sombre tone and solemnity appropriate to a royal procession or ritual:

... on a day
in Athens when the rain-dark hurrying clouds
that drown Apollo in their ragged hearts

and skirt museum walls but can't
douse the red flames of Troy
alight across the face of gold.

The iambic regularity of the final line sets it slightly apart and serves to sound a clear conclusion to the poem. The aural relations between the words lend the stanza both a tensile and propulsive quality: 'Apollo' appears almost inevitably after 'Athens'; 'rain,' 'ragged hearts,' and 'red,' point to 'Troy'; and 'alight' reinforces the sound and sense of 'across,' while the latter intensifies the effect of 'face.' Incidentally, the syntactic ambiguity of 'alight' (is it a past participle attached to 'red flames of Troy' or is it the verb of 'the rain-dark hurrying clouds'? Or both?) lends the final line a double syntactic and semantic force reinforcing the effect of the precise iambic rhythm.[29]

A similar impression of metrical closure is present in many poems that, for the most part, avoid a syllable-stress metre in most of their lines. In 'Birds and Beasts' (CP, 306), for instance, the iambic metre and the pararhymes bring that playful poem's music and theme to a point and, with the surprising irregularity in the penultimate line, swerve away from the sentimentality potential in the personification:

Nearby they cry 'Sleep Well Sleep Well'
to brothers in the woods
and these reply 'We Will We Will'
while the little red bonfire dies
and silence   silence falls

And a single line in 'Dead March for Sergeant MacLeod' (CP, 173) – 'of drums and guns and smoking guns' – recalls with its iambic regularity military marches different from the one being written by Purdy.[30] In all three cases, Purdy tightens up the line with metre in order to achieve an effect of formality and closure. Even a reader without English would sense the presence of two metrics if the poem were read aloud.

Purdy's use of metre and rhyme at a time when, as Ekbert Faas puts it, 'the writing of verse in regular rhyme, metre and stanza has ... almost become an anachronism,'[31] is itself a way of 'alluding' to a tradition and a poetics within a body of poetry, his own, whose primary allegiance is ostensibly to an antithetical poetics, a poetry freer and more open than anything he could envisage during the 1940s but not quite what would later come to be called a poetry of 'open form.' In the poems of the 1950s we can hear Purdy's indebtedness in those lines where his voice is overwhelmed by the voice of a stronger poet, often Dylan Thomas. In the poems of the 1980s and 1990s, Purdy, confident in his voice, often indicates his 'roots' simply by naming, alluding, referring, quoting, or echoing. But throughout his career, his occasional use of the iambic line recalls his first phase and a poetic tradition that he has never forgotten. Measured against the openness of much free verse, Purdy's lyrics, like Layton's, are relatively conservative. The fact that each thinks of poetry primarily *as* lyric speaks for itself and has won them few important followers among the poets of the next generation. Of the poets of some stature, only Dennis Lee, Tom Wayman, and Bronwen Wallace are obviously indebted to Purdy, though others, including Margaret Atwood and Michael Ondaatje, have acknowledged a more general indebtedness. The opening section of *In the Skin of a Lion*, for instance, is set in Purdy country, and some scenes overlap with those in *A Splinter in the Heart*. Purdy's copy of *In the Skin of a Lion* is inscribed as follows by Ondaatje: 'And for Al in Trenton years ago.' And inserted in the book is a letter in which Ondaatje writes, 'I've learned/stolen/been in awe of your work for years and still am/and still steal probably' (November 1980).[32]

Why Purdy turned his back on his early poetry is self-evident: it represented a dead end both personally and in the larger North American poetic tradition. His situation as he struggled to find his own voice and to become a poet was roughly analogous to Eliot's in New England at the beginning of the century, and Eliot's comments, in the essay on Yeats, are relevant here: 'A very young man, who is himself stirred to write, is not primarily critical or even widely appreciative. He is looking for masters who will elicit his consciousness of what he wants to say himself, of the kind of poetry that is in him to write. The taste of an adolescent writer is intense, but narrow: it is determined by personal needs. The kind of poetry that I needed, to teach me the use of my own voice, did not exist in English at all.'[33] Making himself into a poet, Eliot, of course, had the advantage of meeting other aspiring writers at Harvard, and Ezra Pound, a one-man cultural avant-garde in London. Purdy, in a Nietzschean heave, had to remake himself at least until he began corresponding with Birney and, later, having moved to Montreal, met Irving Layton, Louis Dudek, Frank Scott, and Milton Acorn. *Reaching for the Beaufort Sea* describes his situation as a poet in the mid 1950s as follows: 'At this time I had gone beyond my imitations of Dylan Thomas, G.K. Chesterton, Oliver St. John Gogarty (the friend of Yeats), and others, but had not yet reached my ultimate mentor, D.H. Lawrence. Sure, Layton's blunt use of language was having its effect: I was taking shortcuts across vast fields of adjectives, and I was thinking about entirely deleting punctuation. But worst of all, I was imitating the English, the *worst* English poets. The kind of writer who leaves poems open to multiple interpretations in laborious fashion, who deliberately protect themselves with complicated varieties of syntax and prosody' (215). As if this weren't a sufficiently unsparing self-analysis, he describes in 'Disconnections' how before coming East he read Dylan Thomas, T.S. Eliot, Roy Campbell, and Pablo Neruda and then wrote 'pretentiously meaningful poems' trying to emulate them (*ECW*, 207). He could have added, however, that, while the poems in *Pressed on Sand, Emu! Remember,* and *The Crafte So Longe to Lerne* often lack genuine feeling, are ventriloquial, derivative, and occasionally pretentious, they have their moments of strength where we can see a poet struggling with diction, rhythm, and music trying to find his own voice on the other side of influence. Poems like 'In Mid-Atlantic' (*ER*, 8) and 'Invocation' (*ER*, 9) may hum with echoes or imitations of Hopkins and Thomas, but they could only have been written by someone who had absorbed those poets and was on the verge of using them, and everything else he had read over an economically and poetically hungry decade, to write from the heart.[34] Whatever their shortcomings, the three derivative books of the 1950s are Purdy's occasionally impressive graduation exercises from a rigorous poetic curriculum of his own designing. Had he been a painter, these would have been his studio pieces, conventional still lifes and nudes. Among North American writers, only the equally self-educated Whitman would have appreciated the effort involved or the full implication of the author's note at the end of *Emu! Remember*: 'Education from institutions, nil; from approx. 10,000 books, considerably more; from living a great deal more' (16). Combined with Canada's belated Modernism, Purdy's own late education in modern poetry – he was thirty-six years old in 1955 – ensured that the conservative tradition of his youth would always be a presence in his work.

2

D.H. Lawrence in North America

In the preface to *The Collected Poems*, Purdy names only two poets as 'important influences, D.H. Lawrence and Irving Layton ... as examples, not tutors' (xviii). I'm not sure what force the slightly defensive distinction has for Purdy, but I suspect that he wants to emphasize that in confronting Lawrence and Layton he managed to avoid imitating them and, thus, to find his own voice through his reading of their poetry. By calling them 'tutors' as well as 'influences' he is able simultaneously to indicate indebtedness as well as freedom, the tradition and the individual talent. The importance of his encounter with both cannot be underestimated, and each, in different ways, has influenced his major work though, paradoxically, without leaving his voice on it. However, as I shall show below, each left a residue of images and echoes.

The force of Layton's presence can be gauged from Purdy's descriptions of him both in his poetry and in his prose. Purdy's earliest attempt to turn Layton into a poem is 'The Great Man,' an unpublished poem from 1958. He sent it to Birney and admitted that 'The Great Man is, of course, Layton.'[1] A playful, affectionate, and perceptive poem, it presents the title character from four viewpoints: his wife's, a friend's, a critic's, and his own. The wife recognizes that everything in the poet's life, including herself and the children, is secondary to words and poetry; the critic describes him as 'almost a Canadian Catullus / With Freudian guilt'; and the poet thinks of himself as 'that Prince from Serendip / Who was what his mind held.' In 'Disconnections,' Purdy looks back across three decades after their first meeting:

Layton was kingpin for me. Visits to the Côte St-Luc cottage were occasions of subdued excitement. With a face like that of some Semitic Buddha, he would listen with close attention when you tried to explain an opinion to him or had a point to make ... he pontificated about world literature and his own genius, a gift to grateful mankind – it was like listening to God.

Layton was extremely erudite. He devoured critical books that I found boring. Nietzsche was an exemplar; a candle for D.H. Lawrence burned sometimes in a living-room niche at Côte St-Luc. I saw Layton once, hurrying along a sunlit afternoon sidewalk, face buried in a book, oblivious to everything else. I didn't speak to him; that would have amounted to wrecking a ten-mile train of thought. I loved the man. (*ECW*, 190)

The hyperbole seems to beg for deflation, but it's worth noting that Purdy doesn't provide it: his admiration and affection for Layton shine through the intervening decades. Though the essay also registers, with some reluctance, Purdy's reservations about Layton's later poetry, it leaves little doubt that Layton was important to him in three ways. He continued Purdy's education in modern poetry; by his own example he showed Purdy that modern poetry of a high standard was being written in Canada; and he taught him that a Canadian poet could be Laurentian without simply imitating Lawrence's world-view or his poetic. Layton's voice is not Laurentian, and neither is his line; and his poems are freer of Laurentian echoes or allusions than Purdy's.

In any relationship between poets, there are also various intangibles. Simply to be taken seriously by Layton in 1956 must have been of enormous importance to a relatively unsuccessful and unknown poet like Purdy, a thirty-six-year-old who had failed at almost everything he had attempted. The effect of a letter from a major poet as encouraging as this one (1 July 1956), responding to some recent poems, is probably incalculable: 'I thought them the very best things you've done up to now, though you may not agree with me. I think you've at last found the form suitable to your free-swinging imagination. Not only that, it permits you to comment as well as to imagine. What you need is a form that allows you lots of elbow room, to slide in and out of your many moods and complexities, your passionate uncertainties.'[2] What's remarkable here is Layton's anticipation of some of the comments that Purdy's later readers made in response to later poems answering more closely to Layton's description. It's as if Layton writes in response to poems he thinks Purdy is capable of writing rather than to those that were collected a year later in *Emu! Remember*. Whatever the case, it's a remarkably generous and prescient critical performance in which Layton seems to foresee Purdy's Laurentian turn. It's also worth noting what is missing in Layton's letters and in Purdy's memories of their encounters: the older poet never tried to refashion Purdy into a poet in his own image. Some of Layton's images and metaphors have a second life in Purdy's poems – more on this below – but not his voice and poetics.

The one thing Layton couldn't teach Purdy, however, nor with his internationalist orientation as a poet would he have wanted to, was how to write 'in the Canadian grain,' how, that is, to forge a poetic, based on 'conservative verse,' modern poetry, and the Laurentian poetic, that would give voice to the country. The earliest hint of the last in Purdy's work is 'As a Young Man,' published in 1955 in *Pressed on Sand*. Purdy's artist is a 'flawed' young man who

> ... can
> Capture an illusion and hold the grey street
> In his arms without surprise,
> Re-enact tribal genesis on canvas,
> Restore lost Eden in his hollow eyes   13

There are earlier uncollected poems on Canadian historical themes ('Paul Kane,' 'Samuel Champlain,' 'Portrait of Sir William Cornelius Van Horne'), and 'Joe Barr,' the first poem to use the Trenton/Belleville/Ameliasburg material, appeared in 1951, but this is the first poem in which Purdy gives the writer a social function.[3] It is also one of his earliest meditations on poetry.

According to *Reaching for the Beaufort Sea* – written more than thirty years after the crucial encounter – Layton was also important simply because he created the impression through his work and personality 'that anything was possible' and that 'we were all great writers, or would be soon' (213). The editors of *The Complete Poems of E.J. Pratt* may suffer from the delusion that 'E.J. Pratt is widely acknowledged as Canada's most influential poet,'[4] but my suspicion is that Layton had a much greater effect on both the poets and critics who admired him and those who reacted against him. The question really comes down to this: is there a single important poet of Layton and Purdy's generation in whom one can detect Pratt's influence? Reviews of Pratt's books in the era are polite and, among the public and academic guardians of culture, even enthusiastic, but it's obvious from Layton's reviews that his poetry is where the action is, and even the reviewers who attack him recognize that they have encountered the shock of the new.

In the 1960s and 1970s, after Purdy had won the Governor-General's

Award for *The Cariboo Horses* (1965), I suspect that Layton may have been equally important as the one obviously 'strong' poet *against* whom Purdy measured himself. He may have read 'Thomas's *Collected Poems* every day for several weeks while riding' a tram in Vancouver, and he may have imitated him 'slavishly,' but Thomas's voice is simply too idiosyncratic to be useful to another poet, especially one looking for help in finding his own voice. Layton, by contrast, could be imitated and reacted against. And in contrast to some of the other 'contenders' – Avison, Dudek, Souster – he was so obviously 'there' as a challenging presence that could not be avoided. There is evidence of Purdy's early wrestle with Layton in several poems from the 1950s, most obviously 'Poem' (*ER*, 3) and 'At Roblin Lake' (*CLL*, 17–18). The first ends with two images borrowed from Layton's 'The Birth of Tragedy' (if you're going to steal, steal from the best):

> Whatever it means
> Isn't very important now, summed up for me to discover
> In casual rhymes.
> But take a deep breath and feel the angling sunbeams make
> Me a confluence
> Established by vectors of light, like candles burning in space
> For a hunchback prince.

The 'candles burning in space' are from the ending of Layton's much-anthologized poem ('while someone from afar off / blows birthday candles for the world') as is the emphatic 'Me' of the third last line. The 'hunchback' is probably from 'The Cold Green Element,' ('and grew a brilliant / hunchback with a crown of leaves') though it's possible that Thomas's 'The Hunchback in the Park' is also partly responsible. Purdy mentions Thomas's poem in a letter to Birney ([?] March 1955).[5]

The indebtedness of 'At Roblin Lake' is more interesting because, in a manner of speaking, both poets could be said to have tried to hide the evidence of the key image – an 'air rifle' – by removing it from later versions of their poems (the other poem is, of course, Layton's 'Cain'). Layton's poem shows the poet, who in 'The Cold Green Element' and 'A Tall Man Executes a Jig' identifies with dead animals – a toad and a snake – shooting a frog. The following lines are relevant here:

> Taking the air rifle from my son's hand,
> I measured back five paces, the Hebrew

In me, narcissist, father of children,
Laid to rest. From there I took aim and fired.[6]

In the first version of 'At Roblin Lake,' Purdy rewrites the scene as follows: 'This walking-morning I made a shore-capture, / With hands – having no air rifle.' By the time the poem appears in *The Collected Poems* (16), Layton's 'air rifle' has disappeared.

Next morning I make a shore-capture,
one frog like an emerald breathing,
hold the chill musical anti-body
a moment with breath held.

Images from Layton's early poems also reappear in the late seventies in 'Starlings' and 'On Realizing He Has Written Some Bad Poems.' In the first, Purdy reaches back to 'The Cold Green Element' for Layton's image of 'the labels of medicine bottles'; and in the second he returns to Layton's 'brilliant / hunchback' and changes him into 'the jewelled hunchback in my head.'

As I wrote above, Layton may have been a crucial 'example' in another sense as well: he was a Laurentian poet – there was a shrine to Lawrence in his cottage[7] – who had absorbed some of his master's lessons about poetry and about life without committing himself completely to or being overwhelmed by the radical poetics of Lawrence's essay 'Poetry of the Present.' Unlike Lawrence, whom he resembles in many ways, Layton was unwilling to jettison stanzas, metre, and rhyme in the anabasis to the open sea of modern poetry. The poems of his major period – from 'The Swimmer' to 'A Tall Man Executes a Jig' – as well as some of the later underrated lyrics of the 1970s and 1980s reveal a poet who has absorbed the lessons of Modernist poetry without turning his back on what for the sake of convenience I'll continue to refer to as conservative verse. The latter helped him avoid the potential formlessness that inevitably comes with the territory if one follows either Williams (the first part of *Paterson* appeared in 1946) or Lawrence. As is painfully evident from the vast majority of published free-verse poems, only a very strong poet with confidence in his own voice and ability to master the free-verse line can follow Lawrence and Williams in jettisoning tradition and betting everything on the individual talent. Layton may also have sensed that he needed a concept of form stricter than that provided by free verse to accommodate, express, but also restrain the elevated and often hortatory rhetoric of his version of high romantic lyric. Finally, Layton is too much the poet of the single, unified speaking subject to be tempted by Williams's pre-deconstructive dissolution of it in *Paterson*.

To return to Purdy, who, I want to suggest, can only be understood in Canadian poetry facing Layton, it's possible that Layton's poems of the 1950s showed him a way of becoming a modern poet without giving up either the poetry he had grown up with or the poetry of his self-education. In other words, Layton showed him a way of reconciling two equally important aspects of his own evolving poetics. Purdy might have turned his back on Carman, Chesterton, Kipling, and Co., but he would never – and would never need to – emotionally and artistically abandon them. The presence of Alfred Noyes's 'The Highwayman' in five of his poems – including two important late works, 'Pour' and 'Red Fox on Highway 500' (*CP*, 238, 271) – alone testifies to the hold (it's more than nostalgia) this body of now neglected poetry has on his imagination after nearly half a century. In Layton he had found a poet who, despite his antipathy to Eliot's poetry and world-view, had understood Eliot's comments on *vers libre* and made them his own: 'But the most interesting verse which has yet been written in our language has been done either by taking a very simple form, like iambic pentameter, and constantly withdrawing from it, or taking no form at all, and constantly approximating to a very simple one. It is this contrast between fixity and flux, this unperceived evasion of monotony, which is the very life of verse.'[8] We don't need to agree with this as applying to all poets in order to assent to Eliot's general point about the need for variety in the line and poem. It's a lesson Layton seems to have learned by himself and one that Purdy may have absorbed from him during the Montreal years. Certainly his later comments, even when he is critical of Layton, always acknowledge his indebtedness as well as his opinion that the poems of Layton's prime are among the best in the Canadian canon. For instance, he told Charles Bukowski in 1965 that '[Layton] was certainly the best thing that ever happened to Canada tho – Until he came along everyone sounded like your aunt Martha – I guess I ask too much of him – it ought to be enough that he's good without me wanting him to scrape the skies every time he writes a poem' (*BPL*, 102). At roughly the same time, he reviews the 1966 *Collected Poems of Irving Layton* and, having published *The Cariboo Horses*, feels confident enough both to praise and criticize: Layton is a 'marvellous craftsman,' but he is also too subjective, often sentimental, and too judgmental. Still, 'despite obvious faults, these poems are the most substantial body of good work published in the country. You have to accept the bad with the good, and be thankful for both' (*SA*, 211–12). Ironically, the last sentence has been repeated over the years by reviewers of Purdy's own work. Nearly three decades later, in *Reaching for the Beaufort Sea*, he mentions that he thinks the best Canadian poets are 'Klein, Atwood, Birney, Acorn, and Layton ... but not necessarily in that order' (*RBS*, 288). Klein, as I pointed out earlier, is the only one Purdy considered for inclusion in 'Bestiary [II]'; perhaps Layton would have made it had the letter 'L' not already been occupied by Lawrence, though there may be a subconscious hint of the Canadian poet in the first two lines: 'Lawrence! – not for his blustering / Jesus propheteering' (*CP*, 326). On second thought, perhaps it shouldn't surprise us that Purdy's list omits Layton. In the game of king of the castle that strong poets play, each must have recognized the other sometime during the 1960s as the only significant competition within the Canadian canon.

Lawrence, the other 'example' not 'tutor,' is as Purdy has repeatedly acknowledged in poems, essays, and letters, the single most important literary figure in his work *and* life: 'my ultimate mentor' (*RBS*, 215). Since the encounter with Lawrence has been so central, it is worth quoting at some length from one of Purdy's longer descriptions of this encounter in 'Disconnections.'[9]

Over the years there have been so many poets I've loved and still love that it's impossible to mention either their influence or their names. But I can't not mention D.H. Lawrence. His *Birds, Beasts and Flowers* actually changed the way I thought inside a poem. One is not conscious of thinking while doing it, at least I am not ... But Lawrence's mind darted off on tangents in all directions; it seemed continually to duplicate and reduplicate past instants; I have a vision of sparkling electrical fire inside Lawrence's skull. (How can that man be dead?)

When I first read his poem about a goat that had climbed a low tree in Italy – 'like / some hairy horrid God the Father in a / William Blake imagination ...' I could hardly conceive of such lines and such a thought actually alighting, like a bird on a white page. How could his brain skip light-years from goats to William Blake? And be absolutely and shockingly right? ...

Lawrence learned much from Walt Whitman, and I can see how and why he could do so. Yet Whitman's work seems to me nearly mindless cliché by comparison to Lawrence's ... Lawrence was drawn by Whitman's tone, his openness of line, his running on and on wherever thought would take him. Whitman refused to be dictated to by other men's thinking, by traditions of prosody, by the pretentious notion that if one was writing a poem one must say what a poem was supposed to say, must scan and rhyme.

Lawrence knew that a poem could say anything ... So that he wrote his life in his poems, and toward the end of his life he wrote his death. When a poet – myself in this case – is influenced enough by Lawrence, then he escapes all influence, including Lawrence. After DHL, all other influences merge seamlessly into your own work. (*ECW*, 215–16)[10]

On the basis of this acknowledgment one would expect to find Lawrence's influence on the poems of the 1950s and 1960s, but if it's there it's merged 'seamlessly' with Purdy's own evolving prosody. Lawrence's role in Purdy's development is fascinating precisely because until the late 1970s it is so inconspicuous in the major poems in which he found the voice that would deepen and expand in range over the remainder of his career. Between 1955 and 1975 we find echoes, allusions, and references to almost every poet Purdy considers important or whose lines have remained in his memory: Blake, Browning, Cavafy, Neruda, Hopkins, Stevenson, Chesterton, Noyes, Birney, Layton, Muir, Housman, Rilke, Eliot, Jeffers, Keats, Arnold, MacLeish, Pound, Whitman, Ramon Guthrie, Francis Thompson, Auden, and Jarrell. But with the possible exception of three lines in 'Decree Nisi' ('The body that is my sole deed / and contract, the word said / which means all that I am' [*BB*, 20] and the title 'Sons and Lovers' in *Poems for All the Annettes*, Lawrence doesn't appear until 1981 in *The Stone Bird*, Purdy's best single volume since *Wild Grape Wine* in 1968. In *The Stone Bird* there is one poem, 'Bestiary,' influenced by several of Lawrence's, and one about him, 'D.H. Lawrence at Lake Chapala.' Three years later, *Piling Blood* has eight: 'In the Beginning Was the Word,' 'Adam and No Eve,' 'Birds and Beasts,' 'The Elephant Is Slow to Mate,' 'Bestiary [II]: ABC of P,' 'Capitalistic Attitudes,' 'The Death of DHL,' and 'Lawrence's Pictures.' All subsequent collections show Lawrence's presence in some form.

Since Lawrence is obviously more important to Purdy than to Layton as a *poet* – Layton tends to value him as a prophet or sage – I have the impression that Purdy could only let himself write out of and about Lawrence when he was sufficiently established as a poet, sufficiently confident in the stature of his own work and in the poetic and view of life he had developed in response to Lawrence's example. A decade after the three great books of the 1960s – *The Cariboo Horses, North of Summer*, and *Wild Grape Wine* – he seems to have felt that he could engage his mentor openly on common ground without the 'anxiety of

influence.' These are poems simultaneously of dialogue with and homage to the poet who had shown him how to write a 'poetry of the
present' with a line and prosody adequate to the vitality, variability,
tone, timbre, and amplitude of his own voice – what Layton had called
his 'free-swinging imagination' and 'passionate uncertainties.' These
poems could only have been written when he had the confidence that
they could stand side by side with Lawrence's without being overwhelmed by them. In other words the Laurentian poems are simultaneously *hommage* and assertion of independence. This seems to me
particularly true in 'Lawrence's Pictures' and 'The Death of DHL,'
where Lawrence's words and images are taken and placed within a
monologue whose voice is Purdy's. Here Purdy's 'wrestling with the
great dead' (Harold Bloom's phrase)[11] results in the momentary establishing of an equivalence between the two poets as their voices meet in
an implicit dialogue. The risk, of course, is that the language of the
canonical poet will overwhelm the 'ephebe,' as often happens even
when a minor poet simply quotes a major one. How many contemporary poems have been exposed as second-rate simply by ill-advised epigraphs or quotations from Rilke, Yeats, or Stevens?

'Bestiary' (*CP*, 259) provides another, slightly different example of
Purdy's use of Lawrence's poetry. I quote the penultimate stanza.

Rooster boast
two short and one long syllable
sends blood plummeting skyward
where he can no longer go
and declares in rooster
earth is best earth is best
and heart knows that isn't true
and brag-song is grief-cry
earth at best is second-best
he mourns the sky the lost sky
with a metal windvane rooster
dodging lightning atop a northern barn
he is sky-lost
the white stovelid a lost glory
poor flightless bird

The first line is a strong echo of Lawrence's 'Tortoise Shout,' and the
playful, sympathetic, nearly empathetic evocation of the animal world

calls to mind some of the poems in *Birds, Beasts and Flowers*. Purdy has absorbed Lawrence's animal poems to the point that he can use their example to write an original animal poem of his own that in line and voice shows little debt to Lawrence's, even though his poem could not have been written without the latter's example. He has created his own imaginative and prosodic space in the reader's mind with un-Laurentian verbal mannerisms and locutions ('brag-song' and, in the first stanza, the mouth and memory stretching 'jewsharpgutstretching-mouthfartingmusic') to describe the burro's cry. Also sounding the Purdy note is the reference in the poem's close to 'the Cambrian / and Precambrian when there were no wolves / no housepets.' Lawrence, by contrast, ends 'Tortoise Shout' with 'life's unfathomable dawn.' The Precambrian and prehistory never interested him, though they obsess Purdy.

But if we recall Purdy's comments about him, it's obvious, though paradoxically so, that Lawrence could be the central figure behind Purdy's best poems even if these never alluded to or named him. Lawrence's poems taught Purdy that 'a poem could say anything' in almost any style or form or prosody the poet chose. The only poetics or rules that mattered for Lawrence were the ones discovered by the poet during the act of writing. As well, Lawrence offered Purdy the choice of turning his back on the belated tradition within which his poetry had developed (as Lawrence had done after *Love Poems and Others* [1913]) or of using it in any way he wanted. Overall, it was a lesson in freedom that Lawrence, as he acknowledged both in 'Poetry of the Present' and *Studies in Classic American Literature*, had learned from Whitman. A few sentences from the essay summarize the basic characteristics of Lawrence's poetics better than I can:

Perfected bygone moments, perfected moments in the glimmering futurity, these are the treasured gem-like lyrics of Shelley and Keats.

But there is another kind of poetry: the poetry of that which is at hand: the immediate present. In the immediate present there is no perfection, no consummation, nothing finished ... It is obvious that the poetry of the instant present cannot have the same body or the same motion as the poetry of the before and after ...

Much has been written about free verse. But all that can be said, first and last, is that free verse is, or should be, direct utterance from the instant, whole man. It is the soul and the mind and the body surging at once, nothing left out. They speak all together. There is some confusion, some discord. But the confusion and the discord only belong to the reality as noise belongs to the plunge of water. It is no use inventing fancy laws for free verse, no use drawing a melodic line which all the feet must toe. Free verse toes no melodic line, no matter what drill-sergeant. Whitman pruned away his clichés – perhaps his clichés of rhythm as well as of phrase. And this is about all we can do, deliberately, with free verse. We can get rid of the stereotyped movements and the old hackneyed associations of sound or sense.[12]

As Williams, Olson, and Duncan later recognized, Lawrence's writings on poetry were a charter and invitation for what would come to be called 'projective verse,' 'the poetry of open form,' and 'process poetry.' Whether Lawrence would have approved of some of the experiments undertaken in his wake is irrelevant; more to the point is the fact that he made them possible not with a prescriptive manifesto – 'fancy laws for free verse' – but with one that insisted that the only prosody and poetics that mattered had to originate in the poet's most intense subjectivity: the line and the poem's overall form or structure – its narrative and structure of feeling – had to have their genesis in the deepest aspects of the self. The nearly psycho-biological connection between heart, breath, and voice in Olson's projective verse or Duncan's nearly mystical 'composition by field' are attempts to involve 'the whole man' – including mankind – in creating the poem.

For Purdy, Lawrence's example, like Layton's, sanctioned the use of a literary version of his own voice and allowed the shape of the sentence and stanza to be identical with the shape of the feeling-thought, whether in poems of reflection, description, dramatization, or statement. From the perspective of literary history, the ultimate debt may be to Coleridge's conversation poems, but Purdy learned it from Lawrence.[13] I should add, however, that he probably learned it only because he was *ready* to learn it in the sense that something in his imagination answered to Lawrence's words. It may not be far-fetched to see a correlation or relationship between Lawrence's free 'line' and Purdy's restlessness (his vagabondia of the 1930s), walking, his sprawling uncontrolled handwriting, and the style of his mature poems. D.G. Jones points in this direction when he comments that 'if Purdy has a method, it is error, rambling, talking: talking to oneself, talking to others, listening to others talk.'[14] Osip Mandelstam recalls the origins of this 'method' when he points out in his 'Conversation about Dante' that 'both the *Inferno* and, in particular, the *Purgatorio* glorify the human gait, the measure and rhythm of walking, the footstep and its form. The step, linked with breathing and saturated with thought, Dante understood as the beginning of prosody. To indicate walking he utilizes a multitude of varied and charming turns of phrase.'[15] Among the effects of this 'method,' whether in Dante, Wordsworth, Whitman, Stevens, Valéry, or Purdy, is the impression on the reader that the poem is an encounter between the rambling poet and various aspects of what Samuel Johnson called 'the living world.'[16]

In addition to his untheoretical theory, Lawrence offered Purdy the example of poems that must have seemed like a catalogue of potential techniques and approaches: the line based on the poet's voice; a poetry open to every possible subject-matter; poems written in the present tense; poems that deliberately included 'some confusion, some discord' (Whitman's 'Do I contradict myself / very well I contradict myself'); a radical subjectivity; poems involving the reader either through the direct address of a familiar vocative or the use of the imperative; and a shedding of the burden of the poetry of the past by abandoning stanza forms, poetic kinds, and decorum. Purdy's own comments on poetry often sound like paraphrases or extensions of Lawrence's views: '... in my own case I like to think of a continual becoming and a changing and a moving'; 'I mistrust almost entirely "methods" and "schools" of writing –'; 'I generally stick to the concrete or get to it pretty quick'; poetry should reflect 'a living stance, a leaning attitude'; 'There seem to me to be a million ways to write a poem'; '... a poem's validity belongs, principally, to its own particular moment of creation. Therefore, all are a series of moments emerging from their own time. At least they emerge as their own kind of truth, if the impulses that created them were valid in the first place.'[17] More narrowly, many of Purdy's characteristic techniques may be seen as functions of these Laurentian assumptions: grammatically incomplete sentences; a reliance on participles and gerunds to open a poem; verb-driven poems; resistance to closure; the use of 'etc' and the desire to leave nothing out; pervasive enjambment and lack of punctuation; self-contradiction; variable styles from 'the natural speech of living people' (FW, vii) to an ordinary but elevated high style or what Frye calls 'the high style of ordinary speech.'[18]

Williams, of course, had been writing this kind of poetry since the 1920s, but Purdy has admitted his lifelong inability to respond to it: 'W.C. Williams I could learn from if I didn't hafta like him. I'd like the *man*, but the poems ... Besides, I started to read him very late, too late to learn anything.'[19] This is also true of his reading of Whitman. Like Lawrence, Purdy is willing to admit Whitman's historical importance but, again like Lawrence, he finds the transcendentalism sentimental and simple-minded, though as the following letter to George Bowering indicates, he's sometimes more blunt in stating his reasons: 'Why do I detest Whitman? He's monotonous, long-winded and fulla shit' (26 March 1973).[20] And in the passage from 'Disconnections' quoted above he acknowledges that Whitman fathered the revolution in poetry – 'Whitman's openness of line, the running on and on wherever thought would take you,' – but can't stop himself from dismissing him as a 'nearly mindless cliché by comparison' with Lawrence. And a letter to the author (18 December 1992) makes a similar point: 'Sure, Whitman was a revolution in prosody, but did he hafta sound so silly at times.'

By contrast, not only is he able to take Lawrence's slant on life seriously, but Lawrence also offered a liberated prosody and, more important, a view of the poem's line, form, and themes as inseparable from the voice and life of the poet: the good poem is good to the extent that it is a direct, sincere, and authentic utterance of the poet's whole self. There is an impulse that originates in the poet's encounter with life 'that transmits the energy of active thought and feeling to the verse, the need and drive that shape the poem.'[21] As in *Leaves of Grass*, the poems, however diverse, become an on-going journal, however indirect, of the poet's life. A poet's collected poems are a single song of vagabondia or of the open road based on the various events, physical, emotional, and intellectual, in his life. Allen Ginsberg makes this Coleridgean assumption explicit in the preface to his *Collected Poems* when he announces, 'Herein author has assembled all his poetry books published to date rearranged in straight chronological order to compose an autobiography.'[22]

It may not be coincidental that Purdy finally settled on his published name only after the shock of recognition he encountered in reading Lawrence. It's as if having learned belatedly to write about himself in his own voice he was finally able to name himself, a naming that is coextensive with naming his family, place, nation, and mankind itself. It's worth emphasizing how late in Purdy's career this happens: he's over forty when he begins to write the poems that have secured him a place in the anthologies and in the canon. As he writes in the autobiography, 'And for just about anything I can think of, I've been a late-developer, delayed for years at the starting gate. Which means that all my reactions are liable to be slightly different than other people's' (*RBS*, 96). This personal sense of belatedness may be mysteriously related to the near urgency one senses behind the names and naming in the poems about Ameliasburg and about Canada. It's as if he felt the need to assert his name as well as the names of Canadians and Canadian places because, though for different reasons and in different ways, all are threatened by belatedness, anonymity, or oblivion: Al Purdy by his near failure as a man and a writer; Canada by the threat of American cultural and political hegemony.[23] To return to the last line of 'On Canadian Identity,' in 1960, 'Al Purdy,' even more than Canada, was a 'word which ha[d] never yet been said.' In point of fact, there's an onomastic confusion or instability in Purdy's poetry for more than thirty years. The issue isn't sufficiently interesting to make it into Canadian Trivial Pursuit, but it does have sufficient biographical and bibliographical interest to pause over. It begins in 1935 with the publication of three poems in the Trenton Collegiate *Spotlight*: each is under a different name! 'Canada' is by Alfred Purdy; 'This is a Fable, Yes That's True' is by A.W.P.; and 'The Black and Gold' is by Alfred W. Purdy. The last name will be on the cover of all of his poetry books before *The Cariboo Horses* (1965), which is by Alfred Purdy, as is *North of Summer* (1967). The following year, *Wild Grape Wine* reverts to A.W. Purdy, but *Poems for All the Annettes* (second edition) is by Al. Two years later in 1970, *Love in a Burning Bush* is credited to A.W. again before *Sex and Death* (1973) and *Sundance at Dusk* (1976) establish 'Al' permanently on the title-page. That this is more than a librarian's concern is clear from Purdy's testy response to Bukowski calling him 'Albert': 'Don't give me that "Albert" stuff – Name is Al – I used to get Alfred years ago and it made me writhe. Tho I still use it on books, though I know that sounds pretentious' (*BPL*, 24 [late 1964?]). It is impossible to be sure of this, but it's possible that some of the archival material may eventually show that Purdy became 'Al' at roughly the same time that he felt confident enough to begin thinking about writing about Lawrence. It's just a hunch.[24]

Considering the centrality of Lawrence in Purdy's life and work, it is slightly surprising to find so few echoes of and allusions to the large group of American poets many of whom, like Williams and Olson, saw him as the essential precursor. If Marjorie Perloff is right in suggesting two camps for modern American or North American poetry, one flying Stevens's banner and the other Pound's (his followers include Williams and Olson), then Purdy would have to be placed in the latter. David Perkins makes a similar point by placing the Canadian poet 'A.L. Purdy' [*sic*] among those 'also influenced by Williams.'[25] Pound, however, is almost as significant an absence in Purdy's work as Whitman or Williams, both of whom have much more in common with him than we would at first suspect. Purdy refers to him in 'Disconnections' in a passage dealing with his reading in the mid-1950s: 'I was also reading T.S. Eliot and Pound at the time, the former with distaste and respect, the latter because I thought I should and with puzzlement. But "The River Merchant's Wife," "Ballad of the Goodly Fere" were hypnotic, as were some of the short lyrics. (But I avoided "Homage to Sextus Propertius" and the *Cantos* were blessedly in the future)' (*ECW*, 215). In an undated letter to Earle Birney, written in 1955, he admits to being 'knee-deep in Ezra Pound at the moment; but his images are literary, for the most part. An odd blend of simplicity and erudition. But at the present time I simply cannot read *The Cantos*. They are not coherent enough or continuous.'[26] Pound can't be considered a significant influence, though 'The River Merchant's Wife' is probably somewhere behind the original version of 'From the Chin P'Ing Mei' (*CP*, 11) and, as was already mentioned, the subtitle of 'Bestiary [II]' echoes Pound's *ABC of Reading*.[27] There are also poems about Pound in the papers as well as in *Naked with Summer in Your Mouth* ('Pound,' 36).

Purdy treats Olson, perhaps Lawrence's most fervent American follower, almost contemptuously both in the letters and in the prose. *Reaching for the Beaufort Sea*, for instance, describes a Vancouver party at which 'a record was played of the reverend progenitor, Charles Olson, reading something that sounded like a laundry list' (233). Purdy also refers to the Zarathustra of Black Mountain 'as a pretentious charlatan thrown up by his age' (234). Ironically, the poetry aside, Purdy and Olson agree on some minor as well as important issues or concerns, including the high opinion each has of the poet's role in society, though, typically, Purdy's views, unlike Olson's, are expressed for the most part in the poems and rarely in prose. Both admire Herodotus and mention Pausanias: Purdy has written poems about them, Olson has referred to the former as the most important of the Western historians. More importantly, each has what could be called a polyhistoric sensibility. Each, though for different reasons, sees Lawrence as a central figure in Modernism. There are even occasionally lucid sentences in Olson's predominantly tortuous prose that could have been written by Purdy. From 'Human Universe': 'If there is any absolute, it is never more than this one, you, this instant, in action.' From *Mayan Letters*: 'The trouble is, it is very difficult, to be both a poet and, an historian' (Purdy would have been more sparing with the commas).[28]

This one-sided disagreement also involves the nature of the speaking subject in poetry (Purdy's is more humanistic and 'subjective'), the poetic line (Olson's depends more on the typewriter, Purdy's on the rhythms of ordinary speech), and open form. Furthermore, Purdy probably saw in Olson's 'projective verse' a new formalism that was paradoxically also a potential formlessness however much the poets and critics claimed otherwise. But in the end Purdy's low estimate of Olson may involve nothing more than his dislike of Olson's poetry; as he says, 'I want to like a poet because of his or her effect on me now ...' (ECW, 216). Olson would have no effect on him probably because, despite their local and historical concerns, The Maximus Poems are both far more obscure and impersonal (or objective) than the kind of poetry Purdy tends to admire. The early 'Eli Mandel's Sunday Morning Castle' (PAA, 41) and the occasionally exasperated responses to Margaret Avison's poetry make it obvious that Purdy has little patience with obscurity. Not the least important part of his legacy from Housman, Chesterton, Kipling, and Carman is the view of the poet as a man speaking to other men in what Eliot, echoing Wordsworth and Whitman, calls 'the ordinary everyday language which we use and hear.'[29] What Eliot means, of course, and what we find in Purdy is a literary version of 'the ordinary everyday language.' Purdy's poetry is haunted by the dream, which was a reality for Kipling and Carman, of a nearly transparent poetry with a large audience. At the heart of Purdy's poetic, as in Gustafson's, Scott's, and Layton's, is the assumption that the poem is a public speech act addressed to the poet's contemporaries and that poetry can play an essential public role. And, as Purdy insists in the introduction to Bursting into Song (1982), to do that it must be able to be 'understood with a minimum of mental strain by people as intelligent or more so than myself' (11).Whatever their other virtues, Pound and Olson require more, much more than 'a minimum of mental strain.' Williams, of course, is closer in this instance to Purdy than to his American peers.

Finally, there is also an element of cultural nationalism in Purdy's irritation with Olson and the Black Mountain Poets and their followers in Canada, the Vancouver-based Tish group. The majority of these references to Olson come in the letters in which, as in Reaching for the Beaufort Sea, one often senses a nationalist animus against the Black Mountain poets because they represent an American poetic 'invading' Canadian poetry by way of Tish and Warren Tallman. The party in Vancouver again:

In the early Sixties the Tish group in Vancouver was making a small splash in Canadian literature. The group consisted of George Bowering, Frank Davey, Fred Wah, Robert Hogg, Jamie Reid and a few others, and the mimeographed

Tish magazine was their literary outlet. Of those named, only George Bowering has grown much larger than he was then, far beyond his beginnings.

The kindest opinion would be to say that the *Tish* people were 'influenced' by the Black Mountain movement in the US. The unkindest: they were slavish imitators. An American prof, Warren Tallman, who taught at UBC, conferred some legitimacy by writing an article about them called, 'Wolf in the Snow.' (231–2)

Though 'Wolf in the Snow' is not about Black Mountain, Purdy's general point is valid. A letter to the author from 1992 develops these comments on Olson and, by implication, American poetry as follows: 'Olson I never could stand. His rules for prosody would drive me to drink if I needed an excuse. What I've always emphasized to myself and others: ya make up yr own mind about these much-praised people. Don't let em take you in with all the shit. Every country that's power-foremost in the world imposes its own standard on literature, at least in some degree' (18 December 1992). In other words, the *Tish* poets – and with the already noted exception of Bowering does anyone read them anymore? with pleasure? – not only allowed themselves to be 'slavish imitators' of a suspect prosody, but that prosody was of foreign, that is American, provenance.[30] If the Vancouver poets didn't understand the objection, Emerson and Whitman, the fathers of American literature and the stepfathers of all post-colonial literatures, would have: they always insisted that Americans had to struggle to invent their own voice. It's worth recalling Purdy's comment on Lawrence's influence on himself: 'When a poet – myself in this case – is influenced enough by Lawrence, then he escapes all influence, including Lawrence. After DHL, all other influences merge seamlessly into your own work. You learn still, you always learn, but never again are you under a *slavish* obligation to another writer. The obligation then is to a thinker, or to a way of thinking and way of life, not to a practitioner of the craft of writing' (*ECW*, 216; my emphasis).

By writing Talmudic footnotes to Olson's plodding and muddled Torah, the *Tish* poets were unable to offer much beyond echoes of the original revelation from Black Mountain, North Carolina, U.S.A. For a poet like Purdy who gradually realized through the sixties that he was searching for a Canadian voice to write a Canadian poetry, loyalty to Black Mountain was anathema for a variety of reasons, not the least of which involved the question of who would speak for Canada. It would have been interesting to see Purdy's reaction to Bowering's claim, in *Al Purdy*, that Williams was the poet with 'the greatest influence on modern Canadian poetry.'[31] He might have agreed, but with the crucial and deflating qualification that Williams, like Olson, influenced only the minor Canadian poets: Daphne Marlatt not Margaret Atwood, Frank Davey not Michael Ondaatje.

The points of contact between Purdy's poetry, on the one hand, and Williams's and Olson's, on the other, indicate that his disagreement is also part of what could be called a family quarrel within the Pound-Williams line of North American poets. Like Olson and Williams he sees Whitman as the essential precursor. But given his commitment to the short poem, a fairly regular number of stresses per line, his occasional nostalgia for metre and rhyme (what Robert Bly terms the 'Tate-Ransom nostalgia for jails'[32]), and his compulsive revision, he has to stop short of endorsing their poetic, despite the common allegiance to Lawrence.

This may seem to have taken us far from a concern with Purdy's poetry, but the brief detour into Purdy's antagonistic relationship with the American poets in whose 'tradition' he to some extent belongs is necessary if we are to see his work as well as his evolution as a *Canadian* in the larger context of North American poetry. To juxtapose Purdy to Williams and Olson helps us see roads Purdy might have taken after Carman and before the liberating encounter with Lawrence. Instead, he learned from Lawrence's 'poetry of the present' and Laurentian 'free verse' that he could use aspects of whatever modern *and* traditional prosodies he needed in order to speak with his own voice. Poems of the early 1960s like 'Uncle Fred on Côte des Neiges' and 'Archaeology of Snow,' which seem to be edging towards free verse and open form, reveal on closer examination that many of the lines of variable length have three or four stresses and that several of the fragmented lines in sequence make up a single metric unit. 'In the Wilderness,' from *The Cariboo Horses* (35), is a good example of how unobtrusive (and unnoticed) can be Purdy's use of the tradition abandoned by Olson and Williams, represented in this case by a very loose syllabic stress metre:

On the road to Agassiz in winter
of 1962
grandfathers
       young wives
           old children
marching in the savage demolitions of hunger
for their own people
to the mountain prison at Agassiz

where incendiarist husbands and
incandescent nephews and
sons of that pale yellow soap-like stuff
                which is dynamite
are locked away near a town named
for the gentle naturalist
                Louis Agassiz

The number of syllables per line ranges from two in line four to thirteen in line six, though I would argue that three, four, and five are really a single line fragmented for emphasis. With the exception of line twelve – 'which is dynamite' – and line six – 'marching in ...' – the lines carry either two or three stresses. I'm not suggesting that this constitutes a strict metric, only that here, as in most of Purdy's poems, attention, whether conscious or subconscious, has been paid both to the number of syllables and stresses in each line. This is still a free verse ostensibly liberated from any overt or obvious pattern, metric or stanzaic; but if we are attentive to its rhythms we can often notice a near regularity in its stresses as well as the occasional recourse to iambic based lines ('of 1962'). In a later poem like 'Lawrence's Pictures' (*CP*, 324) the pattern is more obvious as the lines have, for the most part, two strong stresses throughout.

From the viewpoint of craft or technique, it's fascinating to watch Purdy pulling his poems in two directions at once and achieving a tensile strength from the presence of two rhythms. He may claim that the 'language I use is as close to my ordinary speaking voice as I can get' but the iambic ghosts in the lines separate them from his 'ordinary speaking voice' by giving them a rhythm and a structure drawn not simply from life but also from the history of poetry. He's enough of a lyric poet to want the individual poem to be if not a well-wrought urn then at least a shapely, relatively self-contained vase with scenes representing those aspects of life in which it originated. Although he would never put it this way, a work of art without form simply reaffirms the formlessness and meaninglessness of the non-human universe: in that respect it represents a surrender of the human imagination. The poem's form and structure may be contingent, provisional, and transient, but, as in Stevens, the poem represents all of our attempts, from an A-frame cottage at Roblin Lake to our relationships, to establish order and therefore project a meaning into what, for Purdy, is essentially 'a cosmic emptiness' (*CP*, 88). Lawrence could live with the radical ontological implications of his poetics of an open form because he was a religious poet confident that his being was grounded in Being, in what Anthony Burgess has called 'certain gods, unconquerable *numina*.'[33] Though there is little doubt that Purdy's vision of life is heavily influenced by Lawrence's, he parts company with him in the profundity of his doubt: Lawrence could never have written that 'there was never any purpose / and there was never any meaning' ('Gondwanaland,' [CP, 320]). The whole topic of belief, origins, and the spiritual dimension of life is one of the most important in Purdy's work, and I return to it below.

3

The Limits of Lyric

Although I have emphasized to this point some of the features of Purdy's lyrics linking them to the conservative line in poetry, there is no doubt that the predominant influences on 'the Purdy poem' have been those originating with the poets who broke with that line, among whom Lawrence is the most prominent. And while Purdy isn't as radical in his poetics as his master, aspects of the grammar and rhetoric of his lyrics regularly show a poet stretching the thematic and formal limits of lyric towards a more open poetry that doesn't simply present itself as 'the result of the creative process' but often mimics 'the creative process itself.'[1] Though Purdy's *œuvre* is impressive in its sheer variety of topics and concerns, it is nevertheless possible to generalize about typical poems. For most readers, the representative Purdy lyric is held together primarily by its speaking subject – ostensibly the poet – and his narrative, which describes or enacts in an often characteristic voice an event encountered by the speaker. The 'event,' I would add, can be either physical (the poet watches a fight in a bar) or mental (the poet reflects on his being in the world), or most often, a combination of both. Whether comic ('At the Quinte Hotel' [*CP*, 109]) or solemn ('Funeral' [*CP*, 242]), the poems are clearly parts of the same individual's world, in roughly the same way that Frost's lyrics – however we deal with Frost's persona – cohere around a recognizable subject. In the poems of the first half of Purdy's career – roughly up to 1980 – there is a balance between descriptive and reflective poems; in the ones of the past two decades, I sense a more reflective bias as the aging poet turns more to memory and musing.

This description, however, leaves the impression that Purdy is more limited thematically and formally than he is. Even a casual reading of

The Collected Poems reveals a remarkable range of variations within the limits described above. The speaker or persona, for instance, has several faces and voices, from the whining, playful, slapstick, and comic to plangent, oracular, and solemn, including the impersonal solemnity and objectivity of 'The Country North of Belleville.' He can be Al the beer drinker and wine maker; Al the beleaguered husband; Al the antiquarian; Al the time traveller; Al the traveller interested in Canadian history; Al the traveller interested in the sheer variety and otherness of the world; Al as Everyman; Al as national conscience and national voice; Al as the voice of poetry. A similar variety appears when we look at the 'kinds' of lyrics he has written: landscape or topographical poems; animal poems; ekphrastic poems; reflexive poems on poetry and art that as a group constitute an *ars poetica*; philosophical or reflective poems; dramatic monologues and 'mask' poems; dialogues; political poems; national odes; and elegies. Few of these are in any obvious sense Laurentian poems, yet Purdy's remarks about the freedom he learned from Lawrence's poetry would lead one to suspect that his poems might not have been as various and as open (to experience, in voice) without Lawrence's example.

At its most dramatic and open the typical Purdy poem creates the illusion that the reader is almost participating in the imagined or real experience described by the first-person speaker who, in Richard Poirier's words, is 'a performing self' discovering himself, as well as the limits of the self, in the complex, dramatic act of discovery that is the poem. In this case, the poem enacts, usually in the present tense, the contours of an experience rather than simply offering a description of it. Perhaps I can best illustrate the point by juxtaposing readings of two poems, 'Detail' and 'Trees at the Arctic Circle,' both published in 1968. The speaker in 'Detail' is a good example of what Hegel calls the lyric poet as 'self-bounded subjective entity,' and the poem itself is 'the result of the creative process' – in other words, a traditional post-Romantic lyric on the model of, say, Wordsworth's 'The Daffodils' or Frost's 'The Tuft of Flowers.' By contrast, 'Trees at the Arctic Circle' is an example of a poem trying to allow the reader to enter into 'the process' or experience as it is being lived through by a speaker who records or enacts his changes of attitude. The first is 'Detail' (*CP*, 113–14).

The ruined stone house
has an old apple tree
left there by the farmer

whatever else he took with him
It bears fruit every year
gone wild and wormy
with small bitter apples
nobody eats
even children know better
I passed that way on the road
to Trenton twice a month
all winter long
noticing how the apples clung
in spite of hurricane winds
sometimes with caps of snow
little golden bells
And perhaps none of the other
travellers looked that way
but I make no parable of them
they were there and that's all
For some reason I must remember
and think of the leafless tree
and its fermented fruit
one week in late January
when wind blew down the sun
and earth shook like a cold room
no one could live in
with zero weather
soundless golden bells
alone in the storm

This is in the tradition of those poems and paintings, romantic and realistic in provenance, in which the artist nudges us beyond the limits of ordinary vision to show that even at its barest and most bleak, the world is still alive and containing visionary or near-visionary moments or 'the possibility of joy in the world's tangled and hieroglyphic beauty' (Robert Penn Warren's 'The Mission'). And although the speaker claims disingenuously, in a deft echo of Frost, that he is making 'no parable' of the fact that he looks at the apples (and sees and transfigures them as 'little golden bells) and that other travellers 'perhaps' didn't look that way, the poem as a whole is a sort of parable, as this kind of poem usually is, about the need to look with attention at the world, even in winter when it is a diminished thing. If Stevens is right that 'the bare image and the image as symbol are the contrast,'[2] then 'Detail' leans towards the second both through its suggestive disclaimer about parables and in its valorized antithesis between the speaker and others. Despite its predominantly present tense, lack of punctuation, and the slight hesitation of the 'perhaps,' the poem is a self-contained and relatively predictable lyric.

'Trees at the Arctic Circle' (*CP*, 84–5), by contrast, is a poem in which the speaker enacts all the phases of his response to the trees, even when this involves him in a complete turn-around from his original viewpoint. He begins with what, for a moment, seems a simple description in the present tense:

> They are 18 inches long
> or even less
> crawling under rocks
> grovelling among the lichens
> bending and curling to escape
> making themselves small
> finding new ways to hide
> Coward trees

This confident and dismissive judgment, hammered in with six participles, persists through the second stanza's contrast of them to taller southern trees:

> I call to mind great Douglas firs
> I see tall maples waving green
> and oaks like gods in autumn gold
> the whole horizon jungle dark

The contrast is heightened by the fact that the southern trees are presented in lines of iambic tetrameter, with the metre seeming to lend them a form and dignity that the arctic trees, presented as it were formlessly, lack. But just as the reader is almost settling into what seems to be the poem's point, the lyric begins to turn against itself and into a simultaneous act of discovery for the speaker and the reader. First there is the tentative opening line of the third stanza, 'And yet – and yet –.' This is followed by two similes – with a surprising hint of a metre in lines 1, 2, and 4 – evoking the arctic trees in a completely different way:

And yet – and yet –
their seed pods glow
like delicate grey earrings
their leaves are veined and intricate
like tiny parkas

The iambic metre of the first, second and fourth lines recalls the iambic lines describing the 'great Douglas firs' and 'tall maples,' with the implication that the 'dwarf trees' are not formless or without beauty and grandeur. The poem gradually develops into a criticism of the speaker for being originally imperceptive of the beauty before him. But Purdy doesn't stop with what might seem the predictable turn to the previously unnoticed muted beauty of the trees; he's more impressed by the fact that the trees 'have about three months / to make sure the species does not die' and that since their roots 'touch permafrost,' 'they use death to remain alive.' They are survivors against great odds, and few things elicit sympathy and admiration from Purdy more quickly than people, animals, or things that have endured or survived despite great difficulties. In what is almost a universe of death or, at least, one in which death is literally never more than two feet away, the trees create beauty and order and struggle to ensure the continuity of their species. The poem is not a 'parable,' but the tenacious trees embody the qualities Purdy admires in humanity: in a universe without any apparent meaning or *telos*, they manage not only to survive but, like the poet, to create an evanescent beauty in the face of an ineluctable transience.

The poem ends with the speaker turning his scorn and near-contempt against himself:

I have been stupid in a poem
I will not alter the poem
but let the stupidity remain permanent
as the trees are
in a poem
the dwarf trees of Baffin Island

These lines are a good example of what Lawrence means when he writes that in free verse 'there is some confusion, some discord. But the confusion and the discord only belong to the reality as noise belongs to the plunge of water.'[3]

'Trees at the Arctic Circle,' simultaneously records and is a process of discovery. The present tense and the speaker's complete change of mind – what Poirier calls 'self-erasure'[4] – create the illusion that we are not so much overhearing an internal monologue as it takes place as participating in an event. But having acknowledged the demands of verisimilitude and reality, the poem also acknowledges those of art, of form, with an ending in which the closing couplet turns the poem back to its opening. We now reread the latter ironically, and recognize that the 'dwarf trees' are as great in what could be called moral and aesthetic stature as the 'Douglas firs.' In *North of Summer*, where the poem originally appeared, the speaker's interest in the trees continues beyond the poem into a 'Postscript to "Trees at the Arctic Circle,"' which claims that some of the trees live 'more than / a thousand years' and a 'Note' to that poem admitting that the poet was wrong, 'the Arctic ground willow does not live 1000 years' (*NS*, 31). As Williams put it in a late letter, 'At times there is no other way to assert the truth than by stating our failure to achieve it.'[5]

I want to end the discussion of this poem by suggesting that the lack of punctuation, the poet's willingness to record his own 'stupidity,' even the title's inclusion of the formal botanical nomenclature of the trees (Salix Cordifolia) all show Purdy trying to open up the lyric form from within both by emphasizing its referentiality and by resisting, even as he points to, its inevitable closure. There is an attempt here, as in so many of Purdy's poems, to show more aspects of the speaking subject than we normally encounter in a lyric. It's as if recognizing the limits of traditional lyric, Purdy is determined to destabilize its diction, grammar, movement, and overall temporal and spatial form in order to expand its horizons of concern and effect; Lee's perceptive reference to 'his command of polyphony' (*CP*, 380) points in the same direction. The result is not a poem of open form or a poetry of process, but, as I wrote, it is doubtful that he could have pushed his lyric in this direction without the example of Lawrence's free verse in *Birds, Beasts and Flowers* or even his self-education in poetry during the 1950s.

Purdy's poetic is not committed to open form or the poetry of process, but the individual lyrics consistently resist the limits of traditional lyric and open it up with various grammatical and rhetorical devices. This has several possible thematic implications. For instance, in creating a tension between closure and openness in many of his poems, Purdy, I would suggest, is enacting on the level of form his own philosophical ambivalence about whether the universe is meaningful or meaningless, closed or open. The order, coherence, and closure of the traditional lyric often imply an equally coherent and meaningful world in which the lyric originates and that, however obliquely or symbolically, its form or narrative mirrors. In opening up the lyric, as well as its speaking subject, Purdy destabilizes, though without undermining completely, these implications. Questions, addresses to the reader, opening dashes or participles, fragmentary or incomplete sentences, overlapping tenses, the use of 'etcetera,' the subjunctive or the conditional, and the use of 'maybe' and 'perhaps' at key junctures result in a poetry that, at its most complex, offers a tense articulation of often nearly contradictory impulses, attitudes, perspectives, and philosophies. By the simple fact of being lyrics, however open or fragmentary, Purdy's poems are assertions of order and meaning; but by destabilizing them in various ways he introduces a counterpoint, whether formal or figural, calling the possibility of meaning or order into question. The reverse is also true, however. Poems that assert meaninglessness or claim to question the possibility of any meaning offer that assertion within the context of a form that by its very existence implies the contrary. We may exist in a universe shadowed by dissolution and death, but the poem, like the dwarf trees at the Arctic Circle, creates a provisional order, temporary beauty, and moral value. In a manner of speaking, both the trees and the poem 'touch permafrost' and 'use death to remain alive.'

Whatever the virtues of 'conservative verse,' by itself it did not allow Purdy a form sufficiently elastic for a full response to reality. It was the wrestle with Lawrence that showed him a way out of the dead-end he had reached. Writing in Lawrence's shadow, Purdy gradually created (1) a speaking subject, a voice, a line, and a poetic form supple enough to express the self in its complex often self-contradictory entirety, something that Layton already sensed as possible in the letter quoted earlier; (2) a lyric form capacious enough to allow the discussion of any topic the poet wants to deal with; and (3) a poetic form to mirror the play of form and formlessness we find in our minds and in our lives. For instance, after 1960 many poems open with participles and dashes and create the impression of a poem somehow continuous with something outside it, something that came before it, something of which it is an extension. Similarly the casual, conversational use of 'etcetera,' for which there are precedents in Byron, Wordsworth, and cummings[6] ('What It Was,' 'Yes and No' [CP, 64, 356]), is like a synecdoche hinting at further things that could have been said or described but weren't. In 'Orchestra' (WS, 37), for instance, a sentence describing the performers begins with an imperative and ends with 'et cetera': 'See now / they are looking for their souls / and they are outside time / ... / in one tumescent moment / solemn as eternity's / endless et cetera.' The opening and closing words are gestures implying that the poem is related to or grounded in a reality, an experience, or a dialogue outside itself even as, on the level of form, it strives towards a certain degree of aesthetic autonomy. In 'Place of Fire,' discussed at length below, a similar slightly self-deflating effect is achieved with an implied dialogue with the reader.

> But you'll have to admit the ritual significance
> of not being above working with your hands?
> You don't admit? Okay, I guess you're right.
> But you must agree it's the hard way
> to gather ingredients for a poem?   CP, 229

Unanswered questions, performing a similar function, occur throughout Purdy's body of work, from the early 'At Roblin Lake' (CLL, 17) and 'For Norma in Lieu of an Orgasm' (PAA, 21) to 'Birdwatching at the Equator' (CP, 264) and 'Questions' (WS, 64). The early 'Hokusai at Roblin Lake' is typical of this class of poems:

> Waking: without moving my head: a grey
> slot of both light and darkness,
> the delicate grey augmented by grey
> the Japanese use on their silk screens;
> and a portion of the universe of
> an ash tree.
> I reach for pen and paper carefully,
> prop head on hand and lie
> so still I cannot move independently
> of the leaves outside
> who tilt and turn from my perspective
> (is truth turned over the same?
> or has it little threadlike supporting laws?)
> which is almost the tree's now:
> feeling the blind tugging at its wrists,
> like love I guess trying to get free,
> and sings such a mother song
> they cannot go ...   PAA, 53

Title, opening participle or gerund, two questions, a parenthesis, and the open ending all work to undermine our sense of the poem as a self-enclosed artefact. And though we probably answer the first parenthetical question with 'probably not,' the poem's overall effect, including the slight confusion in the grammar of the final lines, is to leave us slightly unsure no matter what answer we offer. In public readings, the autonomy of the poems is often further undermined by Purdy's regular refusal to pause between the reading of the poem and his particular and general comments. As a result it is occasionally difficult to be sure where the poem ends and 'life' begins.

The questions in Purdy's poems simply make explicit that all of the poems, from *The Crafte So Long to Lerne* on, are subjective, 'of the moment,' reveal 'a living stance, a leaning attitude' towards reality, and offer at best a 'personal and relative truth.'[7] The poems offer provisional and 'momentary stays against confusion' that are simultaneously questionings of or enquiries into reality, inevitably incomplete attempts to evoke or describe something that can never be known or understood completely. Purdy touches on this in a passage in 'Disconnections': 'There have been several questions that joined the fabric of my own poems. They are questions that many people have asked themselves at one time or another, mostly when young. (Which may indicate that I have lived a permanent adolescence.) Who am I? What am I doing here? What is time? How can one come to terms with death? Those questions are unanswerable questions in any but simplistic terms, unless you evade them entirely with religion. The supernatural has always been the refuge of terrified people' (*ECW*, 218–19).

The questioning of reality often begins, as we saw in 'Trees at the Arctic Circle,' with a questioning of the self. In part, this is simply an extension of the radical emotional or psychological honesty and desire for truth in Purdy's poems. His hesitations, doubts, self-questionings, and self-mockery are part of a rhetoric of authenticity insinuating other opinions, attitudes, and viewpoints into a lyric ostensibly dominated by a single voice. The voice often fragments into several dictions, tones, and moods, with the end result that at the poem's end it expresses and represents a more comprehensive and complex subjectivity than it did at the outset. But Purdy's song of myself – *The Collected Poems* as a single poem – is still more complex because it includes within intensely subjective lyrics not only expected aspects of the self, but attempts to include or imagine the viewpoints of others – real or fictional, animal or human

– ostensibly radically different from the poet. D.G. Jones's description of Purdy's 'method,' briefly mentioned above, is worth quoting in full.

From a highly conventional, formally patterned verse, Purdy developed a more flexible, cursive manner accommodated to the speaking voice, accommodating, that is, substantial variations in tone and diction and the vagaries of oral syntax: the seemingly interminable run-on sentence, the fragment, mixed tenses, and other forms of mixed construction.

It is a method that serves to put things in perspective, but not by adopting a single, bird's eye point of view. Non-linear, it produces a collision or concatenation of different points of view. Fact and fantasy, knowledge and desire, what one has learned and what one immediately perceives, have equal validity and presence. It works to enlarge one's sense of where and what one is. It serves to liberate, not through a simplification of point of view, but through its complication.[8]

The complication of point of view is also evident in the dramatic monologues, but slightly different examples can be found in the large number of animal poems, in the poems in which the poet contrasts his and his wife's approaches to life, and in those poems in which he imagines a representative figure from the past. The justly much anthologized and much admired 'Lament for the Dorsets' (CP, 135), though written in the first-person plural, provides a good example of the last. Looking at a handful of Dorset relics – 'Animal bones and some mossy tent rings / scrapers and spearheads carved ivory swans / all that remains of the Dorset giants' – the poet makes an imaginative leap into their era and history and imagines them repulsing the Vikings, hunting and wondering about the disappearance of the seals. And having done that in the first of the poem's three parts, he follows with the admission that it is as impossible for us 'to imagine them in the past' as it is for them to have 'imagined us in their future.' And yet, imagining them, enacting their lives is precisely what the poem continues to do in the final section where, explicitly asserting the importance of art, it focuses even more narrowly on a single imagined figure and involves the reader in calling him back from the dead:

Some old hunter with one lame leg
a bear had chewed
sitting in a caribou-skin tent
– the last Dorset?

Let's say his name was Kudluk
and watch him sitting there
carving 2-inch ivory swans
for a dead grand-daughter
taking them out of his mind
the places in his mind
where pictures are
He selects a sharp stone tool
to gouge a parallel pattern of lines
on both sides of the swan
holding it with his left hand
bearing down and transmitting
his body's weight
from brain to arm and right hand
and one of his thoughts
turns to ivory
The carving is laid aside
in beginning darkness
at the end of hunger
and after a while wind
blows down the tent and snow
begins to cover him

After 600 years
the ivory thought
is still warm.

Like almost all of Purdy's artist figures, Kudluk is wounded, but it is precisely only because he is wounded that he becomes a sculptor. For the reader familiar with Purdy's body of work, the sculptor and the poem gain some residual or contextual power from other artist poems like 'The Cave Painters' (*ER*, 14) 'Scholarly Disagreements' (*BB*, 15), 'Tent Rings' (*NS*, 68), 'The Sculptors' (*NS*, 75), 'In the Foothills' (*SD*, 83), 'Joint Account' (*LBB*, 159), and 'Carpenter's Notebook Entry' (*PB*, 119). By the time we reach the tactile description of how he gouges the suggestive 'parallel pattern of lines' we have forgotten that the overall description began with the conditional, 'Let's say.' The 'parallel lines' also encourage or confirm implied comparisons between themselves and the poem's lines, between past and present, between Kudluk and Al Purdy, the ivory swans and 'Lament for the Dorsets.' (It's worth adding that the 'parallel lines' also occur in 'The Country North of Belleville,' where they again have an almost talismanic significance, and that, as I shall discuss later, Purdy's creative figures are often associated with tents, caves, skulls, and wombs.) Careful word placement and effective enjambment ease us into the full materiality of the gouging – is there an echo of Birney's 'El Greco: Espolio'? – and we find ourselves almost participating in the inexplicable metamorphosis of the materialization of Kudluk's thoughts. The stanza's pervasive present tense links its description of an imagined past with the coda's ivory swan / thought that is both a relic of it and one of our few means of access to it. The poem about a real or imagined work of art inevitably implicates itself and the reader in questions not only of representation and epistemology, but also about the value and potential 'immortality' of art.[9] Purdy's handling of the topos isn't as assertive or explicit as that of Horace's 'Exegi monumentum' or Shakespeare's 'Not marble, nor the gilded monuments,' but it does deal with the question of how we survive death. In 'Lament for the Dorsets,' the sculptor and poet do it through their art. Or, at least, Kudluk has, and Purdy – the poem's anonymous voice is recognizably his – hopes to. Notice, incidentally, how the poem buries Kudluk and marks the transition into death with two unexpected lines of iambic trimeter: 'blows down the tent and snow / begins to cover him.' The richly suggestive three-line coda, almost a haiku, counters the cold fact of death with the suggestion that 'After 600 years / the ivory thought / is still warm.' By calling the swans 'an ivory thought' the poem reminds us that they – and, by extension, the implied spirit of the 'dead grand-daughter' – are still 'warm' only because a craftsman or artist turned a thought into a carving, just as Purdy, in turn, turned an observation and reflection into a poem.

A different attempt to complicate or extend point of view, one that functions to indicate the cognitive and epistemological limits of the subject, occurs in the animal poems ('Deprivation,' 'Bestiary,' 'Iguana' [CP, 213, 259, 302]). Here Purdy approaches the animal as closely as possible without attempting the impossible task of entering into its mode of being. Like Lawrence, he's satisfied with evoking the animal's radical otherness and the inevitable human failure to transcend the self. 'Iguana,' which begins playfully and comically with comparisons between the iguanas and dead members of the Purdy family, ends on a note of failure.

What can I be but humble
for the reptile and mammal primate
may never touch each other
without fear of opposites
and I feel sad
knowing I will never understand him
nor the races before and after
the starship's rocket landing
understand nothing but now
balanced in the needle's eye
and the impulse to touch God
is as close as I'll ever come   *CP*, 303

The animal poems, like the poems dealing with prehistory, often include a search for origins, for a biological and geological point zero or genesis that, if found, might answer some of the poet's ultimate questions about humanity and the universe. This is part of 'the impulse to touch God.' Purdy is rarely sentimental about nature, and when he treats animals anthropomorphically he calls attention to what he is doing ('What Do the Birds Think?' [*CP*, 103]) or there is usually a slightly ironic ('Adam and No Eve' [*CP*, 303]) or comic-pathetic tone ('Bestiary' [*CP*, 259]). When an animal resembles a man, it is usually the comic or absurd qualities that are emphasized, and we learn as much, if not more, about humanity than we do about animals. The description of dogs in 'Bestiary' is typical in this respect.

Dogs
barking and threatening
harassing each other
then into the mob-gabble and out
again emerges one long wavering howl
so close to the man-howl in extremis
self-pitying man-cry
all is lost all is lost
then moving along the scale down down
the dog-soul plaintive and wavering
saying piteously
I am so lonely so one-single
I have so much personality

such tragic grandeur
then frightening himself into seriousness
a disembodied ghost-voice trembling
among red pomegranate and mango trees
calling Father Dog and Grandfather Wolf
all the way back to the Cambrian
and Precambrian when there were no wolves
no housepets

The relationship in lines 4 to 7 between sound and what I suppose can be called 'dog' sense is impressive, as is the evocation of the emotions and attitudes sounded 'along the scale' in the 'one long wavering howl.' Equally deft is the connecting of the present and various distant pasts by the unchanging groundbass of a howl grounded in time yet timeless. The poem flirts with humanizing the dog but does so only after calling attention to the resemblance (and therefore difference) between dog-cry and 'man-cry.'

An analogous realistic stopping short also occurs in those poems in which Purdy is tempted to but resists treating the animal symbolically. In 'After Rain' (CP, 252–3), for instance, he describes a moment of near revelation outside his house. The first part of the poem evokes a landscape 'bathed in a thick gold glow' in which everything seems transfigured:

– everything thickens
as if someone had stirred
and mixed in another colour
I am almost what I was
a bored child again
experiencing magic
but that's a lie
I never did experience magic

Resisted in the last two lines is the temptation to turn the moment into a type of Romantic epiphany. Instead it remains in both stanzas an instant of heightened beauty described in a figurative language brought back to reality with three slightly brutal references (one too many) to the 'shit-house' and 'shit.' But the second stanza adds, with a casualness that calls attention to itself, one more detail to the picture.

Oh yes one thing more
come to think of it I saw
a blue heron this morning
on the lawn like a fake ornament
but he was blood real
I held my breath and didn't move
and the world stopped shoving
then he stopped being
a work of art and changed
his shape becoming
a bird flying in my mind

The almost irresistible temptation here, as in Don McKay's 'The Great Blue Heron,' is to read the heron through other similar poems from Keats's 'Ode to a Nightingale' and Shelley's 'To a Skylark' to Hopkins's 'The Windhover,' Hardy's 'The Darkling Thrush,' and Milosz's 'Ode to a Bird.' In these and many others like them the bird is given – 'bird thou never wert' – or assumes a symbolic status of a kind Purdy resists here. If, to return to Stevens, 'the bare image and the image as symbol are the contrast,'[10] then Purdy almost always chooses the first. Here, however, he seems to want it both ways, the heron as image and as image suggesting transcendence or immanent symbolism.

Of course there's death
cruelty and corruption
likewise shit in the world
to hell with that
one day at least stands
indomitable as a potato
its light curving
over the roof of the world
a samovar of the sun
enclosing my guest
the great blue heron
including a hunched figure
myself
on some porch steps
between lightning flashes
writing

The colloquial cadences – 'to hell with that' – and the matter-of-fact reality of the simile 'indomitable as a potato' locate the heron in the here and now, though we notice that he now calls it 'my guest / the great blue heron' and that the setting has been expanded to include 'the roof of the world.' Similarly the figurative language and the implication that the speaker is turning the scene into a painting (in his mind) and into a poem nudge the scene beyond simple notation and realism. The first stanza ends with the anti-Wordsworthian emphasis that as a child 'I never did experience magic.' The second doesn't offer an explicit contradiction, but instead offers some of the elements of a scene that, in its own way, is also magical: the unexpected and unnoticed arrival of a blue heron in a commonplace landscape on the rare day when the sun shone and lightning flashed. In what may be an example of what I.A. Richards called 'mnemonic irrelevance,' I can't help recalling that two thousand years earlier, when lightning flashed on a sunny day, Horace interpreted it as a sign from the gods (*Odes* I, xxxiv). Purdy, living in an era that has seen the death of the gods and of the great mythological systems, can only repeat Frost's 'for once, then, something' and write about it. In fact, the poem ends with the heron and the 'hunched figure' of the speaker enclosed in the curve of the light, the latter 'writing.' And what he is writing is 'After Rain.'[11]

Twenty years later Purdy returns to the poem, supplementing it rather than rewriting it, unwilling to leave the situation and the imagery alone, with the result that we have a good example of the sort of internal intertextuality that gives a tacit unity to the apparent sprawl and diversity of Purdy's body of work. The poem is called 'The Last Picture in the World' and is unpublished.[12]

A hunched grey shape
framed by greenery
with lake water behind
standing on our
little point of land
glimpsed from the kitchen window
almost sculpture
except that it's alive
brooding immobile permanent
for half an hour
    a blue heron

– but why 'the last
picture in the world'?
– all I can think of
if I were to die at this moment
that picture would accompany me
wherever I am going
for a little way

Anyone reading the two poems together immediately notices the change in tone: the bravado of the earlier poem has given way to the near resignation of its companion piece. 'A hunched figure / myself' has been replaced by the slightly ominous 'hunched grey shape' of the heron observed now by a speaker less interested in writing a poem about it than in simply observing it and relating it to the death that is twenty years closer than it was when 'After Rain' was written. The situation – heron, speaker, setting – is roughly the same, but the voice in each poem is distinct. The ending is a good example of how the absence of punctuation can reinforce the poem's thematic force.

Like almost all animal poems in the western tradition, Purdy's are as much about humanity as they are about animals. And as the above quotation from 'Bestiary' indicates, however much they may focus on the animal, the poems are also Laurentian meditations on aspects of being that have been lost during humanity's evolution, aspects of the self no longer available either to the poems' speaker or to most of us. The animal poems mark a turn back to origins, the beginnings of life as well as, on occasion, the origins of language. Though this atavistic theme is already implied or present in 'Mountain Lions in Stanley Park' (CH [1965]), 'The Beavers of Renfrew' (SD [1973]), and the original version of 'Iguana' (SD [1973]), it only becomes prominent after Sundance at Dusk (1976). A good example is 'Moonspell' (CP, 268), written after the 1980 visit to the Galapagos Islands, which may have been as important to the development of Purdy's later poetry as the 1965 stay on Baffin Island was to the work of the decade that followed it. Here the poet imagines that he has 'forgotten English / in order to talk to pelicans' and to 'find the iguana's secret / name embroidered / on his ruby brain.' Shedding language, and therefore his humanity, he tries to imagine and enter a mode of pre-conscious being in which morality and the separation of thing and word doesn't exist, in which, as in Genesis and the Kabbalah, there is no gap between the reptile he sees and the sign 'iguana.'

I know I know
my speech is grunts
squeaks clicks stammers
let go let go
follow the sunken ships
and deep sea creatures
follow the *protozoa*
into that far darkness
another kind of light
leave off this flesh
this voice these bones
sink down

The shift in subject from the first person – 'I know' – to the anonymous second-person imperative functions to involve the reader in the salutary and paradoxical drift 'into that far darkness / another kind of light.' The dream-like quality of the closing is achieved by the rhymes and gentle, wave-like cadences ('I know I know,' 'let go let go,' 'go / protozoa') that develop out of the iambic metre of eight of the twelve lines. I also suspect that some of the suggestive quality of the closing comes from the reader's unavoidable association, however vague, of these lines with 'Full fathom five thy father lies' and 'Till human voices wake us and we drown.' I'm not trying to make a point about influence, but about the inevitable free play of the reader as a poem comes in contact with his or her memory of other poems whose emotions, themes, images, or even turns of phrase are inevitably called up, however momentarily, by new work. For readers familiar with Purdy's poetry, 'let go let go' will also arouse 'horizontal' associations with the later 'We Will We Will' in 'Birds and Beasts,' which is the cry of whippoorwills answering their 'brothers,' who have called 'Sleep Well Sleep Well' (*CP*, 306).

Though several of the animal poems are among Purdy's most euphoric celebrations of life and though they regularly show him nostalgic for the modes of unconscious being represented by the animals, he's too tough-minded in the end not to remind himself and us of some of the cruel realities of the natural world. In 'Voyeur' (*WS*, 13–14), for example, he describes the otter playing in the creek running beside his house (in Sidney, British Columbia):

the otter enjoys being what an otter is
and squirms and rolls over in snow

contorts like a circus performer
unselfconscious
does everything but balance a ball
on its nose and would if he had one
Watching the otter I think of all that joy
in living so rarely seen in people

...

What have we lost
– or did we ever have it?
– the otter's squirming explosion of joy
at being so alive champagne bubbles
pop in his birthday whiskers
But I think: who in his right mind
would want to be an otter?

He ends by hinting that a careless duck in the same creek may be the otter's next meal and by worrying about 'blood' in his 'stool.' The playful otter is also a killer, and he, the duck, and the poet all live in the shadow of death. Purdy may have learned something about the animal poem from Lawrence, but the world of these poems is death-haunted ('et in Arcadia ego') to an extent that would have surprised Lawrence: the poems are full of animal skeletons, wounded or dead animals, animals threatened or trapped, as well as animals on the verge of extinction. However hard the poems may try to establish a link between speaker and other, the human and the animal, they have to acknowledge the insurmountable gap and 'fear of opposites' ('Iguana'). There is also the inescapable fact that the poems themselves represent an aspect of being – self-consciousness – antithetical and even inimical to the unselfconsciousness of the animal world. Similarly the building of the A-frame inadvertently results in the deaths of animals unable to adapt to the unusual form and materials in the natural world.

Consciousness is conscience as well as consciousness of difference: Lawrence or Purdy can sing about the animal world and make moral judgments only because he knows there is no turning back:

The eagle's passage sings there
Crossing of the sky on a high wire
salmon leap to find their other selves
black bear amble to breakfast at the river

the sun floats thru a blue notch in the hills

There was never a time
I did not know about such a place
to match the imagined place in my mind
– but I have lived too long somewhere else
and beauty bores me without the slight ache
of ugliness that makes me want to change things
knowing it's impossible   'Depression in Namu, B.C.,' *CP*, 168

The contrast is between there and here, between the eagle's singing and the poet's, the salmon's 'selves' and the poet's self-division, between the animals' acceptance of life as it is ('black bear amble') and the speaker's boredom and desire to change things ('beauty bores'), and the title colours the poem with the speaker's evaluation of his situation. The first stanza is pure present, life as unreflective process; the second is in two tenses, reflecting on the temporal and grammatical level the self-consciousness and self-division of the speaker.

Though I began by suggesting that the animal poems were, like the dramatic monologues and others, a means for the poet to stretch the bounds of his subjectivity or even to transcend it, it should be obvious by now that the poems in which Purdy deals with the radical otherness of people or animals simultaneously show him exploring the limits of the self, the cognitive, epistemological, and emotional boundaries that can only be transgressed in imagination and poetic rhetoric. The lake surface separating the speaker and the fish in 'Deprivations' (*CP*, 213), for instance, can be crossed momentarily in imagination, but the poem ends with the admission that the boundary is not only biological and cognitive but also moral.

I can't return there of course
have only this moment
of childlike rare communion
and sudden overwhelming envy
of things without the heritage
and handicap of good and evil
which they escape easily
with one flick of the tail
And something they do not know:
when I move my slowly stiffening

body and they scatter into diamonds
it is like a small meanness
of the spirit they are not capable of
and that is one difference

Ironically, the unbridgeable gap between self and other – poet and fish, poet and otter – serves to recall what has been lost in the long evolutionary struggle. But even as these poems evoke nostalgically modes of being and ways of life that have been lost, they also register the paradoxical gain inseparable from the loss. This is Purdy's version of the 'felix culpa.' In 'Deprivations' a 'heritage' is also a 'handicap' that brings with it 'a small meanness / of the spirit,' but it also brings with it the moral sense capable of making the judgment. The original version of 'Iguana' contrasts a primitive way of life represented by the reptile's 'apparently meaningful / moving in his own mysterious context / from point A to point B / where he may be found still' with the speaker's more confused, 'apparently pointless' itinerary:

Whereas I am still travelling
and sometimes seem to myself
to be searching still for point A
confusing it with point B
And both change continually
from a poem to a woman to a poem
which might be the same   *SD*, 56–7

The grammar, syntax, style, and lineation enact the sense of the lines, the speaker's existential confusion. At first glance, the slightly garrulous poem seems to suggest that the way of life and the Mexican civilization represented by the iguana are preferable to the speaker's. But if we keep in mind the adverb 'apparently' qualifying both 'meaningless' and 'meaningful,' and if we also notice the freedom that is a concomitant of the speaker's confusion and the poems that result from it, then the poem ends in an equilibrium. As is obvious both here and in 'After Rain' as well as in a substantial number of other poems, Purdy is aware that he can only write nostalgically about what has been lost through evolution and civilization because it has been lost. Whenever any of these animal poems or the poems dealing with prehistory and origins refer to language or naming or creativity they remind us that the poem or poetry in general could not exist had we not 'fallen' into language and self-consciousness. Like Rousseau, Lawrence, Heidegger, and to some extent Olson, Purdy attempts to recuperate through and in language precisely what has been lost because of language: those nearly ineffable modes of emotion, consciousness, and being he sees expressed by the 'Mountain Lions in Stanley Park' (*CP*, 47), the fish in 'Deprivations' (*CP*, 213), or the otter in 'Voyeur.'

I want to finish my discussion of the animal poems by looking at 'Red Fox on Highway 500' (*CP*, 271), in which the poet comes as close to identification and empathy with an animal as anywhere in his published or unpublished work and in which the boundary between self and other is repeatedly challenged by the poem's imagery. Originally published in 1980 in *The Stone Bird*, 'Red Fox on Highway 500' is one of those poems with a particularly complex genesis in which we sense a strongly felt but nevertheless nearly indefinable autobiographical impulse and ambivalent personal emotions. As with dreams, the urgency and anxiety in it cannot be wholly accounted for by the narrative's events. To continue the dream analogy, the reader senses that the poem's manifest content depends for some of its power and suggestiveness on the pressure of images and events that remain absent, either concealed or latent. To the reader familiar with Purdy's body of work, the concentration of what could be called his signature words hints that this might be an unusual poem. 'Gates,' 'fox,' 'hammering,' 'running,' the implied 'highwayman,' and Purdy's grandfather constitute a charged emotional nexus in which are implicated, as I will illustrate, some of Purdy's central emotions, themes, characters, and events. Though the poem is successful in its own right, a look at its genesis as well as its relationship to other relevant poems is interesting because it helps illuminate how Purdy writes a poem and the sorts of subjective associations his mind makes between emotions, objects, individuals, and words. It also shows the poetic equivalent of 'dream work,' the process by which experience is transformed into lyric.

There is a suggestion in *Reaching for the Beaufort Sea*, written more than a decade later, that this poem about a midnight encounter between a man and a fox on a rural highway had its remote beginnings in two events that happened on the day in 1948 that Purdy's Belleville taxi company – Diamond Taxi Service – went bankrupt. In the first, Purdy finds himself chased by 'the last bailiff' trying to repossess the taxi he is driving; in the second, he sees 'a fox dashing out from underbrush, running full-out thirty feet ahead of the car, caught like a moth in the headlights; but unlike a moth, unable to turn right or left away from the road. A prisoner of light, its tail riding straight out behind in the self-created wind ... Is the fox's mate waiting somewhere far behind, alone in the forest, one of the junctures of their lives missed, their coming-together delayed, perhaps for a very long time?' (125–6). The escape from the bailiff has the ring of reality; the encounter with the fox is closer to the dream-like mood of the poem and seems like a prose recasting of it. The two events are connected, however, by the motif of the chase: in the first, it is Purdy who finds himself caught in the lights of the bailiff's pursuing car; in the second, now the pursuer, he observes a fox 'caught like a moth in the headlights.'

It is noteworthy that there are foxes in other Purdy poems, most importantly in the 1956 version of 'Elegy for a Grandfather' (*ER*, 2), and several unpublished poems refer to an encounter with a fox. In an unpublished fragment, for example, the poet indicates how difficult he finds it to 'divide' into poems 'these finite moments / whereby the bird stops midflight / the fox halts in his red running.'[13] Another unpublished and undated poem shows a fascination with the fox and with the idea of the poet as somehow embodying some of its qualities. Lines in the third stanza – 'something like a flash / in the night' – anticipate the opening situation in 'Red Fox on Highway 500' where the speaker sees 'the dream fox ahead of me / his rump a red light flashing.' At this point in the poem's evolution – if the fragment is indeed part of the finished poem – the emphasis is simply on the poet. In the finished poem, we are dealing with the theme of the double, with the fox and the poet equally important and the poet imagining points of identity.[14]

'Red Fox on Highway 500' begins with a situation or event familiar to us from poems as different as Frost's 'Two Look at Two,' Lawrence's 'Snake' and 'Bat,' and Charles Tomlinson's 'The Thought Fox': a man surprised by a meeting with an animal. In this case, driving down a highway at midnight he sees a fox running ahead of him:

> All I saw was the tail of him
> the dream fox ahead of me
> his rump a red light flashing
> in a thousand movie still shots
> (callipygous screenland special)
> forty feet ahead of me
> feet red hammers hammering
> light as air on the highway
> running from death on the highway
> he died or dreamed he did

– his tail a flat red poker
flung straight back toward me
his eyes overtaking his shadow
his tail bisecting the moonlight
he was fox fox fox

The remainder of the three-page poem has the quality of dream, at one point of nightmare, as the speaker imagines similarities between the fox's situation and his own. The fox's desperate running down the highway to escape the car reminds him of undescribed 'childhood nightmares' in which 'the adults chased me.'[15] The poem's situation never changes, but the fourth stanza momentarily collapses the distance and difference between man and fox, and, because of the ambiguity of the first-person pronoun, between them and us: 'So here we are / and here we have been forever / running and running and running.' We had been prepared for this identification since, at the previous stanza's close, the speaker described his situation in lines whose rhythm recalled the rhythm of lines in stanza 1 describing the fox:

so that I could drive to Belleville
keep an appointment in Belleville
and never forget a word   (stanza 3)

light as air on the highway
running from death on the highway   (stanza 1)

In each case, Purdy is echoing the rhythm of lines from Alfred Noyes's 'The Highwayman,' another death-haunted poem about travelling furtively down a road late at night.[16] The choice of Noyes's poem is particularly apposite because it reinforces the hints of transgression, escape, sexuality, violence, and death in Purdy's. Its relationship to 'Red Fox on Highway 500' is cumulative since it is only when we finish Purdy's poem that we understand the extent to which it has used Noyes's. (Further examples of Noyes's influence are listed in the appendix in the section devoted to *The Stone Bird*.)

The final stanza begins with what seems at first an almost visionary moment of contact:

Of course I stopped
and gates of the moonlight opened

and lightly he stepped inside
– it was silent that kind of silence
when live events are waiting
jammed at the doors of time
frozen in silver moonlight
then leaped into flux again
– he had to keep his appointment
and I had to drive to Belleville
both of us had our plans
plans of the utmost importance
for going on living longer
for eating and drinking and sleeping
and maybe loving someone
for killing other animals
for being noble and human
or fox fox fox

As I indicated earlier, Purdy's 'gates' ('doors' in an earlier version) are usually liminal, associated with time, creativity (*RBS*, 287), or death. Here, 'gates of the moonlight' heighten our sense of anticipation that something extraordinary is about to happen, as indeed it does during the subsequent five lines: man and fox seem to meet at midnight in an enchanted and timeless circle of moonlight in an otherwise dark, rural landscape. And then just as suddenly the fox 'leaped into flux again,' and the meeting was over. No moral, no generalization, no parable. Man and fox simply return to their parallel though different lives. By teasing us with a visionary resolution only to displace it with one more faithful to our realistic expectations based on some of the factual markers in the poem ('Highway 500'), the ending satisfies two opposed sets of desires, those associated with dreams and those with reality.

Much of the poem's emotional power comes from our surprise at the depth and complexity of the speaker's reaction to the fox. What could have simply been a normal passing encounter with an animal on a road – something that happens to almost everyone who drives regularly in the country – takes on, almost immediately, a numinous, oneiric quality. Why the poet reacts as he does is quickly sketched in stanza 2, where we sense that seeing the fox's panic and fear ('running from death') activates a vague complex of childhood memories that initiate a process culminating in near identification: both are alone on the road late at night; each is anxious or afraid; each has several identities; and each has a 'mate' waiting for him. More profoundly and elusively, however, they are joined by 'death': the poem begins with the fox 'running from death on the highway' (the speaker's car) and ends with the imagined 'killing [of] other animals.' The poem's related anxieties and fears culminate in the concern with the death and oblivion that await us at the end of our life journey, a journey interrupted in this case by stopping on the road at midnight – Purdy's version of stopping by woods on a snowy evening. If not quite a Hermes figure or a messenger of death, the fox neverthe-less mediates between the road and the woods ('the woods are lovely dark and deep') and like many of Purdy's animals he lives with death ('for killing other animals'). There is also the suggestion that for both, this midnight prefigures that other figurative midnight that is death, an encounter from which neither will return.[17]

But the fox is also associated with death in a more complex and subtle way through Purdy's grandfather, against whose death and disappear-ance the poet has written on several occasions. Ridley Neville Purdy doesn't figure directly in the poem, but his ghost can be found, if we keep in mind other poems, lingering around the images of the 'fox' and the 'poker tail.' For reasons that only Purdy could explain, he has con-sistently associated his grandfather with foxes and, more understanda-bly, with death. In *A Splinter in the Heart*, for instance, Patrick Cameron describes his grandfather as a man who 'said what he thought and what he said was Death' (41). Some readers may recall that in the first version of the 'Elegy for a Grandfather,' the speaker imagines 'the shy fox peo-ple play[ing] with his gnarled grey bones' (*CP*, 9) as Old Rid lies in the ground. And in 'News Reports at Ameliasburg' we are told that 'the fox removes his teeth to a glass for safekeeping' (*CP*, 107), a scene that may recall either the grandfather or Purdy's mother, whose false teeth figure prominently in the late poem about her death, 'On Being Human' (*NSM*, 90). The same collection includes 'Bits and Pieces' (51), in which the story of the encounter with the fox is preceded by the poet's memory of having stolen some coins from his grandfather, and 'Heroes' (61), in which a description of the poet 'driving among the windy townships' is followed by one 'of Old Rid's poker table.' The connection here, between grandfather and fox, is in 'poker,' which here refers to a card game but in 'Bits and Pieces' and in 'Red Fox at Midnight' describes the fox's tail – 'a red hot poker' and 'his tail a flat red poker,' respectively. I also wonder whether there isn't an implied relationship based on the homophonic pun tail/tale: the grandfather's tales and the fox's tail?

Drafts of the poem are interesting because they show Purdy eliminating details that would make it too specific, too clear, or too obviously autobiographical. The developing dream-like mood and setting can be seen as a means for avoiding dealing with real-life individuals and situations that he's too reticent to deal with in public. Purdy's narrative or speaking 'I' is usually subjective, but his subjectivity has limits as to what it will reveal about his private life. Among other things, the typescripts reveal the gradual erasure of certain aspects of the personal. The poem exists in one handwritten version and four heavily revised typescripts each of which has a large number of handwritten changes and additions. In the former, titled simply 'Red Fox,' the focus is on the father-son relationship, and it is the son who will meet the fox, in this case 'a vixen.' The last page (of three) reads as follows:

[My son whose father is guilty
of everything he can think of
including his arrival here]
    [little]
breathing heavily [a moment]
wondering if he['d] heard me
knowing that was ridiculous
but thinking of how [now] still
carrying my memory into the forest
to the slim vixen waiting for him
    [under the frosty moonlight]
joining them like the lost shadow
[and] running between the trees
[and open patches]
while I drove [slowly] south slowly

The crucial lines are the first three, which make the relationship between the poet and the fox more explicit and more psychologically problematic than it is at any other stage of composition. There is a hint of an Oedipal situation and of a second potential triangle or family 'romance' in the woods. But it is unclear what sins the father is 'guilty' of. Are they related in any way to the midnight drive to Belleville or to the possibility that the speaker has left or deserted someone at home just as the fox, in the final version, has a 'mate' in the forest? We know from *Reaching for the Beaufort Sea* that in the prose scene quoted earlier Purdy was running away not only from the bailiff but also from his family. By the time the first draft of the poem is typed, the last stanza is changed to the following:

He is there now
carrying my memory into the forest
to the slim vixen sniffing him
and joins[ing] them like a [shadow] white horror
they carry in their heads
running between the dark trees
[into moonlight]
between patches of moonlight

In the second typescript 'the slim vixen sniffing him' becomes 'the slim distrustful vixen / who knows he is strange,' and in the third she is pushed back into the previous stanza ('wondering where you are') as the poem's ending changes direction and the tone becomes lighter, nearly humorous:

Well I stopped
(I'm very foxitarian)
on the edge of the world
just before we fell off
and kept on driving to Belleville
I said to you
fox ol boy we'll know each other
if we meet somewhere [sometime] [?]
and he said will we ol fool
he said will we?[18]

In the final version, the blurring or confusion between the son and the fox is eliminated, and the simplification allows Purdy to treat the fox as a *doppelgänger*, an *alter ego* to the poet, who, the poem suggests, needs to be 'foxitarian' both sexually and creatively. If he weren't 'foxy,' he couldn't write poems.

I have lingered over the poem partly because it is one of my favourites, and partly because it seems to me one of Purdy's most suggestive, mysterious, and elusive. 'Wilderness Gothic' is in the same category of poems that seem to have what David Shaw has called 'silent meanings.'[19] Some of the effect can be accounted for by the incantatory rhythm (a less confident poet wouldn't have dared to use 'The Highwayman' as extensively) and the recurrent references to dreams, dreaming, and the midnight hour; as in 'Cinderella' we sense that the timeless dream will dissolve – here, 'precisely / at ten minutes after midnight.'

Some of the effect is the result of our impression that the poem raises but doesn't resolve situations and emotional issues relating to the poet's childhood, paternity, marriage, and writing ('it was almost like a poem'). Almost from the start the poem has the quality of dream and seems to be on the verge of saying more, and more explicitly than it does. As I mentioned earlier, traces from 'The Highwayman' contribute to the poem's aura and do more subtly the work that was done in the early drafts by more explicit references.[20] More than Lawrence's fox in the novella of the same name, Purdy's 'eludes any deliberate seeking' ('My Cousin Don') and leaves us thinking, with the poet, 'fox fox fox,' almost as bewildered (and enchanted) as we were in what Eliot calls the first 'bewildering minute' in which you 'give yourself up' to a poem.[21] To use Seamus Heaney's terms, the poem succeeds in keeping us suspended between 'dream-truth' and 'daylight-truth' despite our usual desire to translate it into the latter.[22]

4

Poetry and the Poet

I suggested in the previous section that Purdy's poems attempt to make his subjectivity more comprehensive and to escape the inevitable limits of the subject by incorporating in it other voices, viewpoints, dictions, idioms, and modes of being. In part, this may reflect a dissatisfaction with the limits of lyric itself – what Davie calls 'the insufficiency of lyric' for certain poets – and a desire to write lyrics capable of incorporating a speaker's various moods and aspects, more than one voice and time, and any subject-matter interesting to the poet. This desire to be 'two men if I have to' ('Love Song,' *CLL*, 21) is related in the poems about poetry and art to the post-Romantic idea that the poet or artist differs in some fundamental way from other human beings: he lacks some quality or faculty common to everyone else, but he is compensated for this lack with imagination, negative capability, and the ability to create statues, paintings, or poems. In other words, creativity is a function of what is paradoxically a lack or a potentially pathological condition: it is only because he is different, Purdy suggests in his poems about art and creativity, that he is able to write them – though, we should note that more often than not he also simultaneously doubts their value: 'The Children' (*CP*, 210), a poem about poverty, ends with 'but to hell with poems / to hell with poems.' Purdy is too tough-minded and, for the most part, too suspicious of sentiment to have much time for the *poète maudit*, but he is fascinated by this mystery at the heart of creativity and has returned to it repeatedly in poems written over half a century.

Surprisingly prominent among these are several involving the poet and his wife. The poems in which his wife figures are structurally and thematically organized around a counterpoint between her direct, almost unmediated involvement with life and his more self-conscious, detached, and ironic one ('The Horseman of Agawa' [*CP*, 176], 'Tarahu-mara Women' [*CP*, 344], 'Dog and Hummingbird' [*WS*, 45]). In 'The Double Shadow' (*SD*, 49), for example, he steps

> Out of the house late at night to piss
> somewhat soberly semi-drunken
> with wine and an uncertain self-satisfaction
> at having laboured for hours to place precisely
> in print frogs and fish and birds stuffed
> and mounted and harnessed to an idea
> and despair it still isn't good enough

The second line's trochees and dactyl capture his stumbling movement out of the house, while the oxymoron in lines 2 and 3 evokes his some-what confused state of mind, the result of drinking wine, which has also resulted in some lines in which animals, have been 'stuffed / and mounted and harnessed.' If the 'wine' is meant to hint playfully at poetic inspiration, then its effects are at best ambiguous – semi-drunkenness, 'stuffed' animals, and an 'uncertain self-satisfaction' directed both at his current work as well as, as we shall see from the rest of the poem, the entire poetic enterprise. Momentarily turning his attention away from his poetry and from the insects in the night air ('A Tall Man Executes a Jig'?), he notices, beginning with an 'orderly' line of iambic pentameter,

> the things my wife did in the last few days
> and they are her things
> flash back to her instantly
> cut grass poplars planted car washed
> unsubtle impression of order

He then immediately contrasts this to the only sign of his presence:

> my own is two
> tree stumps chopped apart
> so we don't break an axle coming into the yard
> thinking that's my mark
> the rest are marks on paper

His one 'mark' in the yard is a destructive one, appropriately as self-divided as he is. Hers are positive assertions of order within reality:

> ... her things show herself like a spoor
> traceable back to what she's like
> a serious steady woman

In a poem about the different kinds of marks, signs, and traces we leave behind us, from piss on the ground to letters on a page, she leaves a living 'spoor' (perfect word) on the landscape, he black marks of indeterminate value on a page, marks which the poem's imagery associates throughout with death. A 'spoor,' it is worth recalling, is 'the track, trail, or scent of a person or animal' (*OED*).

> I forget to piss and go inside
> and drink and remember and impatiently
> go outside again standing a rude double shadow
> in the rigid pose natural for centuries
> of necessity philosophic
> among the low roar of bugs
> *knowing I was going to write this afterwards*
> *thinking it could be better than it is*
> and depressed at the slight chance
> ignorant of my own indirections
> photograph that slight chance
> make an instant sculpture of myself
> while I'm pissing   (my italics)

Like the 'two / tree stumps,' the 'double shadow' reminds us of his self-division, detachment, or separation not only from the world around him but even from himself, something evident not only in the existence of the subjective lyric we are reading but in the fact that within the poem he makes 'an instant sculpture of myself / while I'm pissing.' 'The Double Shadow' began with 'piss' and reference to one work in progress, it ends with 'pissing' and another. At each point, as throughout the poem, Purdy uses the word to prevent a poem about poetry from becoming solemn and pretentious. As well, if we accept his Wordsworthian view that the poem can develop from the most ordinary or mundane events, then few events are more common (in every sense of the word) than this one, his equivalent of Yeats's 'rag and bone shop.' There is also the suggestion that writing poems is roughly equivalent to pissing one's life away, a view, incidentally, not that far removed from Freud's suggestion that the idea of writing originated in ejaculation.

The concern with the poem's value, the poet's nature, and his place in modern society recurs in more than fifty poems scattered throughout Purdy's body of work. It is already there in the 1950s in the ambivalent 'House Guest' (*PS*, 5), the romantic 'As a Young Man' (*PS*, 13), and 'Mice in the House' (*CP*, 48), and as recently as 'The Prison Lines at Leningrad,' 'I Think of John Clare,' 'Letter to Morley Callaghan' (*WS*, 4, 62, 75), 'Pound' and 'Do Rabbits –?' (*NSM*, 36, 98), and 'Realism 2' (*TPNA*, 94). As a group, these poems constitute a poetics. With the exception of 'The Cave Painters' and 'Post Script' (*ER*, 14, 15), the poems written before *North of Summer* (1967) are the notes for the more extended and complex 'statements' of the poems of the 1970s and 1980s. And though some of the reviews and other prose writings comment often at some length about poetry, it is in the poems themselves that we can see Purdy engaged most intensely with the problematic, even self-contradictory nature of his vocation. At the heart of Purdy's thinking about poetry are three constitutive and unresolvable contradictions.

1 He's aware that, no matter what theory of language one may hold, the fundamental gap between words and things prevents the poet from ever dealing directly with life and the poem from being anything more than a second-order reality.
2 Purdy's poet or artist is almost always the outsider (a disturbed caveman, a wounded hunter, Purdy himself) whose antinomian work nevertheless articulates the central concerns and values of his society, which in the end it transcends and outlives.
3 Though he thinks of the poem as a public speech act and of poetry as having a public function, he's realistic enough to recognize that the relationship of the Canadian poet to his society in the twentieth century is almost completely different from Hugo's to nineteenth-century France or Akhmatova's to the Soviet Union.

The first of these, the inevitably problematic nature of language, is also the least interesting, as one would expect from a poet with a common-sense, referential view of language and a commitment to plain empirical speech as the basic diction of his poems. Even though Purdy occasionally adverts to the situation, in the end he accepts it as a given, one of the conditions within which the poet, like other people, works. Language may mirror nature, name facts, and describe events imperfectly, but it is all the poet has to work with. He refers to the issue periodically in the poems, but it doesn't nudge him in the direction of the more language-oriented poetry of bp nichol or the later Birney. He would find Mallarmé's and Heidegger's responses to the gap between language and reality incomprehensible and the anxiety of postmodern poets over this issue risible. The issue surfaces in a disguised form, however, in those poems expressing doubt about the status, value, or usefulness of poetry. Their anxiety is in part the result of the following line of thinking: if words and things are only arbitrarily related, then the poem, a verbal construct, has no essential connection to reality and can never be as real or tangible as a piece of sculpture, a chimney ('Place of Fire' [CP, 228]), or a relationship. And if the poem is only a second- or third-order reality that, to quote from one of Purdy's favourite modern poems, 'makes nothing happen,' why do we write and read it? This issue of utility is raised directly in two poems of the 1970s, 'The Children' and 'In the Darkness of Cities' (CP, 210, 214). Each is a confrontation with lives of poverty and desperation which question the poet's implicit belief that poetry can deal with almost any subject and undermine his confidence in poetry's social value and ability to help change reality. 'The Children' ends with an imagined dialogue with a reader worth quoting again:

> and it isn't true
> that Indian kids live like that
> and die like that it isn't true
> somebody's bound to say
> besides it doesn't make a very good poem
> and isn't pleasant either I guess
> but to hell with poems
> to hell with poems

'In the Darkness of Cities' begins with him wondering:

> How does one come to terms with the terrible beggars
> staring straight at tourists near Minos' ruins say
> or looking sideways at you in Oaxaca market ...
> ...
> I mean the very poor poor plentiful as money
> things with withered breasts hands like claws
> in Singapore and Karachi and mud huts in Yucatan
> Indians scavenging garbage dumps behind factories

The answer is that even a poem that is *engagé* can't, and that even the poem as witness is inadequate since the knowledge the poor embody and enact screams in silence – like the starving child in David Siqueiros's 'Echo of a Scream' – that 'all books are nothing.' The poem tries to articulate a response to the situation and a judgment on it, but it ends with an admission of defeat because it can make nothing happen. It can describe a situation and evoke a judgment, but it can't change reality in any direct way.

> And in the face of their knowledge
> all these mere words on paper
> ring soundlessly in the vacuum of inattention
> I know they mean nothing
> as the terrible unaccusing poor know also
> while brightly coloured birds
> fly in and out from lonely caves of my imagination

The last two lines seem to indicate that despite his encounter with this 'knowledge' the poet nevertheless goes on trying to write poems, even when he knows that 'they mean nothing.' Unfortunately, the last couplet seems almost to belong to another poem (perhaps 'Quetzal Birds' in *The Woman on the Shore*), and its vaguely pretty imagery points away too obviously from the poem's nearly unbearable desperation, though it does function to remind us of a more common, safer, and more poetic subject-matter for poetry. As well, 'the lonely caves of my imagination' courts cliché. Still, its general point stands: poetry changes nothing and makes nothing happen.

This is a problem, however, only for the modern poet like Purdy or Adrienne Rich, who, hopeful that poetry still has a public, initiates a dialogue with that public with each poem. One can see a similar concern in Basil Bunting, who, however difficult he may seem, writes in complete sentences and strives for a conversational tone because he believes poetry is a '*sociable* affair'[1] or in William Carlos Williams's desire to write a poem in ordinary language summing up the history and daily life of Paterson, New Jersey. A particularly strong late poem, 'The Prison Lines at Leningrad' (*WS*, 4), describes a situation in which the poet, Anna Akhmatova, because of unusual historical circumstances, is able to play an essential public role *as* poet.

> She speaks for them
>   – the speechless dead
> the woman in her chill misery

who said, 'Could you describe this?'
Akhmatova answering, 'Yes.'

They led her husband off like a dog
already emptiness in his heart
– in hers the poems since, a song
that echoes in soundless prison yards.

Number 300 – is she still here,
mourning husband, mourning child?
– the Neva's ice-choked water spares
no swimmer, cannot hear their cries.

The Peterhof in Baltic mist,
and Peter's statue in greenish bronze:
Stalin inside the Kremlin walls
drills unhearing firing squads.

The Tsars arise to cheer themselves,
that's Nicholas who used to wet the bed;
and hand on hip, standing negligently,
the man with ice pick in his head.

Siberia – the name like an anthem,
is requiem for millions dead;
no Mozart here with his last breath
to choir an immense Russian sadness ...

'Far from your ocean, Leningrad,
I leave my body' – they heard the cry,
those prisoners, their anthem hers:
earth speaks as if earth were alive.

This gem of a poem was probably written in response to Purdy's reading of Akhmatova's 'Requiem' in the two-volume edition of *The Complete Poems* that he reviewed for *Books in Canada*, though he indicates in the review that he had read the poem earlier in Robert Lowell's loose translation. He couldn't have written it with such a quiet mastery of the traditional lyric form without his lifelong apprenticeship in 'conservative verse.' At the poem's heart is the figure of the poet whose life is integrated with the lives of the people around her and with her nation, and whose poems or 'lines' are the literal and figurative extensions of the 'lines' in which people waited outside prison doors and the 'lines' they spoke to each other. Her poem can speak for them because their story is hers. This situation in which the poet is integrated with his society and, in Auden's image ('In Memory of W.B. Yeats'), becomes a 'mouth' for it is the product of exceptional and tragic historical circumstances. Purdy's own homage to Akhmatova is written in a society different in every way, including the fact that it has almost no expectations of the poet at all, if indeed it notices poetry. To recall Jarrell, the modern 'public has an unusual relationship to the poet: it doesn't even know he is there.'[2] And Klein's view of the poet's place in the modern world (in 'Portrait of the Poet as Landscape') is too well-known to need quoting. At century's end, it is arguable that the poet's status and the situation of poetry are even more marginal than they were half a century ago.

The poet's close relationship to her society in 'The Prison Lines at Leningrad' represents an ideal towards which many of Purdy's poems about both poetry and his country aspire. We can see this even in the comedy and gentle self-mocking of 'At the Quinte Hotel' (written in 1968), where the 'sensitive' poet is anxious both about his place in society and about the ultimate value of his poems. He is the outsider, the marginal man whose talent – indicated by his romantic isolation and sensitivity – separates him from the others and yet unites him with them when he has a chance to recite one of his 'Flower poems' ('Arctic Rhododendrons'?). This 'reading' in a bar makes explicit the impulse towards dialogue and conversation underlying a significant number of the poems. I'm thinking particularly of those in which the speaker addresses readers with a familiar or formal vocative or includes them by shifting the first-person pronoun from the singular to the plural. Both are gestures of generalization, attempts to involve the reader in the poet's experiences and views. And though Purdy may have little admiration for Whitman, no other poet reaches off the page more often and more dramatically than the American. This may seem a small point, but as W. Johnson has suggested, the presence of the vocative, the first-person plural, and the second-person pronoun in a modern poem is a relatively reliable indicator of the degree to which the poet is turning away from the in-tense subjectivity, the almost complete inwardness, characteristic of the Romantic, post-Romantic, and symbolist lyric. The appearance of 'you' or 'we' in a first-person meditative or reflective lyric is an explicit indication of 'the need for discourse' or the desire for dialogue. This kind of poem isn't quite covered by Northrop Frye's comment that the lyric is 'preeminently the utterance that is overheard.' We seem to overhear 'To a Skylark,' but the first section of Whitman's *Song of Myself* or Frost's 'The Pasture' or Purdy's 'Place of Fire' (*CP*, 228) speak to us directly. They show the lyric as a form of public address in which its isolation and self-sufficiency are deliberately ruptured,[3] and an implied dialogue takes the place of the expected, overheard monologue. In other words, the 'sensitive man' breaks out of the role expected of him and attempts a dialogue with others. Unfortunately, if predictably in a provincial society, they are moved by his poems but answer his claim that '"the poem oughta be worth some beer"' with 'silence,' leaving him with the knowledge 'that poems will not really buy beer or flowers' (*CP*, 110).

The poem as handshake. The poem as letter. The poem as a dialogue between strangers in which the poet momentarily overcomes his habitual isolation by telling a brief narrative in ordinary language and in a conversational tone about an event from his daily life. If the 'I-You' form of some of Purdy's lyrics is the most obvious indicator of the dialogic or public intention of his poetic, I would suggest that two other signs of this are his reliance on a middle style grounded in every-day diction and speech rhythms and the ground bass or undertow of narrative in many poems. These aren't narrative poems in the sense of the word that would have been understood by Kipling, Noyes, or Pratt, but at their core there is usually an event, some encounter with a thing or person or place. 'Place of Fire' (*CP*, 228), for instance, circles around the building of a fireplace and chimney at Purdy's cottage. After an introductory stanza comparing his chimney to factory chimneys and detailing the local sources of the various kinds of stone used in its construction – 'Norris Whitney's barnyard' – the poem then addresses the reader:

> But you'll have to admit the ritual significance
> of not being above working with your hands?
> You don't admit? Okay, I guess you're right.
> But you must agree it's the hard way
> to gather ingredients for a poem?
> ...
> Symbolic as hell too: you can't beat limestone,
> which Auden said was very important stuff;
> W. Yeats and R. Jeffers kept building towers as well,
> so they could write great poems about it.

I'm just the latest heir of the hearth-warming
tradition, eh?

The casual patter shifts smoothly from chimneys to poetry with the speaker situating himself not only in a tradition of tower or chimney builders – Yeats and Jeffers – but also in a tradition of poets; all three are in his pantheon in 'Bestiary [II].' The third stanza follows this with a characteristic temporal slide from the present to the remote past, from 'the dark tribes ... hovering and worshipping, / stone people who preceded the jukebox people / and before them the first fossil critters.' Through the third stanza it is the hearth or fire that links the speaker to these groups. But the first four lines of the fourth stanza focus our attention instead on the poet as 'a listening lowly high priest, / unacknowledged legislator or something – .' And we also begin to feel some of the intimations of the title, the place of fire as hearth, as a place associated with the household gods or lares and penates, as a link between past, present, and future. But the man who makes these connections is 'a listening lowly high priest' named Purdy who senses the social importance of the hearth and the poem about it. Rilke, who had a remarkable sensitivity to things and places, attributes what he terms 'laric value' to objects like 'a house, a fountain, a familiar tower.' Sensing that a modern technological civilization will no longer be capable of responding in or understanding these terms, he tells Witold von Hulewicz, 'We are perhaps the last to have known such things. The responsibility rests with us not only to keep remembrance of them (that would be but a trifle and unreliable), but also their human or 'laric' value ('laric' in the sense of household gods).'[4]

The poem closes with the following disarming admission:

Of course what I'm doing, or seeming to,
is telling anyone reading this how to write a poem:
so build your fireplace, raise your stone tower,
fall in love, live a life, smell a flower,
throw a football, date a blonde, dig a grave
– in fact, do any damn thing, but act quickly!
Go ahead. You've got the kit.

The speaker equates the *making* of poems with other kinds of fundamental human activity, and suggests that, though the poem originates in the same world, it is ultimately able to include them. I would also suggest that the 'How to Write a Poem Kit' is synonymous with 'How I Write a Poem': I begin with an event in my own life, an event rooted in a particular time and place and involving people I know, and I try to turn it into a speech act that will capture its significance, place it in a historical context, and, finally I tell it to you. Characteristically, a poem of self-explanation and playful self-assertion (a poetic tradition of Yeats, Jeffers, Auden, Purdy?) also contains moments of self-deprecation and doubt about his vocation. The poem may imply that the writing of it resembles the building of a chimney in so far as each is a kind of making, and it may imply that poetry is as normal a part of life as raising a 'stone tower,' but the poem also makes it clear that poetry is dependent on these other activities because it is *about* them.

Before leaving 'Place of Fire,' I want to relate its intimations of the links between the building of a house and the making of a poem to Gaston Bachelard's speculations about the relationship between a house and daydreaming. The connection between Purdy's two kinds of 'building' would not surprise Bachelard, for whom 'the house shelters daydreaming, the house protects the dreamer, the house allows one to dream in peace ... The values that belong to daydreaming mark humanity in its depths.'[5] Also not irrelevant here is Heidegger's view that 'Poetic creation, which lets us dwell, is a kind of building.'[6] For both, 'building,' whether literal or figurative, is an assertion of self, what Bachelard calls 'verticality' and Heidegger 'the measure,' against or within the context of what Heidegger terms 'the heavenly.'[7] Furthermore, neither would be surprised by Purdy's atavistic reference to 'the dark tribes' hovering around their places of fire, since each also thinks of the house or building as having 'cosmic roots' or as grounded in Being, their counterpart to Blake's vision of the universe from the roof of one's own house. I linger over these connections because there's something I can't quite put my finger on or describe adequately in the connection between the building of the A-frame, whose 'A' hints at the coextensiveness of dwelling, Al, Adam, and Alphabet, and the turn in Purdy's poetry away from two decades of apprentice work to his major phase. In building the cottage he began the remaking or reimagining of himself, the record of which is the body of work of the next decade. That Purdy himself recognized the A-frame as particularly significant seems evident from his unpublished description of the cottage during a 1970 CBC radio broadcast titled 'Al Purdy's Ontario': 'And the house itself – a drum for the north wind, a kind of knot in time, tho maybe also a yes. The feeling of being here so briefly, that a step backward or forward would make us both disappear. The A-frame house we built like a wooden cobweb against the black sky.'[8] He may still have thought of himself in 1957 as 'one of the world's losers' (*RBS*, 171), but the writing of 'Elegy for a Grandfather' and the building of the cottage marked the boundary between two phases of his life and career. Paradoxically, the apparent narrowing of his horizons in the double return to the isolation of Prince Edward County helped simultaneously to focus and release his imagination. To adapt Bachelard's terms, the building of the A-frame was the essential precondition for the poetic dreaming that would begin with *Poems for All the Annettes* and eventually include what Blake calls 'his universe.'

As I mentioned in passing, though several poems mention Malcolm Lowry and Dylan Thomas, both of whom Purdy admires, in general, he has almost no interest in the *poète maudit*. Still, the writers and artists in his poems tend to be loners or outsiders like Archilochus, Herodotus, Hokusai, John Clare, Housman, Lawrence, Jeffers, and Milton Acorn. In almost all of these poems there tends to be some self-identification between the poet Purdy and the man he is writing about (there are no women in this patriarchal pantheon). In '"Old Man Mad about Painting,"' for example, he admires Hokusai's *chutzpah* in erecting 'a great fifty-foot / framework of bamboo and red tissuepaper' to paint 'his thoughts on the thing / along with mountain landscapes' (*CP*, 149), even though everyone around him laughs at his creation. Though the painter is living in 'bleak poverty' and though he must know that the wind will eventually topple the structure, he nevertheless persists in giving body to his vision, a vision 'without money value or the least permanence.' The connection between Japanese painter and Canadian poet, both failures into middle age, is made explicit in the poem's second half:

It kind of cheers me
during my own Hour of Despond
when I've failed at everything
scribbling poems on the reverse side
of cost schedules scrounged from garbage
to think of Hokusai in bleak poverty
before he painted a still-life of all Nippon
in the encyclopaedic Mangwa Sketches
and Thirty-Six Views of Mount Fujiyama

'"Old Man Mad about Painting"' was written by a man mad about poetry in the period after he had received the first major public recognition of his career, the 1965 Governor-General's Award for *The Cariboo Horses*. In a manner of speaking he had just produced *his* Mangwa Sketches and could sense that he was leaving behind twenty years of struggle, near poverty, and anxiety about failure. He could also take satisfaction in knowing that like Hokusai, he had remained faithful to his quixotic vision 'during the Hour of the Rat,' an hour that Purdy extended for nearly two decades and that included working in a mattress factory, driving taxi, and loading bags of fertilizer.

Fidelity to one's self and, if one is an artist, to one's vision, no matter how wrenching the emotional and social consequences, is a central concern of almost all the poems about artists, including the autobiographical ones in which Purdy indulges in a playful self-mockery. 'I Think of John Clare' (*WS*, 62) is a homage to three artists – Clare, D.H. Lawrence, and Vincent van Gogh – who, in different though analogous ways, suffered for their art and could not have produced the kind of work they did without that suffering. Their lives are depicted as pilgrimages on a road ending in 'the light,' which is simultaneously their vision and a portent of death. (Similarly 'Realism 2' ends with Purdy and Czeslaw Milosz standing over Mozart's grave and sensing 'that essential darkness / from which light is born' [*TPNA*, 95].) And though Purdy doesn't want to compare his life to their heroic and, in two cases, tragic ones, he ends the poem with lines whose ambiguous syntax allows him to join them:

> I grumble peevishly
> (being none of them)
> in the hangover after youth
> ...
> clamouring for attention
> thinking of Clare DHL and Vincent
> limping toward the light.

It is worth noting that there is no biographical evidence that any of the three limped; Purdy, on the other hand, limps occasionally because of an arthritic knee. The idea that the artist is crippled or different in some fundamental way is already present, as I mentioned, in the poems of the 1950s about poetry and art. But it receives its most powerful articulation in 'In the Caves' (*CP*, 181), a poem that should be read side by side with the very early 'The Cave Painters' (*ER*, 14), 'The Sculptors'

(*NS*, 75), as well as the already discussed 'Lament for the Dorsets' (*CP*, 135). Though a dramatic monologue, its many echoes of and connections to other poems hint at what Tom Marshall calls 'an element of autobiography.'[9] In all of these poems, the artist is an individual either physically wounded or emotionally disturbed and therefore unable to participate fully in the life of the society around him. The vision of 'The Cave Painters' turns them into 'inhabitants of loneliness' who 'became an imperfection.' The Eskimo sculpture in 'The Sculptors' is produced by 'the losers and failures / who never do anything right,' while the ivory swans in 'Lament for the Dorsets' are carved by a crippled hunter.[10] It is important to remember, however, that in the last two poems the speaker admits that this is only how he *imagines* the sculptors. That he imagines them ill or wounded ultimately tells us more about him than it does about them. I would add that the fact that so many of the artists in Purdy's poems are painters and sculptors should be read as indicating his unease, even anxiety about the intangibility and evanescence of poetry, of the word. A rock painting, a sculpture, a canvas are palpably *there* in a way that a poem cannot be. And in 'The Horseman of Agawa' (*CP*, 176), the speaker sees on his wife's face,

> ... the Ojibway horseman painting the rock with red fingers
> and he speaks to her as I could not
> in pictures without handles of words
> into feeling into being here by direct transmission
> ...
> And I change it all back into words again for that's the best I can do
> but they only point the way we came from for who knows where we are   177

In both cases, the poem acknowledges the limitations of poetry, and is therefore a confession of failure. The failure may be endemic to the materials of the art, but that is no consolation to the poet, especially to one like Purdy who is reluctant to make large claims for poetry and in whose work the topos of *aere perennius* is rarely emphasized, especially with reference to his own poems.

'In the Caves' begins with pure sound, the 'shriek' of a mastodon brought down by a group of hunters. Among them is the poem's speaker who, 'when the spears struck,' empathized with the animal to the point that 'I felt the red string of a shriek / leave my body and rise into the sky.' The sense of unity with the dying mastodon results in a feeling of alienation from the tribe, though he also tells us that even before this happened he had been an inept hunter laughed at by the others. Still, the encounter is decisive, and the word 'shriek' punctuates the poem until the speaker is able to translate it from a jagged echo in his mind into, first, a drawing 'in soft earth' made with a stick and coloured with 'blood from my wrist,' and then a wall painting in a cave. The painting, undertaken for reasons he can't understand and of whose value he is uncertain ('It may be useless'), helps him exorcise his own pain, but he also realizes that its meaning and significance, though their origin is subjective, transcend him:

> but there is something here I must follow
> into myself to find
> outside myself in the mammoth
> beyond the scorn of my people
> who are still my people
> my own pain and theirs
> joining the shriek that does not end
> that is inside me now
> The shriek flows back into the mammoth
> returning from sky and stars
> finds the cave and its dark entrance
> brushes by where I stand on tip-toes
> to scratch the mountain body on stone
> moves past me into the body itself
> toward a meaning I do not know
> and perhaps should not

The mysterious painting may have originated in an individual's encounter with death, but its final meaning, which is identical with and as elusive as the meaning of the poem, is a plangent, drawn-out note to which we all respond. He may not know its meaning, but he senses that it unites him with the universe as well as others in his tribe even as it alienates him from them.

Ironically, such a vision of unity is only available after the separating or alienating 'fall' into consciousness undergone by the painter-to-be at the killing of the mammoth. Feeling the death and the death cry more intensely, he becomes conscious or self-conscious of death in a way incomprehensible to those around him as well as to his earlier self. His painting attempts to comprehend the mammoth's death (and perhaps death in general), but it does so only by disrupting a way of life and forms of consciousness now antithetical to his own. In other words, in expressing 'my own pain and theirs' he is also bringing to an end an aspect of their former way of life: his painting as activity and as artefact will eventually make them as self-conscious as the shriek made him. As a painter, he has become like the anthropologist who contaminates and therefore permanently changes the way of life of the village in which he is living in order to study it so that its language and customs won't be lost. A painting / poem that begins with death – Purdy agrees with Heidegger that the fact of death poses the most important question – also, in a manner of speaking, introduces a new awareness of death into the artist's immediate world. To change the metaphor, if artists are the antennae of the race, and the work, whether painting or poem, is the 'tale of the tribe,' then this prehistoric artist is receiving and transmitting a dark, ambiguous, and complex tale. That the 'transmission' will continue through the generations is indicated in the poem in the troubling figure of 'one long-legged grey-eyed boy,' who is fascinated by the artist and is shown at the end sitting outside the cave, waiting.

I have so far emphasized the darker and what could be called a more pessimistic reading because this ambitious poem shows Purdy more pessimistic about the value of art than anywhere else in his poetry or prose. But if we accept the inevitability of the fall as a given of the poem's world and ours, then it is possible to interpret the artist and his work more positively. The work becomes an attempt to interpret 'the shriek' of death and thus, as far as is humanly possible, to answer it. In *Reaching for the Beaufort Sea*, Purdy goes so far as describing poetry as 'the word that slanders death' (285). If the death of the mammoth brings a new awareness of death into the world, so does the wall painting in the womb of the mountain that constitutes an answer to it, just as more generally poems, paintings, and sculptures in Purdy's poems are usually attempts to create something that will survive the death of the artist and offer him and humanity the only immortality available. The poem's imagery relates the killing of the mammoth and the painting of its image on the wall of the cave. It opens with a metaphor evoking the animal as a mountain – 'The grey hairy mountain shrieked' – and closes with an image of the painter standing 'on tip-toes / to scratch the mountain body on stone' inside the cave in what must be either a hill or mountain. There is also a suggestive correspondence between the two scenes, one early, one late, both painted in red. The first shows 'an old woman' cutting out the mammoth's heart; the second, the painter entering into the earth to carve and paint its image on a wall, almost as if offering a mysterious expiatory restitution for the first cutting or carving.

The cave, like the womb, skull, parallel lines, fox, gate, and road is part of Purdy's private lexicon of words whose significance often exceeds their conventional meaning; their full connotative value is often only available if the reader is aware of the poet's entire corpus. Caves, as I mentioned earlier, figure in poems across his entire career: 'The Cave Painters,' 'Twin Heads' (BB, 2), 'Driving the Spanish Coast' (SB, 44), 'Meeting' (SB, 47), 'No Second Spring' (SB, 76). They are also suggested in various poems where the tent or the skull or the womb is presented as cave-like: 'Lament for the Dorsets' (CP, 135), 'On Realizing that He Has Written Some Bad Poems' (CP, 249), 'Homer's Poem' (CP, 3), and 'The Dead Poet' (CP, 369).[11] In all of these, the image carries with it suggestions both of burial and birth, the tomb and the womb; a quest for oneness and a primal unity that is also a point of origin; and a search for the sources of art, which are connected to the nexus of associations raised by the conjoining of life and death in one image. The recent 'A Job in Winnipeg' (TPNA, 17) shows the hold the image, mediated here through Plato, has on Purdy's imagination.

> but I'm standing on the planet
> which is myself
> seeing only my shadow self
> dancing on a cave wall
> in a kind of semaphore
> visible to no one

I also want to suggest that the image of the skull – 'catacombs of the bone brain' (ISOR, [23]) – seems cognate for Purdy with that of the cave, with the head figured as a cave in which a preconscious creativity takes place or into which the poet withdraws to begin the creative process that culminates in the finished work of art. In the recent '"Happiness,"' (TPNA, 66) the speaker pictures himself 'moving from room to room / in my brain with a guttering candle / peering into the silent places' as part of the creative process. There is also a strong suggestion of this in the original titles of Sundance at Dusk and The Stone Bird, 'Dancing (or Dreaming) Skull' and 'The Dreaming Skull' respectively.[12] And I can't help thinking that the image of an enclosure that is partly curved is somewhere behind the occasional representation of the writer as 'a hunched figure' ('After Rain') or as a 'hunchback,' almost as if he becomes the cave or the womb or the skull / brain. The earliest instance of this occurs in the already mentioned 'Poem' (*ER*, 3) in which, in images borrowed from Layton's 'The Cold Green Element' and 'The Birth of Tragedy,' he describes the following scene:

> But [I] take a deep breath and feel the angling sunbeams make
> Me a confluence
> Established by vectors of light, like candles burning in space
> For a hunchback prince.

Twenty years later in 1981, in 'On Realizing He Has Written Some Bad Poems,' Layton hasn't disappeared completely, but he's been absorbed into a complex figure that is Purdy's:

> (and that other
> the jewelled hunchback in my head
> seated brooding in a dark bone corner
> who will not be placated
> by such rewards
> he too has ambitions
> – different ones –)   *CP*, 250

The 'jewelled hunchback' is a metaphor for the poet's better self, the one ambitious for something more than wealth or mass fame. And his situation 'in a dark bone corner' recalls the prehistoric painters in their dark torch-lit caves, the forty-year-old Purdy reading and writing by lamplight in his newly built A-frame at Ameliasburg (*ISOR*, 24), or the poet hunched over his typewriter inside the wind-buffeted tent on Baffin Island. I'm not suggesting that the cave and the skull are synonymous, only that they seem cognate, overlap often in his imagination, and carry similar suggestions of darkness, origins, withdrawal, a secret activity, and a creativity analogous to birth. The fact that *The Collected Poems* opens ('Homer's Poem') and closes ('The Dead Brother') with poems in which the womb/cave/enclosure is the setting would seem to confirm the point. To borrow De Quincey's image, Purdy's poet is the dark interpreter who explores the mysteries in our existence and reports on them to us.

5

Starting from Ameliasburg:
Old Rid, Owen Roblin, and Al

For someone who has travelled compulsively and widely and whose poems are set in places as different as Hiroshima and the Galapagos Islands, Purdy has nevertheless remained very much a poet of beginnings and origins. Few bodies of poetry in this century have as felt a sense of place as his. His small-town Ontario background is well known from interviews, poems, the novel *A Splinter in the Heart* (1990), and the autobiography *Reaching for the Beaufort Sea* (1993). He may refer periodically with disparagement to Trenton and Belleville, but there is a counterbalancing local pride in poems dealing with the area and its past, as well as in his diffident and occasionally reluctant comments about family history. In a letter to Margaret Laurence, for instance, he describes Trenton as 'the dingy reality of my misspent youth,' 'umbilical cord to the past,' and finally, as 'the miserable place' from which he can't escape (31 December 1967, *MLAP*, 78). By contrast, Charles Taylor catches a hint of the local pride, familiar to us from the poems, in his chapter on Purdy in *Radical Tories*, when he describes talking to Purdy about his books:

there's a local history of Prince Edward County by Richard and Janet Lunn which mentions one 'Purdy the sweet singer of Ameliasburg' – a man who went around the settlements in the early nineteenth century, singing for his living. 'It puts me off,' Purdy says, and then mumbles something about not wanting to seem 'a long-haired poet.' Next he shows me another large volume called *Pioneer Life in the Bay of Quinte*, with genealogies of old families, including several called Purdy. There's a McDagg Purdy and a lot of Wellington Purdys, among others. 'I guess they're my people,' Purdy says, diffidently. 'Wellington is my own middle name – it's always embarrassed me.' Yet I suspect he's much prouder than he chooses to let on. 'I'm not an ancestor worshipper,' he says firmly, but then adds quickly; 'One has ambiguous feelings about everything.'[1]

The comment about ancestor worship, or its lack, is confirmed by the general absence of poems about his family. With the crucial exception of his grandfather, Ridley Neville Purdy, Purdy pays little attention to other members of the Purdy family. There are two poems about his mother's death, a poem for a 'brother' who died 'in the womb' (*CP*, 369), and some poems about cousins. More often, the focus is on self and place, the individual rooted *in* the place. A recent poem, originally titled 'Entering My Mother's House' (*TPNA*, 45), lingers over the house rather than on the mother, and foregrounds the speaker's response. In the final version the mother even disappears from the title – '134 Front St, Trenton, Ont.' In 'Gateway,' a poem of the early 1970s, place and self become coextensive by an act of imaginative appropriation that is typical of many of the poems set in the region: 'As much as any place in the world / I claim this snake fence village / of A-burg as part of myself' (*CP*, 202). It's a bold claim made by a confident poet at the height of his powers, and it comes in the form of a poetic statement: an 'r' links the 'world' to 'A-burg,' while 'place' and 'myself' are joined by sibilants also present in the more homely local image of 'snake fence,' which visually embodies the statement in the local and concrete. For all the departures in the poems and the travelling of the 1970s and 1980s, the poet and the poems always return to that part of the world the teenaged Purdy couldn't wait to escape from and in which the rooted adult poet feels curiously marginal.

When in 1957 Purdy and his wife returned to the area and built, with her father's help, their now-famous cottage at Ameliasburg, he was at a turning-point in his career. He may have felt like a failure, but the decade-long wrestle with his past and with modern poetry was about to produce a stream of poems in a voice unmistakable for any other. The poems of the next decade would establish him as an original and major force in Canadian literature. Had he not written a poem after the appearance of *Wild Grape Wine* in 1968 his reputation would be secure on the basis of 'Elegy for a Grandfather,' 'The Country North of Belleville,' 'Transient,' 'Trees at the Arctic Circle,' 'Tent Rings,' 'Listening,' 'Wilderness Gothic,' 'Boundaries,' 'Roblin's Mills [II],' 'Lament for the Dorsets,' and 'My Grandfather's Country.' As I mentioned earlier, the breakthrough involved the creation of a poetic voice – an entire prosody – that is almost an echo of his real one, and an awareness that he could write, that he *had to* write, out of his own life, especially his past. It may not be an exaggeration to say that a key to that past and a metaphor for it was Ridley Neville Purdy, the poet's grandfather whose life story he has written and rewritten at least once a decade for the past half century. 'Elegy for a Grandfather,' for instance, first appears in *Emu! Remember* (1956), and is rewritten in *Wild Grape Wine* (1968) and *The Collected Poems* (1986). Some of the events in the grandfather's life are also dealt with in the 1950s radio play 'Christmas Memory,' *In Search of Owen Roblin* (1974), the novel *A Splinter in the Heart* (1990), and the autobiography *Reaching for the Beaufort Sea* (1993).[2]

The first version of the elegy describes the grandfather's 'wide whale-bone hips' as making 'a prehistoric barrow, / A kitchen midden for mice under the rough sod,' and there is the implication that it is the grandson-poet who excavates the barrow and sorts through the midden's seemingly unimportant refuse (see 'Gateway' [*CP*, 202]) in order to find his poetry's subject-matter. In a manner of speaking, Ridley Neville Purdy (finally named in *In Search of Owen Roblin*) *is* both the region and a pattern for and justification of the kind of radically independent life Purdy chose to live. Every line the poet has written about him bellows 'I AM,' as the grandson tries to achieve in words what is not possible in real life – the resurrection of his grandfather and by extension the history of the region and family in which the grandfather and his grandson are inextricably implicated. In all three versions (1956, 1968, 1986), the elegy is both an epitaph and an attempt at denial: 'Well, maybe he did die, but the boy didn't see it.' And the last two versions emphasize that he lives on in the grandson's memory and, by implication, in the poem. A comment by Purdy about the elegies expresses eloquently his continuing sense of loss: 'I am probably the only person alive who now remembers him. But he never should have died; it is so improbable that he died. I guess what I was doing in the poem was trying to keep him alive forever. Because he is.'[3]

Naming and honouring 'Rid' is both paradigm and prelude to the extended imaginative engagement with regional and national history that we encounter in Purdy's major work. The emotional and mnemonic wrestle with the almost mythic grandfather helps Purdy to find the voice that will 'name' his place, his ancestors, and, as discussed earlier, himself. The two decades of being a 'transient' end with the writing of the first elegy and the building of the A-frame. A poem about the most important death in his life and the nearly simultaneous building of a cottage, appropriately in the shape of the letter A near the town of his youth, both point him in the direction of the poems that will almost silence the 'shriek' and overcome the persistent sense of failure that had been with him since the first poem of his first book: 'My better judgment voted me / Least likely to succeed.' This is not to discount the other poems of the period; but in retrospect they seem like essential preliminaries in which we see Purdy stretching his voice, experimenting with diction, syntax, lineation, and styles in the slow and awkward process of discovering what he needs to write about. Despite some contemporary assertions to the contrary, some poems are more important than others, and at the heart of Purdy's achievement are the poems that start with 'Rid' and Ameliasburg, poems that in Williams's words are 'rooted in the locality which should give [them] fruit.'[4] The later equally ambitious poems about Canada, history, prehistory, and in the broadest sense, spiritual issues, could not have been written without the prior path-breaking engagement with 'Rid,' 'a burg / named after a German dumpling named Amelia' ('One Rural Winter,' [CP, 57]), and the history for which they are synecdoche and metaphor.

As I wrote earlier, it is only after he finds his voice and his subject-matter that Purdy finally settles on what form of his name to use professionally, settles, in a manner of speaking, who he is. In retrospect it seems inevitable that he would sign his work with the name used in everyday life since in his poetics the life and the work are often coextensive. But the final naming of the self can take place only after the great poems of the 1960s that begin his naming and poetic cartography of Ameliasburg, Belleville, Prince Edward County, Baffin Island, and Canada. The order isn't quite that neat since the impulse and ambition, even the sense of national proprietorship, are already evident in 'On Canadian Identity' in the 1962 edition of Poems for All the Annettes; and the fascination with indigenous names ('Dog with Red Eyes and Woman with Moon on her Shoulder') and their disappearance is already present in Pressed on Sand ('Onomatopoeic People,'[10]).[5] But it is only after the Trenton-Ameliasburg poems begin to appear that we sense road maps, surveyors' maps, and historical maps being unrolled on the imagination's long table as the poet, in saying 'I AM,' simultaneously describes a place, names it, recreates it imaginatively, and takes possession of it. The representative poem here is, of course, 'The Country North of Belleville,' one of the finest poems in Canadian literature and one of those works that, like MacLennan's Two Solitudes, Pratt's Brébeuf and His Brethren, Laurence's Manawaka novels, or Atwood's The Journals of Susanna Moodie and Surfacing, recognizes that the national identity and a national literature are still still awaiting definition and direction. It's the kind of poem that reminds us that in every national literature, there are writers with a sense of the nation and of national proprietorship not evident to the same degree, if at all, in many of their peers. Pratt, MacLennan, Laurence, Purdy, and Atwood have it; Callaghan, Layton, Gallant, and Ondaatje don't.

'The Country North of Belleville' is written in what Frye calls 'the high style of ordinary speech,' and, unusually for Purdy, the voice is anonymous to the point that even the three uses of the first-person plural seem to refer to a trans-personal communal subject, a group, community, or nation, rather than a specific speaker. If the term did not have such negative connotations, I would be tempted to call the poem a national ode. 'The Country North of Belleville' opens and closes with an impersonal and slightly formal recital of for the most part Irish and English names of the townships north of Belleville: Cashel, Wollaston, Dungannon and so on. The cadences are impersonal and stately, and the lines have a weightiness appropriate to a public poem concerned with recalling us to our historical origins – 'the country of our defeat' – and enacting in poetic form one of the constitutive myths of nationhood. At the heart of the poem, literally and thematically, is the image of an anonymous and therefore generic farm family leaving its mark on the land while wresting a living from it.

> And where the farms are
>   it's as if a man stuck
> both thumbs in the stony earth and pulled
>
>   it apart
>   to make room
> enough between the trees
> for a wife
>   and maybe some cows and
>   room for some
> of the more easily kept illusions –
> And where the farms have gone back
> to forest
>   are only soft outlines
>   shadowy differences –
> Old fences drift vaguely among the trees
>   a pile of moss-covered stones

gathered for some ghost purpose
has lost meaning under the meaningless sky
      – they are like cities under water
and the undulating green waves of time
      are laid on them –

This is the country of our defeat
      and yet
during the fall plowing a man
might stop and stand in a brown valley of the furrows
      and shade his eyes to watch for the same
      red patch mixed with gold
      that appears on the same
      spot in the hills
      year after year
      and grow old
plowing and plowing a ten-acre field until
the convolutions run parallel with his own brain   *CP*, 61–2

The stanzas framed by the simple catalogues of names encapsulate more than two centuries of rural life, from pioneer days to the present; by not indicating how the farmer ploughs – horses? tractor? – Purdy leaves the scene timeless, and the effect is affirmed by the image of the 'red patch mixed with gold' appearing at the same time every year. (These are the only colours in a poem with an otherwise deliberately black-and-white palette.) And our impression of timelessness is reinforced by the second stanza's tacit comparison, criticized by Bowering,[6] of the men in this country to Sisyphus who rolls 'a big stone / year after year up the ancient hills / picknicking glaciers have left strewn / with centuries' rubble' (62). The farmer's immemorial struggle to impose his order ('meaning under the meaningless sky') is projected against a permanent background that indifferently provides stones to be moved by 'back-breaking' labour or an ineffable beauty that appears whether anyone is looking or not. And in the end it slowly and again indifferently effaces or buries or disguises all traces or 'lines' of human presence.

Resisting this inevitability are the farmer and the poet/speaker, each of whom tries to inscribe the land, with a plough or a pen – note the tell-tale 'parallel' lines – to create meaning but in a way that is co-extensive with and expressive of the landscape they find. I take this to be the force of the haunting couplet, 'plowing and plowing a ten-acre field until / the convolutions run parallel with his own brain –.' The smoothly flowing enjambments of the preceding ten lines evoke the back-and-forth flow of the ploughing until by the final couplet the tempo of our reading echoes the farmer's pace. In what may be another example of 'mnemonic irrelevance' or overinterpretation, I can't help relating the farmer's continuous lines of ploughing, early Greek 'boustrophedon' writing (continuous parallel lines), and Purdy's own enjambed continuous parallel lines trying to express and embody what the farmer is doing. Granting that boustrophedon writing alternates right to left and left to right without a break, something that Purdy's sprawling handwriting can't match, I still find the comparison suggestive. What the farmer achieves, and I'm assuming that it echoes what Purdy is attempting in the poem, is a near oneness – his furrows echoing the land's parallels – with his land, antithetical to the unity of farms that 'are like cities under water / and the undulating green waves of time / are laid on them.'[7] The ploughing adapts itself to the uneven contours of the land as expressively as the writer's lines: each achieves a temporary and provisional order that in Purdy's view of the universe – 'the meaningless sky' – is the best humanity can do. The poet, of course, goes beyond the farmer by incorporating the latter's vision within his own, which expands to include mythic and geologic time.[8] The linking of ploughing and language, it is interesting to note, also occurs in Heidegger's 'The Way to Language,' where the ploughing, or the opening up of the field is treated as a metaphor for the revelation of 'the rift-design in the essence of language.'[9] In each instance, there is a mysterious and undefined connection between being, an almost chthonic language (implied in Purdy), the land, ploughing, and the language we use.

Though I emphasized at the outset that Purdy left the poem's temporal dimension undefined, the poem can also be read historically as reflecting on the disappearance of a way of life. Before the closing catalogue of now almost talismanic names – because ignored and nearly forgotten? or because they belong to our youth? – the anonymous and impersonal speaker describes the country north of Belleville as

a little adjacent to where the world is
a little north of where the cities are and
sometime
we may go back there

                    to the country of our defeat

Wollaston Elzevir and Dungannon
and Weslemkoon lake land
where the high townships of Cashel
                    Mclure and Marmora once were –
But it's been a long time since
and we must enquire the way
        of strangers –   *CP*, 62

I presume that, as in the conclusion to *Sunshine Sketches of a Little Town*, 'we' now live in 'the cities' and rarely return to the country north of Belleville, the country of our own as well as the nation's youth.

Why 'the country north of Belleville' – a town with various parallels in its name – should be 'the country of our defeat' is less clear, though the crucial unsettling phrase is repeated at three key junctures. Is it because the land, on the southern edge of the Laurentian Shield, always reasserts itself, whether seasonally or in ice ages, to overturn attempts to impose human patterns on it? Or is it that the suffering involved in gaining a living from it makes every triumph a Pyrrhic victory in which we lose some of our illusions about life? The speaker describes the young as leaving quickly, 'unwilling to know what their fathers know / or think the words their mothers do not say –.' The speaker is among those who 'sometime / ... may go back there,' but the vague adverb and the conditional are so weak that the reader is justified in not quite believing it. This may account for the lingering feeling of undefined guilt in the closing lines evoked by the reference to the 'strangers' we need to direct our steps home to the harsh and occasionally lovely land often abandoned.

The first-person pronoun is, of course, ambiguous: it includes all those who like Purdy share the personal and historical experience evoked by the poem. For those, like myself, who don't, it points to a complex set of historical experiences that have been constitutive of the country's traditions, values, and myths – traditions, values, and myths that, however indirectly, have shaped our history and ourselves. Like most of the more ambitious Ameliasburg poems, 'The Country North of Belleville' is concerned, as Dennis Duffy has pointed out, with evoking and therefore preventing the forgetting of a crucial cultural and historical tradition, at its most particular rooted in the experiences of the United Empire Loyalists and their descendents.[10] With a handful of exceptions, Purdy focuses on ordinary or historically marginal or even insignificant figures or events. But the cumulative effect of these poems is to bring to life a distinctive Canadian tradition and a Canadian way of being in the world. One way of reading these poems – and they are as different as 'Roblin's Mills' and 'Shot Glass Made from a Bull's Horn' – is as explorations of a past whose traces can still be found in the present. As a group these poems constitute a complex and nuanced emotional, geographical, and historical mapping of a past as intricately layered as the sides of the Niagara River gorge or the cliffs of the Alberta Badlands.

Purdy's most ambitious and sustained effort in this direction is the long poem *In Search of Owen Roblin* (1974), a work more impressive in its parts – it incorporates some previously published lyrics – than as a whole. Though it resembles *Paterson* in some respects, it stands to it in the relation of an epyllion to an epic, and its main strengths are the strong individual lyrics that have been woven into it: 'Elegy for a Grandfather,' 'My Grandfather Talking,' 'Roblin's Mills,' and 'Gateway.' Its main weaknesses are sections that are unintentionally prosaic, several awkward transitions, and a lack of any of the narrative velocity or dramatic energy that is one of Purdy's most obvious gifts in the lyrics. The whole is held together primarily by the speaker's voice, the setting, and the slowly evolving narrative of historical research and self-discovery. In its overall form, the poem attempts to recreate in some detail the complicated process of the poet's search for the past, a search that is part discovery or recuperation and part imaginative recreation. The search focuses on a few square miles, a few hundred people, and less than two centuries of local history. The speaker tries to come into contact with as much of the past as survives: the two local people who still remember Roblin; the nineteenth-century houses and the ruins of the mill; his grandfather's stories of logging in the nineteenth century; and the land itself. And though in the end he finds almost all that remains of Roblin, this is less important than what he discovers in the process about the history of Ameliasburg and about himself. The seeker and the process of searching and interpreting are from the start as important as the declared object of the search, Owen Roblin and his times. To understand both Purdy and Roblin, we need to learn about the village on the margins of history they called home.

The search begins with the grandfather's stories – 'Listen he'd say to me Listen' [11] – and then meanders through a *bricolage* of pioneer books, including *Pioneer Life on the Bay of Quinte*, local maps, deeds and records, photographs, a digression dealing with Vitruvius's description of the building of log cabins in Colchis, and Purdy's own attempts to fill in the extensive lacunae by imagining life in the later nineteenth century. The approach to history is humanistic: we can know what we have made. Whatever patterns of meaning or significance he finds are the result of human will and effort. What he finds, and this is true of all of his historical poems, is people like ourselves. The historical conditions may have been radically different (see 'The Names' [CP, 311]), but the ground bass of humanity sounds very similar to ours.

> Then I went still farther back
> trying to enter the minds and bodies
> of the first settlers and pioneers here
>   – how did they feel and what were their thoughts?
> I tried to feel as they felt and think as they did
> thrown out of their homes farther south
> the new land bleak and forbidding
> promising nothing but work and more work
> some of the new settlers middleaged
> others not more than boys
> knowing how they were trapped
> by the circumstances of loyalty
> and trapped by their own stubbornness
> even their weakness and pride
> But not heroes
> in any conventional sense
> certainly not the brawny men I once imagined
> striding thru the forest that names their names
> still impressed on faces of descendants
> not heroes but people like all of us
> all different and all human   [46]

Though he wants to avoid calling the people of the past 'heroes / in any conventional sense,' there's little doubt about his admiration of their achievement in settling a 'land bleak and forbidding.' Some of the empathy probably has its origin in the fact that he built his own house at a time when his future must have seemed to offer as little promise as theirs did at a similar point in their lives.

Perhaps the poem's most important discovery – and this is its overall theme – is the present's unavoidable debt to the past, even when all that remains of the latter are some traces, a few ruins, and a handful of memories. As in almost all of his historical and prehistorical poems, it is the relationship between the past and the present, and the implications of that relationship for the future that interest Purdy. In *In Search of Owen*

Roblin, his engagement with Roblin, and everything the mill owner represents, becomes a paradigm for our more general relationship to the past. As Charles Taylor suggested in *Radical Tories*, Purdy's emphasis on memory and continuity and on the partnership between generations is conservative and his view of history partly Burkean.[11] In Purdy, as in Burke, the past inevitably conditions the present and the future too.

> In search of Owen Roblin
> I discovered a whole era
> that was really a backward extension of myself
> built lines of communication across two centuries
> recovered my own past my own people
> a long misty chain stretched thru time
> of which I am the last but not final link   [80]

As the earlier reference to Vitruvius, the Roman architect, implies, the links and connections don't stop with the American Revolution and the experiences of the United Empire Loyalists. His lovers recall Tristram and Iseult and Heloise and Abelard, while the village drunks and model citizens 'all have their counterparts in antiquity' [63], and if one digs deep enough in the garbage dump, one may find 'a mammoth's tusk' [55].[12] He is candid, however, in admitting that the connections originate with him and therefore depend upon his perspective on the world. He understands that since the past must be interpreted by someone in the present, there is a strong sense in which all history is present history. The act of interpretation is inseparable from the objects and events being interpreted.

This is the theme of 'Artifact' (*SuD*, 80), a poem written two years after *In Search of Owen Roblin*. It begins with the speaker's discovery of a six-inch-long 'Dull red-pitted stone / maybe granite / shaped like a loaf of bread / found in the backyard.' Unsure whether it is a 'footwarmer for nineteenth century settlers / corn grinder after the last ice age / something Indian women used / for husbands to stub their toes on,' he goes to Toronto to show it 'to various experts.' Despite differing opinions, he never meets the one expert whose interpretation is definitive. As a result, he understands that he will 'never identify it completely.' The poem ends with the following resignation:

> I dont even want to know what it is
> or find that last expert eating artichokes

at the Four Seasons the sonuvabitch
might tell me but I know
he doesn't know it's a gift
from governments of stone.

This record of an exasperated search for the meaning of a small fragment of the past is both comic and serious in its foregrounding of the
acts of interpretation and of the inevitable limitations of some of these
acts.

Like all of Purdy's historical poems, *In Search of Owen Roblin* shows
that it is the individual, willed act of remembering, retrieving, imagining, and recreating that sees or projects patterns of meaning. Owen
Roblin and the entire way of life for which he is a metaphor depend on
the poet's fascination with him and his ability to bring him back to life.
He is honest enough to admit that the fascination is partly egotistic or
narcissistic in origin:

For it wasn't Owen Roblin I was looking for
but myself thru him always myself ...
I am the sum total of all I know
all I have experienced and love
and if that makes me a monster of egotism
bring on your Doctor Freud and Doctor Jung
then go look at the face in your own mirror   [81]

The last line recalls the book's opening pages in which the poet tells the
reader and himself to 'stare back at the mirror' of the ancestral photographs. It reminds us that from the start of the poem we knew, though
perhaps not fully conscious of our knowledge, that any pilgrimage into
the past is ultimately in search of ourselves. Focusing simply on himself,
Purdy admitted as much in a letter to Mike Doyle when he described *In
Search of Owen Roblin* as 'a psychological self-examination.'[13]

The lines that follow offer a vision of the poet as an everyman who
feels himself connected to the entire past, in fact to all of life.

I don't mean solipsistic navel-watching either
but John Donne's 'I am a piece of the main'
meaning a part of everything larger
and all the things I write about I've done myself
oh not with hands, but with my mind

I am a screen thru which the world passes
a thermometer registering pain and sorrow
and laughter sometimes at being ridiculous
a writer – good, bad, or indifferent
embedded in all I've written about
a fly speck in history
dust mote cruising the galaxies
I contain others as they contain me
in the medieval sense I am Everyman
and as Ulysses said of himself in the Cyclops' Cave
                                        'I am Nobody'
and a lover   [83–5]

Purdy may dislike Whitman, but there is more of the 'good grey poet'
here than there is of Donne. The passage is also unusual because
Purdy rarely makes large claims of this kind for the poet or for poetry.
His more usual procedure is to let the poem show or enact what
poetry can do while simultaneously questioning, often explicitly, the
poem's claims. What's troubling here is not the self-assertive and self-
justifying tone, but the difference between this and the rest of the book
as poetry: these lines are the 'Hallelujah Chorus' after nearly eighty
pages of what was predominantly a cello concerto. And the final three
words – 'and a lover' – are simply a mistake threatening to bring
down the inflated rhetoric of what preceded. In fact, it's almost invari-
ably true that when Purdy brings in love or a woman at the end of a
poem not previously concerned with them, he's probably unsure of
how to close.

Luckily the book ends with an understated lyric ('The wheels
stopped') paradoxically describing what is no longer there. The poem
casually and wistfully gathers up a handful of details from the vanished
past (the mill, children at school, gossip). In a long poem that begins
with sepia or black-and-white photographs and often reads as if written
by a poet restricted to a black-and-white palette and shades of grey, it is
appropriate that in the closing lines

The black millpond
                holds them
movings and reachings and fragments
the gear and tackle of living
under the water eye

all things laid aside
> discarded
> forgotten
but they had their being once
and left a place to stand on   [90]

The pure negation of the very suggestive 'black millpond' is what the poet writes against. In a literal sense, the past may indeed be lost to us, but the poet's words attempt to evoke aspects of it – 'the gear and tackle of living' is just right – and keep it alive in the only way we can. Like the oval photograph of its prologue, *In Search of Owen Roblin* offers a partial image of the past resisting the obliterating blackness of the millpond's unseeing oval. And the final poem reminds us of why that past – local, marginal, and provincial – is worth remembering: '... they had their being once / and left a place to stand on.' If much of the past has been lost, something of value still remains: the snake fences, the houses with 'white gingerbread woodwork,' the roads, the village, the grandfather's stories, and intangibles like names, attitudes, and values are their heritage to the future. In this respect, *In Search of Owen Roblin* has an admonitory intention and function. It asserts the importance of the Canadian past for an understanding of the present, however different the present may seem. Purdy's suggestion that he can only understand himself fully by understanding the people and country south-west of Belleville is intended as paradigmatic for his readers. As I suggested in the first chapter, that admonition is more important today than at any other time in our history.

6

History and Nation

The poems dealing with Canadian places and Canadian history are also written against the attitude common since the nineteenth century that, because Canada has no world-historical figures and hasn't been the setting for world-historical events, it has no significant history. It's a sobering reminder that for most of humanity, 1867 is remembered as the year in which Marx published the first volume of *Das Kapital*. Frank Scott's disappointed response to Quebec in the 1920s, after a stay at Oxford, captures the sense of living on the margins. 'Coming back from Oxford, where for the first time in my life I was brought into direct contact with the European tradition, in which one soaked up the human achievements of great individuals and great nations past and present, and where always one was drawn back toward antiquity, I found Quebec presented a totally different kind of challenge. Here nothing great seemed to have been achieved in human terms. I was shocked by the ugliness of the cities and buildings by comparison with those that I had recently lived in, and there seemed so little that one wished to praise or draw inspiration from in our social environment or past history.'[1]

Purdy's historical poems resemble his landscape poems in suggesting that the reader look attentively at what is there before lamenting automatically what isn't. He's not concerned to show that what happened at 'The Battlefield at Batoche' is more important than what happened at Thermopylae or Austerlitz or that in any objective historical sense – if that is possible – 'Remains of an Indian Village' (*CP*, 36) or Arctic 'Tent Rings' (*CP*, 88) are more important than 'The Death Mask' (*CP*, 240) mistakenly identified with Agamemnon. The Canadian characters, events, and objects are important and of value because they constitute the country's past, and we can't understand our present without them: to use a metaphor from *In Search of Owen Roblin*, they are 'a backward extension' of ourselves. Whatever our ethnic backgrounds, however recent our immigration, and whether we know it or not, we stand and build on foundations laid down by Champlain, Big Bear, John A. Macdonald, and Owen Roblin. As Milosz puts it in a poem that begins with an echo of the opening of Livy's *History of Rome*, 'a country without a past is nothing, a word / That, hardly spoken, loses its meaning, / A perishable wall destroyed by flame, / An echo of animal emotions.'[2] The unnamed city of Milosz's poem has a past but fails to recognize it, and the poem, like so many of Purdy's, is written against a general historical amnesia. For Purdy, whatever myth or sustaining fiction of national identity we may have is inevitably grounded in the histories and in the narratives of those who came before. To recall *In Search of Owen Roblin*: 'they had their being once / and left a place' for their ancestors 'to stand on.' To ignore, devalue, or forget them is to undermine our collective social fabric and the constitutive ideological bases of the nation. The nation, as Coleridge emphasizes, is not only the 'sod' under the feet, but also, and perhaps more importantly, the 'language, religion, laws, government, blood' that a people have shared in that place. It is 'identity in these makes men of one country.'[3] And identity is meaningless without and inseparable from continuity. An impressive late poem, 'The Gods of Nimrud Dag' (*TPNA*, 30), suggests that the community's past remains important even if its world-view has altered significantly and it no longer worships the same gods. Looking at a large colour photograph of 'stone heads of gods / on top of a Turkish mountain called Nimrud Dag,' the speaker realizes that though these gods and others are forgotten,

These were the gods of our fathers:
they are not to be dismissed from our own lives,
even if we worship no longer at their shrines
– an unused part of the brain knows them
when the priests' chanting dies
and the moon silent on the silent mountain.

The connection between past and present is still potentially there.

For Purdy, history is the history of the making of a community, and the historical poems often show or imagine a commerce between past and present and present and future. This kind of poem often begins with a simple recuperation of the past both by recording an encounter with what remains of it, and, on that basis, imagining, however momentarily, what it might have been like. The recuperation of the past within the present then becomes, as a poem, a gift to the future. There is something of this in Heidegger's more general view of the effect of creativity or poetry. 'The poetic projection of truth that sets itself into work as figure is also never carried out in the direction of an indeterminate void. Rather, in the work, truth is thrown toward the coming preservers, that is, toward an historical group of men ... Genuinely poetic projection is the opening up or disclosure of that into which human being as historical is already cast. This is the earth and, for an historical people, its earth, the self-closing ground on which it rests together with everything that it already is, though still hidden from itself.'[4] Though Heidegger, who was notorious for his contempt for all things American, would probably not consider Canada a 'nation,' nevertheless his ideas about 'projection' and 'the coming preservers' seem to me applicable to the inevitable future-oriented dimension of the poems of any national poet.

'Projection,' in this context, can be a function of the simple fact of the poem's existence. 'Remains of an Indian Village' is representative. Written in 1961, the poem shows the poet wandering among the 'rotten boards, forest rubble, bones,' all that remains of a settlement slowly being overgrown by the forest around it. He describes the place, his response to it, and expresses an undefined sense of indebtedness or obligation to this particular nearly obliterated past.

> As I observe the wispy legs of children
> running in this green light from
>   a distant star
> into the near forest –
> wood violets and trilliums of
> a hundred years ago
> blooming and vanishing –
> the villages of the brown people
> toppling and returning
> What moves and lives
>   occupying the same space,
> what touches what touched them
>   owes them ...   *PAA*, 57

The emphasis is on the transience of life, and the verse has the overall quality of elegy. Six years later Purdy reprinted the poem in *Wild Grape*

Wine, but in a revised version in which five new lines introduce the above segment, establishing a different context for what follows and making more explicit the relationship between poem and village, poet and Indians, present and past. The 1968 version has the 'double vision' and the layering characteristic of much of the 'historical' poetry after *The Cariboo Horses.* The revision is a small but significant example of an aspect of the development of Purdy's historical vision.

> But I come here as part of the process
> in the pale morning light,
> thinking what has been thought by no one
> for years of their absence,
> in some way continuing them –
> And I observe the children's shadows
> running in this green light from
> > a distant star
> into the near forest –   *WGW,* 119–20

The poem's present tense as well as the closing present participle – 'continuing them' – ensure the scene's 'projection' into the future. The gesture of temporal extension has its spatial counterpart in the cosmic context introduced by 'this green light from / a distant star' literally linking the local and the cosmic. The poem is a complex gesture of historical recuperation as well as an attempt at expiation analogous to other postcolonial poems in which an individual encounters remnants of the cultures that existed in America prior to the arrival of Europeans. Josiah Canning's nineteenth-century 'The Indian Gone' explores the same topos with a similar intention and effect.

> Beneath me in the furrow lay
> > A relic of the chase, full low;
> I brushed the crumbling soil away –
> > The Indian fashioned it, I know.
> But where is he?[5]

Though Canning implicates the reader with a question, I would suggest that the reader is already involved in both poems because, in Vendler's words, the lyric as a genre 'offers itself as a potential speech for its reader to utter, or *lied* to sing ... A lyric is *a role offered to the reader,* the reader is to be the voice speaking the poem.'[6] The lyric 'I,' in other words, is always potentially a double pronoun, existing between and incorporating both the poet as speaker and the reader.

The structuring of the encounter with the past in 'Remains of an Indian Village' becomes a model for later poems, most of which play a variation on the form in dealing with historical or prehistorical material. The narrative situation in 'Tent Rings' (CP, 88) is typical. The poet sees

> Stones in a circle
> on an island in the Kikastan group
> placed there long ago
> to hold down the skirts
> of caribou skin tents
> All over the Arctic
> these tent rings
> going back thousands of years
> in the land where nothing changes

The image is initially primordial and alien, though the fact that the tent rings are the remaining trace of a dwelling helps bridge the temporal and spatial gap between the reader's present and the poem's past. And it is with just such a bridging that the poem as a whole is concerned, as the speaker, in a gesture we're now familiar with from many other poems, tries to imagine the past – of Kikastan, of Canada – before speculating about the future.

> In some sense I think of them
> as still here in the circle
> the small brown men
> they lived so strongly
> with such a gift of laughter
> the morning sun touches
> and glances off
> their sparkling ghosts
> To enter these tent rings
> is mingling with the past
> being in two places
> having visions
> hearing voices
> sounding in your head

almost like madness
summoned by wizard angakoks
a thousand-year-old spell
relayed and handed down
a legacy
from the dead to the living

The poem's grammar – 'they lived' – acknowledges the pastness of the past but then shades into a present tense in the same sentence. Also impressive is the subtle shift in the subject from the first person pronoun – 'I think' – to the infinitive clause – 'To enter these tent rings' – that dominates a sentence whose only personal pronoun is 'your': for a moment, the reader joins the speaker and the ghosts of the original inhabitants inside the tent rings. The quotation's penultimate line – 'a legacy' – is the shortest in the two-page poem and the only one with a single stress. By its end, the poem becomes the will, written by a modern 'angakok,' by means of which the legacy is passed on to the present that, in turn, is imagined as leaving something for the future ('in the future I suppose / the stones will be rectangular'). Though the poem began by acknowledging that tent rings like these exist all over the Arctic, it leaves the reader with the momentary impression that the one described is as unique and historically significant as Stonehenge. Purdy doesn't make that claim and would probably dismiss it as a category error, but that nevertheless strikes me as part of the poem's effect.

'Why does one not hear Americans speak more often of these important things? Because the fools do not believe that they have sprung from anything: bone, thought and action. They will not see that what they are is growing on these roots. They will not look. They float without question. Their history is to them an enigma.'7 This, of course, is Williams, but change the country and it could be Purdy shaking his head in wonder at people not interested in their past, who 'will not see that what they are is growing on these roots.' This is a plea for a historical vision and understanding analogous to a more primal, sensory response to the physical beauty and grandeur of the land itself. In 'The Country of the Young,' the final poem of *North of Summer*, Purdy describes the aged A.Y. Jackson painting

... a picture that says
'Look here
You've never seen this country

it's not the way you thought it was
Look again'

The poem itself becomes a painting as Purdy brings out his palette in an
attempt to match Jackson's.

The colours I mean
for they're not bright Gauguin
or blazing Vincent
not even Breughel's 'Hunters in the Snow'
where you can get lost
and found in five minutes
– but the original colour-matrix
that after a giant's heartbeat
lighted the maple forests
in the country south
You have to stoop a little
bend over and then look up
– dull orange on a cliff face
that says iron deposits
olive leaves of the ground willow
with grey silver catkins
minute wild flower beacons
sea blue as the world's eye –   *NS*, 79; *CP*, 105

Ending with another imperative – 'Look here' – the poem tries to per-
suade the reader to look again, more attentively – as did Jackson and the
Group of Seven – even if that attention requires an effort at first, at a
landscape whose grandeur and beauty he or she may not have yet
remarked or appreciated. The poem's implied readers are those who, in
Williams's words, 'will not look' either at the landscape or, in other
poems, at their own history. The references to Gauguin, Van Gogh, and
Bruegel suggest that someone accustomed to thinking of landscape as it
has been defined within the European tradition of painting, may be unable to see or do justice to the country being painted by Jackson and
described by Purdy. A new palette and a new poetic are needed to
evoke the Canadian landscape and so is a new mode of perception. But
the mention of the European painters also implies that Canadian painting, however different, is inevitably an extension and development of
the European tradition. The Group of Seven's debt to Gauguin and Van

Gogh is well known. The point about the uniqueness of the Canadian landscape isn't a new one; it goes back at least to the mid-nineteenth century and each generation of poets has reasserted it. But Purdy partakes of this tradition while going beyond it and using landscape poems to deal with political, historical, aesthetic and spiritual issues as well.

More often than not, landscape in Purdy is imbued with history. Even in a casual piece of journalism like 'Streetlights on the St Lawrence,' in which he accompanies a ship down the St Lawrence Seaway, he registers the felt pressure of the historical past in a contemporary landscape, and insists that an awareness of it is mysteriously indispensable to our lives.

The St Lawrence, more than any other, is the river of canada. You can't row a boat or swim a stroke there without crossing the paths of Jacques Cartier and Samuel de Champlain. Both are basic to what we were and what we have become.

After the long Atlantic journey, then the immigration station at Grosse Isle, newcomers were ferried with muscle and sweat by bateau and shank's mare to Lower and Upper Canada. Where there was no beer waiting for them. It is difficult not to think of those people on the river, the dispossessed from France, England, Scotland and Ireland; difficult because we are their children, and their children's children. (*SA*, 87)

The first paragraph reminds us of 'official history,' of facts and names that we may have forgotten. The second, however, is a found poem that shifts the focus onto the mass of anonymous and forgotten immigrants who underlie 'what we were and what we have become.' Here, as in 'Grosse Isle' (*NSM*, 9), the later poem based on it, we feel the endurance, exhaustion, and quiet desperation of emigration as we experience history from within.

As I mentioned earlier, the naming of places and people is at the centre of Purdy's poetics. 'On Canadian Identity,' discussed above, is an early example. Some of its concerns recur in another poem that also mentions Illecillewaet in its opening lines.[8] This is an untitled lyric existing only in an undated, heavily corrected typescript. I mention it primarily because its ending makes explicit what the earlier poem is hinting at. It begins with a catalogue of names rolling down the page like boulders down a hill:

[But] name those names
the lilting ones

that dance in high school geographies
Illecillewaet and Temiskaming for instance
Similkameen [and] Calabogie and Laurentides
the magic ones / that cast a spell of inattention /
on pimply classroom adolescents
when I was a pimply adolescent
Rivière du Loup and Trois Pistoles
Kicking Horse Pass and Caribou Crossing
the [flat] borrowed imitations
Brighton Windsor Trenton
native only by indulgence

The list of names is as much a personal topos in Purdy as in Whitman, and the naming of the country is an integral part of each poet's
poetics. Both are equally fascinated by indigenous names that on occasion seem to them somehow closer to the essence of the land than 'the
borrowed imitations' or those that are 'native only by indulgence.'
Whitman's notebooks contain lists of Indian names and words, and he
often preferred aboriginal names like Mannahatta and Paumanok to
the ones in use, New York and Long Island. The names are also a metaphoric shorthand for languages, ways of life, and histories that are
essential aspects of each country's past. It's appropriate that the opening of this manuscript poem offers names in the languages of the three
founding peoples since the remaining two pages name various parts of
the country as a prelude to a slightly pessimistic series of rambling
comments about Purdy and then the nation. These fifty or so lines are
in Purdy's most garrulous style, which is pulled up short by a colon
introducing a closing paragraph in which we can feel the voice of a
visionary or mythopoeic poet struggling to express an almost ineffable vision.

this land this dust this country
to invent and explore and mythologize
and which we finally know
provides some hint to ourselves
this weak flesh this crumbling bone
the fossil mind that signals
and semaphores our lost origins
these northern distances
this floating stone in space

and we the strangers
in our green living room

The familiar cadences of *Richard II* are so powerful here that it is almost impossible not to add, 'This Canada' after 'these northern distances' or 'this floating stone in space.'[9] And I wonder if other readers are tempted to preface the second line with 'And these, poet, shall be thy tasks' 'to invent and explore and mythologize'? I mention the *Aeneid* not to point to an influence – Virgil isn't Purdy's kind of poet, Homer is – but to suggest that there is an analogous programmatic and admonitory intention in Purdy's poetry, whether it is explicit as in this fragment, 'Joint Account,' and 'Arctic Romance,' or implicit as in the Baffin Island poems in *North of Summer* or any of the poems rooted in Canadian experience or touching on history.

In the work of few Canadian writers (Pratt, MacLennan, Hood, Lee) is Canada as prominent as it is in Purdy, and no other writer uses the word 'country' as often as he does. On the simplest and most obvious level, this is evident in those poems that name various towns, cities, and provinces in the process of describing Purdy's experiences in them. (Incidentally, poems dealing with naming and with Canadian places are conspicuous by their absence in the first four books, another indication of how late Purdy found the voice and vision we now think of as distinctly his.) It is almost impossible to overstate the comprehensiveness of this. There are poems about Tofino, the Alberta Badlands, Winnipeg, the country north of Lake Superior, Montreal, Newfoundland, and the Arctic. If the prose is included, then almost every part of the country has been visited and written about. We can see this as early as 'Towns' (*BB*, 8) and as recently as 'Vancouver' (*CP*, 309), 'Oh God Oh Charlottetown' (*NSM*, 57), and 'A Job in Winnipeg' (*TPNA*, 16). The instances are nearly almost countless, almost as if the impulse to name is compulsive and fundamental to his vision. He admits as much in a 1972 letter to Dennis Lee. Responding to Lee's insightful article about him in *Saturday Night*, he comments, 'Yes, I do have this sense of "opening up" the country, writing about places in a way that has not been done here before.'[10] His 1977 review of *Literary History of Canada* reiterates that 'we are our own future: that is, Canadian writers now are mapping the country, both psychologically and physically. It has not been done before, despite the evidence of this History, and I am bound to think the job important' (*SA*, 268). And a marginal note in his copy of the final volume affirms that '*we* are our own tradition. We writers are mapping it' (328).[11]

A similar point can be made about the presence of Canadians in the poems. These range from anonymous figures riding the rails during the Depression ('Transient' [CP, 77]), to ordinary Canadians like the farmer 'Wilf McKenzie' (CP, 190), who appears in a poem and an article, to well-known individuals like Maurice Richard ('Homage to Ree-Shard'), René Lévesque ('A Handful of Earth'), and the country's prime ministers from Macdonald ('On Canadian Identity') to Pierre Trudeau and Brian Mulroney ('A God in the Earth' [WS, 47]). If *In Search of Owen Roblin* shows the poet 'switching identities' as he tries to enter 'bodies of long-vanished people' (ISOR, [48]), these poems offer sketches and portraits of living individuals. Taken together, the poems are a group portrait of the country taken by a man who has travelled extensively, who knows the people and the land well, and whose love for both is obvious.[12]

We feel the last directly and without embarrassment (by the poet or the reader) in the ironically titled 'A Handful of Earth,' which has its origins in an interview Purdy did with René Lévesque (the poem is dedicated to him). As the imperatives and the repeated 'we' indicate, the poem is about our relationship to the handful of earth we call Canada that Lévesque wants to break in two. Engaging separatism, Purdy tries to outflank it by avoiding narrowly political issues and playfully proposing at the outset,

> let us join Quebec
> if Quebec won't join us
> I don't mind in the least
> being governed from Quebec City
> by Canadiens instead of Canadians
> in fact the fleur-de-lis
>   and maple leaf
> are only symbols
> and our true language
> speaks from inside
> the land itself
>   CP, 245–6

He appeals to something that transcends partisan politics and specific policies – the land and the history we have shared for more than two centuries. Shifting between his own experiences and the generic ones like the real and metaphoric building of houses and homes, he offers a moving overview of what we have been and what we are on this handful of earth whose name he won't say but that the reader inevitably supplies. He ends by remembering Lévesque and reiterating what will be lost if the PQ prevails:

I think of the small dapper man
chain-smoking at PQ headquarters
Lévesque
on Avenue Christophe Colomb in Montreal
where we drank coffee together six years past
I say to him now: my place is here
whether Côte des Neiges Avenue Christophe Colomb
Yonge Street Toronto Halifax or Vancouver
this place is where I stand
where all my mistakes were made
when I grew awkwardly and knew what I was
and that is Canadian or Canadien
it doesn't matter which to me

Sod huts break the prairie skyline
then melt in rain
the hip-roofed houses of New France as well
but French no longer
nor are we any longer English
– limestone houses
lean-tos and sheds our fathers built
in which our mothers died
before the forests tumbled down
ghost habitations
only this handful of earth
for a time at least
I have no other place to go

The final line is a simple declarative sentence, emotionally restrained; and yet it has an accumulated strength and a poignant affective quality inherited from the emotionally charged, almost archetypal and 'laral' images of the preceding six lines – houses, fathers, mothers, and everything implied by 'ghost habitations,' the particulars of which are furnished differently by each reader. If rhetoric, in the broadest sense, is concerned with convincing or persuading, then the poetic rhetoric of 'A Handful of Earth' tries to move us – and I assume, Lévesque – to look beyond mere politics to a more comprehensive vision of the nation that perhaps only poetry, fiction and song can articulate. Their words are able to express intuitions and emotions that we may have but find ourselves unable and perhaps unwilling to speak. How many of us in discussing our feelings for something simultaneously as tangible and nebulous as a country are capable of the unsettling honesty of the poem's final line. One of the ironies of today's multicultural politics is that it encourages just such expressions of feeling for the countries we all left while implicitly discouraging them for the country we now live in.

If the lyric is usually the conversation we hold with ourselves, in Purdy's hands it is often also a means to an implicit dialogue with others – in this case, Lévesque and readers who may agree with him or with Purdy or with neither.[13] Ironically, a poem of this kind would seem less unusual to the Quebec politician than it does to English-speaking readers; after all, Quebeckers are accustomed to songs and poems dealing with 'le pays.' 'A Handful of Earth' doesn't seem out of place among Yvon Deschamps's 'Je suis moi,' Robert Charlebois's 'Presqu'Amérique,' Gilles Vigneault's 'Mon Pays,' and French B's 'Je m'en souviens.'[14]

If we stand back from the poem for a moment, I suspect that most of us, if we think about it, are slightly surprised by the ease with which we accept the poet's assumption of authority to address these issues in this manner. I don't mean to imply that the modern poet shouldn't deal with politics or the nation. That would be absurd. But in an era that thinks of political poetry as synonymous with feminist poems (Sharon Olds, Adrienne Rich, Erin Mouré) or poems of Third World politics (Caroline Forché, Eduardo Galeano), the kind of political poem I'm concerned with here – the poem of the nation – is almost anachronistic and in literary history belongs with odes, Romanticism, and the rise of nationalism. As I wrote earlier, if the term were not so much out of fashion, I would call them patriotic poems or national odes, part of a tradition that includes Whitman's 'Starting from Paumanok,' Pratt's *Towards the Last Spike*, Frost's 'Build-Soil,' Akhmatova's 'Requiem,' Tate's 'Ode on the Confederate Dead,' and Milosz's 'In Warsaw.' These are national odes, perhaps doing the work of epic in an era that doesn't believe in epic, or only accepts it in encyclopaedic, 'academic' poems like *The Cantos*, *Paterson*, and *The Maximus Poems*, which seem authoritative because they are so obviously comprehensive and inclusive. Their size and ambition alone proclaim them as poems of 'America.'

The authority in Purdy's poems depends on very different sources. The first, as one would expect, lies in the language of the poem itself. If, as in some of Purdy's more narrowly political and occasional poems, the language is flat, the voice garrulous, and the intention unmatched by the verbal performance, then the question of authority doesn't arise. But there is also what could be called contextual authority. That is, the authority of the individual poem, the poem that works, also derives from and depends upon all those poems, some of which I mentioned earlier, dealing with real individuals and places. The more general poems are extensions and intensifications of the national feeling, implicit or explicit, in those that surround them. In them the poet speaks out of a sense of national proprietorship almost as if his voice were the voice of the nation. In other words, we accept the claim to authority of these ambitious lyrics partly because we read them as grounded in those other poems describing and dramatizing the tale of the Canadian tribe. On the basis of his extensive and deep engagement with the country, the poet has earned the right to speak for it and to it. More intangible than this may be the reader's willingness to attend to the poems because of his admiration for their sheer ambition, rather like the attention one pays to someone doing something none of his contemporaries would dream of doing.

The difficulties confronting a postcolonial writer trying to write what I am calling a national poetry can be appreciated if we compare Purdy's situation to Whitman's in the 1850s. Whatever other obstacles he may have had to overcome, Whitman at least shared a national myth and ideology with his potential readers whose sources were in the democratic or republican dream of 1776. For nearly a century the epic subject had awaited its poet, though Timothy Dwight's *The Conquest of Canaan* (1785) and Joel Barlow's *Columbiad* (1787, 1807) were attempts at the great American poem. Though failures, their presence at least indicated that the idea of a national poem was alive. It took Whitman to realize that the American epic had to be written in an American idiom, that the poem of the democratic revolution needed a revolutionary democratic poetics. The appearance of various 'epic' poems as well as odes on national subjects in the half century before the publication of *Leaves of Grass* (1855) indicates two important things: there was a general expectation that poets would compose poems about public themes, and there was still a large audience for poetry. Even a century later, Lionel Trilling could still describe Robert Frost, on the occasion of the poet's eightieth birthday, 'as a tutelary genius of the nation and a justification of our national soul.'[15] One wonders how many contemporary Canadian writers and critics would feel comfortable referring to 'our national soul'?

In the Canada of the 1960s, the expectation of poems on public or national themes had died with E.J. Pratt, who, as his national lectures and readings testify, may have been the last genuinely popular Canadian poet. Though Margaret Atwood's poetry readings attract equally large audiences this is due primarily to her status as a very popular middle-brow feminist novelist. The decade during which Pratt wrote *Brébeuf and His Brethren* and *Towards the Last Spike* may have been the last period during which a writer could assume at least a minimal homogeneity in his audience's assumptions and values. Ironically, he was writing at the moment when those values, intensified and foregrounded by the experience of the war, were about to be challenged and much of that audience was about to disappear. And because he wrote in an old-fashioned poetic his influence on the poets of the succeeding generation was minimal. He marked the end rather than the beginning of a tradition.

A Canadian poet of the 1950s or 1960s wanting to write a public poetry had the following inheritance to work with: no dominant national myth; no viable modernist tradition of public poetry; and no expectation among serious readers that such a poetry could be written in the second half of the twentieth century. I suspect that because Purdy is such a prominent and familiar figure in our literature, we have forgotten the private and public difficulties he had to overcome to write the most ambitious of his lyrics and to create the poetic world of his *œuvre*. Self-educated and without a strong native tradition to fall back on and develop, he can be said to have almost begun from nothing when he turned to the writing of the poems on which his reputation is based. In a sense, the individual voice is everything because the authority of the poems depends on it alone, there being no national tradition of major public poems functioning as a matrix for them. An equally important absence is a body of national poems, on whatever topics and of whatever quality, that would have been taught and memorized in schools. It is noteworthy that only a poet like Dennis Lee, whose own ambitions are similarly nationalist, has emphasized this aspect of Purdy's work and has written children's poems that can be memorized. Critics with a more North American orientation like George Bowering and Frank Davey seem almost embarrassed by this aspect of the poetry and by critics attentive to it.

As I have emphasized from the beginning, Purdy's national vision, like that of his more metaphysical poems, is rooted in the local and regional. Like Margaret Laurence, Alice Munro, and Margaret Atwood, to name only the most obvious examples, he has had to solve the question of the relationship between the local and the universal. In his case it meant writing about the regional, without remaining merely local or parochial, and finding the national and universal in it without simply using it as a point of departure.[16] One could say that his problem was how to avoid becoming Melville's Pop Emmons. David McFadden may overstate the point, but at least he recognizes that Purdy always looks beyond Prince Edward County. 'I never thought of Yarn [Purdy] as having anything more than a functional interest in the part of the world in which he lived. It's true his poetry reflected his environment, but only directly as it related to him. He was no regionalist.'[17] I would prefer to say that because of his 'double vision' Purdy is never simply a regionalist: Belleville and ancient Greece (Sisyphus) exist side by side and simultaneously in his poems as do Owen Roblin and the Cyclops.[18] *North of Summer*, his Baffin Island book, begins with the following untitled poem:

On the country road these spring days
odd things happen
brown men in mukluks climb
       the snake fences
with Norris Whitney's sheep
near Ameliasburg
and I'm afraid to mention it
at the village store   17

Here, as so often, the solution to 'mere regionalism' is a vision that begins with the concrete particulars of Ameliasburg ('Norris Whitney's sheep' and 'the snake fences') but sees them as coextensive with the rest of the world, or at least those aspects of the world experienced in some way by the 'local' poet. The rasp, reticence, and scepticism of the voice may seem local, but they have to be adaptable to the ordinary higher style of the public oratory of the national poems.

Purdy's attitude to both the local and the national is equally proprietary. Compare the opening of an Ameliasburg poem like 'Gateway' with that of a national poem like 'Joint Account.'

As much as any place in the world
I claim this snake fence village

of A-burg as part of myself
its dusty roads and old houses
even the garbage dump sliding
its sleazy treasure chest of litter
and malodorous last year valuables   CP, 202

The myth includes Canada,
inside the brain's small country:
my backyard is the Rocky Mountain trench
– wading all summer in glacier meltwater,
hunters with flint axes stumble south –
I take deed and title to ancient badlands
of Alberta around Red Deer:
and dinosaurs peer into Calgary office buildings –
Dead Beothucks of Newfoundland track down my blood;
Dorsets on the whale-coloured Beaufort Sea
carve my brain into small ivory fossils
that show what it was like to be alive
before the skin tents blew down –   CP, 159

Though with very different effects, each poem is permeated by a historical sense. Each evokes the spirit of a place through the sensibility of a speaker sensitive to the layers of history – the entire temporal and spatial continuum – embedded in the place he inhabits and imagines. In each there is a sense of plenitude and a simultaneous sense of transience and mortality. 'Gateway' is grounded solidly in the particulars of contemporary Ameliasburg, though the speaker makes a handful of playful excursions into history and prehistory. The 'deed and title' in 'Joint Account' 'includes Canada' to the extent that everything that can be associated with the name is part of the poem's vision, which, incidentally, is communal, as the pronouns of the second verse indicate.

In the long body of the land I saw your own,
the mountain peaks,
the night of stars,
the words I did not speak,
and you did not,
that yet were spoken –

At this point, the joint account is a vision of what is possible and what is desired, and it is sung by the poet speaking as the voice of a potential community that his words are trying to imagine into being. As Purdy once told Acorn, 'I write in my own way toward a society that will not come in my lifetime, perhaps never.'[19] In Frye's terms this is also 'a vision of the nature and destiny of man and the human situation (*quo tendas*).'[20] The associative rhythm is nudging us towards an ideal, towards the paradoxical situation in which unheard and unspoken words are heard and spoken, when it suddenly breaks off and Purdy the realist foregrounds the economic meaning of 'account' to remind us of our real status.

> But reality is an overdrawn bank account,
> my myths and cheques both bounce,
> the creditors close in;
> and all the dead men,
> chanting hymns,
> tunnel towards me underground.

The visionary or mythic account is valid, but so is the other 'account,' which has to do with the economy, unemployment, and other related political questions, and which, in the end, may undermine the poet's vision. It is a measure of the honesty and integrity of Purdy's vision that these poems regularly remind us of the gap between what the country is and the poet's vision of it, as well as his doubts about the possibility of its realization. 'Arctic Romance' seems on the verge of national 'myth-making' before it pulls back and admits that 'there is perhaps some wistfulness included / in all this,' only to once again swerve towards an 'unwritten choreography of a nation' (*CP*, 169). And 'Home Thoughts' follows the *via negativa* of this kind of poetry for nearly two pages before suggesting that 'the only / country in the world whose people / do not dance in the streets very much' may have something

> overlooked by anthropologists
> born of the land itself perhaps
> what is quietly human and will remain so
> when the dancing has ended.   *CP*, 360

The dark side of Purdy's national vision occurs at those moments when he realizes that many are blind to what seems self-evident to him. For example, in 'Man without a Country' (titled in manuscript 'What Is a Canadian')[21] the contrast is between the poet who feels that the country and the people '... are my history / the story of myself / for I am the land / and the land has become me' (CP, 314), and the man of the title, who feels no connection with what is around him and to whom the country's history is devoid of significance.

> But I have heard a man say
>   'This is not a country
>   I am going away from here'
> It was as if he had said
>   'I am no man because –
>   because this is not a country'
> – his face twisted in contempt for himself
> and he spoke of all the great things
> other countries had accomplished
> one country in particular he named
> and said 'Look at them
> their pride their arts and science
> and above all they have not sold out
> to the highest bidder.'

The man remains unnamed, supposedly for personal reasons; but I wonder if there isn't also the intention to let the reader fill in the name with that of someone who fits the poem's description – perhaps even his or her own? In the end he represents all those who, distracted by the achievements of other countries, are unable to see anything of value in their own.

That others have had a vision similar to Purdy's, and not lived to realize it, seems implied by the troubling image at the close of 'Joint Account' of 'the dead men, / chanting hymns' who seem to be moving towards the poet from underground. That they chant 'hymns' lends a solemn and quasi-religious tone to the poet's song as well, while their association with him confers a sort of blessing on his vision from the dead bards of the past or the voices of the land.[22] This is similar to what happens in poems like 'The Sculptors,' 'Lament for the Dorsets,' 'The Country of the Young,' and 'I Think of John Clare,' where Purdy implicitly relates his own poem to the carvings, paintings, and poems he is describing. In both instances, he is situating himself and his work within a community of artists whose vision overlaps with his, each an extension of the other.

'Man without a Country' closes with the poet admitting to feeling 'insulting compassion' for the poem's subject, an emotion that echoes the cold contempt he feels in an almost contemporary poem, 'A God in the Earth,' for the politicians who have failed to build on the visions of the explorers and nation builders. Both poems are flawed by lapses into preaching, but that in itself indicates Purdy's anxiety in the late 1970s and 1980s about the country's future. This is particularly evident in what may be his most despairing political poem, 'The Country of the Losers.' Originally intended to open *The Stone Bird*, it was dropped, together with 'A God in the Earth,' primarily because Purdy's publisher, Jack McClelland, disliked it, and it has never appeared in print. It reads like a litany of disillusionment, as if Purdy found himself agreeing with 'the man without a country' but for reasons the latter wouldn't understand. It's the love letter of a lover whose life-long devotion has not only not been reciprocated but has never even been acknowledged. The unnamed country is twice described as 'mythic' (a favourite adjective in the national poems), but by the poem's end we sense that the word's dominant meaning is 'non-existent' or 'unreal.' There is a similar ambiguity in 'Shot Glass Made from a Bull's Horn,' where the poet refers to 'a mythic country that disbelieves in itself' (*CP*, 271). In both cases the ambiguity serves to remind us of what has not been achieved. Not surprisingly, among the country's failures is the lack of a significant connection with its own past.

> A country ...
> whose fifth-rate politicians
> make tenth-rate speeches
> for a second-rate electorate
> where lovers make love out of boredom
> the silver hinge connecting past and future
> become slobbering enema
> A country soon to be broken apart
> crumbling into separate sand grains
> on the windblown beaches of time
> Who will mourn?[23]

The poem seems to flail in all directions and leaves the impression of a poet concerned less with objectifying and enacting an emotion or an attitude than with getting his anger down on paper. As to the poem's closing question – 'Who will mourn?' – the answer is obvious: if no one else, then at least the man who has written these lines. His anger is testimony to his concern and desperation. There are moments in reading even the more positive of these national odes when they seem great and lonely poems, monuments to a grand and ambitious conception of a nation, a national myth directed at a people who increasingly can barely conceive of Canada as anything more than a political state. The depth of Purdy's political disillusionment in this period can be gauged not only from the tone of this and other poems, but from the fact that in 'A God in the Earth' he includes Pierre Trudeau among

> ... these small men
> who cannot lift the heart
> or stir the blood with visions
> a direction an aim
> if not for the sky then for the earth   WS, 48

Purdy's relationship with Trudeau goes back to the 1967 trip to Cuba, and they had exchanged friendly letters for several years. The note of disillusion with Trudeau and Canadians is particularly strong in the unpublished long poem 'Election Blues, May 22, 1979.' But even here, the poet registers the inevitability of his fate as a Canadian, his inability to conceive of his destiny in any other terms.

> I sit here wondering
> what world would I have chosen
> I mean what country
> if there was a choice
> (but there is no choice)
> where I would not be growing old
> preaching this little homily
> this assessment of things
> as they are to myself
> possibly to make myself
> feel better
> shake off depression
> this footnote to darkness
> But there is no other world
> no other country
> I am here[24]

As is obvious from earlier examples, Purdy usually hints at the nation's identity or its myth; the poems provide some salient details, but leave some of the work of definition to the reader, just as in 'On Canadian Identity' he or she must speak the 'one word which has never yet been said –.' If the myth, the necessary national fiction or narrative, is to be believed, valid, and of value, it will have to be earned, just as the country's beauty will only be perceived by those willing to extend themselves to reach it. At the end of the struggle is something that under other historical circumstances would be known instinctively but that at present can only be hinted at or suggested, as it is in the closing stanza of 'Hellas Express' (*SD*, 72). Here the poet is on a train crossing the border into Greece.

> Winter is reversed at the Macedonian border
> the iron snake pants and lies there
> orange trees have bronze age lights in them
> rivers run south like old brown bones
> in the land of Socrates Alexander and now me
> the latest anonymous arrival
> Greeks are lined up at every window staring
> out at their homeland
> at something not stamped on passports
> when custom officials board the train
> I fumble for it in my breast pocket

Whatever that 'something' may be, the Greeks know it without necessarily having it 'stamped on passports' or even being able to say it. The ambiguity of 'it' (grammar dictates that the pronoun refer back to 'something,' but sense indicates the speaker's passport) suggests that the Canadian speaker is lacking whatever it is that the Greeks possess as naturally and unconsciously as they breathe the air of their homeland. If Purdy's body of work can be said to have an overall intention, it is to leave his Canadian readers with an attitude towards Canada similar to the one the Greeks have for Greece/Hellas in this poem.

It may not be obvious from the way I have approached it, but the engagement with Canadian history and the concern with Canada's 'myth' is ultimately inseparable in Purdy's thinking from the more general concerns with history and prehistory, both of which become more prominent in the poems of the 1980s and 1990s. Though a couple of very early poems show a sense of history as exotic costume drama (see 'Genghis Khan' [*EE*, 27] and 'Mary the Allan' [*PS*, 14]), there is evidence in other poems of a serious and probing interest in problems of historical interpretation and knowledge, and in the relationship of the past to the present. 'Scholarly Disagreements' (*BB*, 15) and the impressive 'On the Decipherment of "Linear B"' (*CLL*, 16) both focus on interpreters of the past – historians and code breakers – to emphasize the difficulties involved in breaking its codes as well as to offer, almost in passing, Purdy's hint that what was important to our ancestors is also important to us.[25] The 'scholarly disagreements' he cites are over historical facts pertaining to Egyptian, Sumerian, Etruscan, and Minoan civilizations. But for Purdy, as for Lawrence, these disputes about the past are less important than his perception, based on the sculpture they left behind, that our ancestors were intensely alive. In lines that we now recognize as an early version of his eventual personal signature – before he settled on its final form and found his voice and name – he describes how

> A slim priestess with bare breasts
> brandishes a snake in affirmation:
> 'I am alive and life is all my meaning!'
> Life that moves and burns fiercely
> as the heat of nails crying out
> against the intolerable status quo of death,
> and even false gods' old advertising –

In a manner of speaking, much of what Purdy has written since is an elaboration of the last five lines. A decade later he rephrases them as follows: 'For [sex and death] are the great themes of human literature, the best literature ... [and] in my book, sex and death must always include love and life' (*SD*, preface). This is sloppy – 'human literature'? Is there any other? – and a bit too pat, but it's accurate as a shorthand account of his dominant concerns.[26] He acknowledges the pastness of the past, but it fascinates him most when it becomes an antique mirror in which we can see ourselves through the mottling, dust, and distortion.

As we saw in *In Search of Owen Roblin*, contemporary life and history often coexist in a single poem. In 'The Cariboo Horses,' for example, the flowing, loping, associative, open style lets past and present flow into each other as the appearance of ordinary 'half-tame bronco rebels' at '100 Mile House' evokes in the speaker memories of different kinds of horses from history. And though the poem begins and ends with real broncos and though it describes them as 'only horses,' its overall effect is to leave one with a very positive impression of them, due in part to our new knowledge of their impressive historical pedigree. They may seem to move in and through a pure present, but the allusions to Kiangs, Onagers, and Quaggas have surrounded them with an aura based on layers of time. In the early 'News Reports at Ameliasburg,' the present and the historical past are joined by prehistory and all three appear in the same poem, as Al Finnegan dreams his way through levels of history and prehistory and mythic, human, and animal modes of being (*PAA* [1968], 70). Often the interdependence of past and present in Purdy's thinking can be inferred from the simple juxtaposition of poems in a book: for example, 'Shot Glass Made from a Bull's Horn' and 'Near Tofino, Vancouver Island' are side by side in *The Stone Bird*, and 'The Strangers' comes between 'At Mycenae' and 'The Uses of History' in *Piling Blood*. I wouldn't want to press the comparison, but the effect of reading the poems of an individual collection or of *The Collected Poems* in the given order is roughly analogous to the paratactic arrangement of details or sections in Pound's *Cantos*. The dominant organizing principle – and perhaps the only one – in each 'work' is the capacious and eclectic mind of the poet and his memory. In Purdy, we always return to a poem about a present experience, but through allusion, comparison, or juxtaposition of poems, the experience becomes situated, grounded, or contextualized in history and thus implicitly evaluated. This may not be precisely what Purdy intended when he said that he takes 'a double view of history' (*SA*, 15–16),[27] but it seems to me closely related to his practice, which often reveals a multiple perspective. If, on the model of *Leaves of Grass*, we think of *The Collected Poems* as a single, evolving poem, then the various individual poems can be read as commentaries on one another, counterpointing, repeating, contradicting, intensifying, restating, and developing Purdy's views of life and history. Every poem that describes, narrates, or enacts a way of life, either past or contemporary, different from Purdy's own should be read as indicating another way of ordering and interpreting reality. In the end, history and life are presented from diverse points of view, and if either can be said to have a meaning that meaning is the sum of the modes of being described and enacted in the poems. Whatever desire Purdy may feel for totality or holistic explanations is deferred for the most part to the more metaphysical and spiritual poems dealing with prehistory or to the more generally reflective poems.

The effect of all this on the specifically Canadian poems is to ground them in world history, to show the Canadian experience, however unique it may seem, as coextensive with similar individual and national experiences, past and present, elsewhere in the world. It is simultaneously shown to be valid and important on its own terms and to be a part of a more general and inclusive context, whether historical or prehistorical. This is a large claim and perhaps unprovable, though readers could try the following experiment. They could read 'Funeral,' 'In the Dream of Myself,' 'A Handful of Earth,' and 'Prince Edward County' (*CP*, 242–8) as a separate group, and then read them again after having read the two poems preceding them in *The Collected Poems*, 'The Death Mask' and 'Along the Ionian Coast' and the one following, 'Monastery of the Caves.'[28] I would emphasize, however, that because Purdy's view of history is not overtly teleological or ideological he doesn't establish connections between past and present – his 'double view' – to suggest an ideological point. Whitman offers an interesting contrast since he almost always reads history as if it were the Old Testament prophesying the coming of the messiah of Democracy.

> I was looking a long while for Intentions,
> For a clew to the history of the past for myself, and for all these chants – and
>   now I have found it,
> It is not in those paged fables in the libraries, (them I neither accept nor reject,)
> It is no more in the legends than in all else,
> It is in the present – it is this earth to-day,
> It is in Democracy – (the purport and aim of all the past,)
> ...
> All for the modern – all for the average man of to-day.[29]

Referring in another poem to 'that old entire European debris,'[30] he sounds almost like Mayakovsky after the 1917 revolution, wondering whether all the cultural artefacts of earlier eras should be destroyed. For both, the present society, whether American or Soviet, is the culmination or fulfilment of the historical process. As a result, almost everything that happened before 1776 or 1917 is regarded as prehistorical and as having little except genealogical interest.

Purdy, by contrast, wants to suggest the fundamental continuity between ostensibly different societies and human beings of various historical (and prehistorical) eras: in other words, a group portrait of the cave painter at Altamira, Archilochus, Bruegel, Hokusai, and Al Purdy would reveal unsuspected points of resemblance, even while acknowledging their inevitable differences. The approach is for the most part humanistic, and its basic assumption can be traced back to Vico: we can know history because it was made by individuals like ourselves. Think back to how often Purdy emphasizes the craftsmanship involved in the making of an object: 'On the Decipherment of "Linear B,"' 'Wilderness Gothic,' 'Pillar of Fire,' 'Carpenter's Notebook Entry,' 'Scott Hutcheson's Boat.' If history has a meaning, it can be found in what we leave behind us. In the form of what we did we hint at what we were: the garbage dumps of Manawaka and Ameliasburg or works of art like Eskimo sculptures and Mycenaean death masks. For Purdy, history's lesson plan has been written by humanity and therefore is inevitably punctuated by similar questions that are repeated over millennia.

These include, of course, the ultimate questions humanity has always posed and been unable to answer. 'Names' (PB, 51) is a representative example. It compares the deaths of 'Marcus Flavinius, Centurion of / the Second Cohort, Augusta Legion' and 'Oberleutnant Conrad Schmidt, minor / cog in General Erwin Rommel's Afrika / Korps,' and begins with the following four lines:

Birthing, begetting and dying
– the great hammers of being,
each one thudding against the skull,
each one obliterating the others –

The fact that these lines are temporally unfixed has the paradoxical effect of relating the events that follow both to the present as well as to all other times. The effect is reinforced by our sense that the weighty, lapidary style of the first two lines gives them a proverbial quality: 'Birthing, begetting and dying [are] the great hammers of being.' Readers familiar with Purdy's body of work will also notice the presence of two of his signature words, 'hammers' and 'skull,' often present in poems dealing either with death or creativity. What follows is in the nature of a historical illustration with a conclusion that once again brings us back to larger metaphysical and moral questions arising out of our historical experience. Because the questions are ultimately transhistorical, time collapses in the poem, and poet, reader, Marcus Flavinius, and Conrad Schmidt confront the same riddle from the same sphinx. In other words, though Purdy recognizes those features of the past that constitute its pastness – everything that differentiates it from today – he's ultimately interested in those aspects and features in which he can see identity and continuity.

> two men about to die,
> who spent their last few moments
> wondering how they could change things
> on the earth they were leaving –   CP, 311–12

Like most questions in Purdy's poems, the ones posed in 'Names' remain unanswered, unless the reader attempts, as I assume most of us do, a provisional response that may have little to do with the practice of formal criticism but is an integral part of our reading. I would suggest that this effect is part of the poem's intention. In fact, enough poems end either with questions or enigmatic lines that this kind of open ending – an ending resisting poetic and *narrative* closure – seems to me an integral part of Purdy's poetic. It's as if recognizing that any ordering of history into narrative form constitutes an interpretation, he wants to ensure that that interpretation remains open: if, as Nietzsche suggests, to believe in grammar is to reveal a latent or residual belief in God, then to believe in story and closure may reveal an equal attachment to teleology. Since narrative is at the heart of Purdy's poetic, several of his most common poetic techniques – various aspects of his grammar, syntax, and rhetoric – function to undermine and forestall some of the epistemological and ontological baggage narrative comes encrusted with. Purdy wouldn't agree with Kroetsch's critically trendy assertion that 'any coherent story has to be a lie,'[31] but he regularly acknowledges that what we know of the past is full of lacunae and contradictions and that any historical discourse – verse or prose – will have to acknowledge these if only by indicating the extent to which imagination has been involved in the account.[32] Where the postmodern critic, having noticed fragments and gaps, seems disabled from seeing anything else, Purdy, more commonsensical and pragmatic, interprets them as part of a complex totality.

One of Purdy's more explicit reflections on history occurs in 'The Uses of History' (CP, 346), one of his more entertaining later poems. It is a humorous treatment of his double vision, his desire to relate past and present. With a title appropriate to an academic volume (see E.H. Carr's *What Is History?*), the poem shows the poet going from the Belleville library to 'the Gatsby Lounge / at the nearby Quinte [Hotel].' The rest of the poem alternates between the poet's reactions to a striptease taking place in the present and his reading

... about the 16th century
Hindu kingdom of Vijayanagar
whose courtesans were so beautiful
that looking deeply into their eyes
caused some men to dance like raindrops
on water and others to howl like dogs

He slowly brings his description of the '16th century' into the present tense while simultaneously comparing the present-day strippers to 'the Venus of Willendorf' and the incomparable 'Verynice' of Vijayanagar. The whole performance is playful and light-handed with one or two memorable comic touches: Purdy, for instance, pursuing his 'scholarly bent' at the Quinte Hotel or comparing his situation to 'Thoreau's at Walden Pond.' As for the uses of history? The poem has shown us an aspect of contemporary society from a new, idiosyncratic, and revealing perspective: at the end of the unexpected history lesson, whose surprising and unnamed origin is Forster's essay 'The Consolations of History,'[33] we see the strippers at the Gatsby Lounge and Vijayanagar's courtesans differently than we saw them at the beginning. And the poet's comparative study of history, as he drank 'a flagon or six,' has revealed something relatively consistent about male attitudes to women through the ages.

As I said, it's an unpretentious comic poem, a companion piece to 'At the Quinte Hotel,' that drama in five scenes about the uses of poetry in contemporary Ontario. But just as that poem had a serious point to make about the poet's relationship to his audience, 'The Uses of History' also tells us something about how Purdy reads and uses history. As with the poetry he reads, he follows his interests and occasionally absorbs what he reads into new poems. Or as he put it in a letter to Bukowski: 'Don't really know fuckall myself nor see any reason why I should. Only a helluva lot of opinions. Things happen, I refract them into poems, which is about all' (*BPL*, 25 February 1965). This should be taken with a shot of brandy and read with the author's note to *Emu! Remember* in which he describes his education as consisting of 'approx. 10,000 books, considerably more' (17).[34] The first is an understatement made with Bukowski's expectations in mind, the second is the overstatement of an autodidact still unsure of himself on a page. (If Purdy had read 10,000 books by 1956, the date of the publication of *Emu! Remember*, that would be more than a book a day if we take his serious reading to have begun at the age of 12 in 1930.) On the other hand, the comment to Bukowski is relatively accurate as a description of how his interests, in this case history, enter the poems.

Though I have compared his procedure to Pound's, a more apt comparison would be to the peripatetic Herodotus, another wanderer on the open road who gathered interesting stories and wove them into a long, rambling narrative as uneasy with teleology as Purdy's *Collected Poems*. I cite the father of European history because he happens to be a favourite of Purdy's and because he figures in two late poems, 'This from Herodotus' (*CP*, 358) and the simultaneously biographical and autobiographical 'Herodotus of Halicarnassus' (*WS*, 44). The first presents a well-known episode from *The Histories* (book VIII, sec. 123–5) involving Themistocles and Timodemus, an episode that probably caught Purdy's attention because it deals with two of his continuing concerns: the fallibility of historical memory and death. After Themistocles had been awarded 'the prize of valour / "for conduct throughout the campaign"' of the war against Xerxes, Timodemus claimed that 'he had earned his honours not / by merit but from the fame of Athens itself.' The poem's moral is that

> after that fraction of time which is
> two thousand five hundred years or so
> the hatred and envy of Timodemus is
> just as much alive as memory of Themistocles
> to the latter's eternal annoyance:
> two men linked together in time
> unable to distinguish the nuances
> between first and second place
> in death which has no nuances

Whether or not Timodemus and Themistocles are equally 'alive' today – I suspect that the latter is the better-known figure – we nevertheless remember them differently: one as a hero who didn't vote for himself in the balloting for the prize of valour, and the other as a spiteful and envious Athenian.

The poem about Herodotus seems to have, even more than the earlier one about Archilochos (*PB*, 58), an autobiographical subtext, though unlike 'Archilochos' it doesn't make any explicit comparisons between the ancient writer and the modern one.[35]

> A reasonable man
> listening to what people say

in the marketplace
at peddlers' stalls
at the docks talking to fishermen
off-shift miners
ploughmen in springtime
taking notes and considering ...

(For gawd's sake
they're talking about a statue
on the main street
for the old bastard
I mean why?
– that sloppy old man
staring at women's legs
wine-bibber
'old father of lies'
buttonholing everyone
asking the world questions ...)

Quietly in a vineyard at Thurii
Herodotus
dreams life never ends
– in the Islands of the Blest
of the Western Sea
all his loves waiting
the fair and not so fair
the dark ones with lips like flames
their faces shining on him
their eyes like springs of light
Let it be so!   WS, 44

This is Herodotus refracted and augmented by Purdy with some images
of the poet himself mixed in or caught between the lines. I'm not sure if
Purdy keeps a notebook, but the individuals interviewed by Herodotus
in the first stanza also appear, two and a half millennia later, in his journalism and poems (see 'Wilf Mackenzie'). And reading 'they're talking
about a statue,' I find myself thinking of the recently named 'Purdy
Lane' in Ameliasburg – connecting the main street to the graveyard – as
well as about the locals' longtime curiosity about the 'sloppy old man /
staring at women's legs / wine bibber' (see 'Spring Song' [CP, 29]). The
poem's double vision allows the historian and the poet to coexist, and

the closing sentence's fiat is both wish and wish-fulfilment. As Purdy half-seriously suggests in 'On Realizing He Has Written Some Bad Poems,'

> my poems
> your obligation is to cause people
> to look at you and glimpse between your lines
> indistinct and ambiguous my own face
> enigmatic almost majestic certainly wise   *CP*, 250

If we see the poet's 'indistinct and ambiguous face' between the lines of his poem about Herodotus, then classical Greece and contemporary Canada exist simultaneously for us.

The connection between the two men includes one other important quality: the work of each yields more questions than answers, and the answers, when offered, are usually provisional. The most prominent word in the poem is the adverb 'why,' and the questions it introduces about history and about life are never adequately answered. What this says about Purdy is that he may be interested in the *meaning* of history, but that he isn't sure there is one beyond the meaning of our individual lives and what we make collectively. As for the ultimate metaphysical or spiritual meaning of our existence, that kind of enquiry is often deflected into the more speculative and philosophical poems dealing with prehistory. It is in these and in the many late poems about death that he raises the large, and ultimately unanswerable questions about origins/creation, evolution, and God.

7

Origins and Being

Though he shows some interest in evolutionary and prehistorical origins in the poems of the 1950s and 1960s ('Barriers' [*PS*, 9], 'Twin Heads' [*BB*, 2]), and though death is a concern – more as a poetic convention, however, than a reality – even in *The Enchanted Echo*, Purdy has written the majority of his more reflective and philosophical poems about origins and dying in the past fifteen years. As a group, these poems represent a significant and to some degree unexpected development in his work, a shift from a predominantly descriptive to a reflective mode of poetry. It's as if responding to the onset of old age – Purdy was sixty-three when *The Stone Bird* was published in 1981 – and the deaths of friends like Milton Acorn, Frank Scott, and Margaret Laurence, Purdy began to recognize the need to go beyond lyrics, however complex, that describe and celebrate life; the larger and perennial questions implied by the 'why' of 'Herodotus of Halicarnassus' could no longer be avoided. It would be inaccurate, however, to suggest that they had been entirely absent from the earlier work, since 'death,' and the images Purdy uses to deal with it, is one of the most frequently used nouns throughout the poetry. Since *The Stone Bird*, however, 'the old questions' have become more prominent as Purdy's imagination has returned to them with greater frequency and increasing urgency in poems dealing with death or, alternately, with the origins of life. Death, it is interesting to note, is mentioned more than ninety times in *The Stone Bird*, *Piling Blood*, *The Woman on the Shore*, *Naked with Summer in Your Mouth*, and *To Paris Never Again*, the books published between 1981 and 1997. Confronted with death, Purdy turns increasingly to biological, geological, and prehistorical speculation, almost as if these and cognate interests are a replacement for the more conventional religions most turn to when confronted with ultimate and usually unanswerable questions. There is a sense in which this group of prehistorical and 'timeless' poems forms a matrix or ground for the contemporary and historical poems with which I have been primarily concerned to this point. Having dealt with personal and historical beginnings, Purdy turns in these poems to the search for origins and presence within which all beginnings (and all being) originate. To adapt Heidegger's terms, place and nation provide a historical sense of 'dwelling,' while origins and being offer an ontological one.

Despite the occasional presence of biblical allusions and images – the residue of his childhood and his reading – Christianity and other religions are prominent by their almost complete absence from these poems, indeed from nearly all of Purdy's poems. It's as if in burying his mother, he buried his interest not only in the United Church of Canada but in Christianity as a whole. The only references to Christianity in the poems are either hostile ('The Funeral' [*CP*, 242]) or bemused ('The Crucifix across the Mountains' [*NSM*, 73]). The latter, based on a travel piece by Lawrence describing crucifixes in the Tyrol, ends as follows:

> And it is a strange feeling for me
> beside Roblin Lake in Ameliasburgh
> to be talking about Jesus as Son of God
> as if he were divine
> and I struggling to be human –

Some of the strangeness has its origin in his awareness that his poems almost never refer to Jesus or Christianity; the very recent 'Minor Incident in Asia Minor' and 'On the Beach' are important exceptions (*TPNA*, 38, 58). Unlike Lawrence, who spent his life wrestling with, rejecting, and revising Christianity – *The Plumed Serpent, The Man Who Died, Apocalypse* – or Layton, whose body of work is a bitterly hostile settling of a two-thousand-year account, Purdy shows neither nostalgia nor interest. His most sustained response occurs in 'On First Looking into Avison's "Neverness,"' a poem unusual both because it deals with Christianity and because it is a rare direct response to another poem. Permeated with biblical imagery, Avison's poem is a meditation on the effect science and the scientific world-view, represented by Leeuwenhoek's discovery with his microscope of 'the one-celled plant,' will have on faith, represented by 'Old Adam, with his fist-full of plump earth, / His sunbright gaze on his eternal hill.' For Avison, Leeuwenhoek represents anyone trying to reconcile the different kinds of origins and knowledge represented by Adam and science, both of which are emphatically described as 'not historical,' though I assume that Adam is so both because his life preceded recorded history and because his story, being biblical, is outside history as such. In the end, Avison has no doubt that if the scientific world-picture replaces the religious one, the result will be catastrophic for the self.

> We sprawl abandoned into disbelief
> And feel the pivot-picture of old Adam
> On the first hill that ever was, alone,
> And see the hard earth seeded with sharp snow
> And dream that history is done.

The context makes it clear that she is describing what she takes to be the modern condition. The poem ends with her version of Yeats's second coming: 'the pivot Adam,' both Adam and Christ, is denied and 'the whole cycle [is] ravelled and flung loose.' There may be a glimmer of hope in the cryptic closing triplet (calling Avison cryptic is almost a tautology, like calling Heidegger difficult). Here there is a suggestion that an extreme form of vision on the other side of blindness will still be able to make out the slowly fading 'outline' of 'Old Adam.' Otherwise, all that is left is the 'unending night' of a world history lacking a sacred dimension.[1]

Purdy's answer offers Adam as an everyman liberated by the problematic knowledge revealed under the crude microscope. He acknowledges Avison's concern, but, unable to find any enthusiasm for her Christian vision, ends the poem with a wry vision of Leeuwenhoek in heaven trying 'to examine sin under his new / model guaranteed for life / microscope.' Contrasted to this slightly comic heaven, is the universe as a whole in which

> my non-plussed Adam
> blurs and becomes anyone
> becomes one-celled organism
> speeding outward past the traffic
> lights at far Centaurus
> looking for his lost leader
> whom he never knew
> > anyway
> a man needs something to believe in

The suggestion seems to be that a man may need something to believe in, but that Christianity has no privileged status in the universe, and God is a 'lost leader' whom we never knew 'anyway.' (The adverb, incidentally, is a good example of a word doing double duty, pointing forward and back at once, and, in this case, linking and therefore intensifying two important clauses.) Almost as provocative are the sexual imagery and subtext of Purdy's response to a poem by a writer whose work is chaste, asexual, or even anti-sexual. The microscope becomes 'a dog penis' (why? perhaps a juvenile provocation to the reader and fellow poet?) searching for 'organisms / (orgasms?),' and of the two lines quoted from 'Neverness' one refers to 'the lust of omnipresence.' And in a self-referential joke, Purdy refers to 'lonesome Adam and no Eve,' which happens to be the title of his poem about the last male turtle in a species about to die out because there is no female for him to mate with. The overall point seems to be that if the best Christianity can provide is a heaven without sex and sin, Purdy will settle for the universe as it is, fallen and unredeemed. Instead of the Bible, he will turn to scientific accounts of origins and endings; instead of biblical teleology, he posits a biological continuity.

It's a playful poem, but it shows us the earth-oriented direction of Purdy's reflections on what Avison calls 'our metaphysic cells,' that is, those aspects of our existence that transcend mere being or that provoke us to ask questions about meaning, origins, and death. As I wrote above, in Purdy this impulse is particularly evident in reflective poems whose focus is predominantly prehistorical. It's as if he rewrites the creation myth and the myth of the fall in evolutionary terms. And though his poems refer to God or the gods as often as Lawrence's, they are ultimately earth-bound and equally vague about the nature and status of the divine. More often than not, 'God' in Purdy's work is a noun without any defining content. He and Lawrence are equally passionate in their celebrations of nature and life, but neither takes the next step towards pantheism (though Laurentian nature worship often comes close) or, even further, towards Whitman's transcendentalism. There's no doubt that there is a powerful will to believe in Purdy, but as has been noticed by most commentators, it is difficult to define his 'religion' precisely. Purdy's comments in his prose and in his letters aren't particularly helpful; when he discusses God he usually refers to the traditional Judaeo-Christian conceptions – which even Frye found problematic on occasion.[2] Writing in 1968 to Margaret Laurence, for example, Purdy comments that 'as to God or god, one can only logically be an agnostic I suppose, but I am an atheist in reality, in practical life, which doesn't preclude thoughts closely akin to religion.'[3] The subordinate clause seems to contradict what preceded, but only until we realize that for Purdy 'God or god' usually refers to the gods of the traditional religions. To understand what he intends by 'thoughts closely akin to religion' we need to turn to the poems themselves – which is as it should be, since as Williams put it, 'The poet thinks with his poem, in that lies his thought, and that in itself is the profundity.'[4] In other words, if we want the poet's ideas (as a *poet*) we should go to the poem and not to his prose: to *Paterson*, not the *Selected Essays*; to *The Collected Poems of Wallace Stevens* and not *The Necessary Angel*.

'The Gossamer Ending,' a poem of the late 1980s, contains perhaps the most explicit and clearest statement Purdy makes about the human condition; that may also be why it isn't a particularly strong poem. But it's a useful point of departure for the more religious poems that attempt to go beyond the humanistic and agnostic impasse in which Purdy deliberately situates himself. The following is the third of five stanzas.

> In the beginning
> we don't know where we came from
> apart from our most recent ancestors that is
> and in the end
> after a million years or so of being dust
> we don't know where we're going to
> only in the middle
> do we have some control over things   WS, 89

(That the stanza is particularly weak becomes obvious when we rewrite it as prose and realize that nothing has been lost.) The poem ends acknowledging the inevitable annihilation of the self, its reduction to dust, though it cushions the blow or distracts us from the full implications of what is said with a figurative style and pathetic fallacy more appropriate to a poem on a different subject: 'a small rain like tears / that can only be imagined by lovers / who do not yet exist / is falling somewhere.' The poem simply goes soft in style and thought, as is often the case when Purdy introduces lovers near the conclusion. There are three things here we should note, however: the poem's inclusive pronouns, its emphasis on 'the middle,' and its simultaneous linking of the middle or the individual life to everything that precedes and follows it, origins (not beginnings) and endings. Most of the reflective or philosophical poems assume this view, which, as we have seen, is also the 'theory' underlying the poems of the present, whether these deal with personal experiences and history or offer celebrations of nature. But as the poem indicates, though Purdy admits that we can't know the origin or the end, his imagination nevertheless can't stop worrying them. It's as if unable to believe in a traditional master narrative, he needs to try to imagine one he can accept. Though to be strictly accurate, endings and eschatology interest him less than origins, and in the poems I want to discuss he has about as much to say about them as the Kalahari Bushmen, whose view of what we could call existential closure is simplicity itself: 'When we die, we die ... The wind blows away our footprints, and that is the end of us.'[5]

The poems concerned with origins are usually prehistorical in setting or orientation and take two forms, which could be called the biological (or evolutionary) and the geological. Both show Purdy trying to find a trans-historical ground for his life and for history, something that will give both the kind of depth they would have were he able to believe in a traditional religion. Having denied himself a sustaining myth of origins, an eschatology, and a *telos*, he is forced to imagine one for himself on the basis of metaphors drawn from the natural sciences. Unable to believe in God's presence and that 'In the beginning was the Word,' he tries to evoke in his own words a primal a-historical, a-temporal presence in nature. Though he could say with Henry Adams 'that what he valued most was motion, and that what attracted his mind was Change,'[6] he nevertheless suffers simultaneously from a metaphysical nostalgia for 'presence,' a ground – his version of Avison's 'pivot Adam' – and for some kind of totality, transcending mere natural and historical process. Unable to believe any of our inherited master narratives, he nevertheless finds himself longing for some of the consolations they offered. Within history itself, some of this finds expression for him in the inevitably limited form of everything involved in the fact and idea of a place and a nation. But ultimately, seeking to transcend historicity and the finitude of life, he can only find origin, totality, and *telos* by imagining them in the form of poems; in other words, through poetic fictions as necessary and as necessarily contingent as Stevens's, though his references and allusions to historical individuals and events often distract us from realizing this. In a very real sense, the poems are 'momentary stays' against the confusion he feels because he no longer believe in Tennyson's 'one far off divine event / To which the whole creation moves.' Pratt, equally fascinated by prehistory, found it ultimately unproblematic because, like history, it could be understood within the context of the Christian revelation, whatever doubts Pratt may have occasionally felt about his faith. The well-known closing stanza of 'From Stone to Steel' – a poem Purdy echoes closely in 'Near Tofino, Vancouver Island' – summarizes Pratt's view:

The road goes up, the road goes down –
Let Java or Geneva be –
But whether to the cross or crown,
The path lies through Gethsemane.[7]

For Purdy, Gethsemane is irrelevant to the prehistoric discoveries at Java, and, in a manner of speaking, his poems swerve around Gethsemane or are written in an attempt to fill the gap or abyss that opened up when he found himself confronted with the death of the gods.What I have called the biological or evolutionary poems, for instance, attempt to imagine the origins of life or states of almost paradisal being, which, though they obliquely remind us of the Old Testament, nevertheless try to avoid its language or imagery. Poems like 'Vertical versus Horizontal' (WS, 8) and 'In the Garden' (CP, 263) try to describe what life might have been like 'in the beginning' either before or just after the arrival of 'man.' Often these kinds of poems offer a relatively idyllic vision of primal unity before the fall into language and more complex forms of human being. 'Vertical versus Horizontal' begins in a casual conversational style and describes how one mammal shifted from a horizontal existence to a vertical one. The second half of the poem is written in a more lyrical style, and is organized in three italicized stanzas, each beginning with a gentle interrogative, 'Remember' (= 'Do you remember?'), which tries to coax the reader into recalling scenes from the first day not available even to the collective unconscious.

Remember the morning?
– our shadows long in the long grass
our bodies swift in the leaping distance
how we overtook our own beginning
in sweetness of dew and morning
and so still we heard god's heartbeat
in the wet near earth

Remember the noonday?
– the trees were green sentinels

and birds warned us of danger
and we raced the west wind over the grasslands
and discovered the east wind in earth's turning
in springtime everything was shining
as if it had just been born
and it had been

Remember the evening?
– how it was in that great blaze of sun
horizon embroidery
blue green purple orange mixed with blackness
being born as a colour
asking ourselves who we were
and knowing anyway
– and quietness in the forest
when leaves talked together
and the words they said
were sleep sleep sleep
and we slept
our bodies joined to each other
and were parallel with the earth
– we slept
and dreamed a strange dream
and woke and were not ourselves

This part is a visionary pastoral in a lilting, flowing rhythm that offers a brief vision of a paradise that seems to have lasted only one day before the fall into an estranging mode of being occurred ('and woke and were not ourselves'). And though the poem doesn't make this explicit, involved in the radical change is the *felix culpa* of the fall into language, which, in other poems, will have to be overcome or reversed if the poet is to hear 'god's heartbeat,' the languages of nature or Being. Such a vision is offered in 'Moonspell' (*CP*, 268), where the speaker imagines himself as able to communicate with the animals on the Galapagos Islands because 'I have forgotten English.' This sensuous poem whose lineation is as delicate yet firm as fine lace ends with the speaker encouraging himself (and perhaps the reader) to

let go let go
follow the sunken ships

and deep sea creatures
follow the *protozoa*
into that far darkness
another kind of light
leave off this flesh
this voice these bones
sink down

The effect of the poem's long tranquil cadences and intricate patterning
of sounds ('and those soft murmurings / of moonlit vertebrae' [a wonderful couplet]) is gradual and incremental, and produces in the end a
beneficent siren call – but a siren call nevertheless – to let go of the complexities of language and human life and drown in a unified and unconscious mode of being similar to what Freud described as an oceanic
feeling.[8] And though neither *The Tempest* nor 'The Love Song of J. Alfred
Prufrock' is alluded to or echoed – unless the near juxtaposition of
'voice' and 'down' is an echo of 'Till human voices wake us, and we
drown' – I assume that images or lines from both drift through most
readers' minds to heighten the emotional power of the close.

'In the Garden' offers another version of letting go, though this time
the return seems to be to Purdy's version of the garden. It's tempting to
see the poem as his rewriting of Genesis 1: 1–19. The poem is worth
quoting in full because it is also a particularly explicit expression of the
poet's 'religious' attitude to nature and, by extension, life as a whole.

Poinsettias blaze red bougainvillaeas burn
the lake is a smooth blue plate
for sun-tongues to lick clean
Once maybe at the very beginning of things
everything was mud-coloured
you could look out and see only grey sand
you could see nothing to send messages
back from it to you
just dirty-coloured seawater
where rain had lashed things in fury
and wind mixed everything up like soft porridge
and only the pole-star shone like a white lever
for gods of the sky to shinny down
on long slender columns of light
and arrive on earth with a cry

Then we had blue and scarlet and silver
then we had vegetable love
whoever was looking for something
dreamed it first of all
then we made a wanting song of sadness
then we made a finding song of joy
when the Moon said 'Here I am Sun'
so he was
and went on sailing up there
all night for the first time

It must have been if you were watching
if you could have watched in the morning
a time to stand naked in rain
a time to feel the fingers of warm rain
touching your new human body
and stammer some praise for it
　　your thanks – and you had to thank someone
why not the earth?
Thank you earth thank you sea thank you sky
the beginnings of human love
when we said:
　　　these things are dear
they are bought with your life
they are yours for only an instant
they are yours unconditionally
then you must give them away

CP, 263–4

As the present tense of the first three lines indicates, we have never left the garden, perhaps the only garden that has ever been available to us. The world as it is will suffice, despite the brevity of our lives, if we approach it with reverence and gratitude. Despite the playful reference to 'gods of the sky' shinnying down 'columns of light,' the divine is present only to the extent that it is immanent in the world, which is not to say that the world is divine or that these poems show any evidence of a worship of nature, however reverential Purdy's attitude may be. If he has a philosophy it is one of immanence and views this existence, our being in the world, and this world – as we experience it – as all there is. Or as he puts it in 'Driving the Spanish Coast' (SB, 44) '"Our Father which art the earth!"'

Usually when Purdy describes flowers in detail, the poem in question concerns itself at some point with modes of perception, both its own and the reader's. Its implicit didactic point is that the reader needs to look attentively at the circumambient natural world, almost as if he or she had never seen it before. Think back to 'The Country of the Young,' where the reader is guided into an appropriate stance: 'You have to stoop a little / bend over and then look up.' The atavistic, evolutionary poems about the beginnings of life try to place the reader within a narrative in which seeing is literally first seeing as we witness / imagine, for instance, the first appearance of flowers. 'Yellow Primavera in Mexico' (*WS*, 87) begins with what seems to be either a synaesthetic description of or a prescription for how our senses should respond to flowers – 'Tasting with both your eyes / hearing with all your blood' – before turning to an imagined scene showing 'little hairy mammals' anticipating the first appearance of a flower. And 'In the Early Cretaceous' (*CP*, 348), though written earlier, imagines the first sighting of a flower and the subsequent proliferation of flowers over the earth. It's as if to illustrate the cleansing of the doors of perception Purdy needs to imagine a time before they were occluded.

> It was not a motionless glory
> for colours leaped off the earth
> they glowed in the sky
> when wind blew great yellow fields
> danced undulating in sunlight
> hundreds of miles of blue flowers
> were dark velvet in starlight
> and maybe some unnamed creature
> stayed awake all night in the
> midst of a thousand miles of colour
> just to see what it felt like
> to have all the blue-purple there was
> explode in his brain
> and alter both present and future

Colour is mentioned or implied twelve times in fourteen lines, and by the end one feels as if one's senses have been saturated to the point that one's response and that of the 'unnamed creature' seem momentarily to merge. Once again the lack of punctuation and the strong flowing enjambment work to create an impression of a unified field or of a densely interconnected set of experiences. The last three lines try to suggest the prelapsarian epiphany that might have happened if 'maybe' an 'unnamed creature / stayed awake all night.' As we recognize by now, the 'maybe' is a characteristic gesture of mild reservation by which Purdy introduces and tags as 'fictive' or imagined a scene from the past. The creature isn't Adam – the poem is set 'before Genesis was written' – but his situation is Adamic and, in the last three lines, even potentially apocalyptic as he absorbs part of the landscape and feels 'both present and future' altered as a result. Again characteristically, the poem ends by bracketing its own revelation as the speaker admits that '... no one will ever know / what it was like / that first time on primordial earth ...'

The admission introduces an elegiac note not wholly absent from other poems of this kind, which, after all, are trying to evoke a landscape or set of experiences that are ultimately unattainable except in our narratives. Perhaps what is most interesting is the hold this idea or scenario has on Purdy's imagination. For a man who has admitted to being an 'atheist,' he is an atheist of the religious kind, with everything that implies.

More than thirty late poems display a strong will to believe that there might be 'a First Cause' (*CP*, 258), 'gods' (*CP*, 218), or an ultimate meaning or *telos* to the universe. God, even when mentioned, is an absent presence, what David Shaw has called an 'empty signifier,'[9] as evasive and elusive as Heidegger's Being or Beckett's Godot. In fact, I suspect that Purdy's use of the word is ultimately misleading, given its traditional cultural connotations and the semantic halo it inevitably wears. Lawrence tried to solve the problem by using the plural, as in 'I refuse to name the gods, because they have no name. / I refuse to describe the gods, because they have no form nor shape nor substance.'[10] Purdy, however, would probably defend his usage in terms that would echo unconsciously Spinoza's defence in the *Ethics* of his use of certain traditional philosophical terms: 'I know that in their common usage these words mean something else. But my purpose is to explain the nature of things, not the meaning of words. I intend to indicate these things by words whose usual meaning is not entirely opposed to the meaning with which I wish to use them' (pt. 3, 20 exp.). The frequent presence of the word 'God' in the poems functions, then, less as a precise referent than as a shorthand hint at what has been lost and whose absence we are trying to fill in various ways. Jacques Derrida's use of certain words 'sous rature' is not irrelevant here.

That Purdy is sensitive to our changed situation is evident in 'In the

Snow' (*SB*, 71). Here he reflects on the tracks in the snow outside his cottage and wonders

> if that footfall
> outside my door might be God
> of course I know it won't be
> but that kid I was wasn't
> so sure as I am now
> Sometimes in the snow
> I followed tracks ending nowhere
> and thought what do I care
> whether some animal or some god
> stopped in the snow thinking
> I shall perform my miracle
> or have a shit?

Initially, I had the impression that the poem was about the speaker's lack of faith in the existence of God. But what it says is more specific and more comprehensive. It offers an overview of the evolution of his beliefs: his younger self might have believed that the 'footfall / outside my door' was a trace of God's presence; the man he is today, can't. The shift is indicated by the change in spelling from upper-case to lower, God / god. Still, the question of whether or not God exists is left undecided when he admits,

> I do not like to investigate
> such matters at all closely
> prefer to retain my options
> of belief or disbelief:

If one reads a significant portion of Purdy's poetry one finds him fluctuating, as one would expect, among a number of positions. In 'In the Snow' he retains his 'options.' In the overlong and meandering 'A Handle for Nothingness,' he seems to be on the verge of reiterating the same position and then points out that '(He is unprovable / but lack of evidence / is evidence *against*)' (*WS*, 23). 'Dead March for Sergeant MacLeod' mentions that God's 'existence is not / beyond doubt,' and, describing the sound of the waves, associates it with 'idiot music idiot questions idiot God?' And 'Gondwanaland,' to be discussed below, goes even further and states that 'there was never any purpose / and there was never any meaning' (CP, 320), even though the poem as a whole is more ambivalent and is haunted by the idea of a maker and the image of an original unity more than simply geological. It is one of several in which the speaker – here anonymous within the 'we' – wants to have it both ways in a poem registering his ambivalence.

In a Heideggerian sense, some of these poems, if they are strong enough as poems, become the ground, presence, and 'dwelling' that they seek. Heidegger's example is Hölderlin but the general point applies to Purdy:

When Hölderlin speaks of dwelling, he has before his eyes the basic character of human existence. He sees the 'poetic,' moreover, by way of its relation to this dwelling, thus understood essentially.

This does not mean, though, that the poetic is merely an ornament and bonus added to dwelling. Nor does the poetic character of dwelling mean merely that the poetic turns up in some way or other in all dwelling. Rather, the phrase 'poetically man dwells' says: poetry first causes dwelling to be dwelling. Poetry is what really lets us dwell. But through what do we attain to a dwelling place? Through building. Poetic creation, which lets us dwell, is a kind of building.[11]

As in the poems about nation and history, the occasionally metaphysical concern with the past is coextensive with a future-oriented intention. A poetry that can imagine 'being / Being' and 'dwelling,' in however temporally remote a setting, shows that such an imagining is still possible even in an alienating world under the sway of instrumental reason. The constants in this are the simultaneous acceptance and celebration of this world and the occasionally sceptical search for meaning on the open road of life as the poet looks for and interprets the various traces that may or may not be implicated in a larger pattern, an encompassing meaning, which, as in the poetry of high Romanticism, is half-discovered and half-created. The search takes him to places as different as the A-frame at Ameliasburg ('On the Flood Plain' [WS, 51]), a 'Rodeo' (CP, 234), the Galapagos Islands ('Darwin's Theology,' 'Iguana' [CP, 268, 302]), and an enormous pre-Cambrian rock on Baffin Island ('Listening' [NS, 50]). What he finds occasionally are various 'spots of time' whose significance he summarizes in 'On the Flood Plain.'

> – it's a matter of separating these instants from others
> that have no significance
> so that they keep reflecting each other

a way to live and contain eternity
in which the moment is altered and expanded
my consciousness hung like a great silver metronome
suspended between stars
on the dark lake
and time pours itself into my cupped hands shimmering

As in Wordsworth or Whitman, the unusual 'instant' depends on the ability of the self – 'my consciousness' – to be alert and creatively responsive to whatever is taking place around him. The self is 'like a great silver metronome' (an image that hints at metre, creativity, and naming ['onomos']), and the poem implies that without it the contiguity, even collapse of time and eternity, self and landscape could not have happened. The poem also implies that the revelation was contingent on two other facts: that the poet took the risk of building his house too close to the lake – 'on the flood plain' – and that he ventured out at an unusual time.

An analogous moment of revelation is convincingly rendered in 'The Darkness' (CP, 277). Published in 1981, ten years earlier than 'On the Flood Plain,' it has the same setting, but where the later poem's sense of space is horizontal, its emphasis is on the vertical as the speaker, chasing a porcupine from the house, pauses to look up at the 'great ocean' of the night sky. With admirable control, the poem moves from the chase, to a memory of dead animals on highways, to standing on the porch and looking at the night sky and reflecting on the speaker's place in the universe and finally, in a return to the opening, to death. If the evolutionary and geological poems are temporally comprehensive, this one is spatially so as the speaker's mind encompasses 'billions of miles' and feels momentarily that it has touched 'the far edge of the cosmos.' He acknowledges that he may be 'deceiving' himself or 'pretending,' but the impulse to find 'some lost kind of coherence' is genuine and permanent. Mentioning 'religion,' though 'not the conventional stuff,' he closes the long main part of the poem with an admission that he has never found what he is looking for among people.

... some lost kind of coherence
I've never found in people
or in myself for that matter
only in the unhurried natural world
where things are uncrowded by things

> with distance between animals
> star distance between neighbours
> when the grouchy irritable universe
> fumbles with understanding
> and a god's coherence.

Notice how the idea of distance, order, and coherence is reinforced by the lineation with each line forming a syntactically self-contained unit with no enjambment overriding the integrity of clauses or phrases. The poem ends with what seems a prayer to the 'spirit of everyplace / guardian beyond the edge of chaos' for some sort of revelation. This isn't made explicit, but the imagery of the closing lines seems to suggest as much.

> I am waiting here
> until the dark velvet curtains
> are drawn and the scrap of darkness
> I clutched in one hand
> has changed to light

The closing movement, the last three lines of which were accidentally dropped in *The Collected Poems*, is a plea or prayer by a man anticipating his own inevitable death and 'waiting here' for something implicit in but ultimately comprehending the 'coherence' he has occasionally experienced in his life. A poem that seemed initially to be an animal poem – an answer perhaps to Lawrence's essay 'Reflections on the Death of a Porcupine' – about the deaths of animals ends with a vision that includes, like Layton's 'A Tall Man Executes a Jig,' the animal, the human, the cosmic, and the divine.

It's not surprising that a poet whose focus is so insistently 'this-worldly,' even on occasion materialistic or phenomenalist in his outlook, and who thinks of the historicity and finitude of life as the norm, should also turn to geology when looking for permanence or a transcendent ground for being. After all, the earth's rocks are our oldest palpable reality and carry with them physical traces of earlier eras, non-human sounds, and even the heat from events that occurred millions of years ago. In poems such as 'Listening' (*NS*, 50), 'Lost in the Badlands' (*CP*, 295), 'The Stone Bird' (*SB*, 107; *TPNA*, 115), and 'Gondwanaland' (*CP*, 318) Purdy is able to touch the distant past, to stand, for instance, approximately where at 'the end of the Cretaceous' the dinosaurs walked in the Alberta badlands. Of an event imagined to have taken place 'In the Early Cretaceous' (*CP*, 348), only the rocks remain; the animals and plants are at best part of the fossil record. The rocks and the fossils literally help collapse the distance between past and present in a way that is impossible with any other aspect of the prehistoric past. In these poems, the sense of time is often spatial and is defined by the layering or sedimentation of rock. The almost unimaginable age of rock, for example, offers the temptation of an origin that is also a substantial presence, while the fossil record and our ability to map the movement of the continental plates from the breakup of Pangaea to the present creates the illusion that there may be not only patterns and designs but an ultimate designer and *telos*.[12] Thus to descend into the Alberta Badlands ('Lost in the Badlands') is to descend through time while seeing its work incarnated or embodied on the face of the cliff. This isn't quite transcendence, but it is a direct way of coming in touch with what is left of the primordial past. A different and less obvious contact is made in 'Listening' (1967) and 'The Stone Bird' (1981, 1997) both of which deal with the same event, though written fifteen years apart. They describe how the poet lies down to put his ear against 'a mountaintop of gneiss and granite' on Baffin Island to listen to the sound of the earth. In the first poem, he writes of

Listening
where solid granite slopes down
into the water into that silence
at the mountain's foot
my ear following its configurations
into the earth-stone
beneath the sea bottom and on
into another silence
where any impossible sound might be
interpreted as God's voice

The unstopped flow of the lines enacts their sense as the descent down the page mirrors the descent into the centre of the earth towards what 'might be / interpreted as God's voice.'

In 'The Stone Bird' this is expanded, but 'God' is replaced by the earth.

once on an arctic island
at Kikastan in Cumberland Sound

in a moment of desolation
I laid my head flat against the island
a mountaintop of gneiss and granite
with ice floes silent nearby
and heard the heart of the world

                                                    beating
                    It was a singing sound
steady and with no discernible pauses
a song with only one note
like some stone bird with such a beautiful voice
any change of pitch would destroy it
...
                    – that body-sound is earth sound
a singing sound of the past:
radioactive clouds condensing
rain beating the new planet
chemicals interacting on each other
to produce one-celled life
then dinosaurs then mammoths
                    and volcano rumblings[13]

Kikastan may not be Mount Sinai, but what Purdy hears there is as close as he ever comes to hearing what he calls in 'Listening' 'God's voice,' amplified, so to speak, and elevated with a couple of lines of iambic pentameter, an evocative use of long vowels and sibilants, and one telling placing of a word – 'beating.' And although God disappears from the second recension of this experience, it is worth pausing to look at some of the figural implications of the poem.[14] Though God is traditionally associated with light, height, ascent, and the Word, here he is literally grounded, as in Lawrence, in darkness, depth, descent, and silence. In other words, whatever or whoever it is that the poet hears is completely immanent and inseparable from the earth. By implication, the New Testament's 'on this rock' is rewritten as 'in this rock,' while the multilingual paraclete steps aside for the stone bird and 'a song with only one note.' It's not the St Matthew Passion, and Purdy's vision won't satisfy anyone wanting a vision of salvation or concerned with eternal life, but together with the epiphanic moments in some of the other poems, this is all that Purdy can offer with any assurance to the question teasingly and playfully left hanging in 'Iguana,' – 'before Jehovah, what?' His Laurentian answer is 'the song of life,' in which all of life is included, even everything associated with 'those dark blood-stained gods / plotting against life.' The last claim isn't quite convincing, but is necessary to the poem's attempt at a thematic inclusiveness.

The speaker understands, however, that his more prosaic contemporaries will judge him as claiming too much for this experience since

> a specialist of eye ear nose and throat
> ... would say it's a body sound
> he would say blood capillaries indigestion
> but the specialist would miss something
> everything

The choppy rhythm created by the end-stopped lines and the piling up of nouns in the first line establish a visceral contrast between the specialist's diagnosis – attentive to detail and fact – and the poet's vision in the preceding two stanzas, which had a large number of sibilants and pervasive run-on lines. In response, all the poet can do is reassert that what he heard was 'the song of life' itself and that it may be heard anywhere – even 'in the supermarket' – 'in a moment / of grace' as long as we 'Listen.' The poem is simultaneously our record of it and an antiphonal Te Deum sung anxiously to a 'God' who disappeared between versions of what is essentially the same poem. As well, it is another reminder to the reader of forgotten or neglected modes of perception and being. Heidegger again: 'For, to be sure, although we do remain always and everywhere in correspondence to the Being of being, we, nevertheless, rarely pay attention to the appeal of Being. The correspondence to the Being of being does, to be sure, always remain our abode. But only at times does it become an unfolding attitude specifically adopted by us.'[15]

'Gondwanaland' shifts the search for meaning to a level more general than what we find in 'The Stone Bird' as the narrative voice changes from an 'I' to an anonymous 'we.' It is an ambitious poem whose grandeur of intention in theme and form is almost realized in the performance; there is a potentially great poem here struggling, like one of Michelangelo's Slaves, to find its final shape. Though relatively closely organized, with the first and last stanzas forming a frame and the whole united by images of drifting, shifting, floating, and changing, the poem still has a curiously amorphous and undefined quality to it as if the poet couldn't make the parts relate quite as closely and as evocatively as he wanted. Whether or not Purdy wants the poem read as antithetical to 'Listening' and 'The Stone Bird,' it seems to me almost inevitable that most of his serious readers will do so, sensing links of imagery and theme among them. All three are among what I have called Purdy's geological poems, but 'Gondwanaland' could be said to destabilize the entire series by being about continental drift and plate tectonics as well. Though it begins and ends with stanzas about what humanity has done with rock or stone – 'stone as art forms' – much of the poem tries to evoke what could be called a history of rock from Gondwanaland's breaking away from Pangaea, through the shifting of mountain ranges and the sedimentation of levels of rock. This forms the almost timeless background for the curiously intrusive and unconvincingly evoked human drama of the lives of 'perhaps two lovers – / their identity doesn't matter / – but maybe you and I.'

The stanzas dealing with the nearly timeless telluric background have a grim, sombre, austere, monumental, and impersonal quality; the two dealing with humanity are lighter in cadence and movement and ultimately celebratory in mood. We can get a sense of this by reading the ending of the sixth stanza together with the whole of the seventh.

> far in the future a crew of
> skeletons replacing living men
> under earth's dying sun
> crews of fossil mariners
> riding ships of floating stone
> without meaning or purpose
> for there was never any purpose
> and there was never any meaning –
>
> Only that we listened to the birds
> or saw how the sun coloured the sky
> and were thoughtful in quiet moments
> Sometimes in these short lives
> when our minds drifted off alone
> moving in the space vacated by leaves
> to allow sunlight to pass thru
> at the wind's soft prompting
> there was reasonable content
> that we were aware of only afterwards
> and clapping our hands together like children
> we broke the spell

The 'crews of fossil mariners' being carried on 'floating stone' in some distant future are Purdy's version of the ship of death. The statement that there has never been any 'meaning or purpose' seems, momentarily, substantiated by the next stanza, which offers a vision of life whose 'meaning' or being is immanent, or exists only in its 'becoming,' and even that awareness comes to us 'only afterwards.' If we look for it elsewhere we will find only the history of floating land masses under whose surface we can read a Domesday book of human and animal fossils. In an early draft of the poem the fossils are described as carrying 'messages from the builders / and the stone gods.' The fifth stanza, which now begins 'Sedimentary rock / where a fallen leaf / prints itself on stone / and dies forever' reads as follows in a typescript version: 'Sedimentary rock / where a fallen leaf / prints itself on stone / with messages from the builders / and the stone gods / and dies forever.' By eliminating 'the builders' and 'the stone gods,' the published poem denies any possibility of locating an origin or *telos* anterior to or transcending life itself. In its final version, the poem offers nothing beyond the hope of a 'reasonable content' on earth itself and an acceptance and celebration of life as it is.[16]

If the poem stopped here, it wouldn't differ substantially from several others similar in concern that we encountered earlier. But the final, almost gnomic triplet pushes our reading in a slightly different direction: 'Cairn on an arctic island / blind shape turned seaward / what sails rise there?' This has the lapidary quality of an epitaph, and the cairn's location certainly suggests one. It also recalls the poem's opening stanza, which celebrates

The planet's basic stone
and what they did with it
those old ones
– stone as art forms
shaped rearranged caressed worshipped
unknown men hammering stone on stone
common stuff from deep within
                        earth's mantle
at Machu Picchu Sacsahuayman Carnac
artisans of the finite

What 'the old ones' did with rock, including Auden's 'In Praise of Limestone,' foreshadows what another 'old one,' a poet named Purdy, does with reality: he transfigures it into an artefact simultaneously embodying 'the finite' and yet resisting and seemingly overcoming finitude, overcoming death. (The participle 'hammering' – it rarely appears in poems not about death – alerts us immediately to one of the poem's hidden motifs.) In other words, meaning and purpose exist *on* the 'ships of floating stone,' which may or may not be simply floating or drifting. The structures the old ones left behind them, the 'cairn on an arctic island' – the rough-edged line begs to be read out loud – and the poem itself (it could have been titled 'In Praise of Rock') all constitute momentary stays against drift, transience, meaninglessness, and death. As to the question, 'what sails rise there?' the answer is probably 'other ships of floating stone / with other cairns and other poems.' The poem's massive, sometimes sprawling stanzas figure the floating land masses, while its heavily enjambed lines enact their sense of drift, with the result that even while the poem has a recognizable structure, it is a structure that answers to the poem's view of life as fundamentally unpatterned and nearly amorphous without human creativity.

For Purdy, poetry is *poesis*, and a poem is something made, like an Inuit cairn, because of human desire, will, and craft. The poet is like the carpenter in 'Carpenter's Notebook Entry' (*PB*, 119): his work is coextensive and connected with the realm of necessity – in this case the building of a house – but it is simultaneously also free from it and a supplement to it. Thus the carpenter carves 'a unicorn with a clasp knife / at one end of the gable roof' after having finished the work he was paid to do. Like the poet, who can never be sure whether anyone will read his work or, having read it, see its value, the carpenter takes pleasure in simply having created it and knowing that, for a short term, it will outlive him, thus granting him a paradoxical 'immortality.' I emphasize the idea of poetry as a making, a craft, and the poet as a *homo faber*, because I don't want Purdy to be misinterpreted as making neo-Romantic claims for poetry of the kind we associate with Shelley, Yeats, or Layton.

Where does this leave 'Gondwanaland,' that grave and ponderous meditation on mortality? As in 'The Darkness,' 'what this comes to is religion / not the conventional stuff.' It's as unconventional, personal, and radically 'protestant' as Lawrence's since its epiphanies and 'coherence' depend ultimately, as Purdy recognizes, on the self. 'The Darkness' may refer to 'a god's coherence' and an early version of 'Gondwanaland' may refer to messages from 'the stone gods,' but the only account we have – and can have – of religion or meaning is the poem itself. In a manner of speaking, whatever it is that the poet is 'waiting' for in 'The Darkness' is already available in the poem since his mind has already encompassed the universe. The implications of the poem's epistemology, like the specialist's anticipated comment in 'The Stone Bird,' turn us back to the poet. For him, for us, what gives the universe its coherence, in this poem and anywhere else, is his (and our) imagination, however troubling and finally unsatisfactory we may find the self as the ground of ultimate value and being. These poems simultaneously express the desire for presence, unity, and totality and show their impossibility except in subjective terms. In the end, it is only the transfigurative power of language that momentarily convinces us that there is a 'coherence' and what Charles Taylor calls 'a human-independent ontic order'[17] or that the 'song of life' can be heard by anyone who will listen, and, if heard, will mean what the poet claims for it. We may want to follow Taylor in trying to save the vision from subjectivity by separating the 'matter' of the poem from what he would call its 'subjective manner,' but that may not be possible in dealing with visionary experience and figurative language.

To point this out doesn't seem to me to call the more positive moments of Purdy's vision into doubt. Instead, this allows us to see them as parts of an evolving vision, a single poem recording moments of affirmation and questioning, of faith and celebration as well as doubt and near despair. It is also an inevitable reminder of the problematic conditions under which every post-Romantic 'religious' poet writes: this is as true of Wordsworth and Whitman as it is of Rilke, Milosz, and Purdy. It is no exaggeration to say that the poets of the spirit in the twentieth century have as often written of doubt as of faith: the affirmations of the latter have often been glimpsed only through a full engagement with the former. Purdy is no exception. Almost every poem celebrating and accepting life as it is or enacting / embodying being, also contains a hint of doubt – often indicated by nothing more than a verbal mood, a 'perhaps,' a 'maybe' – or else is answered elsewhere in *The Collected Poems* by a poem reluctant to make any religious claims on life at all. I don't want to go as far as Trilling did when he called Frost 'a terrifying poet,' but I do see Purdy as a writer aware of the limitations of his affirmative or religious vision because of his awareness of and inability to comprehend – in both senses of the word – 'the terrible things of human life.'[18] And, as one would expect, the most prominent among these is death, which from *The Enchanted Echo* on is a pervasive theme in the poems.

Not surprisingly, a radical unease about poetry and about life often appears in poems dealing with suffering and, especially, death. In many of the celebratory poems, death is simply an inevitable part of life to be accepted with all the other aspects of our existence. The gentle ending of 'The Darkness' is a good example, and the early 'Spring Song' (*PAA* [1962], 27) makes a similar point but with a resilient humour. But there is another side of Purdy – a tragic Proteus – whose response is less resigned, less willing to accept what is inevitable. A comment made to Earle Birney in 1971 about Rilke points us to this aspect: 'Rilke is sort of 'accept,' 'accept!' which I don't like. (I'm fucked if I'll accept a lot of things.) A kind of roseate look at depression and death. One accepts, but one dammit doesn't have to like it, stoicism is too damn Greek for me. I want to be the cat yowling on the backyard fence sometimes.'[19] Rilke's attempt, especially in the *Duino Elegies*, to treat death as the inevitable complement of life is well-known. In a letter to his Polish translator, he wrote that 'AFFIRMATION OF LIFE AND AFFIRMATION OF DEATH REVEAL THEMSELVES AS ONE. *To concede the one without the other is, as is here experienced and celebrated, a restriction that finally excludes all infinity. Death is our reverted, our unilluminated*, SIDE OF LIFE: *we must try to achieve the greatest possible consciousness of our existence, which is at home in* BOTH OF THESE UNLIMITED PROVINCES, *which is* INEXHAUSTIBLY NOURISHED OUT OF BOTH.'[20] In another letter, in which he consoles a young wife abandoned by her husband, Rilke writes of a death 'not accepted as an extinction, but imagined as an altogether surpassing intensity.'[21] What I have called Purdy's acceptance of death certainly doesn't go this far towards a mysticism that seems like a substitute for a Christian attitude to death Rilke is no longer able to accept. But in Purdy's case, the resigned, melioristic, quietist acceptance of poems like 'The Darkness,' 'Gondwanaland,' and, more recently, 'Questions' (*WS*, 64) is challenged by the anger, frustration, and resistance of poems dealing with meaningless suffering and death; the following are representative – the several versions of 'Elegy for a Grandfather,' 'Evergreen Cemetery' (*CP*, 33), 'Dead Seal' (*CP*, 96), 'My Cousin Don' (*CP*, 333), and 'The Smell of Rotten Eggs' (*CP*, 366). If they were published as a group, their collective epigraph could be Thomas's 'Rage, rage against the dying of the light.' If juxtaposed to the other poems, they serve to remind us how close to naturalism Purdy's 'vision' can be. An optimistic or positive version of this can be found in a fragment from Euripides that Purdy quotes on two occasions in the 1990s:

And every seed
Earth-gendered back to earth shall pass,
And back to heaven the seeds of sky;
Seeing all things into all may range
And, sundering, show new shapes of change,
But never that which is shall die.   *RBS*, 197

But an acquiescent and celebratory attitude to the world disappears if one has little to celebrate or if one is overwhelmed by despair ('In the Darkness of Cities,' 'Tarahumara Women,' 'Sestina on a Train' [*CP*, 214, 344, 50]). At that point, the affirmations of nature poems and atavistic imaginings of origins begin to seem like near pastoral evasions of what William James calls 'the evil facts' that are 'a genuine portion of reality.'[22] Without the ballast of the 'creatural realism' of this second group, the affirmations of the earlier poems – however fine the poems may be – don't seem earned, as if an affirmation and acceptance of life were being offered without 'a full look at the worst' (Hardy, 'De Profundis').

Another way of putting this would be to say that the pulling of 'the dark velvet curtains' of death at the ending of 'The Darkness' (*CP*, 277) is charged with greater significance and emotion if we remember not only the deaths of animals mentioned earlier in the poem but also the more troubling ending of 'The Smell of Rotten Eggs':

I have always tried to avoid unpleasant things
bad smells – death – physical pain
and never been able to
flowers stink beauty rots gods die
we can hardly seize one good instant
of sunlight for ourselves and hold onto it
in our minds before it turns monster
It is no panacea
to describe these various aspects of horror
and no help to name the names of things
nevertheless I name names   *CP*, 366

'The Darkness' doesn't become a better poem *as poem* if we recall these or similar lines, but its vision, and Purdy's vision as a whole, gains in stature because of the gain in emotional comprehensiveness and consequent complexity and profundity. It doesn't make his vision tragic, but it establishes a constitutive counterpoint between, on the one hand, its small and large affirmations and, on the other, 'the terrible actualities of life' and its tragedy.[23] Faced with 'the massed nothingness' of the night sky in 'The Darkness' and the 'savagery' of a friend's death in 'The Smell of Rotten Eggs,' the poet responds with the words that he knows can't even offer a 'panacea.' Nevertheless, like an old mill, tent rings, ivory swans, a chimney, and rock paintings, the poems offer an assertion of human order and potentially lasting and transcendent value in the face of 'the abyss of time and the tragedy of human transience.'[24]

I want to close by suggesting that the elegies and the more general poems about death should be read as continuous with the historical poems and those concerned with being. They are all engagements with loss, their verses shadowed by a plangent awareness of human transience. Even as the poems protest against or resist death's 'all oblivious enmity' (Shakespeare's Sonnet 55), the poet recognizes the futility of the gesture, since the majority of poems and poets are eventually forgotten. I would even extend this point to those poems that are clearly acts of acceptance and celebration. However affirmative they may seem, the affirmation is often clearly conditional, dependent as it is on the self's imagination, the contingency of the moment, and the reader's awareness, provided by other poems in the volume, that *this* moment cannot be separated from what Shakespeare calls 'the dark backward and abysm of time.' The latter doesn't frighten Purdy, but he recognizes that he writes against it and the oblivion it implies. I assume this is what he means when he calls poetry 'the word that slanders death' (*RBS*, 285). Perhaps it's particularly appropriate to end a reading of Purdy's poetry with a discussion of being and death since the topics, more obviously than any others, conflate the distance between the local and the universal, Ameliasburg and Alexandria. In these late poems, perhaps more obviously than ever before, the Canadian poet stands on his roof and surveys the universe in poems 'reflecting the present reiterating the past / reconnoitring the future' (*CP*, 314).[25]

We seem to have travelled far from Ameliasburg, but it may be a sign of our lingering provincialism if we can't imagine that a poetry that is simultaneously a poetry of the nation and a poetry of Being can be written anywhere, even in a 'burg / named after a German dumpling named Amelia' (*CP*, 57), or by anyone, even Al 'something or other.'

8

Conclusion: The Future of the Past

Canada has always, in my memory, *always* been on the verge of dissolution.

... to be a world poet, so-called, I think you hafta come from a country a place and a time, and be somewhat involved in those concerns. Of course you can easily refute that concept, but it's mine and I'm stuck with it.

Al Purdy[1]

The present is not always the future that the past had in mind. However prescient or open-minded our best and worst writers may have been about the future of a country they often called the Dominion of Canada, none, while they were doing their portion of nation building, could possibly have anticipated the contemporary nation: a country that, on the one hand, has been described for several years running by the United Nations as the best place to live in the world and, on the other, is constantly calling its existence into question and even seems perpetually on the verge of dissolution. The ideas of nation and nationalism that they passed down are today at best ghost narratives within our contemporary literature, history, and systems of education. And multiculturalism, the fashionable if self-contradictory 'nationalism' of the end of the century, is challenging even the residual validity of these.

The old masters would not have been surprised, however, by the fact that the literature they had started and nurtured, in journals and anthologies that they knew to be colonial and second-rate, had finally produced a poet fit for our occasions and whose work expressed our sense of being in the world as Canadians – a point of view on the world and a way of being human rooted in the Canadian landscape, experience, and history. As I have argued throughout this book, this is one of Purdy's major claims on our attention and one of the bases of his substantial reputation and his historical importance. He represents the culmination and fulfilment of an important, even constitutive, strand in our national and literary histories. Paradoxically because he is also the best Canadian poet to have yet appeared, he also represents – with the best poets of his generation (Layton and Avison) – a beginning, a point at which Canadian poetry can enter without embarrassment the imaginary anthology of international contemporary poetry. Though the distinction is an artificial one, nevertheless it is necessary to emphasize again that his importance for us as a national poet is ultimately inseparable from the fact that we can make this claim for him as a first-rate poet. As I mentioned earlier, if his best poems didn't convince and move us *as* poems spoken in an inimitable voice, then his vision of the nation would be only slightly more relevant than Wilson MacDonald's. Nor would poets as different as Dennis Lee and Tom Wayman be interested in the particular national patrimony envisioned in his body of work. The presence of Margaret Atwood, George Bowering, Patrick Lane, and Dennis Lee as speakers at the Al Purdy Tribute at Toronto's International Authors Festival in October 1997 was a reminder of a certain lineage within Canadian literature, and Lee's reading of 'The Country North of Belleville' pointed to one of the reasons for Purdy's centrality – the poet as someone for whom our being in the world and our being in the world as Canadians are inseparable.

Among the ironies of this achievement is that it occurs in what one could call an era of irony that flies the banner of postmodern and postcolonial ideology for which terms like nation and national poetry are either radically redefined or offered in quotation marks. A cursory reading of the Canadian anthologies of the past two decades shows that, with the expected exceptions, the images, myths, rhetoric, and narratives of nation are no longer present even as ghosts. Words like 'nation,' 'country,' and 'Canada,' and their cognates have disappeared from the poetic vocabulary as completely as Augustan epithets did at the turn of the nineteenth century. The impersonal vocative, the 'you' with which Purdy invokes a community and a nation, as well as the inclusive 'we' that performs the same function, have been replaced in the work of the younger poets by pronouns referring almost always only to a lover, a family member, or a personal relationship. This reduction in scope and ambition is particularly noticeable in the poetry of women, where politics and history have become gender-specific and politics has been reduced to, in Mary di Michele's words, 'what we consciously choose to value, how we are *determined* to live.'² Such a narrowing of the limits of lyric can, of course, be defended as simply a return to what lyric poetry has always done best, the subjective account or reflection of a specific experience. And there's no doubt that many of Purdy's poems fit comfortably in this particular line in the history of the genre.

Yet, in the end, Purdy's reputation as a poet would not be as substantial as it is had he not stretched the boundaries of the Canadian lyric in order to do more with a poem than one saw in and expected from his contemporaries. Like Lawrence, Neruda, and Milosz he refashioned the forms that he inherited in order to make them expressive of his particular vision, his particular Canadian way of being in the world. He did this at a time in the Canadian experience when one could still respond affirmatively to the question 'Is poetry still an essential and necessary way in which that truth happens which is decisive for our historical experience, or is poetry no longer of this character?'³

Looking back on the second of Heidegger's questions from the vantage-point of the end of the century, I am tempted to answer that Canadian poetry 'is no longer of this character' and that Purdy's major work, the poems written between 1960 and 1985, stands now as a reminder of visionary historical and political possibilities acted on by neither Canadians nor the state nor most of our poets. It is in this context that I call him the first and last of our poets. Nearly countless readings, authors' festivals, and literary prizes may be of value, but they do not have a necessary connection with a truly national literature or the vision of a nation. If his poems of the 1960s, when Purdy developed his voice and his poetic, can be said to have been part of the nationalist current of that era, the poetry written during the past twenty years, but especially since *The Stone Bird* (1981), is written implicitly against the political, aesthetic, and ideological currents of the past two decades. Simply by remaining wholly indifferent to fashion and loyal to the vision he first articulated in the 1960s, Purdy found in the 1980s that his new poems constituted an implicit reminder of the road abandoned and of possibilities undeveloped by the majority of the younger Canadian writers. (An analogous relationship exists between Hugh Hood's shamefully neglected series *The New Age* and Rudy Wiebe's historical novels and contemporary Canadian fiction.) The entire issue may, of course, be irrelevant if today we choose to answer 'no' to the first of Heidegger's challenging questions: 'Is poetry still an essential and necessary way in which that truth happens which is decisive for our historical experience?' I suspect that even Purdy and Layton, the Canadian modernists who made the largest claims for poetry, would probably see those claims today as part of a particular historical moment. There is a sense in which the several elegies for writers in Purdy's last four collections are also a collective lament for Canadian poetry, or, if that overstates the case, for the kind of writing he believes in and the national vision implicit in it. The absence of any potentially major poets under thirty-five might lend support to the former assertion.

This pessimistic conclusion about poetry and nation would seem belied by the optimistic afterword of *To Paris Never Again* (1997), his most recent collection, until one notices the temporal shift in the following passage from the present to some vague almost ahistorical future:

... I think of that United Nations agency that listed Canada first among the best countries in the world in which to live. I forget how that listing was phrased. It doesn't matter anyway; I knew it all along – the United Nations didn't tell me a thing. I expect it to go on, move forward into the future, a country recognizable as the one I've been talking about here. Its people, of course, will be shaped by time and resemble only distant relations of their forebears. But they will be there, anyway, all of us will – in shapes we really can't anticipate, another presence among people on the street, like the memory of a white bird on the wind. The land will remain too. And all of us, the shape-changers, the transitory immortals, evolution's animals, we shall be there as well. (127)

The first-person-plural pronoun and the oracular tone carry us from a specific historical moment to a timeless future, from a particular political and historical identity to what is at best a generic one – 'the transitory immortals, evolution's animals' – in which all our historical markings are lost. It seems to me that there are two possible interpretations here; for the sake of neatness they can be called the optimistic and the pessimistic, and readers attentive to the implications of my title will know which I prefer. The optimistic reading would see the shift from the temporal to the timeless as evidence of the poet's awareness that the forms of the future cannot be predicted, that the best he can do is point us in a certain direction and indicate its general outlines. The pessimist would reply that Purdy's swerve away from history in the second part implies something darker, something the poet as a historical dark interpreter would rather leave unsaid: of course, 'we' will still be here in the future, but I'm not sure that we will be here as Canadians. A Canadian state may still exist, but it won't be a nation.

Annotating the Poems of Al Purdy: Quotation, Allusion, Echo, and (Some) References

Why do poets in particular resent the attribution of the influence of other poets? The customary answer to this is that it gives them the appearance of being second-hand. That may be one of the aspects of what seems to me to be the true answer. It seems to me that the true answer is that with a true poet his poetry is the same thing as his vital self. It is not possible for anyone else to touch it ... And, of course, I am no more interested in influencing people than you are. My interest is to write my own poetry just as yours is to write your own poetry.

Wallace Stevens to Richard Eberhart, 20 January 1954[1]

If someone had shown me the above title eight years ago, just before I began research on this book, I would have anticipated a relatively short list or catalogue of the various literary traces in Purdy's poems. Like most of Purdy's readers and critics I tended to think of him as a 'native,' 'redneck,' or 'democratic' poet rather than as a 'cosmopolitan,' 'paleface,' or 'aristocratic' one (the familiar terms are A.J.M. Smith's, Philip Rahv's, and W.H. Auden's), with the concomitant assumption that it was only the second group who wrote conscious of the relationship of the individual talent to the tradition of poetry in English. In other words, when I thought of 'literary' Canadian poets, those whose work would at some point need the kind of annotation we take for granted with Arnold or Eliot, the names that came to mind were A.J.M. Smith, Ralph Gustafson, A.M. Klein, and Margaret Avison. This is a view of Purdy, and I suspect a relatively common one, based on a number of factors. Purdy, like Whitman, has made no secret of his lack of formal education: no other major Canadian poet dropped out of school as early as he did (grade 10). There's also the often anti-intellectual persona of the interviews, public readings, and critical prose. For instance, although the preface to *The Collected Poems* (1986) surveys Purdy's life and career and comments on some of the poets who were essential influences, it closes on a completely different note:

In a world so abundant with both good and bad things, in which my own unique lighted space of human consciousness burns and flickers, at this moment when the past and future converge to pinpoint now, at an age when the body says, 'Slow down, you silly bugger,' there are still important things in my life, and still poems I want to write.

Which is a very long sentence: it makes me thirsty for a beer or two. And it occurs to me that if I were aboard a rowboat floating in the middle of all the beer I've drunk in a lifetime, I'd never be able to see the shore. (xviii)

This leaves the reader with an image of the poet similar to the one in 'At the Quinte Hotel,' a poem written in 1968 and a staple of Purdy's public readings ever since. As I wrote earlier, the poem is set in a hotel not far from Purdy's Ameliasburg home, and dramatizes, in the first person, an encounter in a bar between a poet, who sounds like Purdy, and his ultimately uncomprehending 'public.' Like several other of his well-known poems, this one seems grounded in and directly expressive of his experiences, and its primary allegiance seems to be to life rather than art. The absence from it of any allusions, quotations, or echoes from other poems reinforces this impression. The poetics implicit in the poem are much closer to Whitman and Williams than to Eliot or Avison.

But that this represents only one side of Purdy becomes obvious if we juxtapose the poem to 'The Uses of History,' written in the early 1980s. Both are set in bars; both explore the relationship between the poet and his immediate environment; and both evince the same poetic. Yet, as I pointed out above, the later poem refracts the events in the lounge through the speaker's reading in history, and counterpoints the strip-tease and its effect on the 'patrons' to events in 'the 16th century / Hindu kingdom of Vijayanagar' and the local stripper to a legendary concubine as well as to 'the Venus of Willendorf.' Along the way, the poet playfully, with tongue in allusive cheek, compares his situation to 'Thoreau's at Walden Pond.' It would be tempting, but misleading, to attribute the presence of literary and historical allusions and references to the poet's growing maturity as a poet, his growing willingness to layer and mediate his experiences through other texts. Even a cursory glance at the published and unpublished poems of the 1940s, 1950s, and 1960s reveals not only a poetry engaged in and struggling with the Canadian, English, and American traditions but also poems reflecting on both poetry and, ekphrastically, on art. There is also the evidence of the letters, reviews, and prefaces, all of which reveal a poet educating himself and discovering a poetic. A representative comment occurs in the little-known preface to *A Handful of Earth* (1977): 'Northrop Frye's dictum that poems are created from poems seems to me partially true, in the sense that if other people's poems hadn't been written you couldn't have written your own. In that sense, what each of us writes balances and juggles the whole history of literature, and we are for that moment the "midland navel stone of the earth."' The style may be closer to Whitman than to Eliot, but 'balances and juggles the whole history of literature' is just another way of talking about tradition and the individual talent.

As my chronologically arranged catalogue shows, the poems written before *Poems for All the Annettes* (1962) are often overwhelmed in a variety of ways by the poets Purdy has been reading in his attempt to get beyond the dead end represented by Bliss Carman, the tutelary genius of *The Enchanted Echo* (1944). Many of the poems in *Pressed on Sand* (1955), *Emu! Remember* (1956), and *The Crafte So Longe to Lerne* (1959) show Purdy trying out voices and styles, going to school in modern poetry from Hopkins to Layton. One often has the impression of a poet trying to kick-start a poem into being by imitating some of the powerful (and, with Hopkins and Thomas, inimitable) poets he has been reading. The poems in the collections of the 1950s seem in retrospect derivative, exercises in imitation; in the terms of Milton's definition of 'Plagiare,' they are a 'kind of borrowing ... not bettered by the borrower' (*Iconoclastes*, XXIII). Once Purdy finds his own voice with *Poems for All the Annettes* (1962), *The Cariboo Horses* (1965), *North of Summer* (1967), and *Wild Grape Wine* (1968), his own line, voice, rhythm, and imagery are either free of influence or absorb and subdue the tradition to his own measure. Occasional traces of other poems are still present, but they occur less frequently and are always subordinate to Purdy's voice. And although I haven't kept count of the various intertextual presences in each of the three periods of Purdy's work, I have the strong impression that there are proportionally fewer in the collections between *Poems for All the Annettes* (1962) and *The Stone Bird* (1980) than in the periods that precede (1938–62) and follow (1980 to the present).

Purdy's third period begins with *The Stone Bird* (1980), published in his sixty-first year, and is characterized by a more open and frequent use of borrowed images and quotations. It's as if having established himself and confident of his own talent, Purdy can now imagine a new relationship between his body of work and the tradition of western poetry within which he has struggled to find a place for it. There is an anticipation of this in 1978 in the 'Introduction' to *Being Alive: Poems 1958–78*; 'Bestiary [II],' which lists and offers impressionistic responses to poets Purdy admires, is the most obvious sign in the poems of this change in attitude. Similarly significant is the more open engagement with D.H. Lawrence, one of his acknowledged masters and perhaps the most important influence on his view of poetry and life. If I'm right, Purdy could address Lawrence in a poem and continue the dialogue in a variety of forms only after he had written the major poems that established his reputation. Looked at from another viewpoint, Purdy could only risk incorporating the words of the poems of his heroes – from Archilochus to Yeats, Auden, and Lawrence – when he was confident that his own poetic voice would not be overwhelmed by theirs. By juxtaposing Purdy's voice to Akhmatova's ('The Prison Lines at Leningrad' [*WS*, 4]), Lawrence's ('The Death of DHL' [*CP*, 321]) and Yeats's, Auden's, and Rilke's ('Touchings' [*NSM*, 102]), the later poems tacitly suggest that he now belongs in their company. In Purdy's case, the Freudian/Bloomian *agon* with one's predecessors ends when the ephebe or later poet feels confident enough to address them as equals – or perhaps simply to address them at all.

The following catalogue of annotations lists the various kinds of intertextual presence that I have found in Purdy's published and unpublished poems. With the former I have tried to be comprehensive, even listing quotations or allusions I have so far been unable to trace. With the unpublished work, of which there is a great deal especially from the 1930s and 1940s, I have chosen poems important either because they tell us something about Purdy's reading or because aspects of them reappear in work published later. As will be obvious, for the most part I restrict my annotations to traces or residues – allusions, echoes, and quotations – of literary texts. But in order to make the catalogue more useful to those interested in tracing Purdy's reading, I have also sometimes annotated references to novelists, poets, and travel writers, though I am less interested in references than I am in allusions. For the most part, however, I have annotated epigraphs, references, quotations, allusions, instances of parody or pastiche, and echoes of rhyme, rhythm, metre, and syntax patterns. In some cases I have the impression that my reach has exceeded my grasp to the point that I might be accused of what I.A. Richards called 'mnemonic irrelevance.' Needless to say, I shall be grateful to receive corrections and supplements and to include them with due acknowledgment in any revised edition, monograph on Purdy's reading, or perhaps on an Al Purdy web site.

The system of annotation is self-explanatory. Each book has a roman numeral; individual poems have Arabic numbers (the page number or location of the poem is given in parentheses after the title); the details annotated in a poem are assigned separate letters. Thus when I cross-reference to VII. 3. A – VII is *Poems for All the Annettes*, 3 is 'Spring Song,' and A is 'Include me out of it all?' In citing or noting texts I have kept, for the most part, to the following rule: poems that are well-known are simply named or quoted without reference to a text or edition (for example, Marvell's 'To His Coy Mistress'); less well-known poems, by the Australian-English music critic W.J. Turner (1889–1946), for instance, are provided with a brief citation in the text and a full one in the bibliography. If no date is indicated for a poem that exists only in manuscript that means that the manuscript is undated and that I have been unable to date the manuscript on internal evidence.

I Poems Uncollected or Unpublished (1938–66) (from the Purdy Papers at the University of Saskatchewan and at Queen's University)

1. 'Bliss Carman' (Saskatchewan, mss 4/3/7)
A. This is an unpublished three-page indirect tribute to Carman, a celebration of the return of spring written in the earlier poet's style. The poem is part of a hand-bound collection titled 'Song of the Restless Ones' and dated 26 April 1942: 'Once more the Lord of April / Has tossed his chains aside / And o'er the sleeping swampland / Has crossed the great divide.' Carman's presence is so pervasive in the poems, even as late as 1950, that it would be tedious to catalogue it beyond calling occasional attention to a particularly obvious example to document the case. See, for instance, 'Defence Counsel' (*Canadian Forum*, Aug. 1948, 115) and 'Mallards' (*Canadian Forum*, Sept. 1948, 140).
2. 'Abstract Plans' (*Canadian Forum*, Oct. 1948, 160)
A. 'We shall build our cottage where running water gleams,
   And plant the ground with roses and sow the day with dreams.'
   Compare the opening lines of W.B.Yeats's 'The Lake Isle of Innisfree.'

3.   'Winter Harbour' (*Canadian Poetry Magazine*, Summer 1949, 17)
A.   The poem's organizing image of a ship gradually being absorbed, almost magically, by ice may owe something to Duncan Campbell Scott's 'The Piper of Arll' as well as to Charles G.D. Roberts's 'The Stranded Ship.'
4.   'Poem' (*Canadian Poetry Magazine*, Christmas 1949, 11)
A.   The entire poem is a meditation on G.K. Chesterton's 'Lepanto,' a Purdy favourite. See VII.6.
5.   'Spanish Hilltop' (*Canadian Forum*, June 1950, 67)
A.   'Here, on top of a hill, is El Greco'
     See XV.6.
6.   'Paul Kane' (*Canadian Forum*, May 1951, 43)
A.   'If one should ask, "What is Canadian art?" / Then lead him to the north, the solemn land, / Where Thomson left his brush beside a northern lake ... / And take that stranger gently by the hand: / Here's Morrice with his half-Parisian style, / And Emily Carr whose totems drink the rain: / Then lead your skeptic through the painted past / To where the Indians wait, and say, "Here's Kane."'
7.   'Ex-Lawrencians' (Saskatchewan, mss 4/1/3)
8.   'After You, G.V. Catullus (and Irving Layton)' (Saskatchewan, mss 4/1/3)
A.   Compare the title of Archibald MacLeish's poem, 'You Also, Gaius Valerius Catullus' (*Collected Poems, 1917–1982*, 395). See V.2.B and XXII.11.
9.   '"A la Recherche du Temps Perdu"' (Saskatchewan, mss 4/1/3). See I.11 and IV.2.
10. 'Aspirin for Transients (On a poem by Wallace Stevens)' (Saskatchewan, mss 4/1/4)
A.   Although there is a Canon Aspirin in 'Notes toward a Supreme Fiction' ('It Must Give Pleasure,' v, vi), Purdy's poem is probably written in response to the concern with order in 'Anecdote of the Jar' and 'The Idea of Order at Key West.'
11. 'Proust Again' (Saskatchewan, mss 4/1/4). See I.9, IV.2.
12. 'Word-Symbols' (*Canadian Forum*, June 1957, 69)
A.   'A Renoir's sun shadowy woman inside me / Deciding she likes it there, and Ingres' / Women that Gully Jimson might have done.'
     Gully Jimson is the painter-hero of Joyce Cary's *The Horse's Mouth*.
13. 'Stencils' (*Canadian Forum*, April 1958, 14)
A.   '... but gently I intrude / the Skelton [*sic*] of Yeats' shrieking bird / I saw die.'

The allusion is probably to 'Sailing to Byzantium,' though the bird in that poem doesn't 'shriek,' it sings 'of what is past, or passing, or to come.' Another possibility is the line 'Juno's peacock shrieked' from 'Meditations in Time of Civil War' (*Collected Poems of W.B. Yeats*, 228). I owe the suggestion to W.J. Keith.

14. 'Recommended Reading: Joe Hill and Robinson Jeffers' (Saskatchewan, mss 4/2/9a)

A. 'I read once about Hokusai painting a / big landscape on paper propped 50 feet high that / the first wind blew down ...'
See Purdy's 'Japanese Painter' (*WGW*, 81; XI.9.A.); the title was later changed to '"Old Man Mad about Painting"' (*CP*, 149).

B. 'And reading Robinson Jeffers ...'

15. 'Ezra Pound' (Saskatchewan, mss 4/3/9)

A. 'It took him 77 years to discover / he doesn't know a damn thing ...'
Since Pound was born in 1885, the poem might have been written in 1962. For a later poem about Pound, see 'Pound' in *NSM*, XXV.3.

16. 'The Genealogy of the Sons of Gilbert' (Saskatchewan, mss 4/3/9)

A. 'and she died on the Idaho plains around 1880 / leaving some letters from Canada behind / the sort of sentimental stuff / found in poems by James Whitcomb Riley / or novels by Harold Bell Wright / authors triple named to conquer one dimension.'
A later line indicates that the poem was written in 1965, shortly after two distant American cousins, John and Hazel Master, had given Purdy *The First Purdys in Canada*, a history of the Purdy family.

17. 'Muskoke [*sic*] Elegiac' (Saskatchewan, mss 4/3/14)

A. This is a sequence of sixteen poems. A reference to the death of Winston Churchill in poem 10 dates it as written after 24 January 1965.

B. [1] 'Lady, till the curfew rings / To dispossess us of the things / Let's head out for muskoka.'
Compare Andrew Marvell's 'To His Coy Mistress.'

C. [3] 'Dusk, and the bright air falls / like light from the leaves, the needles.'
Compare Thomas Nashe's 'Summer's Last Will and Testament': 'Brightness falls from the air; / Queens have died young and fair; / Dust hath closed Helen's eye.' (ll. 1588–1600).

D. [9] 'Looney with sunlight, van [*sic*] Gogh stood and stared / into the wicker inferno, and stared until / those manic eyeballs blazed in contemplation. / What made a dowdy chair become volcanic?'
See Van Gogh's painting 'The Chair and the Pipe,' also called 'Van Gogh's Chair.' See also XXVI.10.B.

E.   [10] 'Monroe and Einstein, Churchill, Hemingway: / built their lives
     in time and time said no.'
F.   'Mortal! At the crack of that one word / we rise to our inheritance'
     Compare Keats's 'Ode to a Nightingale': 'Forlorn! The very word is
     like a bell.'
G.   [11] 'Rilke, master of ripeness, and the things' / celebrant, rapt, be
     near us in limbo' and 'Oh Rilke, work your lovely fraud / for we
     who are your music must applaud'
     See VIII.5.A, XX.7.A, and XXVI.11.
H.   [16] 'If there's one thing that really cleans you out / it's blas-
     phemy. / Wasn't much to it; I mean I heard Frye, / looked through
     Blake, and thought I'd have a go.'
18. 'After Yeats's "Lapis Lazuli"'
A.   This was probably written at the same time as 'At Evergreen Ceme-
     tery'; the latter was published in *Canadian Forum*, Dec. 1958, 205.

II   *The Enchanted Echo* (1944)

1.   'The Enchanted Echo' (11)
A.   In diction, syntax, and overall style the poem is derivative Carman.
2.   'The Lights Go On' (13)
A.   The poem alludes to Ben Jonson's 'Song: To Celia': 'The streets
     where Shakespeare strolled and Jonson strayed / With Celia long.'
     The poem also refers to 'Herrick's song.'
3.   'Erinna's Song' (14)
A.   Again, Carman's is the predominant influence, but the last stanza
     may echo William Wordsworth's 'She Dwelt among Untrodden
     Ways' and, closer to home, Duncan Campbell Scott's 'Delos.'
4.   'Summons to Vagabonds' (16)
A.   See Carman's 'Vagabond Song' as well as various other 'vagabond'
     poems from the *Songs from Vagabondia* and its successors.
5.   'Votaries of April' (18)
A.   The opening – 'Oh, up my lads, 'tis April' – is clearly from A.E.
     Housman, while later phrases such as 'the chant of Arcady' and 'a
     Piper's song' echo Carman.
6.   'Ghenghis Khan' (27)
A.   The poem has five stanzas of five lines each with the third and
     fourth lines ending with the same word: 'From Cathay unto Europe,
     / The rock frontiers of Europe.' The repetition and rhythm remind
     me of Alfred Noyes's 'The Highwayman': 'He whistled a tune to the

window, and who should be waiting there / But the landlord's black-eyed daughter / Bess, the landlord's daughter, / Plaiting a dark red love-knot into her long black hair.' See also XVI.1, XX.12.A.

7. 'The Sprite' (28)
A. The poem mentions Sappho. See also XIV.1.

8. 'Tamerlane the Limper' (29)
A. The reference to 'Samarcand' (a name that occurs frequently in Purdy's early work) could be a memory of Carman's 'The Ships of Yule': 'With figs and dates from Samarkand.' W.J. Keith has drawn my attention to James Elroy Flecker's very popular *The Golden Journey to Samarkand* (1913).

9. 'A Remembrance' (33)
A. Again, the poem is an imitation of Carman.

10. 'Dramatis Personae' (38)
A. See Hardy's 'Haunting Fingers (a Phantasy in a Museum of Musical Instruments),' where the instruments speak of their former owners, as here the furniture and parts of the room discuss their former occupants.

11. 'François Villon' (42)
12. 'The Age of Machines (With apologies for Mr Kipling)' (57)
13. 'Earth's Benediction' (62)
A. The final line, 'a pilgrim bound for the quiet sea,' could pass for Carman.

III *Pressed on Sand* (1955)

1. 'I See No Hand' (3)
A. 'No men in the tide-walking town of time could / Clamber from the phoenix flesh'
Both 'the tide-walking town of time' and 'phoenix flesh' echo Dylan Thomas. 'Tide' is a frequent noun in Thomas's poems and occurs on seven occasions in a compound form (for instance, 'tide-looped' in 'I make this in a warring absence' [*Collected Poems 1934–1952*, 78]). He uses 'phoenix' twice in 'Unluckily for a Death' (91). For other echoes of Thomas's poems see Peter Stevens's 'In the Raw: the Poetry of A.W. Purdy,' *Canadian Literature*, no. 28 (Spring 1966), 24.
B. 'You! you over there, collapsed on your awkward stilts, / We shall run together again.'
The first line has echoes of T.S. Eliot's 'The Waste Land,' 'Stetson! / You who were with me in the ships at Mylae!' and of Irving Lay-

ton's 'Whatever Else Poetry Is Freedom,' 'And now I balance on wooden stilts and dance / ... / Space for these stilts! More space or I fail!' (*Collected Poems*, 175)

W.J. Keith has also drawn my attention to Yeats's 'High Talk': 'Processions that lack high stilts have nothing that catches the eye. / What if my great-granddad had a pair that were twenty-foot high, / And mine were but fifteen foot, no modern stalks upon higher' (*CPWBY*, 385). For a confirmation that Purdy knows the poem see '"Malachi Stilt-Jack Am I"' in *Cariboo Horses* (51) – the title is a quotation from the same Yeats poem (VIII 9).

2.   'Far Traveller' (7)
A.   Bliss Carman
3.   'Barriers' (9)
A.   'Black kraken country' and 'ultramarine' are from Malcolm Lowry, the former from the poem 'No Kraken shall be found till sought by name,' the latter from the novel *Ultramarine*. Purdy quotes from the poem in his essay 'Malcolm Lowry' (see *Starting from Ameliasburgh*, 247).
B.   Compare 'weed-forged fetter' to William Blake's 'mind-forged manacles' in 'London.'

IV   *Emu! Remember* (1956)

1.   'Poem' (3)
A.   There are several echoes of Irving Layton's 'The Birth of Tragedy' and 'The Cold Green Element' (*CP*, 64, 175): 'birds' wings' recalls 'robins' wings,' and 'grasses grow green' recalls 'green air,' from 'The Birth of Tragedy'; 'candles burning in space / For a hunchback prince' conflates images from both: 'while someone from afar off / blows birthday candles for the world' ('The Birth of Tragedy') and 'One of those / for whom the lightning was too much / and grew a brilliant / hunchback with a crown of leaves' ('The Cold Green Element'). See also Layton's 'The Poet Entertains Several Ladies': 'The solid hunchback, the poet said ...' (*CP*, 85, 87). Incidentally, I wonder whether Layton's line 'blows birthday candles for the world' doesn't echo Yeats's 'Bid me strike a match and blow' from 'In Memory of Eva Gore-Booth and Con Markiewicz (*CPWBY*, 263).' See XIX.1.A.
2.   'Proust' (7)
A.   For earlier references to Proust see I.9 and I.11.

3.   'In Mid-Atlantic' (8)
A.   The poem seems written in the shadow of Gerard Manley Hop-
     kins's 'The Wreck of the Deutschland,' though Hopkins's presence
     is less a matter of style than of the overall mood of peril and a hand-
     ful of suggestive details: the 'midnight' of stanza 4 calls to mind
     Hopkins's note that the ship went down 'between midnight and
     morning'; 'halls of trembling glass' brings together Hopkins's 'I am
     soft sift / In an hourglass' and the dominant rhyme of the fourth
     stanza, wall/fall/tall, which is recalled in Purdy's 'halls.' The 'sup-
     plicating shapes' and the 'Sea voices crying in the night outside'
     remind me of the nun's cry. Finally, 'carrion gods of the water' bor-
     rows the adjective of Hopkins's sonnet 'Carrion Comfort.'
4.   'Invocation' (9)
A.   The compound adjectives – 'foot-heart-beat audible / And terror-
     telling,' 'sky-falling torrents,' 'The horse-clopping, the bell-ringing
     time of earth, / The cloud-beaten, wind-bullied hammers of blood'
     – recall Hopkins and Thomas. Incidentally, Thomas uses the word
     'hammer' seven times in various poems. Purdy, as I suggested ear-
     lier, often uses the word and its variants when dealing with death.
5.   'The Cave Painters' (14)
A.   'Ticked in the salmon sky and soundless wood' echoes Dylan Tho-
     mas's 'In the torrent salmon sun' ('Author's Prologue,' *Collected
     Poems 1934–52*, ix).
6.   'Post Script' (15)
A.   '... like a proud Queen' echoes A.J.M. Smith's well-known 'Like an
     Old Proud King in a Parable.'
B.   'At Valladolid in drizzling rain'
     Compare Browning's 'How It Strikes a Contemporary': 'You saw go
     up and down Valladolid / A man of mark.'
7.   'Flies in Amber' (16)
A.   The archaic spellings in the last three lines may owe something to
     Birney's 'Anglosaxon Street' and 'Mappemounde' (*The Collected
     Poems of Earle Birney*, I, 74, 92).

V   *The Crafte So Longe to Lerne* (1959)

1.   The title is from the opening line of Chaucer's *Parliament of Fowls*:
     'The lyf so short, the craft so long to lerne.' In *The Collected Poems of
     Al Purdy* the title becomes *The Crafte So Long to Lerne*.
2.   'Villanelle [plus 1]' (4)

A. The epigraph 'Disdain, my verse, the language of the age ...' is from John Heath-Stubbs's 'The Language of the Age' (*The Triumph of the Muse*, 1).

B. There is a reference to 'Catullus' as one who 'once defined bad taste / In pimps and whores.' Purdy probably read Catullus in the Horace Gregory translation he mentions in the 1966 review of *The Collected Poems of Irving Layton* (*SA*, 211). See also I.8. and XXII.11.

3. 'From the Chin P'ing Mei' (12)

A. *Chin P'ing Mei* is a sixteenth-century Chinese novel.

4. 'On the Decipherment of "Linear B"' (16)

A. 'And over the island a south wind blowing ...'
The line is probably taken from Leonard Cottrell's *The Bull of Minos*. Cottrell quotes John Pendlebury's *The Archaeology of Crete*: '"And, in the last decade of the fifteenth century on a spring day, when a strong south wind was blowing which carried the flames of the burning beams horizontally northward, Knossos fell ..."' (187).

B. '"Horse vehicle, painted red, supplied with reins."'
The first four words are quoted in Cottrell from the translation of a tablet 'from the armoury of Knossos' (240).

5. 'At Roblin Lake' (17)

A. The speaker's capture of a frog in the third stanza – 'This walking-morning I make a shore-capture, / With hands – having no air rifle' – seems a response to Layton's 'Cain,' in which the speaker shoots a frog in the back after 'Taking the air rifle from my son's hand.' In *The Collected Poems*, Purdy rewrites the couplet, without reference to Layton's 'air rifle,' as 'Next morning I make a shore-capture, / one frog like an emerald breathing,' (17). It's worth noting that Layton drops the 'air' from 'air rifle' in *A Wild Peculiar Joy*.

B. 'What the wall said to Belshazzar'
See Daniel 5: 25: 'The words inscribed are: "Mene mene tekel u-pharsin."'

6. 'Passport' (21)

A. References to 'Marlowe, Webster.'

7. 'Love Song' (21)

A. 'Shining taller than Holofernes' glinting spears ...'
See the apocryphal book of Judith, though there is no reference to 'glinting spears.'

B. '(Unlike the man delivering beer from Porlock's Grocery).'
The allusion to Coleridge is made explicit in the next line: 'Coleridge knew you and maybe Shelley.' Coleridge refers in the prefa-

tory note to 'Kubla Khan' to 'a person on business from Porlock' who interrupted his attempt to transcribe the lines he had dreamt during 'a profound sleep.' See XV.5.B.

8. 'Gilgamesh and Friend' (23)
A. The poem offers a summary of the action and characters of *The Epic of Gilgamesh*. See also 'My Grandfather' (XXVI.8) and 'Becoming' (XXVI.9).

VI   *The Blur in Between* (1962)

1. 'Twin Heads' (2)
A. Compare Layton's 'Maurer: Twin Heads' (*CP*, 152).
2. 'Bullfrogs' (16)
A. 'their counterpoint / would move Bliss Carman / to iambic hexameter; / rouse Archibald Lampman / to competitive fever.'

VII   *Poems for All the Annettes* (1962)

1. 'Uncle Fred on Côte des Neiges' (11)
A. Compare Layton's 'Family Portrait' (*CP*, 203).
B. Poe may be behind the line 'the crème nepenthe.'
C. The spacing and parentheses in the closing lines may owe something to e.e. cummings. See 'O sweet spontaneous' and 'who's most afraid of love? thou.'
2. 'Negroes on St. Antoine' (19)
A. See Arthur Koestler's *The Gladiators* (213) for a possible echo of 'Spartacus / waiting for ships to come and staring / alone across the Straits of Messina.'
3. 'Spring Song' (27)
A. 'Include me out of it all?'
The comment 'Include me out' has been attributed to Sam Goldwyn.
4. 'Likes and Opposites' (35)
A. Compare Cavafy's 'Waiting for the Barbarians,' though I should mention that I don't know when Cavafy's poem first appeared in English.
5. 'Eli Mandel's Sunday Morning Castle' (41)
A. 'in the salley gardens'
See Yeats's 'Down by the Salley Gardens.'
6. 'O Recruiting Sergeants!' (51)

A. '(a Persian at Marathon, / a Turk at Lepanto)'
    The Lepanto reference probably has its source in G.K. Chesterton's
    poem of the same name, already written about in 'Poem' (see above,
    I.4).
7. 'On Canadian Identity' (47)
A. The quotation 'The high school land' is from Earle Birney's 'Canada:
    Case History: 1945,' while 'A dull people' is from Layton's 'From
    Colony to Nation' (*CP*, 159). I have been unable to identify the third
    quotation, 'A bridge between old land and new,' though it 'feels'
    like Hugh MacLennan. See his letter to George Barrett: 'I see Canada
    as a bridge – a bridge with the ends unjoined' (quoted in Elspeth
    Cameron's *Hugh MacLennan: A Writer's Life*, 155).

VIII   *The Cariboo Horses* (1965)

Though the collection comes without a dedication, the following
note in the Purdy Papers at the University of Saskatchewan indicates that Purdy had one in mind: 'Proposed dedication of *Cariboo*.
To: Charles Bukowski, A.E. Housman, W.H. Auden, Robinson Jeffers, Catullus and Callimachus of Alexandria.' (mss 4/1/4)
1. 'The Cariboo Horses' (7)
A. 'clopping in silence under the toy mountains / dropping sometimes
    and / lost in the dry grass / golden oranges of dung –'
    Compare Pablo Neruda's 'Their rumps were like planets or oranges'
    ('Horses' [*Poems of Five Decades*, 181]).
B. The poem may also owe something to the sense of wonder sur-
    rounding the horses in Edwin Muir's 'Horses' (1925) and 'The
    Horses' (1946) (*Collected Poems*, 19–20, 246–7). In an interview with
    Gary Geddes, Purdy also indicated a debt to Ted Hughes's 'A
    Dream of Horses' (*Lupercal*, 23) and Philip Larkin's 'At Grass' (*Col-
    lected Poems*, 29)
2. 'Malcolm Lowry' (9)
3. 'Song of the Impermanent Husband' (27)
A. Compare D.H. Lawrence's 'Song of a Man Who Is Not Loved,'
    'Song of a Man Who Is Loved,' 'The Song of a Man Who Has Come
    Through' (*Collected Poems of D.H. Lawrence*, 222, 249, 250), all from
    Look! We Have Come Through!
4. 'Portrait' (29)
A. This is obviously a portrait of Layton.
5. 'Mountain Lions in Stanley Park' (33)

A. Compare Rainer Maria Rilke's 'The Panther' (*The Selected Poetry of Rainer Maria Rilke*, 25), D.H. Lawrence's 'Mountain Lion' (*CPDHL*, 401), and Ted Hughes's 'The Jaguar' (*New Selected Poems 1957–1994*, 4).

6. 'In the Wilderness' (35)
A. 'With a Pillar of Fire by day / and a Pillar of Fire by night'
   See Exodus 13: 21: 'And all the time the Lord went before them, by day a pillar of cloud to guide them on their journey, by night a pillar of fire to give them light.'

7. 'Lu Yu (A.D. 1125–1209)' (40)
A. '"marketplace the in / drink more One"'
   Though Lu Yu, a major poet of the Sung era, wrote over 10,000 poems, Purdy told me that the line is his own.

8. 'Ballad of the Despairing Wife' (44)
A. Purdy's note '(After Creeley),' dropped in *Love in a Burning House* (1970), indicates that the poem is a companion piece to Robert Creeley's 'Ballad of the Despairing Husband' (*The New American Poetry*, 80–1).

9. '"Malachi Stilt-Jack Am I"'
A. See Yeats's 'High Talk': 'Malachi Stilt-Jack am I, whatever I learned has run wild, / From collar to collar, from stilt to stilt, from father to child. / All metaphor, Malachi, stilts and all' (*CPWBY*, 385–6). I owe the point to W.J. Keith. See III.1.B.

10. 'A Power' (53)
A. '"a country 29 days from now and we / were a long coming here just then so ..."'
    Compare T.S. Eliot's 'Journey of the Magi': 'A cold coming we had of it' (*The Complete Poems and Plays 1909–1950*, 68).

11. 'The Viper's Muse' (56)
A. '"Canada hath need of thee in this hour she / is a fen"'
    Compare Wordsworth's 'London, 1802': 'Milton! thou shouldst be living at this hour: / England hath need of thee: she is a fen / Of stagnant waters.'
B. 'Ananias' / planet riseth silent gibbous yonder / over Parnassus'
    Compare the last line of Browning's 'Home-Thoughts, from the Sea': 'While Jove's planet rises yonder, silent over Africa.' I owe both to W.J. Keith.

12. 'Dylan' (66)
A. See XI.1 below.

13. 'The Country North of Belleville' (74)

A. Compare Edwin Muir's 'The Difficult Land' (*Collected Poems*, 237–8).
14. 'Death of John F. Kennedy'
A. 'I mourn for Caitlin ...'
    The allusion is to the death of Dylan Thomas.
15. 'Wine-Maker's Song' (96)
A. '"We are the dead / drunk short hours ago / we truly serious and
    sober looked you / straight in your damned eyes ..."'
    The lines parody John McCrae's 'In Flanders Fields': 'We are the
    Dead. Short days ago / We lived, felt dawn, saw sunset glow, /
    Loved and were loved, and now we lie / In Flanders fields.'

IX   *North of Summer* (1967)

1. 'The North West Passage' (20)
A. 'Martin Frobisher / "Admiral of the Ocean-Sea" who was / "hurte
    ... in the Buttocke with an Arrowe"'
    This may be a misquotation from Captain Luke Fox's *North-West
    Fox or Fox from the North-west Passage*, 52. The passage in Fox runs as
    follows and describes Master James Hall: '... they shote him through
    both buttockes, with a Dart.' It's also possibly from a source I
    haven't located.
B. 'in search of dead sailors / suspended from Ariadne's quivering
    cord / ... / and the Minotaur's bull-roar'
    The allusions are to the myth of Theseus, Ariadne, and the
    Minotaur.
2. 'Arctic River' (22)
A. The poem has an epigraph from C.F. Hall's *Life with the Esquimaux:
    A Narrative of Arctic Experience in Search of Survivors of Sir John Frank-
    lin's Expedition*, 357.
3. 'Eskimo Graveyard' (26)
A. As L.R. Early has shown in 'Birney and Purdy: An Intertextual
    Instance,' the poem is indebted in several ways to Birney's 'Novem-
    ber Walk.' Purdy reviewed *Near False Mouth Creek* in *Fiddlehead*
    (Summer 1965), the volume in which Birney's poem first appeared.
4. 'Canso' (34)
A. 'Swung by the heels like / Achilles / dipped in mountains'
    As an infant Achilles was dipped in the Styx by his mother, Thetis,
    who hoped to ensure his immortality. Unfortunately, his heel, by
    which she held him, remained vulnerable.
B. 'On the sea bottom under us / Sedna / mother of all sea mammals'

'I was reading Inuit mythology around that time, which is probably
– almost certainly – the source of Sedna.' (Letter to author, 24 Jan.
1996)

5. 'Odysseus in Kikastan' (40)
A. 'If sirens sing on the Arctic islands / they come equipped with a
    pair of flippers / blubber lips for drinking tea'
    The allusion is to the *Odyssey*, XII, 175–200.

6. 'When I Sat down to Play the Piano' (43)
A. 'sans dignity / sans intellect / sans Wm. Barrett / and damn near
    sans anus' parodies 'Sans teeth, sans eyes, sans taste, sans every-
    thing' (*As You Like It*, II.vii.166). 'Wm. Barrett' refers to Barrett's
    popular study of existentialism, *Irrational Man*.
B. 'Horatius at the bridge' probably owes less to history than to
    Macaulay's *Lays of Ancient Rome* (1842).
C. '"Lo tho I walk thru the valley of / the shadowy kennels"'
    Compare Psalm 23: 'Yea, though I walk through the valley of the
    shadow of death, I will fear no evil.'

7. 'Still Life in a Tent' (47)
A. 'Or Erewhon and Atlantis'
    Samuel Butler, *Erewhon* (1872) and *Erewhon Revisited* (1902)

8. 'Listening' (50)
A. Cynthia Messenger has suggested to me a general indebtedness
    here to F.R. Scott's 'Lakeshore.'

9. 'South' (60)
A. 'I think of Schopenhauer's "The World / as Will and Idea" and /
    whatever the hell the rest of it is'
    This is a rare reference to a work of philosophy.
B. 'a toast to the pessimists / like Housman and Schopenhauer / and
    the optimists / such as Leibniz and Robert Browning'

10. 'At the Movies' (77)
A. 'watch Gary Cooper and Burt Lancaster / in a technicolour western
    shootemup'
    The film is *Vera Cruz* (1954).

11. 'The Country of the Young' (79)
A. The title, repeated in the closing lines, may owe something to
    Yeats's 'Sailing to Byzantium': 'This is no country for old men. The
    young / In one another's arms ...' I owe the suggestion to Cynthia
    Messenger.
B. 'The colours I mean / for they're not bright Gauguin / or blazing
    Vincent / not even Breughel's "Hunters in the Snow."'

X   *Poems for All the Annettes* (1968)

1.   'House Guest' (27)
A.   The poem is about Milton Acorn and contains references to Freud, François Villon, Marcus Aurelius, and Nietzsche.

XI   *Wild Grape Wine* (1968)

1.   'Dylan' (39)
A.   'and the force that thru the green fuse / is liable to get the strap-hanger's face slapped'
   Compare Dylan Thomas's 'The force that through the green fuse drives the flower' (*CP 1934–52*, 9). See also VIII.12 above.
2.   'Further Deponent Saith Not' (41)
A.   Compare A.M. Klein's 'In re *Solomon Warshawer*,' the last line of which is 'And further deponent saith not' (*Collected Poems of A.M. Klein*, 234).
3.   'My '48 Pontiac' (48)
A.   In a letter to James Dickey (29 July 1975), Purdy acknowledges a debt to Dickey's 'The Auto Wreckers': 'I wrote one called "My '48 Pontiac" strongly modelled on yours about the auto wreckers' (Queen's, box 1).
4.   'Wilderness Gothic' (51)
A.   'wrestles with Jacob'
   See Genesis 32: 24.
B.   The unexpected reference in the third stanza to 'the whole Durer landscape' establishes the possibility of a link between the poem and Marianne Moore's 'The Steeple-jack,' which opens with 'Durer would have seen a reason for living / in a town like this.' Though Moore's is a very different poem, it is also set by the water (a sea instead of a lake) and involves a workman on a church spire doing a job that is potentially dangerous. See *The Faber Book of Modern Verse*, [1936] 139–41. I cite this edition because Purdy owned it. The version in *The Complete Poems of Marianne Moore* (1967) was heavily revised in 1961.
C.   There is also a possible echo of W.H. Auden's 'Family Ghosts' in the third line of the third stanza: 'gothic ancestors peer from medieval sky' may recall 'The strings' excitement, the applauding drum, / Are but the initiating ceremony / That out of the cloud the ancestral face may come' (*Collected Poems*, 47).

5.   'The North West Passage' (56)
     This is not the same poem as 'The North West Passage' in *North of Summer*.

A.   The first section begins with an epigraph from John Ross (1777–1856):
     '"– let them remember that ice is stone / a floating rock in the stream –"'
     The line is from Sir John Ross's *Narrative of a Second Voyage in Search of a North-West Passage and of a Residence in the Arctic Regions during the Years 1829, 1830, 1831, 1832, 1833*, 152: 'But, let them [readers] remember that ice is a stone; a floating rock in the stream, a promontory or island when aground, not less solid than if it were a land of granite.'
          There is also a memory of these lines in 'Gondwanaland' (XXII.12.A and C).

B.   The fourth section opens with another quotation from Ross:
     '"– being informed / that we were Europeans / they answered / that they were men –"'
     In Ross, 'Europeans' is followed by '(Kablunae),' (212).

6.   'Return from Kikastan' (61)

A.   "Foxe his farthest"'
     See Captaine Luke Fox, *North-West Fox or Fox from the North-west Passage*.

7.   'Three Thousand' (76)

A.   '– tho I disagree with John Donne / in some ways man is certainly an island –'
     Donne's famous image occurs in the seventeenth Meditation: 'No man is an *Iland*, intire of it selfe; every man is a peece of the *Continent*, a part of the *maine*.' See XIV.6.A.

8.   'A Walk on Wellington Street (*Or: How Much Land – ?*)' (78)

A.   The last three words of the subtitle allude to Tolstoy's story, mentioned in 'The Cartography of Myself' (*SA*, 17), 'How Much Land Does a Man Need?' See XXII.15.A.

9.   'Japanese Painter' (81)

A.   The poem is about the painter and wood-engraver Katsushika Hokusai (1760–1849), who was nicknamed 'Old Man mad on drawings.' In *The Collected Poems*, the title is changed to 'Old Man Mad about Painting' (149). Hokusai is originally referred to in 'Recommended Reading: Joe Hill and Robinson Jeffers' (I.14.A). See also XIII.5.A.

10. 'Dark Landscape' (95)
A. '"To live a life is not to cross a field"?'
   This is the final line of Boris Pasternak's 'Hamlet' (*Doctor Zhivago*, 523).
B. 'Vancouver Montreal and Toronto'
   In the typescript, the line reads 'Vancouver Little Gidding and Toronto.' For another allusion to 'Little Gidding' see XXIV.12.A. Purdy has also indicated a debt to Vachel Lindsay's 'Spring Comes on Forever,' though I have been unable to find a poem with that title in Lindsay.
11. 'The Runners' (110)
A. The epigraph is taken from an episode in *Eirik the Red's Saga*. See *The Vinland Sagas: The Norse Discovery of America*, 95–6. See also XV.6.B.
12. 'Liberal Leadership Convention' (122)
A. 'and don't affect time's winged chariot a damned bit'
   Andrew Marvell, 'But at my back I always hear / Time's winged chariot hurrying near' ('To His Coy Mistress').
13. 'My Grandfather's Country' (125)
A. 'Thru towns named for an English novel / ... / – Ivanhoe'

XII   *Love in a Burning Building* (1970)

1. 'Social Poem' (62)
A. '"Traveller Beware of the water and food / travelling thru lands of the sun / if a strange woman speaks be sure to be rude / and all political opinions shun. [Anon]"'
   In this case 'Anon' is Purdy (letter to the author 7 Jan. 1996).
B. 'or reject you like Lawrence did that woman / in the train-poem who desired sin with him?'
   See Lawrence's 'In a Spanish Tram-Car' (*CPDHL*, II, 617).
2. 'Letters of Marque' (78)
A. 'I want to say nothing / but poems that land / with little jumps in your mind / the places where your eyes / are like crushed gold foil / quivering as if a bird had landed / then returned to me'
   Compare Hopkins's 'God's Grandeur': 'The world is charged with the grandeur of God. / It will flame out, like shining from shook foil; / It gathers to a greatness, like the ooze of oil / Crushed.' (*The Poems of Gerard Manley Hopkins*, 66). But see also Layton's 'Reconciliation': 'and in the tinfoil air / I doubly marvel ...' (*CP*, 43).

XIII   *Sex and Death* (1973)

1. 'Dead March for Sergeant MacLeod' (10)
A. 'Does Gray's / Elegy still seem very important now'
   See Thomas Gray's 'Elegy Written in a Country Churchyard.'
2. 'Johnston's on St. Germain' (16)
A. '(Or: *comfort me with bagels*)
   See Song of Songs 2: 5: 'Stay me with flagons, comfort me with apples: for I am sick of love.'
B. 'the body odour of race sprang from new box springs I made'
   W.J. Keith has directed my attention to Klein's 'Political Meeting':
   'The whole street wears one face, / shadowed and grim; and in the darkness rises / the body-odour of race.' (*CPAMK*, 308)
C. 'Like Cortes and Balboa in Homer's Chapman'
   'Homer's Chapman' is probably by way of Keats's 'On First Looking into Chapman's Homer.'
3. '"Sizwe Bansi Is Dead"' (20)
A. This is the title of a play by Athol Fugard.
4. 'Flying over Africa' (28)
A. 'the storybook country / of Rider Haggard and Joseph Conrad'
   Purdy is probably thinking of Haggard's *King Solomon's Mines* (1886) and *She* (1887) and Conrad's *Heart of Darkness* (1902).
B. '"Fingerprints prove you Greystoke" / says Edgar Rice Burroughs ...'
   This is a quotation from the closing scene in Burroughs's *Tarzan of the Apes* (1914).
5. '"Old Man Mad about Painting"' (34)
A. The title is a translation of the nickname of Katsushika Hokusai (1760–1849), Gwakiojn or 'Old man mad about painting or mad on drawings.' He published his *Hundred Views of Mount Fuji* in 1835. See I.14.A and XI.9.
6. 'Freydis Eriksdottir in Greenland' (36)
A. The poem is based on a handful of pages in 'The Saga of the Greenlanders.' See George Johnston's translation *Thrand of Gotu: Two Icelandic Sagas*, 166–9. See also Purdy's comments on the sagas in (a) his review of Farley Mowat's *Westviking* and Helge Ingstad's *Land Under the Pole Star* (*SA*, 216–21), and (b) his review of George Johnston's translation of *The Faroe Islanders Saga* (*Canadian Literature*, no. 67 [Winter 1976], 104–6).
7. 'Coffee with René Lévesque' (48)

A. 'I think of Drummond's quaint habitants / "hewers of wood and drawers of water"'

The reference is to W.H. Drummond's dialect poems, the first volume of which was *The Habitant and Other French Canadian Poems* (1897). The quoted words, however, are biblical: Joshua 10: 14.

8. 'Lampman in Heat' (64)

A. See Lampman's 'Heat.' Purdy commented in a letter to John Newlove that of Charles G.D. Roberts, Archibald Lampman, Bliss Carman, and Duncan Campbell Scott, 'all but Scott are shit.' (1 Jan. 1976; Queen's, box 2)

9. 'Beat Joe McLeod' (65)

A. 'and say Gil do you really want that paragon / compleat angler ...'

Izaak Walton, *The Compleat Angler* (1653). See also 'Lights on the Sea' (*SA*, 31–4) for a prose version of the events and characters in the poem.

10. 'Street Scene' (73)

A. 'the forked man stands in his skin and smiles'

There is a possible echo of Lear's description of man as 'a poor, bare, forked animal' (*King Lear*, III.iv.102). And given Purdy's interest in Malcolm Lowry's poetry, it is also possible that he was remembering 'Delirium in Vera Cruz': 'Am I that forked rashed image?' (*Selected Poems of Malcolm Lowry*, 32).

B. The situation in the poem of a spectator watching a horse being tormented by its driver and slowly discovering his empathy with it has two significant predecessors, one literary, one actual: it occurs in Fyodor Dostoevsky's *Crime and Punishment*, and was a cause of Friedrich Nietzsche's collapse into madness. See also Blake's couplet in 'Auguries of Innocence': 'A horse misused upon the road / Calls to heaven for human blood.'

11. 'Athens Apartment' (75)

A. 'Browning's "wise thrush" who / sang "each song twice over" ...'

'That's the wise thrush; he sings each song twice over,' ('Home-Thoughts, from Abroad').

12. 'Ephesus' (76)

A. 'the good / luck birds sing Grimm's / fairy tales to their unborn'

13. 'I Am Definitely on the Side of Life I Said to Pausanias' (81)

14. 'In the Foothills' ['In the Caves' in *The Collected Poems*] (83).

A. Ramon Guthrie's 'The Making of the Bear' and 'This Stealth' (from *Maximum Security Ward*, 134–9, 58–9), both of which deal with caves and cave art, may have suggested some details of Purdy's poem.

Purdy has recommended this relatively obscure volume to friends. The book was published in 1970.

B. It's also possible that Purdy is remembering W.J. Turner's 'In the Caves of Auvergne,' which was published in the same volume as 'Epithalamium for a Modern Wedding,' a poem he has misquoted from memory on at least two occasions. See *The Dark Fire*, 23, 36. See also XXV.17.E.

15. 'The Pope's 1968 Encyclical' (88)

A. 'I go down eventually / into the valley of the shadow of death' See Psalm 23.

16. 'Literary Feuds in Montreal' (90)

A. I'm guessing that Louis Dudek is the friend who tells the speaker, '"Read Pound and Williams / you've got a lot to learn / from them ..."' If I'm right, then the poem is a sort of companion piece to the earlier 'Portrait' (*CH*, 29), a similar settling of accounts with a figure from the past, in this case Irving Layton, whose *Collected Poems* Purdy reviewed in *Quarry* in 1966 (see *SA*, 208–12).

17. 'Power Failure in Disneyland' (91)

A. There are references in the first stanza to 'the great Russian poet Dubrovsky' and 'Ezra Pound.'

B. 'parfit gentil tiger' See Chaucer's 'General Prologue' to *The Canterbury Tales*: 'He was a verray, parfit gentil knycht' (l. 72).

18. 'The Time of Your Life' (97)

A. 'and under / its patchwork quilt time moves / in a drift of birds a dream of horses' See Ted Hughes's 'A Dream of Horses' in *Lupercal* (1970).

19. 'The Hiroshima Poems' (111)

A. The 'Hiroshima Poems' section of the volume has the following epigraph by Randall Jarrell: 'They said, "Here are the maps"; we burned the cities.' This is the closing line of Jarrell's 'Losses' (*Collected Poems*, 145–6). See XXIV.1.A.

20. 'Survivors' (116)

A. '– is it presumptuous to feel like Matthew Arnold / When he wrote *Dover Beach* / "Where ignorant armies clash by night"'?

21. 'Whose Mother?' (118)

A. 'And please lord help us not / Walt Whitman's mother not again / out of the cradle endlessly metrical ...' See Whitman's 'Out of the Cradle Endlessly Rocking.'

XIV *In Search of Owen Roblin* (1974)

Since the volume is unpaginated, the page references are in square brackets.

1. [17]
A. 'and Lesbos' singer in her sunny islands / stopped when the sun went down –'
   As in II.7. the allusion is to Sappho.
2. [34]
A. 'a Roman architect and military engineer / named Vitruvius described the method of log building / used by the Colchis people / on the south shore of the Black Sea: / "They lay timbers ... / ... / ... wood chips and mud."'
   This is a rough translation of a passage in Vitruvius' *On Architecture* (vol. I, bk. 2, 81).
3. [40]
A. 'Back here at home on Page 263 / of *Pioneer Life on the Bay of Quinte.*'
   See *Pioneer Life on the Bay of Quinte*. The book was reprinted in 1976 by Mike Publishing of Belleville, and it is probable that Purdy is referring to this edition.
4. [72]
A. 'So I don't understand Tristan and Isolde very well / I don't know much about those others / whoever it was swam the Hellespont / or that lost monk and nun chastely / marooned in the Middle Ages / Abelard and Heloise I think.'
   The swimmer of the Hellespont was Leander, trying to reach Hero on the other side. Purdy probably knew Christopher Marlowe's poem 'Hero and Leander,' since he refers to Marlowe and his work on several occasions.
B. '"And did you once see Shelley plain?"'
   The quotation is from Robert Browning's 'Memorabilia,' which has an 'Ah,' where Purdy has the opening conjunction.
5. [77]
A. 'And did I once see Owen Roblin plain?'
   See the previous note.
6. [81]
A. 'I don't mean solipsistic navel-watching either / but John Donne's "I am a piece of the main"'
   See XI.7.A.
7. [85]

A. 'I contain others as they contain me'
    The line may echo Whitman's famous triptych in 'Song of Myself':
    'Do I contradict myself? / Very well then I contradict myself, / (I
    am large, I contain multitudes.)'
B. 'in the medieval sense I am Everyman / and as Ulysses said of him-
    self in the Cyclops's Cave / "I am Nobody"'
    The reference and quotation are from the *Odyssey*, IX, 364–7.
8. [90]
A. 'the gear and tackle of living'
    Compare Hopkins's 'Pied Beauty': 'Glory be to God for dappled
    things – / ... / And all trades, their gear and tackle trim' (*PGMH*, 69).

XV *Sundance at Dusk* (1976)

1. 'The Children' (24)
A. 'The plague of Egypt in Churchill'
    See the various plagues in Exodus, chapters 7–10.
B. 'Well just imagine just supposing / Mother Goose lived here /
    whispering stories to the dead children / ... / while Hickory Dick-
    ory Dock solemnly / concurs and Humpty Dumpty never / fell
    before Peter Rabbit became rabbit stew'
    See Beatrix Potter's *The Tale of Peter Rabbit* (1901).
2. 'Homage to Ree-shard' (36)
A. 'now sullen castrated paranoid Achilles / with sore heel in a
    Montreal pub retired / to muse on wrongs and plot revenge'
    See Achilles's withdrawal from the fighting in the *Iliad*, especially
    books 9 to 17.
B. 'I fled Him down the nights and down the days / I fled Him down
    the arches of the years / I fled Him down the labyrinthine ways /
    of my own mind –'
    This is an unacknowledged quotation, without punctuation, of the
    opening of Francis Thompson's 'The Hound of Heaven.'
3. 'Shall We Gather at the River' (44)
A. The title is from the popular hymn.
B. 'to think of that unprovable God / meeting me at the river / and
    saying nothing not a word / just sitting comfortably on his golden
    throne / the second-best one in muddy shallows'
    I have a hunch that by describing God's throne as 'the second-best
    one' Purdy may have opened the Shakespeare door in his memory –
    the will's well-known reference to 'my second-best bed' – with the

result that the subsequent lines may owe something to 'As flies to wanton boys are we to th' gods; / They kill us for their sport' (*King Lear*, IV.i.36). Compare 'where little green gun-slingers / of frogs were shooting down bugs.'

4. 'Eleanor' (47)
A. 'who calls the sun to stand at noon?'
   See Joshua 10: 12–13: 'Then spake Joshua to the LORD in the day when the LORD delivered up the Amorites before the children of Israel, and he said in the sight of Israel, Sun, stand thou still upon Gibeon; and thou, Moon, in the valley of Ajalon.

   And the sun stood still, and the moon stayed, until the people had avenged themselves upon their enemies. Is not this written in the book of Jasher? So the sun stood still in the midst of heaven, and hasted not to go down about a whole day.'

5. 'Ritual' (52)
A. '*in illo tempore* beyond my own time slightly / and my gods apart from Eliade's'
   The Latin phrase is from Eliade's *Myth and Reality* (11): 'But the myth of the origin of death narrates what happened *in illo tempore*, and, in telling the incident, explains *why* man is mortal.' Eliade contrasts mythic time or the mythic world-view with its modern opposite.
B. ''Person from Porlock'
   See V.7.B.
C. There are also references to T.S. Eliot, Lawrence, Dylan Thomas, Henry Kelsey, and Eliade.

6. 'Stop Watching' (60)
A. 'and consider Domenico Theotocopoulos / in the stained-glass shroud of Toledo / dead five hundred years'
   Purdy's earliest poem about El Greco is 'Spanish Hilltop,' published in *Canadian Forum* in June 1950 (see I.5). The lines quoted here are used, slightly changed, in 1984 as the epigraph to 'There is of course a Legend' (*PB*, 53). The first two words are dropped, and the final line is altered from 'dead five hundred years' to 'dead 370 years' (see XXII.9).
B. 'consider the two Scots runners / sent by their masters to explore Newfoundland'
   See 'The Runners' (*WGW*, 110; see XI.11)
C. Incidentally, 'Stop Watching' was originally part of a fifteen-poem sequence – 'A Mirage of Poets' – with each poem having the name

of a Canadian poet in the title. Its original title was 'John Newlove's Soliloquy of Optimism while the Last H-Bomb Falls at McClelland & Stewart.' Purdy's table of contents gives the following short titles for the poems: 'Souster's Pastoral,' 'Layton's Ode,' 'Glassco's Meditation,' 'Newlove's Soliloquy,' 'Dudek's Critique,' 'Ondaatje's Contemplation,' 'Gustafson's Epithalamium,' 'Acorn's Paean,' 'Cohen's Madrigal,' 'Birney's Monody,' 'Scott's Lament,' 'Pratt's Epic,' 'Lee's Elegy,' 'Nowlan's Memory' (Queen's, box 15).

7. 'Murder of D'Arcy McGee' (82)
A. 'In Cote des Neiges [*sic*] Cemetery / the bald detective lurking in forget-me-nots / slips handcuffs on a skelton'
    Compare Michael Ondaatje's description of Billy the Kid's buried corpse: 'The arms would be cramped on the edge of what was the box. And a pair of handcuffs holding ridiculously fine ankle bones. (Even though dead they buried him in leg irons).' (*The Collected Works of Billy the Kid*, 97)
8. 'Rodeo' (85)
A. 'Another bronco refuses to do anything at all / just stands there somewhat reminding me / of a friend saying "It's better not to be born"'
    The quotation is a free translation of the famous line (1225) in Sophocles' *Oedipus at Colonus*: 'Not to be born is, past all prizing, best.' See also XXV.15.
9. 'Place of Fire' (90)
A. 'Symbolic as hell too: you can't beat limestone, / which Auden said was very important stuff; / W. Yeats and R. Jeffers kept building towers as well'
    Auden writes about limestone in 'In Praise of Limestone.'
B. 'unacknowledged legislator or something'
    The allusion is to Shelley's 'Poets are the unacknowledged legislators of the world' in 'A Defence of Poetry.'
10. 'The Statue in Belleville' (94)
A. The poem is anticipated by 'Short History of X County' in *The Crafte So Longe to Lerne* (3).
B. Purdy indicated in a letter to James Wright that this poem was inspired by Wright's 'Two Poems about President Harding' (*Above the River: The Complete Poems*, 127–9). 'When I read the Harding poem I wrote one about the "Fixer" in Belleville (Ont, that is, where I come from – I'm writer in rez at Loyola, Mtl.). Saying that, should also say I've pubbed some fifteen books myself. "The Fixer" in

Belleville was a guy named Mackenzie Bowell who got to be P.M. here in 1895, was Grand Master of the Orange Lodge then, which helped with votes.' (9 Mar. 1974; Queen's, box 1)

11. 'Trousers in a Cloud' (108)
A.   Compare the title of Vladimir Mayakovsky's *A Cloud in Trousers* (1914–15). The source of the title is particularly appropriate since the poem is dedicated to and is about Milton Acorn, a communist.

XVI   *At Marsport Drugstore* (1977)

1.   'Pour' (23)
A.   There are two allusions to Alfred G. Noyes's 'The Highwayman': 'like an out-of-date highwayman with blisters / on both feet' and 'if hell bars the way we fail to keep on coming.' Compare Noyes' '"I'll come to thee by moonlight, though hell should bar the way."' See II.6.A and XX.12.A.

XVII   *No Second Spring* (1977)

1.   As Purdy told Margaret Laurence, the title is take from 'Loch Lomond.' John Lennox identified the source as the third stanza of 'Loch Lomond': 'But the broken heart it kens nae second spring again' (*MLAP*, 357).
A.   'The noon day shadow of man / that lengthens and dies at evening' may contain a memory of Eliot's 'Sweeney Erect': 'The lengthened shadow of a man / is history, said Emerson' (*CPP 1909–60*, 23).

XVIII   *A Handful of Earth* (1977)

1.   'Starlings' (16)
A.   'like arrows   labels on medicine bottles read backwards'
     The phrase 'labels on medicine bottles' is from Layton's 'The Cold Green Element': 'The ailments escaped from the labels / of medicine bottles are all fled to the wind.'

XIX   *Being Alive* (1978)

I.   'On Realizing He Has Written Some Bad Poems' (188)
     'the jewelled hunchback in my head / seated brooding in a dark bone corner'

As in 'Poem' (*ER*, 3), the allusion is to Layton's 'The Cold Green Element,' 'a brilliant / hunchback with a crown of leaves' and perhaps to 'The Poet Entertains Several Ladies' (see IV.1.A).

XX   *The Stone Bird* (1981)

1. According to a letter from Purdy to the author, the epigraph – '... the irresistible anxiety to discover what the orange whistles and the invisible globes on the other side of death were like' – is from Gabriel García Márquez's *One Hundred Years of Solitude*, but I have been unable to find it in the text.
2. 'The Dead Poet' (13)
A. '– and the shadow in Plato's cave'
    Plato's *Republic*, book VII, 515–B. Purdy discusses the poem in a letter to Earle Birney (14 Nov. 1979): 'Of course Plato's Cave is slightly different: I meant to refer to myself as a shadow of life, without carrying it any further – which I could do / But as the shadow in Plato's Cave, the shadow of life if you prefer, I do remember "the small dead one." Does that help any?' (Queen's, box 2, folder 37)
3. 'Journey to the Sea' (15)
A. 'blue robes and blue sandals / spread out before us / like the altar cloths of heaven' echoes W.B.Yeats's 'He Wishes for the Cloths of Heaven' (*CPWBY*, 81).
4. 'Bestiary' (17)
A. The portraits of the burro in the first stanza and of the rooster in the third may owe something to Lawrence's 'The Ass' and 'Turkey-Cock' (*Birds, Beasts and Flowers, CPDHL*, I, 377–80; 369–72]).
5. 'South of Durango' (20)
A. '... Graham Greene and Evelyn Waugh / who hated Mexico'
    See Greene's *The Lawless Roads* (1939) and *The Power and the Glory* (1940) and Waugh's *Robbery under Laws: The Mexican Object Lesson* (1939). See also XXVI.15.A.
B. The poem's closing image of '... Voltaire and Mme. du Chatelet / equipped with measuring devices' is drawn from E.M. Forster's essay 'Voltaire's Laboratory' (*Abinger Harvest*, 222–36). For a more extended use of Forster's essay see the note on 'Voltaire' at XXII.3.A.
6. 'Figures of Earth' (22)
A. 'he provides no salvation / no loaves nor fishes'
    See Matthew 14: 17.
7. 'D.H. Lawrence at Lake Chapala' (25)

A.   'Try to simplify your life'
     If we consider the number of references to Rilke in Purdy's work,
     it's not unlikely that this opening line is an allusion and reply to the
     famous closing sentence of Rilke's 'Archaic Torso of Apollo': 'You
     must change your life.' See I.17.G and XXV.17.G.
B.   'Apotheosis takes over / and he says he's like "some horrid hairy
     God / the Father in a William Blake imagination"'
     This is a quotation from D.H. Lawrence's poem 'She-Goat,' describ-
     ing Lawrence's sometime friend John Middleton Murry, one of the
     models for the character Gerald Crich in *Women in Love*. Purdy
     reverses the order of 'hairy horrid' (*CPDHL*, I, 383). See XXV.17.C.
8.   'In the Garden' (31)
A.   'Then we had vegetable love'
     Compare Marvell's 'To His Coy Mistress': 'My vegetable love
     should grow / Vaster than empires and more slow.'
9.   'Driving the Spanish Coast' (44)
A.   'Robert Browning sailing past Cadiz Bay / into which sunset ran
     reeking / in order to make a poem / (Home-Thoughts, from
     Abroad)'
     The last three words of the second line are taken directly from
     Browning's 'Home-Thoughts, from the Sea' ('Sunset ran, one glori-
     ous blood-red, reeking into Cadiz bay'). 'Home-Thoughts, from
     Abroad' precedes it in the volume *Dramatic Romances and Lyrics*. See
     XXIII.5.C and XXIII.6.
10. 'Near Tofino, Vancouver Island' (58)
A.   'I seize her by the hair and climb / high up some Quasimodo
     stairs / rest safe at last in Notre Dame'
     See Victor's Hugo's *Notre Dame de Paris* or *The Hunchback of Notre
     Dame*.
B.   'The man Neanderthal departs / and drives his car along the
     sand'
     Compare E.J. Pratt's 'From Stone to Steel': 'The snarl Neanderthal is
     worn.'
11. 'Hail Mary in Dawson City' (62)
A.   'as we pass a mountain / with a raven perched there / so close to
     the wingtip / I ask if he's been talking / to Edgar Poe lately'
     Edgar Allan Poe's 'The Raven'
12. 'Red Fox on Highway 500' (66)
A.   Alfred G. Noyes's 'The Highwayman' has influenced the metre,
     rhythm, and syntax at three places in the poem: 'light as air on the

highway / running from death on the highway / he died or dreamed he did'; 'His shadow black as a monster / his shadow a soundless monster'; 'so that I could drive to Belleville / keep an appointment in Belleville / and never forget a word.' On one of the typescripts Purdy had even used one of Noyes's most famous lines – 'The road was a ribbon of moonlight over the purple moor': 'forty feet ahead of me / feet red hammers hammering / pounding away at the highway / light as air on the highway / the road a ribbon of moonlight' (Queen's, box 12). See also II.6.A.

B. It is worth repeating that the fox recurs several times in Purdy's body of work – see 'Seasons' (*SB*, 98) – and that Purdy reviewed two books with 'fox' poems, Margaret Atwood's *The Animals in That Country* and Bill Howell's *The Red Fox*. There's also the possibility that the writing of the Lawrence poems may have brought Lawrence's novella *The Fox* to mind. Other possible echoes are included in the discussion in chapter 3. There is also a similarity in situation between Purdy's poem and the final stanza in Randall Jarrell's 'Field and Forest': 'There in the middle of the forest is the cave / And there, curled up inside it, is the fox. / He stands looking at it. / Around him the fields are sleeping: the fields dream. / ... / The boy stands looking at the fox / As if, if he looked long enough – / he looks at it. / Or is it the fox that's looking at the boy? / The trees can't tell the two apart' (*CP*, 335).

See also James Dickey's 'Blood' (*The Whole Motion: Collected Poems: 1945–92*, 218), another poem about a meeting under the moon between a man and a fox. 'Superhuman deer' and 'a hammering day-and-night sign / of that country' could have been written by Purdy.

13. 'Inside Gus' (74)

A. '"Believe in nothing and poems."'
Purdy informed me in a letter (20 Jan. 1996) that the quotation is from one of Ralph Gustafson's poems, but I have been unable to locate it.

14. 'Writer-in-Rez' (102)

A. There are references to Huysmanns [*sic*] and John Cleland's *Fanny Hill* and the marquis de Sade's *120 Days of Sodom*.

XXI *Bursting into Song* (1982)

1. 'Thomas Morton' (56)

A. The epigraph '"*a kind of pettifogger*" – *[to be exiled or gaoled]*' is from William Bradford's *History of the Plymouth Colony*, 205: 'But this Morton abovesaid, having more craft than honesty (who had been a kind of pettifogger of Furnival's Inn) in the others' absence watches an opportunity (commons being but hard amongst them) and got some strong drink and other junkets and made them a feast'; 'to be exiled or gaoled' isn't in Bradford.

B. 'Doc Teunissen' was the chair of the English Department at the University of Manitoba when Purdy was writer in residence.

C. '(memo: read Hawthorne on the subject)'
The allusion is to Hawthorne's story 'The May-pole of Merry Mount.'

D. 'Who sees Tom Morton plain? Not me, sirs!'
See XIV.5.

XXII   *Piling Blood* (1984)

1. 'Piling Blood' (13)
A. Because references or allusions to classical music are rare in Purdy's work (see XXII.17.A: 'Doug Kaye' [*PB*, 139]), it may be worth quoting the closing lines of this poem – 'I reached home / turned on the record player / and faintly / in the last century / heard Beethoven weeping' – and asking an unanswerable question – which work did Purdy have in mind? Beethoven is also mentioned in 'The Son of Someone Loved' (*CP*, 340).

2. 'Menelaus and Helen' (19)
A. '*Was this the face that launched a thousand ships, / And burned the topless towers of Ilium?*'
As Purdy indicates, the epigraph is by Christopher Marlowe, though he doesn't cite the source, *The Tragical History of the Life and Death of Dr Faustus* (V.i. 98–9).

B. It is worth noting that in a letter to George Galt (11 Jan. 1983), Purdy mentions that reading E.M. Forster's *Pharos and Pharillon* inspired him to reread Homer's two epics, a rereading that is probably behind several Trojan, Mycenaean, and Homeric poems of the following decade. (Queen's, box 2)

3. 'Voltaire' (24)
A. The poem is based on the first part of E.M. Forster's essay 'Voltaire's Laboratory: 1. How They Weighed Fire' (*Abinger Harvest*, 222–9). The lines Purdy puts in quotation marks are taken verbatim from

the essay (223 and 226–7). The interest in Voltaire, not the sort of individual to whom Purdy is usually attracted, may have something to do with Auden's poem 'Voltaire at Ferney' (*CP*, 199). Also, see XX.5.B.

4. 'In the Beginning Was the Word' (32)
A. Though the title is an unacknowledged quotation from John (1:1), Purdy is more interested, as the epigraph from D.H. Lawrence indicates – '*In the Beginning was* not *the Word* / – *but a Chirrup*' – in Lawrence's recasting and 'de-Christianizing' of the gospel. Lawrence deals with the opening of the fourth gospel twice, once in *Etruscan Places* – from which the epigraph is taken – and once in 'St John' (*Birds, Beasts and Flowers, CPDHL*, I, 328–30). Incidentally, Lawrence's exact words are, 'And in the beginning was not a Word, but a chirrup' (*Etruscan Places*, 126).

5. 'Adam and No Eve' (37)
A. Like many of Purdy's Galapagos animal poems, this one owes something in conception and mood to Lawrence's tortoise poems in *Birds, Beasts and Flowers* (*CPDHL*, I, 352–67).

6. 'Birds and Beasts' (39)
A. Compare the title of Lawrence's *Birds, Beasts and Flowers*, one of Purdy's favourite books of poetry. See also *Margaret Laurence – Al Purdy: A Friendship in Letters*, 167.
B. 'Mourn ye rugged Newfoundlanders and Albertans / and mourn ye bereft westcoasters likewise'
Compare the opening of Shelley's 'Adonais': 'I weep for Adonais – he is dead! / Oh, weep for Adonais! Though our tears / Thaw not the frost which binds so dear a head!'
C. 'jug-jug for dirty ears'
T.S. Eliot, 'The Waste Land,' '"Jug Jug to dirty ears."' (*CPP 1909–1950*, 40, l. 103). See XXV. 8.

7. 'How It Feels to Be Old' (41)
A. '(Dylan notwithstanding)'
The allusion is to Dylan Thomas's 'Do not go gentle into that good night.'
B. 'with the dog star overhead / and music on the waters'
Compare *The Tempest* (I.ii. 390–2): 'Sitting on a bank, / Weeping again the King my father's wrack, / This music crept by me upon the waters.' Shakespeare's lines are also quoted by Eliot in the third part of 'The Waste Land' (ll.191 and 257).

8. '"The Elephant Is Slow to Mate –"'? (49)

A. The title is taken, as Purdy indicates, from Lawrence; it is the title of one of Lawrence's *Pansies, CPDHL*, I, 465.

B. '"the whole science / of venerie at his fingertips"'
I have been unable to trace this quotation, and Purdy no longer remembers the source.

C. 'the excretory office (as Yeats would have it) / a site of enemas and noisome exhalations'
The reference is to W.B.Yeats's 'Crazy Jane Talks with the Bishop': 'But love has pitched his mansion in / The place of excrement;' (*CPWBY*, 294).

9. 'There Is of Course a Legend' (53)

A. 'Domenico Theotocopoulos / in the stained glass shroud of Toledo / dead 370 years –'
See above, I.5 and XV.6.

10. 'Archilochos' (58)

A. 'When he was promised Lykambes' daughter, / by her father, and then refused her, / Paros Island rang with his fury –'
The reference is to Archilochos' poems 71, 42, 202, 89, 159, 166, 97a, 167. The numbers refer to Archiloque, *Fragments* (Paris: Les Belles Lettres, 1958).

B. '... he died in battle / (with a brand new shield)'
The allusion is to poem 13, in which Archilochos admits that he threw down his shield in battle and ran. See also XXV.10.

11. 'Bestiary [II] / *ABC of P*' (65)

A. The poem is a tribute or *hommage* to many of Purdy's favourite poets: Auden, Blake, Byron ('So We'll Go No More –'), Catullus, Donne, Homer, Housman, Jeffers, Keats, Kipling, Lawrence, Neruda, Thomas, Yeats. The manuscript at Queen's University also includes stanzas dedicated to Emily Dickinson and A.M. Klein (box 7, folder 2). Compare the proposed dedication to *The Cariboo Horses* (VIII.1). As I mentioned earlier, the overall form, based on the poet's comments on a succession of poets, has two possible sources: Carman's 'The Green Book of the Bards' (*Pipes of Pan*) and Auden's *New Year Letter*. The subtitle parodies Ezra Pound's *ABC of Reading*.

B. '"Lay Your Sleeping –" et cetera,'
From Auden's 'Lullaby': 'Lay your sleeping head, my love, / Human on my faithless arm.'

C. '– here face down beneath the sun' is from MacLeish's 'You, Andrew Marvell' (*CP, 1917–82*, 150). See XXV. 12.

See also XXV.17.B.

12. 'Gondwanaland' (88)

A. 'The planet's basic stone / and what they did it with it / those old ones:'
Compare the opening of Auden's 'Musée des Beaux Arts,' one of Purdy's favourite poems: 'About suffering they were never wrong, / The Old Masters.' See also Randall Jarrell's 'The Old and the New Masters': 'About suffering, about adoration, the old masters / disagree' (CP, 332).

B. 'Cairn on an arctic island / blind shape turned seaward / what sails rise there?'
The 'cairn' may have its origin in several references to cairns in Sir John Ross's *Narrative of a Second Voyage in Search of a North-West Passage* (see 146 and 649, 650), a volume quoted from in 'The North West Passage' (see XI.5.A). Though this is really a stretch, I can't shake the feeling that Swinburne's 'A Watch in the Night' is also present: 'Watchman, what of the night? – / Storm and thunder and rain, / Lights that waver and wave,' (*Swinburne's Collected Poetical Works*, I, 687). The same warning should be kept in mind with the suggestion that Isaiah 21: 11 is also perhaps present somewhere behind this closing triplet: 'He calleth to me out of Seir, Watchman, what of the night? Watchman, what of the night? The watchman [sic] said, The morning cometh, and also the night: if ye will inquire, inquire ye: return, come.'

C. The image of 'riding ships of floating stone' may be an echo of 'let them remember that ice is stone / a floating rock in the stream –' the epigraph from John Ross to 'The North West Passage' (see XI.5.A). Incidentally, there is an earlier version of this key passage in 'In Sullen March' (*LBB*, 87): 'computers already know / that life is death's / trembling green-leafed coffin / sailing outward like a ship / booming across great waves of eternity / where the reflection of yourself and myself / puts on pants and panties every morning at 8 a.m.'

D. 'Gondwanaland' as a whole may also owe something to Auden's 'In Praise of Limestone.'

13. 'Death of DHL' (92)

A. The poem is almost a collage of Lawrence's last letters and Frieda Lawrence's account of his last days in *Not I, But the Wind*, especially the chapter 'Nearing the End' (287–96). The relevant letters are those to Maria Huxley (21 Feb. 1930) and to E.H. Brewster (?27 Feb. 1930).

The lengthy final paragraph is taken, with some changes, from the last two pages of Lawrence's *Apocalypse*.

B.   'Slippers beside the bed, / formed in the shape of living feet.'
I can't resist making the irrelevant connection with Heidegger's commentary on Van Gogh's painting of shoes in 'The Origin of the Work of Art' (*Poetry, Language, Thought*, 33).
There are also references to Eric Gill, Norman Douglas, Aldous and Maria Huxley, and H.G. Wells.

14.   'At Mycenae' (108)

A.   'Perhaps a ploughman down below / stopped his horse in wonderment'
Compare Auden's 'Musée des Beaux Arts': 'In Breughel's *Icarus*, for instance: how everything turns away / Quite leisurely from the disaster; the ploughman may / Have heard the splash.' Williams's 'Landscape with the Fall of Icarus' (in *Pictures from Brueghel*) should also be noted. (I owe the last suggestion to Cynthia Messenger.) Note, by the way, that Purdy has not been consistent in his spelling of Bruegel over the past half century.

B.   'where we cannot leave / and where we cannot stay / are stone and earth and clouds / and flesh for just a day'
Compare Shakespeare's *Cymbeline* IV.ii.258.

15.   'The Strangers' (110)

A.   'How much sunlight does a man need?'
The line adapts the title of Tolstoy's story 'How Much Land Does a Man Need?' See its earlier appearance in 'A Walk on Wellington Street' (XI.8.A) and in Purdy's essay 'The Cartography of Myself' (*SA*, 17).

16.   'The Son of Someone Loved –' (126)

A.   'Include Breughel's Fall of Icarus / as exception / where such logic is umbilical / the boy drowns like a footnote / (notice also that uncanny turning away / from the event which Auden pointed out)'
The reference, once again, is to Auden's 'Musée des Beaux Arts.' See 'At Mycenae,' XXII.14.A.

B.   'Anyway it was a mistake / it happened in another country / of witches magicians satyrs undines / a negotiated settlement is contemplated'
The second line seems to be an allusion to Marlowe's *The Jew of Malta* (IV.i.40–2), though I suspect that like most readers Purdy remembered it from the epigraph to T.S. Eliot's 'Portrait of a Lady': '*Thou hast committed – / Fornication: but that was in another country, / And besides, the wench is dead.*'

17. 'Doug Kaye' (139)
A. '... and also hearing / *Amor ti vieta* ... / ... and *E lucevan* / *le stelle*'
The first is Loris's tenor aria from act II of Umberto Giordano's opera *Fedora* (1898); the second is Cavaradossi's tenor aria from act III of Giacomo Puccini's *Tosca* (1900). I owe these references to Father Owen Lee.
B. 'and thinking / of life being "nasty brutish and short"'
This famous quotation is from Thomas Hobbes's *Leviathan*, part I, chapter xiii: 'No arts, no letters, no society, and, which is worst of all, continual fear and danger of violent death, and the life of man solitary, poor, nasty, brutish, and short.'

XXIII *The Collected Poems of Al Purdy* (1986)

1. 'Homer's Poem' (3)
This is a dramatic monologue spoken by Odysseus, who seems to shift among three positions: the womb, the cave of Polyphemus, and the inside of the Trojan horse.
A. The repeated 'I have no name' echoes not only 'My name is Nobody' (*Odyssey*, IX, 365) but also Purdy's own *In Search of Owen Roblin* [85]: 'I contain others as they contain me / in the medieval sense I am Everyman / and as Ulysses said of himself in Cyclop's [*sic*] Cave "I am Nobody."'
2. '"– Great Flowers Bar the Roads"' (353)
A. The dedication to P.K. Page points to 'Stories of Snow' as the source of the quotation: 'And stories of this kind are often told / in countries where great flowers bar the roads / with reds and blues which seal the route to snow –' (*The Glass Air: Selected Poems*, 42).
B. '"In countries where –"'
This fragment is also from Page's poem.
C. 'he wakes to dream / and dreams himself / into those inner rooms / one cannot enter waking ...'
Compare Page: 'in that warm metamorphosis of snow / as gentle as the sort that woodsmen know / who, lost in the white circle, fall at last / and dream their way to death.' I also suspect that 'he wakes to dream' carries more than a hint of Roethke's 'The Waking': 'I wake to sleep, and take my waking slow.' There is also a passing reference to Job and his wife.
3. 'Yes and No' (356)
A. The epigraph – '*Yes* – : *I love the word* / *and hear its long struggle with*

no' – is from Brendan Kennelly's poem 'Yes' (*A Time for Voices: Selected Poems*, 24).

4.   'This from Herodotus' (358)

A.   The poem is based on the following passage in Herodotus: 'After this division of the loot, the Greeks sailed away to the Isthmus to award the prize for that Greek who in the war had been most worthy of it. When the commanders came and gave their several votes at the altar of Poseidon, deciding the first and second choice out of all the forces, everyone voted for himself, thinking that he indeed had been the bravest of all; but the most votes agreed in giving second place to Themistocles. So the votes for first place were all singles, but Themistocles was far ahead in the vote for second' (*The History*, book 8, section 123, 601–2.) See also XXIV.5.

5.   'On First Looking into Avison's "Neverness"' (359)

A.   The title alludes and refers to Keats's sonnet 'On First Looking into Chapman's Homer' and to Margaret Avison's 'Neverness,' which Purdy interprets and responds to in his poem. The several quotations in the poem are from Avison. See XXV.17.H.

B.   'lonesome Adam and no Eve'
     See Purdy's poem 'Adam and No Eve' (*PB*, 37).

C.   'looking for his lost leader / whom he never knew'
     'The Lost Leader' is Browning's famous poem about what he saw as Wordsworth's apostasy. The poem comes one page before 'Home-Thoughts, from Abroad' and 'Home-Thoughts, from the Sea' in Browning's *Dramatic Romances and Lyrics* (1845).

6.   'Home Thoughts' (360)

A.   The title may be indebted to the two Browning poems mentioned in the previous note and in 'Driving the Spanish Coast' (*SB*, 44; XX.9.A).

7.   'For Steve McIntyre' (363)

A.   'like *Thalassa* for Xenophon and the Greeks'
     There are also references to Proust, Woolf, Dostoevsky, Cervantes, and Joyce.
     For '*Thalassa*' see Xenophon's *Anabasis* (book IV, chapter 7, section 24, 77).

XXIV   *The Woman on the Shore* (1990)

1.   'Blood Pressure Blues' (vii)

A.   The dream-like quality of the first two stanzas as well as the anticipation of death may owe something to Randall Jarrell's well-known 'The Death of the Ball Turret Gunner' as well as to his other war poems: 'From my mother's sleep I fell into the State, / And I hunched in its belly till my wet fur froze. / Six miles from earth, loosed from its dream of life, / I woke to black flak and the nightmare fighters' (*Collected Poems*, 144). It is worth recalling that a line from Jarrell's 'Losses' (145–6) is the epigraph to Purdy's 'Hiroshima Poems' (see XIII.19.A). There may also be the memory of James Dickey's 'The Firebombing' (*The Whole Motion: Collected Poems: 1945–1992*, 193). In a 1968 review of *The Poems of James Dickey*, Purdy called it 'a quite remarkable poem' (34). There is also a Dickey poem titled 'Falling' about a stewardess who falls out of an airplane (243).

2. 'The Prison Lines at Leningrad' (4)
A. The poem begins with and quotes from the situation Akhmatova describes in 'Requiem': 'In the terrible years of the Yezhov terror I spent seventeen months waiting in line outside the prison in Leningrad. One day somebody in the crowd identified me ... "'Can you describe this?" And I said: "I can."' ('Instead of a Preface,' *Poems of Akhmatova*, 99). Purdy reviewed the collected poems for *Books in Canada* (*SA*, 386–90).

3. 'Seven Ways of Looking at Something Else' (11)
A. The title may owe something to Wallace Stevens's famous 'Thirteen Ways of Looking at a Blackbird.'
B. 'she is beyond my conception of her / yet only possible because of me / sweet shadow in the bedroom / my rebellious beloved satellite orbiting me / yearning to be free'
The idea and the image in these lines are similar to Rupert Birkin's description in D.H. Lawrence's *Women in Love* of the ideal male-female relationship as the 'equilibrium' of 'stars' (*Women in Love*, 148).

4. 'A Handle for Nothingness' (19)
A. '"Hail Brother – Hail Camerado" / and shit like that'
That Purdy has Whitman in mind here is confirmed by a parenthesis on the poem's last page – '(Whitman notwithstanding).' Purdy's disagreement with George Bowering over Whitman may be relevant here: Bowering: 'Why do you detest Whitman? ... I find it amazing, partly because Whitman made you.' Purdy: 'Why do I detest Whitman? He's monotonous, long-winded and fulla shit.' (Letters of 18 and 26 Sept. 1973 [Queen's, box 2]).

5. 'Herodotus of Halicarnassus' (42)

A.   The poem refers to several episodes described in *The History*, including Xerxes's flogging of the Hellespont (book 7, section 35, 482). See also XXIII.4.A.

6.   'The Others' (53)

A.   Purdy acknowledged during a reading in Toronto (20 June 1991) that the poem was indebted to Edwin Muir's 'The Animals' (*CP*, 207). A comparison of the opening lines suggests a connection. Purdy: 'We are not alone in the world.' Muir: 'They do not live in the world.'

7.   'On the Death of F.R. Scott' (58)

A.   Compare the last line 'What's right? / Frank Scott knew' with the last line of Hugh MacDiarmid's 'Audh and Cunaide': 'What life is? What is it anyway? / ... Audh knew!' (*Collected Poems*, II, 1048). It is also possible that Purdy is recalling 'Tom Paine knew' from MacLeish's 'America Was Promises' (*CP, 1917–1982*, 328).

8.   'I Think of John Clare' (62)

A.   'John Clare / and his "Meet me in the green glen –"'
See Clare's poem 'Meet Me in the Green Glen' (*John Clare* [the Oxford Poets], 418).

9.   'Questions' (64)

A.   'What shall we say to Death / you and I / when time is short and breath / scant for you and I?'
When challenged by the author over the use of the final 'I' after the preposition, Purdy replied that there was a precedent in Robert Graves's 'Counting the Beats' (letter to the author, 1 June 1989). In fact, all of Graves's first-person pronouns in the poem are grammatical: 'What care you or I?'; 'Always you and I' and so on (*Collected Poems 1975*, 165). W.J. Keith has alerted me to the possibility of an echo of *Hamlet* ('He's fat and scant of breath' [V.ii.290]) in 'short and breath / scant for you and I?'

10. 'Lawrence to Laurence' (71)

A.   'On my workroom wall an original letter / from DHL that reads / "Dear M, / I send you / by this post, registered M.S., / An article I did on the Indians / *and the* Bursum Bill"'
The lines are from a letter to Robert Mountsier (31 Oct. 1922), but there are no italicized words in the original. The Bursum Land Bill was a federal bill that threatened to deprive the Indians of their land (*The Cambridge Edition of the Letters of D.H. Lawrence*, IV, 334).

11. 'Springtime' (83)

A.   The title is followed by the parenthetical phrase '(after Housman).'

There is no specific poem by Housman that Purdy is imitating, though there are two lines that could almost be mistaken as Housman's ('almost' because I don't think the English poet ever uses the noun 'fuss'): 'As for dying – when it's over / there'll be time to make a fuss.'

12. 'In the Desert' (85)

A. At two points in the poem Purdy seems to be remembering Eliot's 'Little Gidding,' a poem he alluded to in 'Dark Landscape' in *Wild Grape Wine* (see XI.10.B): (a) 'A single figure / but impossible to say / whether it was male or female / crossing the sand dunes shouting'; (b) 'I said welcome / and knew this messenger from the desert / was someone I had been waiting for / and clasped them in my arms / the stranger.' The original indecision whether 'the stranger' is 'male or female' and the closing description of the figure as 'them' as well as the oneiric or visionary quality of the passages hints at a debt to the second section of 'Little Gidding': 'And as I fixed upon the down-turned face / That pointed scrutiny with which we challenge / The first-met stranger in the waning dusk / I caught the sudden look of some dead master / Whom I had known, forgotten, half recalled / Both one and many; in the brown baked features / The eyes of a familiar compound ghost / Both intimate and unidentifiable' (*CPP 1909–1950*, 140).

B. I also wonder whether there is an echo of Archibald MacLeish's 'Winter Is Another Country' here as well: 'The hands beyond the reach of hands, the name / Called out and never answered with my name / The image seen but never seen with sight' (*CP, 1917–1982*, 371).

XXV *Naked with Summer in Your Mouth* (1994)

1. 'Grosse Isle' (9)

A. The epigraph is from W.H. Auden's 'On This Island' (*CP*, 112). The imperative with which each verse opens – 'Look stranger' – is also Audenesque; see the title of his 1936 volume *Look, Stranger!* as well as 'The Bonfires' ('Look there!') and 'Consider' ('Consider this and in our time') (*CP*, 53, 61).

B. See also the opening chapter of Susanna Moodie's *Roughing It in the Bush* as well as Atwood's 'Further Arrivals' in *The Journals of Susanna Moodie*.

2. 'Capitalistic Attitudes' (11)

A. The poem contains several passing references to Ralph Gustafson and Russian poets: Pasternak, Mayakovsky, Alexander Pushkin, Alexander Voznesensky, and Aleksander Blok ('The Twelve').

3. 'Pound' (36)

A. The poem quotes from Pound's wartime broadcasts and twice from 'The River Merchant's Wife: A Letter.'

   The first quotation is from the broadcast of 30 Apr. 1942 and can be found in *'Ezra Pound Speaking': Radio Speeches of World War II*, 115; the second is from the broadcast of 7 Dec. 1941, and is on page 22. See also I.15.

4. 'Yeats' (38)

A. The poem quotes from Yeats's letter to his sister about the death of Swinburne: '... meeting his sister in the street on the morrow of Swinburne's death (April 1909), Yeats stopped her to say: "I am the King of the Cats."'(Quoted by Joseph Hone, *W.B. Yeats (1865–1939)*, 232).

5. 'On Robert Frost' (40)

A. '"Archie couldn't do it! / Hemingway couldn't do it! / Williams couldn't do it!"'I have been unable to find the source of this quotation.

B. 'He once said that "Free / verse is like playing tennis / without a net"'
   Frost commented in an interview, 'I've given offense by saying I'd as soon write free verse as play tennis with the net down.' (See 'Conversations on the Craft of Poetry,' in Elaine Barry, *Robert Frost on Writing*, 159.)

C. '– well Shapiro says "No passion"'
   I have been unable to find this quotation in Karl Shapiro's comments on Frost.

6. 'Flight of the Atlantis' (45)

A. 'Cities principalities powers'
   Compare Kipling's well-known 'Cities and Thrones and Powers' and Ephesians 6: 12: 'For we wrestle not against flesh and blood, but against principalities, against powers, against the rulers of the darkness ...'

7. 'The Booby Hop' (51)

A. 'as if to say / with Wendell Holmes / "Build thee more stately / mansions O my soul –"'
   The quoted lines are from Oliver Wendell Holmes's 'The Chambered Nautilus' (*American Poetry: The Nineteenth Century*, I, 557).

Holmes's lines probably carry an echo of John 14: 2: "In my Father's house are many mansions.'

8. 'Procne into Swallow' (65)

A. Though the poem's mood is playful, it assumes that the reader knows the myth of Procne, Itys, and Philomela. An earlier, indirect allusion to it by way of T.S. Eliot's 'The Waste Land' occurs in 'Birds and Beasts' (*PB*, 39); see XXII.6.C. Purdy may also know the myth from Ovid's *Metamorphoses*, book VI, 438–674.

9. 'Procne into Robin' (70)
See previous note.

10. 'Archilochus in the Demotic' (71)

A. '... and wrote / "Horseman Pass By" on Pergamum vellum'
The quotation is from W.B.Yeats's 'Under Ben Bulben,' where it appears as part of a closing triplet: '*Cast a cold eye / On life, on death. / Horseman, pass by!*' The poem also mentions Pindar, Simonides, Homer, Pound, and 'Margaret A.'
Also see XXII.10.

11. 'The Crucifix across the Mountains' (73)

A. The poem is based on D.H. Lawrence's essay 'The Crucifix across the Mountains' in *Twilight in Italy*, from which it takes three quotations. See *Twilight in Italy and Other Essays*, 92, 95, 97.

12. 'On My Workroom Wall' (76)

A. 'Don Coles' poem which says so much about the / lost "Forests of the Medieval World."'
See Coles's *Forests of the Medieval World*, 35.

B. 'Tiff Findley's verse from Euripides / which says "never that which is shall die."'
The Euripides quotation is from Findley's *Inside Memory: Pages from a Writer's Workbook*, 259, where his father and mother quote the fragment. The line is also used as the epigraph for *The Wars*.

C. 'MacLeish's "You, Andrew Marvell" / – and I too follow shadows around the world / at Petra and Ecbatan and Sumer and Palmyra'
MacLeish's poem mentions Petra and Palmyra but not Sumer or Ecbatan. MacLeish's poem is also quoted in 'Bestiary [II]; see XXII.11.C.

13. 'Incident Involving William Blake' (79)

A. This is a rare found poem based on Blake's letter to Thomas Butts (16 Aug. 1803) describing his fight with a soldier. Purdy omits several sentences. (*The Letters of William Blake*, 62–6.)

14. 'Pneumonia' (84)

A.   '"To be or not to be?"'
     See *Hamlet*, III.i.56.
B.   '"What is it in men that women / do require? The lineaments of
     gratified desire"'
     See William Blake's 'Several Questions Answered' (*The Poems of
     William Blake*, 167).
C.   'it's also the earth of Yeats & Garcia Marquez / of Sakharov & Frank
     Scott & Margaret Laurence / Sairey Gamp and MacDiarmid's
     Audh / asleep in Iceland / in her resting place of stones'
     For Sairey (or Sarah) Gamp see Dickens's *Martin Chuzzlewit*. For
     Audh, see MacDiarmid's 'Audh and Cunaide': 'Audh, the deep-
     minded, mother / Of Hebridean chiefs, / Who, widowed, went to Ice-
     land / And sleeps in one of its cold reefs.' (*CP*, II, 1047). See XXIV.7.A.
15. 'On Being Human' (90)
A.   '"It would have been better / if he'd never lived at all"'
     The quotation is from Purdy's poem 'My Cousin Don': '"He might
     better not have lived at all," / his sister said, and "What was he
     alive for?"' (*PB*, 101). See also XV.8 for the source in Sophocles's
     Oedipus at Colonus.
16. 'Do Rabbits –?' (98)
A.   'Our romantic human orgasm / has been likened to / the fall of
     Troy: / "A shudder in the loins / engenders there / The broken
     wall, / the burning roof and tower / And Agamemnon dead"'
     Though the lineation is eccentric, almost as if Purdy is attempting to
     wrench Yeats's lines out of their pentameter into his own free-verse
     lineation, the quotation is from 'Leda and the Swan.'
B.   'But leave off the grandiose: / is there an artistic equivalent / (apart
     from D.H. Lawrence) / for the tortoise's slow dance / of tumes-
     cence and detumescence'
     Purdy is again thinking of Lawrence's tortoise poems. See above
     XXII.5.
17. 'Touchings' (102)
A.   '"the best lack all conviction / and the worst, / are full of passionate
     intensity"'
     This is from Yeats's 'The Second Coming,' though the lineation is
     altered and Purdy substitutes an 'and' for Yeats's 'while.'
B.   '"And now at Kermanshah the gate"'
     This is verbatim from MacLeish's 'You, Andrew Marvell,' though
     Purdy eliminates the break between the fourth and fifth stanzas. See
     also XXII.11.C.

C. '"– like some hairy horrid God the Father / in a William Blake imag-
    ination"'
    See D.H. Lawrence's 'She-Goat' (*CPDHL*, I, 383). See XX.7.B.
D. 'And all the limbo-faces draw near / to gaze down on you like Lay-
    ton's ex-wives'
    Purdy is thinking of the description of a sleeping Irving Layton
    observed by two of his ex-wives and his daughter-in-law in Elspeth
    Cameron's *Irving Layton: A Portrait*, 461.
E. '"I have stood upon a hill / and trembled like a man in love / a man
    in love I was and / could not speak and could not move"'
    As the previous line indicates, this is from W.J. Turner's 'Epitha-
    lamium for a Modern Wedding,' (*The Dark Fire*, 37). Turner's stanza
    is slightly different: 'I have stared upon a dawn / And trembled like
    a man in love, / A man in love I was, and I / Could not speak and
    could not move.' The stanza is also quoted in the essay 'On Bliss
    Carman' (*SA*, 322). See also XIII.14.B.
F. '"Time that is intolerant"' etc.
    This is from Auden's 'In Memory of W.B. Yeats,' though Auden
    later cut the lines from the poem.
G. '"Whoever has no house now will never have one / whoever is
    alone will stay alone"'
    This is from Rainer Maria Rilke's 'Autumn Day.' There is a comma
    in Rilke after 'now,' and the first words of each line are capitalized.
    Purdy is using Stephen Mitchell's translation. See *The Selected
    Poetry of Rainer Maria Rilke*, 11. See also VIII.5.A, XX.7.A, and
    XXVI.11.
H. '"Leeuwenhock [sic] peered through his magic window / ... / of fir-
    mament that was before Adam"'
    This is from Margaret Avison's 'Neverness,' though Avison capital-
    izes the first words of all three lines and has a definite article before
    'Adam.' See also 'On First Looking into Avison's "Neverness"'
    (XXIII.5).
I. I should mention that Purdy's note to the poem indicates that 'the
    quotes are from memory, and would be verbatim only if my mem-
    ory was perfect (which it isn't)' (129).
18. 'Country Living' (106)
A. 'Spring with Pablo Neruda / and I peering out the bathroom / win-
    dow at some imaginary / female and he sez to her / "I want to do to
    you what / spring does to the cherry trees"'
    I have been unable to trace the quotation from Neruda.

19. 'A Sorrow for Tom' (108)
A. 'Not like Shelley's "Adonais" / when Keats had "gone / where all things bright and fair / Descend"'
Shelley's words are slightly different: 'For he is gone, where all things wise and fair / Descend' (24–5).

20. 'The Farm in Little Ireland' (116)
A. 'Hobbes' "sudden glory" of laughter'
The quotation is from *Leviathan*, part I, chapter 6: 'Sudden glory is the passion which maketh those grimaces called laughter.'

21. 'Reassessment' (118)
A. '... that black ship / mentioned by Lawrence'
The reference is to Lawrence's 'The Ship of Death' (*CPDHL*, II, 716), though Lawrence never describes it as a 'black' ship. Purdy may be confusing Lawrence's ship and Philip Larkin's ship of death in 'Next, Please': 'Only one ship is seeking us, a black- / Sailed unfamiliar, towing at her back / A huge and birdless silence. In her wake / No waters breed or break' (*CP*, 52).

22. 'Neanderthal' (123)
A. As Purdy indicates in a note, the several quotations are all taken from the *New York Times Book Review*, 4 July 1993. The piece is a lead review by Malcolm W. Browne of three books about the origins and descent of humanity ('The Way We Were?' 1, 21).

XXVI   *To Paris Never Again* (1997)

1. 'Lament for Bukowski' (9)
A. '"perne in a gyre"' is from Yeats's 'Sailing to Byzantium.'
B. 'the dark gods' occurs in several works by Lawrence, notably *The Plumed Serpent*.
C. '"the golden men / who push the buttons / of our burning universe"' is from a poem by Bukowski that I have been unable to trace.
D. According to Purdy, 'the King of the Jews on his cross / composing dirty limericks for Pop' is from Bukowski, but I have been unable to locate the poem.

2. 'Travel Article' (13)
I have been unable to trace the travel article from which the three quotations about 'those stone age people / in the Orkney Islands' are drawn.

3. 'A Job in Winnipeg' (16)

A. 'and the son of man hath nowhere / to lay his head'
   Matthew 8: 20: 'The foxes have holes, and the birds of the air have
   nests; but the Son of man hath not where to lay his head.'

4. 'Muss i denn' (21)
   A popular Bavarian song; the title can be translated as 'Do I have
   to?' I owe the reference to Annick Hillger.

5. 'Bruegel's Icarus' (23)
   The poem is a response to the painter's 'The Fall of Icarus' (Musées
   Royaux des Beaux Arts, Brussels) and to a lesser extent W.H.
   Auden's well-known 'Musée des Beaux Arts.'

A. Both '"a boy falling out of the sky" / in Auden's poem' and
   '"expensive delicate ship"' refer to Auden's poem.

B. '"Round up the usual suspects"'
   This famous line is spoken by the French captain played by Claude
   Rains in the film *Casablanca*.

C. 'Sam Spade / and Philip Marlowe'
   The former is the private eye in Dashiell Hammett's *The Maltese
   Falcon*, while the latter appears in several works by Raymond
   Chandler.

D. 'Hunters in the Snow' and 'Peasant Wedding'
   Two other paintings by Bruegel. The first is in the Kunsthistorisches
   Museum, Vienna. The second could be either the 'Peasant Wedding
   Dance' (Institute of Arts, Detroit) or the 'Peasant Wedding Feast'
   (Kunsthistorisches Museum, Vienna).

6. 'Ode to a Dead Burro' (26)

A. '"even tenor of our ways"'
   See Thomas Gray's 'They kept the noiseless tenor of their way'
   ('Elegy Written in a Country Churchyard').

7. 'Her Illness' (44)

A. 'where Kurtz had been sighted'
   See Joseph Conrad's *Heart of Darkness*.

8. 'My Grandfather' (47)

A. 'Gilgamesh and Enkidu'
   See *The Epic of Gilgamesh* as well as 'Gilgamesh and Friend' (V.8) and
   the next entry.

9. 'Becoming' (48)
   For 'Gilgamesh et cetera' see previous entry.

10. 'The Names the Names ...' (51)

A. '"they flee from me"'
   See Thomas Wyatt's 'They flee from me that sometime did me seek.'

B. 'Van Gogh's painting' is 'Café Terrace at Night' (Kroller-Muller Museum, Otterloo, the Netherlands). It is reproduced on the cover of *Rooms for Rent in the Outer Planets*. See I.17.D.

11. 'House Party – 1000 B.C.' (60)
    The poem is based on Rilke's 'Alcestis.' See I.17.G.

12. 'Aphrodite at Her Bath' (78)

A. 'and time that is intolerant / of beauty as well as / the brave and innocent.'
    See the original version of Auden's 'In Memory of W.B. Yeats':
    'Time that is intolerant / Of the brave and innocent, / And indifferent in a week / To a beautiful physique, / Worships language and forgives / Everyone by whom it lives; / Pardons cowardice, conceit, / Lays its honours at their feet.' (*The English Auden: Poems, Essays, and Dramatic Writings, 1927–1939*, 242).

B. See also the quotations from the songs 'Clementine' and 'Drink to Me Only with Thine Eyes.'

13. 'Realism 2' (94)
    The poem is a response to Czeslaw Milosz's 'Realism' (*Facing the River*, 30) from which it also quotes.

14. 'January at Roblin Lake' (101)

A. '(I think of Coleridge / "the ice did split / with a thunder fit" / but Coleridge he / was no help at all)'
    See 'The Rime of the Ancient Mariner': 'The ice did split with a thunder-fit; / The helmsman steered us through!'

15. 'In Mexico' (103)

A. 'thinking of Graham Greene / who disliked Mexico / and Waugh who felt much the same'
    See Greene's *The Lawless Roads* and Waugh's *Robbery under Laws: The Mexican Object Lesson*. See also 'South of Durango' (XX.5).

Notes

Preface

1 'The Collapse of the Canadian Poetry Canon,' *Canadian Literary Power*, 95.
2 *Soul Says: On Recent Poetry*, 2.
3 *Making It Real: The Canonization of English-Canadian Literature*, 4.
4 'Democratic Vistas,' *Complete Poetry and Collected Prose*, 932.
5 'The Poetry of Al Purdy: An Afterword,' 390.
6 *From There to Here*, 238.
7 *Soul Says*, 7.
8 *On Poetry and Poets*, 17.
9 'Poetry of the Present,' *The Complete Poems of D.H. Lawrence*, I, 181; *Al Purdy*, 94.
10 James Boswell, *The Life of Samuel Johnson, L.L.D.*, 947.

I Poetry, Nation, and the Last Canadian Poet

1 'Democratic Vistas,' *Complete Poetry and Collected Prose*, 971.
2 *Letters to the New Island*, 174.
3 'Dedication,' *The Collected Poems 1931–1987*, 78.
4 *Under Briggflatts: A History of Poetry in Great Britain, 1960–1988*, 163.
5 'A Man's life of any worth is a continual allegory.' To George and Georgiana Keats, 13 February 1819.
6 *Harsh and Lovely Land*, 90.
7 For Dworkin, see *A Matter of Principle*, 231; for Taylor, 'A Canadian Future,' *Reconciling the Solitudes*, 26–7.
8 John Gray, *Berlin*, 99.
9 'Before 1967, 80 per cent of Canada's immigrants used to come from Europe

or from countries of European heritage; by 1991 almost 75 per cent came from Asia, Africa, Latin America and the Caribbean.' V. Seymour Wilson, 'The Tapestry Vision of Canadian Multiculturalism,' 413. According to the 1996 census figures, between 1986 and 1996, 53 per cent of all immigrants came from Asia and the Pacific rim.

10 See Melville H. Watkins's 'Technology and Nationalism': 'National boundaries defined by vernaculars are as defenceless against information moving with the speed of light as against the inter-continental ballistic missile. The attempt to cram nationalism as content into the new media tends to produce the barbarous and the ludicrous – "Canadian content" rules being a case in point' (290–1).

11 It is worth emphasizing that to tolerate something is not the same as respecting it. As Jacob T. Levy points out, 'Without question it is possible to be tolerant of every religion simultaneously. But it is not possible to affirm the positive value of each religion simultaneously. To a non-believer, a great many religions must seem foolish and misguided at best, dangerous at worst. To the deeply committed believer, faiths other than one's own ... are seen as mistaken on some of the most important questions of human life.' ('The Multiculturalism of Fear,' 277–8).

12 A cartoon in a daily newspaper offers a pointed illustration of this. Two men are talking. The first says, 'If you're right ... if Canada will inevitably be absorbed into the United States ... Do you think we'll at least be recognized as a distinct society?' The second answers, 'Get real.' (*Globe and Mail*, 7 March 1997, D18).

13 Quoted by V. Seymour Wilson, 'The Tapestry Vision of Canadian Multiculturalism,' 415.

14 'The Idea of a Canadian Tradition,' *Unsupported Assertions*, 19.

15 Isaiah Berlin, *Vico and Herder: Two Studies in the History of Ideas*, 211. John Gray, *Berlin*, 98.

16 Letter to Jack McClelland (4 April 1965). McClelland and Stewart Papers, McMaster University, box 40, MacLennan file.

17 Davey, 266. Also relevant and surprising is the following comment by Jack McClelland in a letter to Pierre Berton: 'As a post-nationalist ... I believe in Canadian unity and the survival of the country, but I am no longer satisfied that it can be achieved with the freight of any consideration of economic and political independence' (3 Jan. 1978. McClelland and Stewart Papers, McMaster University, box 73, file 22). A similar pessimism marks Walter Gordon's *A Choice for Canada: Independence or Colonial Status* (1966) and James and Robert Laxer's *The Liberal Idea of Canada: Pierre Trudeau and the Question of Canada's Survival* (1977).

18 See *Reconciling the Solitudes: Essays on Canadian Federalism and Nationalism*: 'A Canadian Future,' 26–7; 'Shared and Divergent Values,' 182–3.

19 *Multicultural Citizenship*, 6.

20 This status is implicitly acknowledged in the Supreme Court decision of 3 October 1996 in which Algonquin 'ancestral rights' are recognized.

21 *Thinking English Canada*, 73.

22 *Lament for a Nation*, 3–4.

23 Fernand Braudel's unease with the word 'identity' is worth noting: 'The title of a book is never entirely neutral. So was I right to call this book *The Identity of France*? The word "identity" appealed to me, but has not ceased to torment me over the years. The title alone raises once more, from an oblique angle, all the problems I have just described and a few more besides' (23).

24 *Under Briggflatts*, 163.

25 'And to imagine a language means to imagine a form of life' (*Philosophical Investigations*, no. 19, 8e).

26 Braudel, 23.

27 Purdy Papers, Queen's University, box 2.

28 'Cadence, Country, Silence,' 154.

29 *Soul Says*, 7.

30 'Cadence, Country, Silence: Writing in Colonial Space,' 155.

31 'Two Canadian Poets: A Lecture,' 27.

32 Quoted in Brown, *On Canadian Poetry*, 120. See also Roberts's letter to Carl Klinck in which he describes how his father 'had the vision of what Canada should be and might become, – *he* filled me with that vision, till I burned to express *Canada*' (quoted in Klinck's *Giving Canada a Literary History: A Memoir*, 13).

33 *The Bush Garden*, 129.

34 See Charles Taylor's comment that 'faced with this model [the American model of a nation], it is natural for Canadians to wonder whether we have an identity. For we have not and could never have one of this kind. In this respect we are more like a European country; that is, we have a greater ideological spread in our politics, and no one set of ideas can be held up to be "Canadian values" or to be the foundation of a "Canadian way of life." A Committee on Un-Canadian activities could only be a joke at the expense of our neighbours. But if the American model does not fit, the European one does not either; for these nations are for the most part united by language, by culture, and often by a long history' (*Reconciling the Solitudes: Essays on Canadian Federalism and Nationalism*, 25).

35 'The Fathers in 1867 announced "a new nationality." It was to be a pan-

Canadian nationality. It was to be that of a composite, heterogeneous, plural society, transcending differences of ethnic origin and religion among its citizens. It was also to be an open society, recruiting its population through large-scale immigration' (Frank Underhill, 'Foreword,' *Nationalism in Canada*, ed. Peter Russell, xvii).

36 'Two Canadian Poets: A Lecture,' 26.

37 'We have made Italy, now we have to make Italians' (quoted by E.J. Hobsbawm, *Nations and Nationalism since 1780*, 44). He made the comment at 'the first meeting of the parliament of the newly united Italian kingdom.'

38 'Nationalism in Canadian Literature,' 243. A page earlier, Watt quotes Aldous Huxley's comment, 'Nations are to a very large extent invented by their poets and novelists.'

39 Ibid., 242.

40 'What Is a Nation?' The following definitions are quoted in Eric Hobsbawm, *Nations and Nationalism since 1780*, 8. Of historical interest is Stalin's 1912 definition: 'A nation is a historically evolved, stable community of language, territory, economic life and psychological make-up manifested in a community of culture' (5).

41 'What Is a Nation?' 19; *The Identity of France*, 25.

42 Quoted by D.G. Jones, *Butterfly on Rock*, 4. For a soft version of the influence of a place on a people, see Goethe's comment to Eckermann: '... great influence over the inhabitants of a country has been conceded to its vegetation. And surely, he who passes his life surrounded by solemn lofty oaks must be a different man from him who lives among airy birches ... Nevertheless, this much is certain: not only the inborn peculiarities of a race, but also soil and climate, aliment and occupation, combine to form the character of a people' (Eckermann, *Conversations with Goethe*, Thursday, 2 April 1829, 306). I call it a soft version because Goethe emphasizes an interaction between self and soil over any simple geographical determinism.

43 Quoted by Will Kymlicka in *Multicultural Citizenship*, 63.

44 *A Vision beyond Reach*, 4.

45 *The Canadian Identity*, 85.

46 'Disunity as Unity: A Canadian Strategy,' *The Lovely Treachery of Words*, 21.

47 'Is There an English-Canadian Nationalism?' 112.

48 A letter from Jack McClelland to Purdy (11 Feb. 1977) reveals that Purdy originally wanted to dedicate *No Other Country* (then titled 'Al Purdy's Canada,') to Lévesque. The publisher was opposed to dedicating a book about Canada to a politician committed to separatism: 'If it is not a cynical dedication, do you really think you should be dedicating AL PURDY'S CANADA [*sic*], to a man who despite any respect we may hold for him, is determined

to destroy the very country you have written about' (McClelland and Stewart Papers, McMaster University, box 95, Purdy file).

49 'Alternative Futures: Legitimacy, Identity, and Alienation in Late-Twentieth-Century Canada,' *Reconciling the Solitudes*, 62–3.

50 'Shared and Divergent Values,' *Reconciling the Solitudes*, 158.

51 Bill Ashcroft, Gareth Griffiths, and Helen Tiffin, *The Empire Writes Back*, 19.

52 Ralph Waldo Emerson, 'The Poet,' *Essays and Lectures*, 465.

53 Whitman, 944.

54 *On Canadian Poetry*, 20.

55 Though my discussion is not concerned with painters and composers, the general point applies since both groups have engaged the question of a Canadian painting and a Canadian music.

56 The work of Paterson Ewen, though less familiar, may be an even more apposite example from the plastic arts.

57 See Carolyn Masel's comment about landscape in Canadian and Australian literatures: 'Both countries reserve actual places as places of peculiar authority: the North in Canada and the Outback (the bush) in Australia. These huge and topographically various sites are reserved places of sacred character, irrespective of the fact that the large majority of people have no familiarity with them whatsoever ...

Furthermore, in both countries the cultural anxiety about one's relation to the land is heightened by the presence, or else the hauntings, of precolonial populations, whose closer daily contact with the landscape they inhabited has meant that they have been inscribed by their postcolonial successors as more authentic dwellers in the landscape' ('Late Landings: Reflections on Belatedness in Australian and Canadian Literatures,' 162).

58 'The Poet in Quebec Today,' in Dudek and Gnarowski, eds., *The Making of Modern Poetry in Canada*, 265.

59 Frye, 'Haunted by Lack of Ghosts: Some Patterns in the Imagery of Canadian Poetry,' 39–40; Bowering, *Al Purdy*, 29.

60 'The Canadian Poet's Predicament,' 120–1.

61 'Haunted by Lack of Ghosts,' 40.

62 *Aesthetics: Lectures on Fine Art*, I, 272.

63 *Technology and Empire*, 17.

64 Often unnoticed, or undiscussed, by advocates of the pluralistic, postcolonial view of tradition is the fact that not only does most indigenous 'writing' exist in translation, but the majority of its literary critics are amateurs – in both senses – with little or no access to the original languages. So-called scholars who wouldn't tolerate an expert in English literature who couldn't speak the language have no reservations about posing as experts on 'the indigene'

whose culture they know second-hand. Yet without fluency in the native languages, an individual simply cannot make crucial anthropological and cultural distinctions and judgments. He or she lacks the basic tools of the profession. A consequence of this is that he or she also lacks the basis for a genuine respect for a culture since respect can only be based on knowledge of the living world of the other. Without that knowledge we remain in the world of various kinds of translations. And, for better or worse, translation is always a distortion and an appropriation of sorts, a means of transferring a work from its original tradition – particularly easy if that tradition is now partial because its roots have been destroyed or debased – to that of the language of translation. If the works enter the dominant 'tradition,' they do so on the latter's terms, the very language of recuperation serving simultaneously to undercut the work's relationship to its sources and to overlay its meaning with associations and connotations embedded in another language. The postcolonial distinction between the 'English' of the imperial centre and the appropriated and adapted 'english' of the new nation doesn't resolve the dilemma of this form of cultural practice as neatly as the theoretical distinction promises. Etymology is always a form of linguistic conditioning and even cultural determinism.

65 'Unhiding the Hidden,' 43.
66 *Thinking English Canada*, 64.
67 'Hawthorne and His Mosses,' 195–7.
68 'Cadence, Country, Silence: Writing in Colonial Space,' 159.
69 Ibid, 165.
70 'Removal from the Wings,' 12–13.
71 *Memoirs*, 54. The passage is italicized in the original.
72 *The Phenomenology of Mind*, IV, A, 3, 237–40.
73 'Disunity as Unity: A Canadian Strategy,' *The Lovely Treachery of Words*, 31.
74 James Breslin, *Mark Rothko*, 283.
75 *In the American Grain*, 226. Also of interest is Marianne Moore's description of this 'America' as 'the wild man's land; grassless linkless, languageless country in which letters are written / not in Spanish, not in Greek, not in Latin, not in shorthand, / but in plain American which cats and dogs can read!' I'm embarrassed to say that I don't recall the source of the quotation.
76 Quoted by Watt in 'Nationalism in Canadian Literature,' 238.
77 'Hawthorne and His Mosses,' 196.
78 *Headwaters of Canadian Literature*, 237. A similarly realistic view of Australian poetry can be found in Vivian Smith's section of *The Oxford History of Australian Literature* (ed. Kramer and Mitchell): 'No Australian poet has been responsible for any formal innovations or revolutions in technique; and it is

probably true to say that until recently the main struggle of Australian poets has been on the level of content: to accommodate their visions of Australia, its landscape, flora and fauna and the experience of Australian living, to the poetic moulds and patterns inherited from Europe and America' (271).

79 Ibid., 211.

80 'The Idea of a Canadian Tradition,' *Unsupported Assertions*, 11–12.

81 'Standards in Australian Literature,' *The Oxford Anthology of Australian Literature*, 280–1.

82 'The Narrative Tradition in English-Canadian Poetry,' *The Bush Garden*, 145.

83 Elspeth Cameron, *Hugh MacLennan: A Writer's Life*, 107.

84 'Mr Smith and the Tradition' ('Introduction' to *Other Canadians*), in Dudek and Gnarowski, eds., *The Making of Modern Poetry in Canada*, 58–9.

85 Ibid, 54.

86 Saying this, I do not wish to be misinterpreted as denying Pratt's historical importance or not respecting his work. Unfortunately, because of the neo-Victorian nature of his poetic, he is a figure of almost no influence, a dead end poetically for anyone influenced by him. His importance within the tradition lies in the fact that he wrote about Canadian themes and that like Roberts and Carman before him he showed that one could be a Canadian and a poet of note.

87 Quoted by Lawrence Bourke in *A Vivid Steady State: Les Murray and Australian Poetry*, 46–7.

88 Illecillewaet is a 'glacier, mining district, village and river flowing into Columbia River at Revelstoke, Kootenay, British Columbia' (Armstrong, *The Origin and Meaning of Place Names in Canada*, 140). It means 'swift water.'

89 Purdy Papers, Queen's University, box 3, Lee file.

90 Purdy Papers, Queen's University, box 13, Birney file.

91 *Canadian Forum*, May 1951, 43.

92 'After a Hundred Years Canadian Poetry Certainly Is ...,' 715.

II   The Poetry of Al Purdy

1 'Epics,' *Collected Prose*, 213.

2 Quoted by Robert Lowell in 'Randall Jarrell, 1914–1965,' *Collected Prose*, 93.

1   Bliss Carman's Shadow

1 'Introduction,' *The Use of Poetry and the Use of Criticism*, 34. See also Jon Stallworthy's description of Louis MacNeice's reading of Yeats at the age of

seventeen: 'For the first time, he had fallen under the spell of a living writer, a spell that, for all his later reservations about Yeats, would never let him go' (*Louis MacNeice*, 90).

2 John Coldwell Adams, *Sir Charles God Damn: The Life of Charles G.D. Roberts*, 189. The royalty statement from Ryerson Press is dated 17 Feb. 1937. Of 1,000 copies, only 157 had been sold.

3 *The Witness of Poetry*, 56.

4 'Al Purdy,' *Canadian Writers and Their Works*, vol. 7, 145.

5 *The Autobiography of William Carlos Williams*, 106. Pablo Neruda admits in his *Memoirs* that he published his first volume, *Crepusculario* (1923), at his own expense (49).

6 Birney Papers, University of Toronto, box 15, Purdy file, 22 Nov. 1947.

7 *Letters of Wallace Stevens*, 106.

8 Quoted in 'Concrete and Abstract,' in Preminger, ed., *Princeton Encyclopedia of Poetry and Poetics*, 149.

9 'Al Purdy's Contemporary Pastoral,' *Canadian Poetry*, no. 10 (Spring–Summer 1982), 35.

10 As was mentioned earlier, Stevens, in his twenties and still struggling to find his poetic voice, admired the songs of vagabondia of Carman and Richard Hovey. Had he published a collection of poems at that point in his career, it would probably have been as embarrassing to him later as *The Enchanted Echo* is to Purdy. Robinson Jeffers's *Flagons and Apples* (1912) is also an apt comparison.

11 Birney Papers, University of Toronto, box 94, Purdy file, 27 July 1967.

12 'The Road Not Taken,' in Brodsky, Heaney, and Walcott, *Homage to Robert Frost*, 104.

13 'Reflections on *Vers Libre*,' *Selected Prose of T.S. Eliot*, 36.

14 For a recent example of this kind of poem, see W.S. Merwin's *Lament for the Makers: A Memorial Anthology*, in which the poet pays homage to his predecessors in this century.

15 Vendler, 'Anxiety of Innocence,' 34.

16 Purdy Papers, Queen's University, box 7, file 2. At one point, Purdy considered including stanzas about A.M. Klein, G.K. Chesterton, Emily Dickinson, and Andrei Voznesensky. The Klein quatrain made it into an early typescript before being crossed out by pen:

> Klein my token Canadian
> he was race, Jewish over all else
> he was the Jewish [of] the non-Jewish
> he was all men inside themselves.

The Chesterton stanza is equally flat, beginning badly and going nowhere after that, though Purdy does manage a reference to 'Lepanto.'

> Chesterton is hard to explain,
> to myself or anyone:
> but Lepanto and all those cider [wine] songs,
> and the paradox of Hilaire Belloc.

Dickinson is in the original list of poets to be included, but Purdy seems to have given up after one hand-written draft:

> Women? Hard to find any but Dickinson
> Emily of that ilk. Token woman
> introvert [indecipherable]
> somehow a death-lover without children

17 Michael Kirkham, *The Imagination of Edward Thomas*, 168.

18 Purdy Papers, Queen's University, box 1, 4 Sept. 1974.

19 Purdy Papers, Queen's University, box 1. Interesting here is A.M. Klein's very different defence of rhyme: 'The purpose of rhyme is to afford the poet the thrill of living dangerously. Trapeze without net' (*Notebooks: Selections from the A.M. Klein Papers*, 124). See also Auden's witty comment that 'the poet who writes "free" verse is like Robinson Crusoe on his desert island: he must do all his cooking, laundry and darning for himself. In a few exceptional cases, this manly independence produces something original and impressive, but more often the result is squalor – dirty sheets on the unmade bed and empty bottles on the unswept floor' (*The Dyer's Hand*, 22).

20 Only Blake and Keats are named in both poems.

21 Purdy had intended to pay tribute to some of his mentors in a dedication, later abandoned, to *The Cariboo Horses*: 'To: Charles Bukowski, A.E. Housman, W.H. Auden, Robinson Jeffers, Catullus and Callimachus of Alexandria.' (Purdy Papers, University of Saskatchewan, mss 4/4, 236). It is noteworthy that Lawrence is omitted. In the end, the book was published without a dedication.

22 'Nil nimium studeo, Caesar, tibi velle placere, / nec scire utrum sis albus an ater homo.'

23 See Donald Davie, *Under Briggflatts: A History of Poetry in Great Britain, 1960–1988*, 206. See also Frost's comment, 'I should like to be so subtle at this game as to seem to a casual person altogether obvious.' The key word in the sen-

tence is, of course, the adjective 'casual' (quoted by Richard Poirier in *Robert Frost: The Work of Knowing*, x).

24 See Murray's 'Coolongolook Timber Mill,' which ends as follows: '– a city man bought / the mill land for ten times / its price, and let the mill / fall down. But I have kept it' (*Times Literary Supplement*, 2 Jan. 1998, 24). See also Frye: 'Similarly Canada is a land of ruins to an extent that the less spacious countries of Europe would not dare to be: ghost towns at exhausted mines or the divisional points of old railways remind us how quickly our economy can scrap not merely a building but an entire city' ('Canada: New World without Revolution,' *Divisions on a Ground*, 172).

25 'Anxiety of Innocence,' 31.

26 Gates in Purdy's poetry are usually associated with death: see 'From the Chin P'Ing Mei' and 'Gateway,' one of his more important poems (*CP*, 11, 202). See Geddes's interview for Purdy's comments on the genesis of the poem ('A.W. Purdy: An Interview,' 69–70).

27 Birney Papers, University of Toronto, box 254, Purdy file, 28 Nov. 1976.

28 *The Lucid Veil*, 120. See also Purdy's comment to R.G. Everson: 'I look at Birney's poem "Bushed" as an example of somewhere near the way I'd like to write. Behind the poem is a whole universe of meaning waiting for the reader, as also in many of Yeats's poems' (quoted in Elspeth Cameron, *Earle Birney: A Life*, 404).

29 Ralph Gustafson's 'Agamemnon's Mask: Archaeological Museum, Athens' records Gustafson's response to the same object (*The Moment Is All: Selected Poems 1944–83*, 29).

30 Other interesting examples occur in the second stanza of 'Time Past / Time Now'(*CP*, 317) where the near-regularity of six-syllable lines is expressive of the drone and routine of the lives of the speaker's ancestors; and in the closing four lines of 'At Mycenae' (*CP*, 293) where the trimeter and the rhyme bring the poem to a point with a final image that is pure Renaissance lyric.

31 *Towards a New American Poetics*, 18.

32 Both the book and the letter are in the Purdy Collection at University College, University of Toronto.

33 'Yeats,' *Selected Prose of T.S. Eliot*, 248.

34 I wonder if any other readers hear 'The Wreck of the Deutschland' in 'In Mid-Atlantic'?

2 D.H. Lawrence in North America

1 Birney Papers, University of Toronto, box 15, Purdy file, ? Feb. 1958.

2 Purdy Papers, University of Saskatchewan, box 4, folder 43, 1 July 1956.

3 *Canadian Forum*, May 1951, 43; *Canadian Forum*, Sept. 1951, 125; *Canadian Poetry Magazine*, 17, no. 4 (Summer 1954), 8–9; *Canadian Poetry Magazine*, 14, no. 4 (Summer 1951), 16–17.

4 *Complete Poems*, vol. I, xi.

5 Birney Papers, University of Toronto, box 15, Purdy file.

6 'Cain,' *Collected Poems*, 179. Purdy also mentions an 'air pistol' in 'Norma, Eunice and Judy,' (*No Other Country*, 117): 'I'd bought an air pistol for my son in London, and during the entire eastward journey he sprayed lead pellets at motorists going in the other direction.' The piece was written in 1974; 'At Roblin Lake' was first published in 1959.

7 See 'Poets in Montreal,' *No Other Country*, 118.

8 'Reflections on *Vers Libre*,' *Selected Prose of T.S. Eliot*, 33. The following comment is also of interest: '... the ghost of some simple metre should lurk behind the arras in even the "freest" verse; to advance menacingly as we doze, and withdraw as we rouse' (34).

9 The following, from a letter to Margaret Laurence (1 Feb. 1970), is also relevant, in part because it helps date Purdy's interest in Lawrence. 'That brought Lawrence to mind, D.H. Since the more I read him the more I know he's the poet that talks in the language and uses the thoughts I aim towards. Not just death, but that too, since it's always so mixed with life – I mentioned his poems to you before, and do now emphatically again. I wish you'd get his two vol collected from library and read quickly, particularly "Birds, Beasts and Flowers", then return to the poems that seemed good' (*MLAP*, 167).

10 Compare the following on influence from earlier in the article: 'Birney's most obvious influences are Chaucer and Joyce, but as a man who reads widely he has been influenced by nearly everybody. And he has absorbed the influences seamlessly, with the exception of things such as "Anglosaxon Street" – that paean of exuberant wordplay and joyous Anglo-Saxon double-talk' (191).

11 *A Map of Misreading*, 24.

12 *The Complete Poems of D.H. Lawrence*, I, 182–4.

13 I owe the point to Michael Kirkham's *The Imagination of Edward Thomas*, 168.

14 'Al Purdy's Contemporary Pastoral,' 41.

15 *The Collected Prose and Letters*, 400.

16 Walter Jackson Bate, *Samuel Johnson: A Life*, 50. For Stevens and Valéry on the connection between walking and poetry see *Letters of Wallace Stevens*, 844, and Gerald Bruns's *Modern Poetry and the Idea of Language*, 87, respectively.

17 Geddes, 'A.W. Purdy: An Interview,' 67; *Reaching for the Beaufort Sea*, 289; Geddes, 67; 'Charles Bukowski: *It Catches My Heart in Its Hands*,' *Starting from Ameliasburgh*, 191; ibid, 190; *A Handful of Earth*, [8].

18 *The Well-Tempered Critic*, 44.

19 Letter to the author, 18 Dec. 1992. See also David McFadden's perceptive exchange with Chesley Yarn (Purdy) about Williams in *A Trip around Lake Ontario*, 91.

20 Purdy Papers, Queen's University, box 23, Bowering file.

21 Kirkham, 151. Donald Davie would call this 'subjective syntax' (*Articulate Energy*, 67).

22 Ginsberg, xix.

23 Describing his travels across the country as a journalist for *Maclean's* in 1971 and 1972, Purdy writes as follows: 'I loved it. And felt I was mapping the country, long after those early cartographers, traversing the savage land Stan Rogers sang about. Not mapping it the way they did, but naming things, saying I was there, adding something personal to the map's cold nomenclature of heights and distances. I hope that doesn't sound silly or trivial. But we weave ourselves and our lives around such real yet mythical places, strange multitudinous sounds in our ears seeping home into memory.' (*RBS*, 249–50).

24 See also 'Allah. W. Purdy' in 'Notes on a Fictional Character,' in *Selected Poems* (1972), 76, and 'Al something or other' in *Canadian Forum*, May 1966, 40–1.

25 *A History of Modern Poetry: Modernism and After*, 510.

26 Birney Papers, University of Toronto, box 15, Purdy file.

27 The second stanza, later dropped, reads as follows:

> Now while I am writing at my desk –
> The day's business – she does not come
> And sit quietly until I finish.
> She did not walk to the gate with me
> This morning and stand there watching;
> She has gone through the gate herself,
> And I accompanied her part of the way –
> Now I must busy myself with accounts.
> When I finish I shall be an old man.   *CLL*, 12

For the sake of completeness, it is worth adding that Eliot surfaces in allusions to *The Waste Land* in 'I See No Hand' (*PS*, 8); 'Birds and Beasts' (*CP*, 306); and 'The Son of Someone Loved' (*CP*, 341); in a reference to Little Gidding in the first version of 'Dark Landscape' (*WGW*, 95); and in an allusion to 'Little Gidding' in 'In the Desert,' (*WS*, 85). There is also the curious comment in *Reaching for the Beaufort Sea* that 'T.S. Eliot received the Nobel more for his "influence" on literature than the actual merit of his own work' (289).

28 Charles Olson, *Selected Writings*, 55, 130.

29 'The Music of Poetry,' *Selected Prose of T.S. Eliot*, 110. Two other comments from this essay are relevant here: 'The music of poetry, then, must be a music latent in the common speech of the poet's place' (112); 'Every revolution in poetry is apt to be, and strives to announce itself to be a return to common speech' (111).

30 For Louis Dudek's objection to the influence of the Black Mountain school see Davey's *Louis Dudek / Raymond Souster*: 'Of a manuscript by Victor Coleman he wrote, "the whole thing is merely an import from USA, and from Vancouver, of that goddamned new style foisted on the ignorant young by Olson, also partly Creeley"'(28).

31 *Al Purdy*, 39. This comment on Williams's influence, however, is far less contentious than his description of H.D.'s 'The Walls Do Not Fall' as 'maybe the best poem of our time'(24).

32 Quoted by Ekbert Faas, *Towards a New American Poetics*, 20.

33 'Introduction,' *D.H. Lawrence and Italy*, xiii.

3   The Limits of Lyric

1 Anthony Burgess, 'Introduction,' *D.H. Lawrence and Italy*, xi. See also Marjorie Perloff: 'Throughout the sixties and well into the early seventies, the debate between modernism and postmodernism in poetry (or "closed" versus "open" poetry, or poetry as "product" versus poetry as "process") revolved around two questions: the question of verse form ("fixed" versus "free") and the question of "transcendence" versus "immanence" or "presence"' (*Poetic License: Essays on Modernist and Postmodernist Lyric*, 237).

2 *Opus Posthumous*, 161.

3 'The Poetry of the Present,' *The Complete Poems of D.H. Lawrence*, I, 184. Lawrence's non-fictional prose also includes passages in which the writer is honest enough to show his 'confusion.' The following passage is from *Etruscan Places*: 'But we see a little bit of wall, built perhaps to cover a water-trough. Our guide goes straight towards it. He is a fair, good-natured young man, who doesn't look as if he would be interested in tombs. We are mistaken, however. He knows a good deal, and has a quick, sensitive interest, absolutely unobtrusive, and turns out to be as pleasant a companion for such a visit as one could wish to have' (34).

4 *Poetry and Pragmatism*, 11.

5 *Selected Letters*, 304. Pasternak's 1929 poem to Akhmatova is also worth citing on this point: 'I think I'm choosing words / Resembling your primordial being / And if I am mistaken, it's all the same to me, / I will still not part

from my mistakes' (quoted in Roberta Reeder, *Anna Akhmatova: Poet and Prophet*, [334]). Finally, there is also an interesting resemblance between the poem and Yevgeny Yevtushenko's 'Dwarf Birches' in which the birches speak collectively about their situation 'under the nails of frosts' and compare themselves to 'Parisian chestnuts' and 'haughty palms' that send them 'moral support' (*The Collected Poems 1952–1990*, 209). Though Yevtushenko's poem was written in 1966, it doesn't seem to have been published in English in that decade. An interesting comparison could be made as well between Purdy's poem and Leopardi's classic 'La ginestra' ('Broom or the Desert Flower').

6 Byron: 'Hail, Muse! *Et caetera. –*' (*Don Juan*, Canto III, 1); Wordsworth: 'And all the sad etcetera of the wrong' (*The Prelude*, 1850 version, VIII, 442); cummings: 'my sweet old etcetera' I owe these examples to Winifred Nowottny's *The Language Poets Use*, 30–1.

7 *Bursting into Song*, [11]; *Starting from Ameliasburgh*, 191; *Bursting into Song*, [11]. There are many examples in the prose of Purdy's insistence on change and relativity as constitutive in our lives. The following from 'Disconnections' is characteristic and also valuable for his description of himself as a 'humanist': 'Between Margaret Atwood, Earle Birney, and myself there is some degree of similarity. The outmoded label of humanist applies to all three of us, but is misleading. Each has a different degree of sophistication, and I am possibly rather crude compared to the other two. Or perhaps more direct? In any event, I doubt that any of us hold conventional religious beliefs, except to the extent that all humanistic feeling and ontological philosophy might be considered religious. But in the course of this small inquiry itself, I've come to be dubious about the insights I've obtained. It's as though I was an observer trying to define and describe the solar system, but can't do it accurately because I'm sitting on one of the planets.' (*ECW*, 213).

8 'Al Purdy's Contemporary Pastoral,' 41.

9 Purdy may be describing real 'ivory swans' since *Sculpture/Inuit* (plate 19) shows a pair of joined swans, from the 'Dorset culture,' with parallel lateral lines scored over their entire 6.1 centimetre length. Purdy's swans are '2-inch.' It is worth adding that in an earlier draft the lines 'and one of his thoughts / turns to ivory' read 'and one of his thoughts / fused with ivory.'

10 *Opus Posthumous*, 161.

11 Other blue herons: 'Late Rising at Roblin Lake,' 'Moonspell,' 'Purely Internal Music,' (*CP*, 71, 268, 352); and for comparison, Michael Ondaatje's 'Birds for Janet – the Heron' (*The Dainty Monsters*, 12); Margaret Laurence's *The Diviners*; Douglas LePan's 'Images of Silenus' (*Weathering It: Complete Poems*, 98); Margaret Atwood's *Surfacing* (chapters 7, 13, 14); and John Updike's story

'The Afterlife,' in which the heron is described as 'an angel' (*The Afterlife and Other Stories*, 13).

12 Letter to the author, 6 Oct. 1997.

13 Since it is unlikely that most readers will know the poem, I will quote it in full:

> To have spent one's life lighting a fire
> to rage thru the alphabet
> – It is a small thing
> but what would you have?
> How divide these finite moments
> whereby the bird
> stops midflight
> the fox halts in his red running
> the sun and moon are forgotten trinkets
> in the mind twist of a word?
> Some might say it is enough
> this game of words
> that love and truth are enough
> and perhaps beauty
> but all of them are only angles of vision
> to light a fire
> at a place that is nowhere
> with fuel that does not exist
> thru which a bird is flying
> and cannot stop [crossed out]   Queen's University, box 7, file 5

14 Queen's University, box 12, folder 135.

15 The 'nightmare' is described in some detail in *Reaching for the Beaufort Sea*, 13–14. At the age of three, Purdy wandered out of the house looking for his mother and got lost at the local market.

16 Other echoes, other 'influences': 'The Death of Animals,' a much earlier poem (*BB*, 6) has the following couplet: 'Fox in deep burrow suddenly imagined / A naked woman inside his rubric fur'; Irving Layton's 'free and gallant' fox in 'Predator' in *Balls for a One-Armed Juggler* (a book Purdy reviewed; he refers to the poem and the fox [*SA*, 207]); Dylan Thomas's 'To Follow the Fox' and 'In Country Sleep' (*Collected Poems*, 44); Bill Howell's *The Red Fox*, which Purdy reviewed twice (*Books in Canada*, Nov. 1971, 22, and *Canadian Literature*, no. 54 [Autumn 1972], 86–90). The reference to a 'hammer' and 'hammering' in James Dickey's 'Fox Blood' is also suggestive:

'That's the bush my hand / Went deeply through as I followed. / Like a wild hammer blazed my right thumb / In the flash and moonlight. / My thumb, a hammering day-and-night sign / Of that country' (*The Whole Motion: Collected Poems*, 218–19).

17 Another, less significant echo from a very early poem occurs in '(callipygous screenland special)'; the only other times Purdy uses 'callipygous' are in 'Towns': 'And Toronto, O city of callipygous whores / for whom I lusted' (*BB*, 8); and 'Ballad of the Despairing Wife': 'your behind / than which however Callipygous' (*CH*, 46).

18 Purdy Papers, Queen's University, box 12, 'Red Fox on Highway 500' file.

19 *The Lucid Veil: Poetic Truth in the Victorian Age*, 14.

20 It is worth noting that for Purdy hammering and its cognates are often associated with death and poetry or creativity, as if all the references to hammers and hammering are ultimately and mysteriously related to the hammering of typewriter keys and coffins. As a result, a line like 'red hammers hammering / light as air on the highway' has a slightly different force for a reader aware of the associations it has for Purdy. In the early 'Further Deponent Saith Not' (*CP*, 124), for instance, the speaker who is hammering a nail is convinced that there is someone at the door 'who wishes to deliver my death certificate.' 'Wilderness Gothic' describes a man on a church steeple 'hammering in the sky. / Perhaps he will fall' (*CP*, 134). 'Names' describes 'Birthing, begetting and dying' as 'the great hammers of being, / each one thudding against the skull / each one obliterating the others –' (*CP*, 311). And 'My Cousin Don' ends with the poet, trying to find something of value in the life of a cousin who committed suicide, admitting that it 'escapes my hammering mind' (*CP*, 334).

21 Letter to Stephen Spender, quoted in 'Remembering Eliot,' *T.S. Eliot: The Man and His Work*, 55–6.

22 Seamus Heaney, *The Government of the Tongue*, 106. For the sake of completeness, I should also mention that the brief prose version of the encounter with the fox in *Reaching for the Beaufort Sea* (125–6) begins on the same page as references to an unwritten novel about Ridley Neville Purdy and 'poker playing.' I rest my case.

4   Poetry and the Poet

1 Quoted in Donald Davie, *Under Briggflatts: A History of Poetry in Great Britain, 1960–1988*, 42.

2 *Kipling, Auden, and Co.*, 305.

3 W.R. Johnson, *The Idea of Lyric*, 8.

4 *Selected Letters 1902–1926*, 13 Nov. 1925, 394–5.

5 Bachelard, *The Poetics of Space*, 6–7.

6 Heidegger, *Poetry, Language, Thought*, 215.

7 Bachelard, 17; Heidegger, 221.

8 Purdy Papers, Queen's University, box 14, file 69. I quote from Purdy's script, a combination of prose and poetry.

9 *Harsh and Lovely Land*, 92. See also Stan Dragland's suggestive reading of it in 'Al Purdy's Poetry: Openings' in *The Bees of the Invisible*, 104 ff.

10 Two comments by George Swinton in *Sculpture of the Inuit* are relevant here. With reference to the Dorsets, Swinton suggests that 'art seems to have been a highly specialized activity. In fact, the pieces are so highly developed and so exquisitely carved that they are difficult to imagine as the work of occasional carvers ... but are more likely the work of specialists (artists, or shaman-artists) who practised a well-known and carefully handed-down tradition of craftsmanship and image making' (114). He also records a conversation with the supervisor of the Rankin Inlet ceramics project who points out that 'Tiktak who was badly hurt when the mine was here, who is deaf, weak, and elderly' 'would have nothing and be nobody' (23) but for his artwork.

11 There is also this fine abandoned fragment, undated, among the papers: 'Among the ambiguities / of myself / a red wall of leaves / drowning the crimson sky / a series of caves / no ending of them / far back where the pictographs / begin / or in the dust / where they end / a flake of mica / in the mind / surrounded by bones / beyond all these / you' (Queen's University, box 13, file 35).

12 Letter to Jack McClelland, 29 Jan. 1976 (McClelland and Stewart Papers, McMaster University, series A, box 52, Purdy file); letter to Earle Birney, 2 Feb. 1976 (Birney Papers, University of Toronto, box 254, Purdy file).

5 Starting from Ameliasburg: Old Rid, Owen Roblin, and Al

1 *Radical Tories*, 93.

2 There are also the poems 'My Grandfather Talking – 30 Years Ago' (*CP*, 72) and 'My Grandfather's Country' (*CP*, 146), first published in 1965 and 1968, respectively. Since much of Purdy's energy went into the writing of radio plays in the 1950s, there is a strong possibility that this also influenced the turn in his poetry late in the decade toward a more idiomatic voice and the concrete and mundane incident or event.

3 *Transitions III: Poetry*, 282.

4 *The Autobiography of William Carlos Williams*, 175.

5 For those who value comprehensiveness, the first mention of 'names' in Purdy's poetry occurs in 1935 in the following stanza from 'Canada' (by Alfred Purdy, Form 2A): 'The pioneers of long ago / Who made this land today / As pass the years that come and go / Their names will ever stay' (*Spotlight*, 17). *Spotlight* was Purdy's high school literary magazine or yearbook . There is a 1935 copy of it in the Purdy Papers, Queen's University, box 13.

6 'But he says it is also a place where the labours of lives have been as futile as those of Sisyphus (Purdy still loves to import the easy classical names at times)' (*Al Purdy*, 87). Earlier in the book Bowering suggests that Canadian poets should replace European mythologies with 'existing Indian cosmology' (29). As I argued in part 1, this seems to me a questionable prescription. Paul de Man offers in *The Rhetoric of Romanticism* a different reason why the modern poet should avoid classical mythology when he suggests that the use of 'Hellenic myths' is an admission of failure, an evasion in the face of reality (7).

7 As I wrote earlier, parallel lines occur in several other poems. Compare the following from 'The Road to Newfoundland' (*CP*, 139):

> My foot has pushed a fire ahead of me
> for a thousand miles
> my arms' response to hills and stones
> has stated parallel green curves
> deep in my unknown country.

Also of interest are the closing lines of 'Vertical Versus Horizontal'

> *– and quietness in the forest*
> *when leaves talked together*
> *and the words they said*
> *were sleep sleep sleep*
> *and we slept*
> *and bodies joined to each other*
> *and were parallel with the earth*
> *– we slept*
> *and dreamed a strange dream*
> *and woke and were not ourselves*   WS, 9

8 A recent poem, 'Bruegel's Icarus' (*TPNA*, 23), repeats the antithesis of farmer and artist but mediates it through a painting, one of Purdy's favourites, 'The Fall of Icarus.'

9 Heidegger, *Basic Writings*, 407–8.

10 It's worth keeping in mind that 'German settlers ... outnumbered the British among the original United Empire Loyalists in Upper Canada' (V. Seymour Wilson, 'The Tapestry Vision of Canadian Multiculturalism,' 412).

11 *Radical Tories*, 92–3.

12 See also *A Splinter in the Heart* for a juxtaposition of the Trenton dump and the 'kitchen middens' of Sumer and Babylon (120).

13 Purdy Papers, Queen's University, box 1, 9 Sept. 1974. After calling the work 'a psychological self-examination,' Purdy goes on, 'I think it doesn't come off completely, tho perhaps partially.'

6   History and Nation

1 Louis Dudek and Michael Gnarowski, eds., *The Making of Modern Poetry in Canada*, 265.

2 'A Legend,' *The Collected Poems*, 103.

3 *Inquiring Spirit*, 335 [*Table Talk*, I, 150–1: 28 May 1830].

4 'The Origin of the Work of Art,' *Poetry, Language, Thought*, 75.

5 John Hollander, ed., *American Poetry: The Nineteenth Century*, vol. 1, 658.

6 Helen Vendler, '*Tintern Abbey*: Two Assaults,' in *Bucknell Review: Wordsworth in Context*, quoted by Timothy Bahti in *The Ends of Lyric*, 6.

7 *In the American Grain*, 113.

8 Purdy Papers, Queen's University, box 13, general file.

9 An earlier use of these Shakespearean lines occurs in MacLennan's *Barometer Rising*: '... this anomalous land, this sprawling waste of timber and rock and water where the only living sounds were the footfalls of animals or the fantastic laughter of a loon, this empty tract of primordial silences and winds and erosions and shifting colours, this bead-like string of crude towns and cities tied by nothing but railway tracks, this nation undiscovered by the rest of the world and unknown to itself, these people neither American nor English ...' (79). Purdy also uses Shakespeare's lines in an unpublished long poem, 'Election Blues' (1979).

10 Purdy Papers, Queen's University, box 3, Lee file, 18 July 1972.

11 Also relevant is a letter to Birney in which Purdy asks, 'Doesn't it add up, the various parts, to a Canadian whole? You are certainly not going to give me, nor is any one, the components of a unique national identity, other than such memories, history etc.' (Birney Papers, University of Toronto, box 137, Purdy file, 26 Nov. 1970).

12 The sketches of individuals are particularly prominent in the articles where Purdy often writes about an area and a way of life – fishing in British

Columbia, ranching in Saskatchewan, being a sailor on the St Lawrence Seaway – primarily by describing individuals and recording his conversations with them. One of his best is 'Dryland Country' (*SA*, 69–78), which deals with the plight of Saskatchewan ranchers being moved off their land to make way for the Grasslands Park. The closing paragraph is a good example of the multi-historical aspect of Purdy's imagination: 'It takes a small leap of the imagination to realize that all of this brown land, soon turning to green and gold, was once the Bearpaw Sea seventy million years ago. Hereford and Charolais and other cattle breeds have replaced the dinosaurs. As pronghorn deer have replaced camels and titanotheres. In a much later time, whites have replaced the Indians and Métis. It's impossible to conceive an equal leap into the future or whether there will still be men at all in that distant time. But if there are, I hope some may be ranchers' (78). Though he drifts into time travel, the paragraph never loses touch with the present and, more important from an editorial viewpoint, the subject of the piece, ranching.

13 The article 'Bon Jour' in *Starting from Ameliasburgh* (100–9) has a longer account of the meeting with the Quebec premier as well as Purdy's adventures in and response to separatism and the province of Quebec. A number of details, images, and lines appear in both the poem and the article.

14 This was pointed out to me by Professor Ursula Mathis of the University of Innsbruck in a discussion following her lecture 'Language and Identity: A Critical Analysis of the Quebec "Chanson"' at the University of La Laguna (Canary Islands) on 11 Dec. 1996.

15 'A Speech on Robert Frost: A Cultural Episode,' 154.

16 See F.T. Flahiff's 'Afterword' to Sheila Watson's *The Double Hook*, 'She thought, according to her own account, about a problem and a place. Whether or not it was possible for a writer in Canada in the first half of the twentieth century to write about a particular place without remaining merely regional – this was the problem. "[H]ow do you? how are you international if you're not international? if you're very provincial, very local, and very much a part of your own milieu ..."' (126).

17 *A Trip around Lake Ontario*, 97.

18 Ralph Gustafson's comments on the regional are pertinent here: '... the village pump, one's own backyard is the place of poetry ... Move that into myth, into universality if you will, but start elsewhere at grave poetic peril' ('Worthwhile Visitations,' rev. of *Notes and Visitations: Poems 1936–1975*, by George Woodcock, *Canadian Literature*, no. 71 (Winter 1976), 91.

19 Purdy Papers, Queen's University, box 2, Acorn file, 6 June 1973.

20 *The Well-Tempered Critic*, 49.

21 The original version is included in a letter to Jack McClelland, 18 Oct. 1982 (McClelland and Stewart Papers, McMaster University, series A, 1982 ff., box N–R, Purdy file).

22 The ambiguity of the adjective 'underground' destabilizes the ending even more; there's no doubt that it modifies 'the dead men,' but its proximity to 'me' creates the momentary impression that the speaker is himself somehow already underground as well, that his 'hymn' has already failed.

23 Purdy Papers, Queen's University, box 11.

24 McClelland and Stewart Papers, McMaster University, box 95, Purdy file, 2 June 1979.

25 In *The Well-Tempered Critic*, Frye writes that 'the poetic process ... [is] the largely subconscious free-association of words by sound out of which the schemata of poetry develop' (66). I wonder whether there wasn't something of subconscious free-association in Purdy's mind in conceiving 'On the Decipherment of "Linear B"'? I'm interested particularly in the relationship between the name of Michael Ventris, the man who did the deciphering, and 'the south wind blowing' in the poem's closing line. Both Ventris's name and the south wind that blew as Knossos burned are historical facts, but the etymological (*ventus*) and euphonic coincidence between the two as well as the formal fact that they frame the poem seem to be the result primarily of aesthetic concerns.

26 Compare the following exchange between a poet and a potential reader in Graham Greene's *The Honorary Consul*: '"You seem to have written a hell of a lot about death." "Yes. I think about half my poems are about death," Aquino said. "It's one of the two proper subjects for a man – love and death"' (136).

27 See also 'The Double Shadow' (*SD*, 49) and the early poem 'Love Story' (*CLL*, 21): 'I can be two men if I have to.'

28 Purdy's general comment about how he arranges poems in individual collections is worth noting, though it doesn't relate to my point: 'Generally I try to find contrasting poems, i.e., place a cynical poem next a romantic one, more rhythmical one next to poem not so rhythmical ...' (to Margaret Atwood, Purdy Papers, Queen's University, box 2, Atwood file, 17 June 1973.)

29 'I Was Looking a Long While,' *Complete Poetry and Collected Prose*, 512.

30 'Spain, 1873–74,' ibid., 591.

31 Neuman and Wilson, *Labyrinths of Voice: Conversations with Robert Kroetsch*, 12.

32 The main failing of some of these historical or historico-mythic poems is inseparable from their strength: in trying to show the various ways in which the past resembles the present, Purdy occasionally diminishes its strangeness, its otherness in emphasizing the similarities rather than the differences.

33 *Abinger Harvest*, 183–6. 'Verynice' is Purdy's addition to the historical account since Forster leaves the wealthy courtesan anonymous.

34 Purdy's style in the letters is relatively consistent from correspondent to correspondent. Any change is immediately noticeable. A comment like the one quoted here seems to me to show Purdy trying to accommodate his style to Bukowski's, which is always closer to the idiom of the bar. On the other hand, if he occasionally writes *down* to Bukowski, the letters to Margaret Laurence show him more restrained and self-conscious than he is usually. The ones to George Woodcock fall somewhere in between. But since the range of subject-matter is so limited – they rarely touch on personal topics – we don't really get a full or accurate impression of either man. When the collected letters appear, they will surprise many with their range of styles and the variety of interests or topics discussed.

35 'Archilochos' ends as follows: 'Archilochos the soldier, he was us. / Three thousand years? I can still hear / that commonsense song of the shield: / a loser who managed to be victorious, / his name is a champagne cry in my blood.' Although this excerpt has five lines, the poem is written in quatrains similar to those in 'Bestiary [II].'

7   Origins and Being

1 Pertinent here is Frye's comment that metaphorical language, the language of paradox, is a way of detaching the self from the ordinary world and preparing it for *kerygma*. See *The Double Vision*, 17–21.

2 See ibid., 74 ff.

3 Purdy Papers, Queen's University, Laurence file, 6 July 1968. The letter is not included in *Margaret Laurence–Al Purdy: A Friendship in Letters*. The note on the author to *Emu! Remember* has the following sentence: 'Religion, show me' (17).

4 *Paterson*, 5. This is preceded by a more famous sentence: 'The poet does not, however, permit himself to go beyond the thought to be discovered in the context of that with which he is dealing: no ideas but in things.'

5 Quoted by Bruce Chatwin, *The Songlines*, 25.

6 *The Education of Henry Adams*, 931.

7 Pratt, *The Complete Poems of E.J. Pratt*, I, 260. The following stanza from the same poem seems to have been in Purdy's mind when he wrote the last stanza of 'Near Tofino, Vancouver Island':

The snarl Neanderthal is worn
Close to the smiling Aryan lips,

The civil polish of the horn
Gleams from our praying fingertips.

...

The man Neanderthal departs
and drives his car along the sand
(with seat belt buckled)
upright a little longer maybe
who loved a little
   thought a little
    and drank a lot
bequeathed the stars some Latin names
    which they forgot –   *CP*, 270

8 *Civilization and Its Discontents*, 1.
9 *The Lucid Veil*, xviii.
10 'Name the Gods,' *The Complete Poems of D.H. Lawrence*, II, 651. See also 'The Gods! The Gods!' and 'There Are No Gods' on the same page.
11 '... Poetically Man Dwells ...' in *Poetry, Language, Thought*, 215.
12 'Dante and his contemporaries did not know geological time. Paleontological clocks were unknown to them: the clock of coal, the clock of infusorial limestone, the clocks of sand, shale and schist' (Osip Mandelstam, 'Conversation about Dante,' *The Complete Prose and Letters of Osip Mandelstam*, 422).
13 There is a prose version of this scene in 'The Cartography of Myself': 'And once there was a mile-long Arctic island, my home for three weeks of summer: I lay with my ear flat against the monstrous stone silence of the island, listening to the deep core of the world – silence unending and elemental, leaked from a billion-year period before and after the season of man' (*SA*, 17).
14 In the unpublished 'Arctic Diary,' Purdy writes, 'Travelling across these wild boreal landscapes is like confronting God, even if you don't believe in him' (8). The manuscript is in Purdy's possession.
15 *What Is Philosophy?* 74–5.
16 Purdy Papers, Queen's University, box 7, file 5. For 'content' see *In Search of Owen Roblin*: 'If the result wasn't home it was a place to camp / and whatever gods there were / who permitted pain and defeat / also allowed brief content' [24]. And also 'The Strangers': 'Almost lighthearted, misgivings hidden / from himself, summer like a spell, the year / a war ended, happiness nearly impossible, / if such a thing was ever possible, / small content only now and then, / the wagon a wooden star ahead in his mind' (*CP*, 337).
17 *The Malaise of Modernity*, 86.

18 Trilling, 'A Speech on Robert Frost: A Cultural Episode,' 156–8.
19 Letter to Earle Birney, 5 June 1971. Purdy Papers, Queen's University, box 2, Birney file.
20 Quoted in J.B. Leishman's commentary to *Duino Elegies*, 93.
21 Ibid, 122.
22 'The Sick Soul,' *The Varieties of Religious Experience*, in *Writings 1902–1910*, 151.
23 Trilling, 158.
24 John Updike, 'On Rereading *The Age of Innocence*,' 18.
25 For an early vision of Ameliasburg as a village not only related to but containing history because of the poet's dream, see 'News Reports at Ameliasburg' (*CP*, 106).

8   Conclusion: The Future of the Past

1 Marginal note to Northrop Frye's 'Conclusion' in Purdy's copy of *Literary History of Canada*, vol. 3, 325 (Purdy Collection, University College, University of Toronto); letter to Earle Birney, 11 June 1980, Birney Papers, University of Toronto, box 254, Purdy file.
2 'Introduction,' *Anything Is Possible*, 5.
3 'The Origin of the Work of Art,' *Poetry, Language, Thought*, 80. I have substituted 'poetry' where Heidegger writes 'art,' but the substitution doesn't distort either the meaning or the force of his question.

Appendix. Annotating the Poems of Al Purdy: Quotation, Allusion, Echo, and (Some) References

1 *Letters of Wallace Stevens*, 815.

Bibliography

Only books and articles quoted or referred to are listed. For a more complete bibliography see *The Annotated Bibliography of Canada's Major Authors*, volume 2, ed. Robert Lecker and Jack David, Toronto: ECW Press, 1980, and Louis Mac-Kendrick's 'Al Purdy,' in *Canadian Writers and Their Works*, volume 7.

Primary Sources

Some of the entries are followed by the abbreviation used in the body of the text.

Poetry

At the Marsport Drugstore. Sutton West, Ont.: Paget, 1977.
Being Alive: Poems 1958–1978. Toronto: McClelland and Stewart, 1978. [*BA*]
The Blur in Between: Poems 1960–61. Toronto: Emblem, 1962. [*BB*]
Bursting into Song: An Al Purdy Omnibus. Ed. Marty Gervais. Windsor, Ont.: Black Moss, 1982.
The Cariboo Horses. Toronto: McClelland and Stewart, 1965. [*CH*]
The Collected Poems of Al Purdy. Ed. Russell Brown. Toronto: McClelland and Stewart, 1986. [*CP*]
The Crafte So Longe to Lerne. Toronto: Ryerson, 1959. [*CLL*]
Emu! Remember. Fredericton: Fiddlehead Books, 1956. [*ER*]
The Enchanted Echo. Vancouver: Clark & Stuart, 1944. [*EE*]
A Handful of Earth. Coatsworth, Ont.: Black Moss, 1977. [*HE*]
In Search of Owen Roblin. Toronto: McClelland and Stewart, 1974. [*ISOR*]
Love in a Burning Building. Toronto: McClelland and Stewart, 1970. [*LBB*]
Moths in the Iron Curtain. Sutton West, Ont.: Paget, 1979.
Naked with Summer in Your Mouth. Toronto: McClelland and Stewart, 1994. [*NSM*]

North of Summer: Poems from Baffin Island. Toronto: McClelland and Stewart, 1967. [*NS*]

No Second Spring. Coatsworth, Ont.: Black Moss, 1977.

On the Bearpaw Sea. Burnaby, B.C.: Blackfish, 1973.

On the Bearpaw Sea. Rev. ed. Toronto: Red Maple Foundation, 1994.

Piling Blood. Toronto: McClelland and Stewart, 1984. [*PB*]

Poems for All the Annettes. Toronto: Contact, 1962. [*PAA*]

Poems for All the Annettes. Rev. ed. Toronto: Anansi, 1968.

The Poems of Al Purdy. New Canadian Library. Toronto: McClelland and Stewart, 1976.

Pressed on Sand. Toronto: Ryerson, 1955. [*PS*]

The Quest for Ouzo. Trenton, Ont.: M. Kerrigan Almey, 1970.

Rooms for Rent in the Outer Planets: Selected Poems 1962–1996. Ed. Al Purdy and Sam Solecki. Madeira Park, B.C.: Harbour Publishing, 1996.

Selected Poems. Toronto: McClelland and Stewart, 1972.

Sex & Death. Toronto; McClelland and Stewart, 1973. [*SD*]

The Stone Bird. Toronto: McClelland and Stewart, 1981. [*SB*]

Sundance at Dusk. Toronto: McClelland and Stewart, 1976. [*SDu*]

To Paris Never Again. Madeira Park, B.C.: Harbour Publishing, 1997. [*TPNA*]

Wild Grape Wine. Toronto: McClelland and Stewart, 1968. [*WGW*]

The Woman on the Shore. Toronto: McClelland and Stewart, 1990 [*WS*]

Prose

Ed. and intro. to Acorn, Milton. *Dig Up My Heart: Selected Poems 1952–83*. The Modern Canadian Poets. Toronto: McClelland and Stewart, 1983.

Ed. and intro. to Acorn, Milton. *I've Tasted My Blood: Poems 1958–1968*. Toronto: Ryerson, 1969.

'After a Hundred Years Canadian Poetry Certainly Is ...,' *Queen's Quarterly* 76, no. 4 (Winter 1969), 710–18.

The Bukowski/Purdy Letters: A Decade of Dialogue 1964–1974. Sutton West, Ont. and Santa Barbara: Paget, 1983.

Cougar Hunter: A Memoir of Roderick Haig-Brown. Vancouver: Phoenix, 1992.

'Dennis the Ed.' *Descant*, no. 39 (Winter 1982), 22–4.

'Disconnections.' *Essays on Canadian Writing*, no. 49 (Summer 1993), 180–222. [*ECW*]

Ed. and intro. *Fifteen Winds: A Selection of Modern Canadian Poems*. Toronto: Ryerson, 1969. [*FW*]

'Fraser Sutherland and His Poems.' In *Madwomen*, by Fraser Sutherland. Windsor, Ont.: Black Moss, 1978.

Margaret Laurence–Al Purdy: A Friendship in Letters. Ed. John Lennox. Toronto: McClelland and Stewart, 1993. [*MLAP*]

Morning and It's Summer. Montreal: Quadrant, 1983.

Ed. *The New Romans: Candid Canadian Opinions of the U.S.* Edmonton: Hurtig, 1968.

No One Else Is Lawrence (with Doug Beardsley). Madeira Park, B.C.: Harbour Publishing, 1998.

No Other Country. Toronto: McClelland and Stewart, 1977. [*NC*]

The Purdy–Woodcock Letters: Selected Correspondence 1964–1984. Ed. George Galt. Toronto: ECW, 1988.

Reaching for the Beaufort Sea. Ed. Alex Widen. Madeira Park, B.C.: Harbour Publishing, 1993. [*RBS*]

A Splinter in the Heart. Toronto: McClelland and Stewart, 1990. [*SH*]

Starting from Ameliasburgh: The Collected Prose of Al Purdy. Ed. Sam Solecki. Madeira Park, B.C.: Harbour Publishing, 1995. [*SA*]

Ed. and intro. *Storm Warning: The New Canadian Poets*. Toronto: McClelland and Stewart, 1971.

Ed. and intro. *Storm Warning 2: The New Canadian Poets*. Toronto: McClelland and Stewart, 1976.

Intro. *Wood Mountain Poems*, by Andrew Suknaski. Toronto: Macmillan, 1976.

Reviews, Critical Essays, and Books on Al Purdy

Bowering, George. *Al Purdy*. Toronto: Copp Clark, 1970.

Coles, Don. 'Image and Archetype: *The Woman on the Shore*.' *Books in Canada* 19, no. 3, April 1990, 34.

Doyle, Mike. 'Proteus at Roblin Lake.' *Canadian Literature*, no. 61 (Summer 1974), 7–23.

Dragland, Stan. 'Al Purdy's Poetry: Openings.' In *The Bees of the Invisible*. Toronto: Coach House, 1991, 90–112.

Duffy, Dennis. *Gardens, Covenants, Exiles: Loyalism in the Literature of Upper Canada/Ontario*. Toronto: University of Toronto Press, 1982, 115–30.

Early, L.R. 'Birney and Purdy: An Intertextual Instance.' *Canadian Poetry: Studies, Documents, Reviews*, no. 23 (Fall–Winter 1988), 1–13.

Geddes, Gary. 'A.W. Purdy: An Interview.' *Canadian Literature*, no. 41 (Summer 1969), 66–72.

Jones, D.G. 'Al Purdy's Contemporary Pastoral.' *Canadian Poetry: Studies, Documents, Reviews*, no. 10 (Spring–Summer 1982), 32–43.

Lee, Dennis. 'The Poetry of Al Purdy: An Afterword.' In *The Collected Poems of Al Purdy*. Ed. Russell Brown. Toronto: McClelland and Stewart, 1986, 371–91.

MacKendrick, Louis. 'Al Purdy.' In *Canadian Writers and Their Works*, volume VII. Ed. Robert Lecker, Jack David, and Ellen Quigley. Toronto: ECW, 1990, 133–90.

Marshall, Tom. *Harsh and Lovely Land: The Major Canadian Poets and the Making of a Canadian Tradition*. Vancouver: University of British Columbia Press, 1979.

Stevens, Peter. 'In the Raw: The Poetry of A.W. Purdy.' *Canadian Literature*, no. 28 (Spring 1966), 22–30.

Taylor, Charles. *Radical Tories: The Conservative Tradition in Canada*. Toronto: Anansi, 1982.

Woodcock, George. 'On the Poetry of Al Purdy.' In Al Purdy, *Selected Poems*. Toronto: McClelland and Stewart, 1972, 8–15.

General

Adam, Ian, and Helen Tiffin, eds. *Past the Last Post: Theorizing Post-Colonialism and Post-Modernism*. Calgary: University of Calgary Press, 1990.

Adams, Henry. *Novels, Mont-Saint-Michel, The Education*. New York: Library of America, 1983.

Adams, John Coldwell. *Sir Charles God Damn: The Life of Charles G.D. Roberts*. Toronto: University of Toronto Press, 1986.

Akhmatova, Anna. *Poems of Akhmatova*. Trans. Max Hayward and Stanley Kunitz. London: Collins and Harvill, 1974.

Allen, Donald M., ed. *The New American Poetry*. New York: Grove, 1960.

Alvarez, A., ed. *The New Poetry*. Harmondsworth: Penguin, 1962.

American Poetry: The Nineteenth Century. 2 vols. Ed. John Hollander. New York: Library of America, 1993.

Archiloque. *Fragments*. Texte établi par François Lasserre. Traduit et commenté par André Bonnard. Paris: Les Belles Lettres, 1958.

Armstrong, G.H. *The Origin and Meaning of Place Names in Canada*. Toronto: Macmillan, 1930.

Ashcroft, Bill, Gareth Griffiths, and Helen Tiffin. *The Empire Writes Back: Theory and Practice in Post-Colonial Literatures*. London: Routledge, 1989.

Auden, W.H. *Collected Poems*. Ed. Edward Mendelson. New York: Random House, 1976.

– *The Dyer's Hand*. New York: Vintage, 1968.

Avery, Donald, and Roger Hall, eds. *Coming of Age: Readings in Canadian History since World War II*. Toronto: Harcourt Brace, 1996.

Bachelard, Gaston. *On Poetic Imagination and Reverie: Selections from the Work of Gaston Bachelard*. Trans. Collette Gaudin. Indianapolis: Bobbs-Merrill, 1971.

– *The Poetics of Space*. Boston: Beacon, 1969.

Bahti, Timothy. *The Ends of Lyric: Direction and Consequence in Western Poetry.* Baltimore: Johns Hopkins University Press, 1996.

Barry, Elaine. *Robert Frost on Writing.* New Brunswick, N.J.: Rutgers University Press, 1973.

Bate, Walter Jackson. *Samuel Johnson.* New York: Harcourt Brace Jovanovich, 1977.

Berger, Carl. 'The True North Strong and Free.' In *Nationalism in Canada.* Ed. Peter Russell. Toronto: McGraw-Hill Ryerson, 1966, 5–26.

– *The Writing of Canadian History.* Toronto: Oxford University Press, 1976.

Berlin, Isaiah. *Against the Current: Essays in the History of Ideas.* London: Hogarth, 1979.

– *Vico and Herder: Two Studies in the History of Ideas.* London: Hogarth, 1966.

Bhabha, Homi K. 'DissemiNation: Time, Narrative, and the Margins of the Modern Nation.' In *Nation and Narration.* Ed. Homi K. Bhabha. London: Routledge, 1990, 291–322.

Birney, Earle. *The Collected Poems of Earle Birney.* 2 vols. Toronto: McClelland and Stewart, 1975.

Blake, William. *The Letters of William Blake.* Ed. Geoffrey Keynes. Oxford: Clarendon, 1980.

– *The Poems of William Blake.* Ed. W.H. Stevenson. London: Longman, 1971.

Bloom, Harold. *The Anxiety of Influence.* New York: Oxford University Press, 1973.

– *A Map of Misreading.* New York: Oxford University Press, 1975.

Borrello, Alfred, ed. *A Concordance of the Poetry in English of Gerard Manley Hopkins.* Metuchen: N.J.: Scarecrow Press, 1969.

Boswell, James. *The Life of Samuel Johnson L.L.D.* New York: Modern Library, n.d.

Bourke, Lawrence. *A Vivid Steady State: Les Murray and Australian Poetry.* Kensington: New South Wales University Press, 1992.

Bradford, William. *Of Plymouth Plantation, 1620–1647.* New York: Modern Library, 1952.

Braudel, Fernand. *The Identity of France.* Vol. 1. *History and Environment.* London: Collins, 1988.

Breslin, James. *Mark Rothko.* Chicago: University of Chicago Press, 1993.

Brodsky, Joseph, Seamus Heaney, and Derek Walcott. *Homage to Robert Frost.* New York: Farrar, Straus and Giroux, 1996.

Brown, E.K. *On Canadian Poetry.* Ottawa: Tecumseh, 1973.

Browning, Robert. *Poems and Plays.* 5 vols. London: Dent, 1968.

Bruns, Gerald L. *Modern Poetry and the Idea of Language: A Critical and Historical Study.* New Haven: Yale University Press, 1974.

Burgess, Anthony. 'Introduction.' *D.H. Lawrence and Italy: Twilight in Italy, Sea and Sardinia, Etruscan Places.* London: Heinemann, 1972.

Cameron, Elspeth. *Earle Birney: A Life*. Toronto: Viking, 1994.
– *Hugh MacLennan: A Writer's Life*. Toronto: University of Toronto Press, 1981.
– *Irving Layton: A Portrait*. Toronto: Stoddart, 1985.
Carman. Bliss. *Pipes of Pan*. Boston: Page, 1906.
Carman, Bliss, and Lorne Pierce. *Our Canadian Literature: Representative Verse English and French*. Toronto: Ryerson, 1935 [1922].
Carman, Bliss, Lorne Pierce, and V.B. Rhodenizer. *Canadian Poetry in English*. Toronto: Ryerson, 1954 [1934. 1922].
Chamberlin, J. Edward. *Come Back to Me My Language*. Urbana: University of Illinois Press, 1993.
Chatwin, Bruce. *The Songlines*. London: Picador, 1988.
Clare, John. *John Clare* [the Oxford Poets]. Ed. Eric Robinson and David Powell. Oxford: Oxford University Press, 1984.
Coleridge, Samuel Taylor. *Inquiring Spirit*. Ed. Kathleen Coburn. Toronto: University of Toronto Press, 1979.
Coles, Don. *Forests of the Medieval World*. Erin: Porcupine's Quill, 1993.
Cottrell, Leonard. *The Bull of Minos*. London: Evans, 1971 [1962].
Dante. *Literary Criticism of Dante Alighieri*. Lincoln: University of Nebraska Press, 1973.
Davey, Frank. *Canadian Literary Power*. Edmonton: NeWest Publishers, 1994.
– *From There to Here*. Erin, Ont.: Press Porcépic, 1974.
– *Louis Dudek/Raymond Souster*. Vancouver: Douglas & McIntyre, 1980.
– *Post-National Arguments: The Politics of the Anglophone-Canadian Novel since 1967*. Toronto: University of Toronto Press, 1993.
Davie, Donald. *Articulate Energy*. London: Routledge and Kegan Paul, 1955.
– *Under Briggflatts: A History of Poetry in Great Britain, 1960–1988*. Chicago: University of Chicago Press, 1989.
Daymond, Douglas, and Leslie Monkman, eds. *Canadian Novelists and the Novel*. Ottawa: Borealis, 1981.
De Man, Paul. *The Rhetoric of Romanticism*. New York: Columbia University Press, 1984.
Dickey, James. *The Whole Motion: Collected Poems, 1945–1992*. Hanover: Wesleyan University Press, 1992.
Di Michele, Mary, ed. *Anything Is Possible: A Selection of Eleven Women Poets*. Oakville, Ont.: Mosaic, 1984.
Donoghue, Denis. *Reading America: Essays on American Literature*. Berkeley and Los Angeles: University of California Press, 1987.
Dudek, Louis, and Michael Gnarowski, eds. *The Making of Modern Poetry in Canada*. Toronto: Ryerson, 1967.
Dworkin, Ronald. *A Matter of Principle*. Cambridge: Harvard University Press, 1985.

Eckermann, Johann Peter. *Conversations with Goethe*. Trans. John Oxenford. London: Dent, 1970.

Eliade, Mircea. *Myth and Reality*. New York: Harper and Row, 1963.

Eliot, T.S. *The Complete Poems and Plays 1909–1950*. New York: Harcourt, Brace and World, 1962.

– *On Poetry and Poets*. London: Faber, 1969 [1957].

– *Selected Prose of T.S. Eliot*. Ed. Frank Kermode. London: Faber, 1975.

– *The Use of Poetry and the Use of Criticism*. London: Faber and Faber, 1967 [1933].

Emerson, Ralph Waldo. *Essays and Lectures*. New York: Library of America, 1983.

Erkkila, Betsy. *Whitman the Political Poet*. New York: Oxford University Press, 1989.

Faas, Ekbert. *Towards a New American Poetics*. Santa Barbara: Black Sparrow Press, 1978.

Ferry, Anne. *The Title to the Poem*. Stanford: Stanford University Press, 1996.

Findley, Timothy. *Inside Memory: Pages from a Writer's Workbook*. Toronto: HarperCollins, 1990.

Forster, E.M. *Abinger Harvest*. Harmondsworth: Penguin, 1967 [1936].

Fox, Captaine Luke. *North-West Fox or Fox from the North-west Passage*. London: Alsop and Fawcet, 1935.

Freud, Sigmund. *Civilization and Its Discontents*. London: Hogarth, 1969 [1930].

Frye, Northrop. *The Bush Garden*. Toronto: Anansi, 1971.

– *Divisions on a Ground*. Toronto: Anansi, 1982.

– *The Double Vision*. Toronto: University of Toronto Press, 1991.

– 'Haunted by Lack of Ghosts: Some Patterns in the Imagery of Canadian Poetry.' In *The Canadian Imagination: Dimensions of a Literary Culture*. Ed. David Staines. Cambridge: Harvard University Press, 1977, 22–45.

– *The Well-Tempered Critic*. Bloomington: Indiana University Press, 1963.

Ginsberg, Allen. *Complete Poems 1947–1985*. New York: Penguin, 1995.

Gordon, Walter. *A Choice for Canada: Independence or Colonial Status*. Toronto: McClelland and Stewart, 1966.

Grant, George. *Lament for a Nation*. Toronto: McClelland and Stewart, 1965.

– *Technology and Empire*. Toronto: Anansi, 1969.

Graves, Robert. *Collected Poems 1975*. London: Cassell, 1975.

Gray, John. *Berlin*. London: Fontana Press, 1995.

Guignon, Charles, ed. *The Cambridge Companion to Heidegger*. Cambridge: Cambridge University Press, 1993.

Gustafson, Ralph. *The Moment Is All: Selected Poems 1944–83*. Toronto: McClelland and Stewart, 1983.

- 'New Wave in Canadian Poetry.' *Canadian Literature*, no. 32 (Spring 1967), 6–14.
- 'Worthwhile Visitations.' Rev. of George Woodcock. *Notes and Visitations: Poems 1936–1975. Canadian Literature*, no. 71 (Winter 1976), 89–92.
Guthrie, Ramon. *Maximum Security Ward*. New York: Farrar, Straus & Giroux, 1970.
Hall, C.F. *Life with the Esquimaux: A Narrative of Arctic Experience in Search of Survivors of Sir John Franklin's Expedition*. Edmonton: Hurtig, 1970.
Hallberg, Robert von. *American Poetry and Culture 1945–1980*. Cambridge: Harvard University Press, 1985.
Heaney, Seamus. *The Government of the Tongue*. London: Faber, 1988.
- *Preoccupations: Selected Prose 1968–1978*. London: Faber, 1980.
- *The Redress of Poetry*. London: Faber, 1995.
Heath-Stubbs, John. *The Triumph of the Muse*. London: Oxford University Press, 1958.
Hegel, G.W.F. *Aesthetics: Lectures on Fine Art*. 2 vols. Trans. T.M. Knox. Oxford: Oxford University Press, 1975.
- *The Phenomenology of Mind*. Trans. J.B. Baillie. New York: Harper & Row, 1967.
Heidegger, Martin. *Basic Writings*. Ed. David Farrell Krell. San Francisco: Harper, 1993.
- *Poetry, Language, Thought*. Trans. Albert Hofstadter. New York: Harper Colophon, 1971.
- *What Is Philosophy?* New York: Twayne, 1958.
Herodotus. *The History*. Trans. Donald Grene. Chicago: University of Chicago Press, 1987.
Hobsbawm, Eric. 'Introduction: Inventing Traditions.' *The Invention of Tradition*. Ed. Eric Hobsbawm and Terence Ranger. Cambridge: Cambridge University Press, 1983.
- *Nations and Nationalism since 1780*. Cambridge: Cambridge University Press, 1993.
Hone, Joseph. *W.B. Yeats (1865–1939)*. Harmondsworth: Penguin, 1962.
Hood, Hugh. *Unsupported Assertions*. Toronto: Anansi, 1991.
Hope, A.D. 'Standards in Australian Literature.' *The Oxford Anthology of Australian Literature*. Melbourne: Oxford University Press, 1983, 269–81.
Hopkins, Gerard Manley. *The Poems of Gerard Manley Hopkins*. Ed. W.H. Gardner and N.H. Mackenzie. London: Oxford University Press, 1967.
Horace. *The Odes and Epodes*. Trans. C.E. Bennett. Cambridge: Harvard University Press, 1968.
Housman, A.E. *Collected Poems*. Harmondsworth: Penguin Books, 1961.
Hughes, Ted. *The Hawk in the Rain*. London: Faber, 1957.

– *Lupercal*. London: Faber, 1960.

– *New Selected Poems 1957–94*. London: Faber, 1997.

James, William. *Writings 1902–1910*. New York: Library of America, 1987.

Jarrell, Randall. *The Complete Poems*. New York: Farrar, Straus & Giroux, 1969.

– *Kipling, Auden & Co*. New York: Farrar, Straus & Giroux, 1980.

Johnson, W.R. *The Idea of Lyric*. Berkeley: University of California Press, 1982.

Johnston, George, trans. *Thrand of Gotu: Two Icelandic Sagas*. Erin, Ont.: Porcupine's Quill, 1994.

Jones, D.G. *Butterfly on Rock: A Study of Images and Themes in Canadian Literature*. Toronto: University of Toronto Press, 1970.

Keith, W.J. *Canadian Literature in English*. London: Longman, 1985.

Kennelly, Brendan. *A Time for Voices: Selected Poems*. Newcastle upon Tyne: Bloodaxe Books, 1990.

Keohane, Kieran. *Symptoms of Canada: An Essay on Canadian Identity*. Toronto: University of Toronto Press, 1997.

Kirkham, Michael. *The Imagination of Edward Thomas*. Cambridge: Cambridge University Press, 1986.

Klein, A.M. *The Collected Poems of A.M. Klein*. Ed. Miriam Waddington. Toronto: McGraw-Hill Ryerson, 1974.

– *Notebooks: Selections from the A.M. Klein Papers*. Ed. Zailig Pollock and Usher Caplan. Toronto: University of Toronto Press, 1994.

Klinck, Carl F. *Giving Canada A Literary History: A Memoir*. Ed. Sandra Djwa. Ottawa: Carleton University Press, 1991.

Koestler, Arthur. *The Gladiators*. Trans. Edith Simon. London: Hutchinson, 1965 [1939].

Kramer, L., and A. Mitchell, eds. *The Oxford History of Australian Literature*. Melbourne: Oxford University Press, 1981.

Kroetsch, Robert. *The Lovely Treachery of Words: Essays Selected and New*. Toronto: Oxford University Press, 1989.

– 'Unhiding the Hidden: Recent Canadian Fiction.' *Journal of Canadian Fiction*, III, no. 3 (1974), 43–5.

Kymlicka, Will. *Multicultural Citizenship*. Oxford: Oxford University Press, 1996.

Lampman, Archibald. 'Two Canadian Poets: A Lecture.' *Masks of Poetry: Canadian Critics on Canadian Verse*. Ed. A.J.M. Smith. Toronto: McClelland and Stewart, 1962, 26–44.

Larkin, Philip. *Collected Poems*. London: Marvell Press and Faber, 1988.

Lawrence, D.H. *Apocalypse*. New York: Viking Press, 1967.

– *The Cambridge Edition of the Letters of D.H. Lawrence*, Vol. IV. *1921–24*. Ed. Warren Roberts, James T. Boulton, and Elizabeth Mansfield. Cambridge: Cambridge University Press, 1987.

- *The Complete Poems of D.H. Lawrence.* 2 vols. Ed. Vivian de Sola Pinto and Warren Roberts. New York: Viking, 1964.
- *D.H. Lawrence and Italy: Twilight in Italy, Sea and Sardinia, Etruscan Places.* London: Heinemann, 1972.
- *Etruscan Places.* Harmondsworth: Penguin, 1971.
- *Twilight in Italy and Other Essays.* Ed. Paul Eggert. Cambridge: Cambridge University Press, 1994.
- *Women in Love.* Ed. David Farmer, Lindeth Vasey, and John Worthen. Cambridge: Cambridge University Press, 1987.

Lawrence, Frieda. *Not I, but the Wind ...* New York: Viking, 1934.

Laxer, James, and Robert Laxer. *The Liberal Idea of Canada: Pierre Trudeau and the Question of Canada's Survival.* Toronto: James Lorimer, 1977.

Layton, Irving. *Collected Poems.* Toronto: McClelland and Stewart, 1965.

Lecker, Robert. *Making It Real: The Canonization of English-Canadian Literature.* Toronto: Anansi, 1995.

Lee, Dennis. 'Cadence, Country, Silence: Writing in Colonial Space.' *Boundary 2.* III, no. 1 (Fall 1974), 153–68.
- 'The Poetry of Al Purdy: An Afterword.' *The Collected Poems of Al Purdy.* Ed. Russell Brown. Toronto: McClelland and Stewart, 1986.

LePan, Douglas. *Weathering It: Complete Poems 1948–1987.* Toronto: McClelland and Stewart, 1987.

Levitt, Joseph. *A Vision beyond Reach: A Century of Images of Canadian Destiny.* Ottawa: Deneau, n.d.

Levy, Jacob. 'The Multiculturalism of Fear.' *Critical Review,* X, no. 2 (Spring 1996), 271–83.

Lindsay, Vachel. *Collected Poems.* New York: Macmillan, 1925.

Lowell, Robert. *Collected Prose.* New York: Farrar, Straus & Giroux, 1987.

Lowry, Malcolm. *Selected Poems of Malcolm Lowry.* Ed. Earle Birney. San Francisco: City Lights, 1962.

MacDiarmid, Hugh. *Complete Poems.* 2 vols. Ed. M. Grieve and W.R. Aitken. Manchester: Carcanet, 1993, 1994.

McFadden, David. *A Trip around Lake Ontario.* Toronto: Coach House, 1988.

MacLeish, Archibald. *Collected Poems, 1917–1982.* Boston: Houghton Mifflin, 1985.

MacLennan, Hugh. *Barometer Rising.* Toronto: McClelland and Stewart, 1969 [1941].

MacMechan, Archibald. *Headwaters of Canadian Literature.* Toronto: McClelland and Stewart, 1974 [1924].

Macrae, Marion. *The Ancestral Roof.* Toronto: Clarke Irwin, 1963.

Magnusson, Magnus, and Hermann Palsson, eds. *The Vinland Sagas: The Norse Discovery of America.* New York: New York University Press, 1966.

Mandelstam, Osip. *The Complete Prose and Letters*. Ed. Jane Gary Harris. Ann Arbor: Ardis, 1979.

Masel, Carolyn. 'Late Landings: Reflections on Belatedness in Australian and Canadian Literatures.' In *Recasting the Sun: Writing after Colonialism*. Ed. Jonathan White. Baltimore: Johns Hopkins University Press, 1993.

Melville, Herman. 'Hawthorne and His Mosses.' In *The Shock of Recognition*. Ed. Edmund Wilson. New York: Modern Library, 1955, 187–204.

Merwin, W.S. *Lament for the Makers: A Memorial Anthology*. Washington, D.C.: Counterpoint, 1996.

Milosz, Czeslaw. *The Collected Poems 1931–1987*. New York: Ecco Press, 1988.

– *Facing the River*. New York: Ecco Press, 1995.

– *The Witness of Poetry*. Cambridge: Harvard University Press, 1983.

Moore, Marianne. *The Complete Poems of Marianne Moore*. New York: Macmillan, 1967.

Morton, W.L. *The Canadian Identity*. Toronto: University of Toronto Press, 1961.

Muir, Edwin. *Collected Poems*. London: Faber, 1968 [1963].

Murray, Les. *The Rabbiter's Bounty: Collected Poems*. New York: Farrar, Straus & Giroux, 1991.

Neruda, Pablo. *Memoirs*. Trans. Hardie St Martin. New York: Farrar, Straus & Giroux, 1977.

– *Poems of Five Decades*. Trans. Ben Belitt. New York: Grove, 1974.

Neuman, Shirley, and Robert Wilson. *Labyrinths of Voice: Conversations with Robert Kroetsch*. Edmonton: NeWest, 1982.

Nowottny, Winifred. *The Language Poets Use*. London: Athlone Press, 1962.

Olson, Charles. *Selected Writings of Charles Olson*. Ed. Robert Creeley. New York: New Directions, 1966.

Ondaatje, Michael. *The Collected Works of Billy the Kid*. Toronto: Anansi, 1969.

Page, P.K. *The Glass Air: Selected Poems*. Toronto: Oxford University Press, 1985.

Pasternak, Boris. *Doctor Zhivago*. New York: Pantheon, 1958.

Perkins, David. *A History of Modern Poetry: Modernism and After*. Cambridge: Harvard University Press, 1987.

Perloff, Marjorie. *Poetic License: Essays on Modernist and Postmodernist Lyric*. Evanston, Ill.: Northwestern University Press, 1990.

Pioneer Life on the Bay of Quinte. Belleville, Ont.: Mika Silk Screening, 1972.

Pocock, J.G.A. 'Removal from the Wings.' *Times Literary Supplement*, 20 Dec. 1996, 12–13.

Poirier, Richard. *Poetry and Pragmatism*. Cambridge: Harvard University Press, 1992.

– *Robert Frost: The Work of Knowing*. New York: Oxford University Press, 1977.

Pound, Ezra. *'Ezra Pound Speaking': Radio Speeches of World War II*. Ed. Leonard W. Doob. Westport, Conn.: Greenwood Press, 1978.

Powe, B.W. *A Canada of Light*. Toronto: Somerville House, 1997.

Pratt, E.J. *Complete Poems*. Ed. Sandra Djwa and R.G. Moyles. Toronto: University of Toronto Press, 1989.

Preminger, Alex, ed. *Princeton Encyclopedia of Poetry and Poetics*. Princeton: Princeton University Press, 1974.

Reaney, James. 'The Canadian Poet's Predicament.' In *Masks of Poetry: Canadian Critics on Canadian Verse*. Ed. A.J.M. Smith. Toronto: McClelland and Stewart, 1962, 110–22.

Reeder, Roberta. *Anna Akhmatova: Poet and Prophet*. New York: St Martin's Press, 1994.

Reid, Dennis. *The Concise History of Canadian Painting*. Toronto: Oxford University Press, 1988.

Renan, Ernest. 'What Is a Nation?' In *Nation and Narration*. Ed. Homi K. Bhabha. London: Routledge, 1990, 8–22.

Resnick, Philip. *Thinking English Canada*. Toronto: Stoddart, 1994.

Ricks, Christopher. *The Force of Poetry*. Oxford: Oxford University Press, 1984.

Riddel, Joseph N. *The Inverted Bell: Modernism and the Counterpoetics of William Carlos Williams*. Baton Rouge: Louisiana State University Press, 1974.

Rilke, Rainer Maria. *The Selected Poetry of Rainer Maria Rilke*. Ed. and trans. Stephen Mitchell. New York: Random House, 1982.

– *Duino Elegies*. Ed. and trans. J.B. Leishman and Stephen Spender. New York: Norton, 1963.

Roberts, Michael, ed. *The Faber Book of Modern Verse*. London: Faber, 1936.

Ross, Sir John. *Narrative of a Second Voyage in Search of a North-West Passage and of a Residence in the Arctic Regions during the Years 1829, 1830, 1831, 1832, 1833*. London: A.W. Webster, 1835.

Rotstein, Abraham. 'Is There an English-Canadian Nationalism?' *Journal of Canadian Studies*, XIII, no. 2 (Summer 1978), 109–28.

– 'The Twentieth Century Prospect: Nationalism in a Technological Society.' In *Nationalism in Canada*. Ed. Peter Russell. Toronto: McGraw-Hill Ryerson, 1966, 341–63.

Russell, Peter, ed. *Nationalism in Canada*. Toronto: McGraw-Hill Ryerson, 1966.

Saul, John Ralston. *Reflections of a Siamese Twin: Canada at the End of the Twentieth Century*. Toronto: Viking, 1997.

Schiller, Friedrich von. *Naive and Sentimental Poetry, On the Sublime*. Trans. Julius A. Elias. New York: Ungar, 1966.

Scott, F.R. *The Collected Poems of F.R. Scott*. Toronto: McClelland and Stewart, 1981.

Sculpture/Inuit. Toronto: University of Toronto Press, 1971.

Shaw, W. David. *The Lucid Veil: Poetic Truth in the Victorian Age*. Madison: University of Wisconsin Press, 1987.

Smith, A.J.M., ed. *Masks of Poetry: Canadian Critics on Canadian Verse*. Toronto: McClelland and Stewart, 1962.

– *On Poetry and Poets*. Toronto: McClelland and Stewart, 1977.

Smith, Barbara Herrnstein. *Poetic Closure: A Study of How Poems End*. Chicago: University of Chicago Press, 1968.

Spender, Stephen. 'Remembering Eliot.' In *T.S. Eliot: The Man and His Work*. Ed. Allen Tate. New York: Delta, 1966, 38–64.

Staines, David. *Beyond the Provinces: Literary Canada at Century's End*. Toronto: University of Toronto Press, 1995.

– *The Canadian Imagination: Dimensions of a Literary Culture*. Cambridge: Harvard University Press, 1977.

Stallworthy, Jon. *Louis MacNeice*. London: Faber, 1995.

Stevens, Wallace. *Letters of Wallace Stevens*. Ed. Holly Stevens. New York: Knopf, 1972.

– *Opus Posthumous*. New York: Vintage Books, 1982.

Sutherland, John. *Essays, Controversies and Poems*. Ed. Miriam Waddington. Toronto: McClelland and Stewart, 1973.

Swinburne, A.G. *Swinburne's Collected Poetical Works*. 2 vols. London: Heinemann, 1924.

Swinton, George. *Sculpture of the Inuit*. Toronto: McClelland and Stewart, 1992.

Taylor, Charles M. *The Malaise of Modernity*. Toronto: Anansi, 1991.

– *Multiculturalism: Examining the Politics of Recognition*. Ed. Amy Guttman. Princeton: Princeton University Press, 1994.

– *Reconciling the Solitudes: Essays on Canadian Federalism and Nationalism*. Ed. Guy Laforest. Montreal: McGill-Queen's University Press, 1993.

Taylor, Charles. *Radical Tories: The Conservative Tradition in Canada*. Toronto: Anansi, 1982.

Thomas, Dylan. *Collected Poems 1934–1952*. London: Dent, 1952.

Thompson, Francis. *The Poems of Francis Thompson*. London: Hollis and Carter, 1946.

Trilling, Lionel. 'A Speech on Robert Frost: A Cultural Episode.' In *Robert Frost: A Collection of Critical Essays*. Ed. James M. Cox. Englewood Cliffs, N.J.: Prentice-Hall, 1962, 151–8.

Turner, W.J. *The Dark Fire*. London: Sidgwick and Jackson, 1918.

Updike, John. *The Afterlife and Other Stories*. New York: Knopf, 1994.

– 'On Rereading *The Age of Innocence*.' *New York Review of Books* XLII, 30 Nov. 1995, 16–19.

Vanneste, Hilda M.C., ed. *Northern Review, 1945–1956: A History and an Index*. Ottawa: Tecumseh, 1982.

Vendler, Helen. 'Anxiety of Innocence.' *New Republic*, 22 Nov. 1993, 27–34.

– *On Extended Wings*. Cambridge: Harvard University Press, 1969.
– *Soul Says: On Recent Poetry*. Cambridge: Harvard University Press, 1995.
– 'Tintern Abbey: Two Assaults.' *Bucknell Review* ('Wordsworth in Context').
   Ed. P. Fletcher and J. Murray. Lewisburg, Pa.: Bucknell University Press, 1992,
   172–90.
Vitruvius. *On Architecture*. Ed. Frank Granger. New York: Heinemann, 1931.
Watkins, Melville H. 'Technology and Nationalism.' In *Nationalism in Canada*.
   Ed. Peter Russell. Toronto: McGraw-Hill Ryerson, 1966, 284–302.
Watson, Sheila. *The Double Hook*. Toronto: McClelland and Stewart, 1989.
Watt, F.W. 'Nationalism in Canadian Literature.' In *Nationalism in Canada*. Ed.
   Peter Russell. Toronto: McGraw-Hill Ryerson, 1966, 235–51.
Welsh, Alexander. *Roots of Lyric: Primitive Poetry and Modern Poetics*. Princeton:
   Princeton University Press, 1978.
Whitman, Walt. *Collected Poetry and Complete Prose*. New York: Library of Amer-
   ica, 1982.
– *Notebooks and Unpublished Prose Manuscripts*. Volume 4: *Notes*. Ed. Edward F.
   Grier. New York: New York University Press, 1984.
Williams, Robert Coleman, ed. *A Concordance to the Collected Poems of Dylan Tho-
   mas*. Lincoln: University of Nebraska Press, 1967.
Williams, William Carlos. *The Autobiography of William Carlos Williams*. New
   York: New Directions, 1951.
– *In the American Grain*. New York: New Directions, 1956 [1925].
– *Selected Letters*. Ed. John C. Thirlwall. New York: McDowell, Obolensky, 1957.
Wilson, Edmund, ed. *The Shock of Recognition*. New York: Modern Library, 1955.
Wilson, V. Seymour. 'The Tapestry Vision of Canadian Multiculturalism.' In
   Coming of Age: Readings in Canadian History since World War II. Ed. Donald
   Avery and Roger Hall. Toronto: Harcourt Brace, 1996.
Wittgenstein, Ludwig. *Philosophical Investigations*. Oxford: Blackwell, 1976.
Wright, James. *Above the River: The Complete Poems*. New York: Farrar, Straus &
   Giroux and University Press of New England, 1990.
Xenophon. *Anabasis* (and *Symposium* and *Apology*). Trans. Carleton L. Brownson
   and O.J. Todd. London: Heinemann, 1961.
Yeats, W.B. *Letters to the New Island*. Ed. George Bornstein and Hugh Witemeyer.
   Basingstoke: Macmillan, 1989.
Yevtushenko, Yevgeny. *The Collected Poems: 1952–1990*. Ed. Albert C. Todd,
   Yevgeny Yevtushenko, and James Ragan. New York: Henry Holt, 1991.

Index